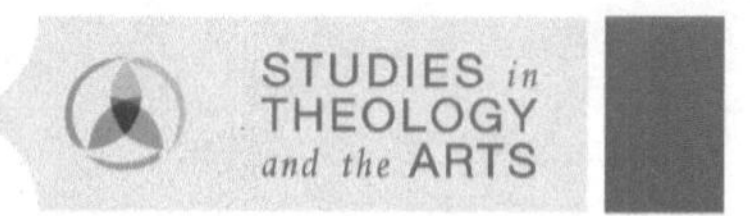

SEEING IS BELIEVING

THE REVELATION OF GOD THROUGH FILM

Richard Vance Goodwin

FOREWORD BY
Craig Detweiler

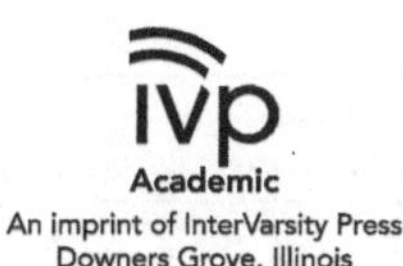

An imprint of InterVarsity Press
Downers Grove, Illinois

InterVarsity Press
P.O. Box 1400 | Downers Grove, IL 60515-1426
ivpress.com | email@ivpress.com

InterVarsity Press® is the publishing division of InterVarsity Christian Fellowship/USA®. For more information, visit intervarsity.org.

Cover design and image composite: Autumn Short
Interior design: Daniel van Loon

ISBN 978-1-5140-0200-1 (print) | ISBN 978-1-5140-0201-8 (digital)

Library of Congress Cataloging-in-Publication Data
A catalog record for this book is available from the Library of Congress.

28 27 26 25 24 23 22 | 8 7 6 5 4 3 2 1

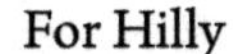

For Hilly

Contents

Foreword

Craig Detweiler

As a filmmaker, why have I invested so much time in teaching? I love the creative process, writing scripts, capturing sacred moments with a camera on location. Yet there is also a creative alchemy in the classroom. Students take what we proffer and transform it into something more. Their creative responses to our courses are profound and encouraging gifts, taking theories forward, adapting them to new contexts.

Richard Goodwin has done the reading, honored his sources, and earned his PhD. Yet *Seeing Is Believing* arrives as something new—a more immersive theology of film from down under.

This doctoral thesis also reveals all Goodwin gleaned from Robert K. Johnston's formative work in *Reel Spirituality* (2000), *Useless Beauty* (2004), and *God's Wider Presence* (2014). Like Goodwin, I've internalized my mentor's teaching on Psalm 19 and the wisdom in Ecclesiastes so completely that the lines between Johnston's thinking and my research blur.

Seeing Is Believing connects Hollywood's cinematic visions to the dreams of Jacob at Bethel (Gen 28). Goodwin invites us to reflect on and interpret our prior experience with new eyes. He's that sharp student awakening the teacher or filmmaker to what we were trying to say. That's a gift that the best artists, prophets, and professors offer—clarifying lenses.

Goodwin corrects his predecessors' tendencies toward "reading" a film. Instead, he focuses our attention on images, emotions, and the body—affect as revelation. My own thesis at Fuller Theological Seminary, supervised by Rob Johnston, focused on audience reception—how reviewers on the Internet Movie Database responded to film.[1] Kutter Callaway's doctoral work, also

---

[1] Craig Detweiler, *Into the Dark: Seeing the Sacred in the Top Films of the 21st Century* (Grand Rapids, MI: Baker Academic, 2008).

overseen by Johnston, listened carefully to film scores.[2] In highlighting an extended shot in *Silent Light* or a musical montage in *Magnolia*, Goodwin underlines the importance of film style. He brings David Bordwell and Kristin Thompson's foundational contributions to film studies into theology and film.[3]

This book treats cinematography as text. It moves from the carefully modulated Word in *Ordet* to the spontaneous Image (like a lens flare) in *Silent Light*. We pause in wonder and awe before the monolith in *2001: A Space Odyssey* and consider Rudolf Otto's notions of the numinous. That same mystery animates sci-fi epics like *Arrival*, *Blade Runner 2049*, and *Dune*. Story is subsumed within set design. Such evocative spaces make us want to return to the place, like Jacob going back to Bethel in Genesis 35. Goodwin brings us back to canonized classics in theology and film with new frames.

I'm so intrigued by Goodwin's concluding questions. Are some stylistic cinematic choices more inherently spiritual? How do the camera movements and lighting schemes in *Ordet* encourage divine encounters? If the crosscut editing in *Magnolia* can underscore our interconnectedness, does the splicing in a Michael Bay film separate us from our fellow filmgoers? Can the right polyphonic score express the spiritual bonding that occurs in communion? Perhaps the breaking of narrative conventions in *The Tree of Life* makes us more open to the Spirit. These are important questions in an era of abundant images saturated with sounds. Style communicates far more than subtext. While the future of filmgoing is in flux, the future of theology and film looks bright thanks to the illumination provided in *Seeing Is Believing*.

[2]Kutter Callaway, *Scoring Transcendence: Contemporary Film Music as Religious Experience* (Waco, TX: Baylor University Press, 2013).

[3]David Bordwell and Kristin Thompson, *Film Art: An Introduction* (Reading, MA: Addison-Wesley, 1979).

Acknowledgments

When the final credits roll, I'm often struck by just how many people it takes to make a movie. One person is acknowledged as the auteur, yet most movies truly are a collaborative effort. The same is true of this book. It may be my name on the cover, but the truth is that several others have played a hand in bringing this work to fruition. These are my credits, my chance to thank them.

This book started out life as my doctoral dissertation. My sincere thanks go to my doctoral supervisors, Drs. Murray Rae and Hilary Radner, without whom this project would never have seen the light of day. Both are accomplished scholars gracious enough to guide me, a fledgling academic, through the long and sometimes arduous process of writing a PhD dissertation. Murray was a dependable source of profound insight and gentle critique. His considerable theological prowess ensured a level of rigor and sophistication to my argument sorely lacking in its earlier stages. Hilary brought much-needed film studies expertise to the project, showing remarkable generosity and broad-mindedness as I sought to incorporate the insights of her discipline into the unlikely area of theology. She agreed to supervising a project that many film scholars would be reluctant to touch, so I am truly grateful to her for her openness. Without her, this project would never have happened. Both Hilary and Murray have been unwavering in their encouragement, which at times was a lifeline.

The University of Otago was an ideal place to study. If it were not for the flexibility to study at a distance and, even more importantly, the generous scholarship granted, undertaking this doctorate would simply not have been feasible. The staff in the Department of Theology and Religion, Graduate Research School, Distance Learning Office, and library were efficient, professional, and personable—all of which made studying at a distance through Otago a rich educational experience. I'm now a proud graduate of this fine institution.

Speaking of fine institutions, I also owe a great deal to Fuller Theological Seminary, a community of scholars, colleagues, students, and alumni that has played a significant role in my development, both personally and professionally. Fuller's Robert K. Johnston, Kutter Callaway, and former faculty member Craig Detweiler—to me, the "Dream Team" in my particular field—deserve special mention. It was Rob's innovative approach to revelation and to film that provided the primary impetus for my interest in this same area. Rob also encouraged me in my scholarly journey at a time when my academic skills were rudimentary. Kutter's excellent theology of film music also helped give shape to my inchoate research interests, inspiring me to include film form and affect as part of my research. He's also a good friend and unofficial mentor, roles that have been every bit as valuable to me on this journey. And at a time when doctoral study seemed little more than a pipe dream, Craig's pragmatism and trademark enthusiasm were a spur toward taking on the challenge. To have him pen the foreword to my book is not only an honor, but also seems fitting.

I've appreciated the way David McNutt from InterVarsity Press has expertly overseen the journey from dissertation to book and kindly coached me through that process. I'm also sincerely grateful to IVP's Studies in Theology and the Arts advisory board—a who's who of theology and the arts—for accepting this project for publication. I'm honored to have had my work greenlit by scholars and artists of the highest caliber.

Thanks to staff and students at Pathways College of Bible and Mission for making my main postdoctoral gig a real joy. I appreciate the financial support of the J. H. Baldwin Fund, and I'm heartened by the trustees' vision for funding theological education for members of Open Brethren heritage churches and Christian Community Churches of New Zealand. Some of the data used in the introduction comes courtesy of the Alister Hardy Trust and their Religious Experience Research Centre based at the University of Wales Trinity Saint David, an important resource for anyone studying religious experience. Another invaluable resource was Auteur House, one of the few remaining DVD rental stores in the Waikato, New Zealand. Thanks to Richard Swainson's brilliantly curated collection (and expert advice), I have been able to access quality films that online streaming services don't bother to obtain.

I belong to a thriving worshiping community, Raleigh Street Christian Centre in Cambridge, New Zealand. Many of my best friends are part of this church, people who have made life during and beyond my doctoral studies not only manageable but also enjoyable. These sisters and brothers have taken an interest in my research, prayed for me, watched cricket with me, babysat my kids, taken me fly-fishing, made meals for my family, and countless other acts of friendship. Thanks for the *koinonia.*

I'm blessed with a wonderful family. My parents, Gwenda and Brian, have been a source of strength and support to me. My siblings too—Nick, Ingrid, Luke, and their respective families—have all helped me in various important ways. My sons, Joel and Caleb, are a delight and continually help me recover my *joie de vivre.* And my deepest gratitude goes to my wife, Hilly, whose unflagging support is a godsend. She backs me unreservedly even when my own confidence falters, so this project is dedicated to her.

Korōria ki te Matua, ki te Tama, ki te Wairua Tapu.

Introduction

It wasn't just that the movie was emotional; it felt somehow *spiritual.* "Somehow," because at the time I wasn't sure how to interpret the experience of seeing *Magnolia* (Paul Thomas Anderson, 1999) for the first time, much less describe it. Indeed, what surprised me most about the experience was how something so seemingly meaningful, loaded with apparent significance, could defy articulation. Seeing this movie was meaningful, yes . . . but *what* did it mean? Any so-called message from the film I *could* identify seemed entirely beside the point. Its power wasn't just in the message. When I was an undergraduate majoring in media studies, it was just one of dozens of worthy films assigned for viewing, yet the experience of watching *this* movie lodged itself more firmly in my memory than most. I was profoundly moved by *Magnolia* in ways that involved affect, yet transcended it too.

Many films have moved me since, and occasionally I've had experiences similar to that memorable first viewing of *Magnolia.* I'm not the only one either. C. S. Lewis had comparable experiences in response to literature, the hills near his childhood home, and even his brother's miniature "sand saucer" garden (though not, as far as I'm aware, movies).[1] Reflecting on these, Lewis wrote, "Until religion comes and retrospectively transforms [numinous experience], it usually appears to the subject to be a special form of aesthetic experience."[2] That's true, I think, of how I initially understood my *Magnolia* moment. It wasn't until years later, having read and eventually studied under theologian Robert K. Johnston, that I came to interpret these as more than "a

---

[1]C. S. Lewis, *Surprised by Joy* (London: Fount, 1998).

[2]C. S. Lewis, *God in the Dock: Essays on Theology and Ethics* (Grand Rapids, MI: Eerdmans, 1970), 175. On the other hand, some have argued that "so-called 'religious experience' is simply aesthetic or moral experience inappropriately described." David Brown, *Divine Generosity and Human Creativity: Theology Through Symbol, Painting and Architecture* (London: Routledge, 2017), Kindle.

special form of aesthetic experience"—I came to see them as moments of divine revelation.[3] Johnston gave me the words to make sense of my experience. I thus became convinced that, watching *Magnolia* for the first time, I had had "an encounter with the sacred itself, with that which lies beyond the natural but which gives meaning to it . . . an experience of God, with the divine who is outside of and independent of the world, even if known from within the world."[4] What had initially befuddled me I came eventually to construe as divine revelation.

Others, of course, have had similar film-viewing experiences, whether they describe them as divine revelation or not. Theologian Kutter Callaway recalls an agnostic woman who attended his church-based film discussion group in the hope of making sense of a recurring dream in which a mysterious voice called to her. After their discussion of *Stranger Than Fiction* (Marc Forster, 2006), in which the anonymous voice narrating the protagonist's life was likened to God, the woman enthused that "now I know who it is that has been speaking to me all this time."[5] Filmmaker Justin Wells describes in a Facebook post an apparently revelatory experience occasioned by seeing *The Shape of Water* (Guillermo del Toro, 2017):

> *The Shape of Water* comprises one of the most profound experiences I've had in cinema. . . . [It] was a very emotional experience for me. I thought I was sitting down to a nice escapist fantasy/sci-fi film. Little did I know it would stick its finger right into my soul. . . . I think if anyone ever asks me why I am not an atheist, I'll just tell them to watch that film.[6]

As a result of seeing *The Keys of the Kingdom* (John M. Stahl, 1944), a longtime atheist ceased trying to outrun "the Still Small Voice [of God] which never gave up" and instead surrendered in faith to that voice.[7] Despite his atheism, one lapsed Catholic cites *2001: A Space Odyssey* (Stanley Kubrick, 1968) as a film capable of eliciting "feeling for . . . a life force or a spirit of man" that he

---

[3]Robert K. Johnston, *Reel Spirituality: Theology and Film in Dialogue*, 2nd ed. (Grand Rapids, MI: Baker Academic, 2006), 74-78.

[4]Johnston, *Reel Spirituality*, 242.

[5]Kutter Callaway, *Scoring Transcendence: Contemporary Film Music as Religious Experience* (Waco, TX: Baylor University Press, 2013), chap. 5, Kindle.

[6]Justin Wells, Facebook, March 3, 2018.

[7]"Account No. 000959," in *Archive of the Alister Hardy Religious Experience Research Centre* (Lampeter, UK: University of Wales Trinity Saint David, March 8, 2018; 1970), www.uwtsd.ac.uk/library/alister-hardy-religious-experience-research-centre/online-archive.

describes as "somewhat of a religious experience."[8] To her surprise, one Christian woman, for whom the arts and nature often mediate "glorious transcendence," was profoundly touched by *Close Encounters of the Third Kind* (Steven Spielberg, 1977). She recalls, "I was speechless throughout... Spielberg must be a visionary—promoting to us a concept of the power of God in a form easily recognizable to us in modern media—i.e. the film and UFOs."[9] Another Christian woman recalls being inwardly prompted against her better judgment to see *Richard III* (Laurence Olivier, 1955), her response to which was that she "felt that Something, Somewhere KNEW WHAT IT WAS DOING."[10]

Not all such experiences are uniformly positive. A young agnostic reports being so terrified by *The Picture of Dorian Gray* (Albert Lewin, 1945) and the image of the eponymous portrait, that as a last resort, "I prayed to the Being that I had rejected to help me; I said the Lord's prayer, the only one I could remember. Immediately [*sic*] a quiet peace stole over me, I just can't explain it."[11] As a young man, filmmaker Paul Verhoeven had a terrifying experience of the numinous while watching *King Kong* (Merian C. Cooper, Ernest B. Schoedsack, 1933).[12] *New York Times* columnist Ross Douthat writes that Verhoeven's "experience actively propelled him away from anything metaphysical; the raw carnality of his most famous films, he suggested later, was an attempt to keep the numinous and destabilizing at bay."[13] These experiences vary in content, valence, affect, impact, and interpretation. But all are instances in which cinema seems to mediate an encounter with or experience of something, or indeed someone, beyond the immanent plane of ordinary material existence.

[8]"Account No. 000878," in *Archive of the Alister Hardy Religious Experience Research Centre* (Lampeter, UK: University of Wales Trinity Saint David, March 8, 2018; 1970), www.uwtsd.ac.uk/library/alister-hardy-religious-experience-research-centre/online-archive.

[9]"Account No. 003759," in *Archive of the Alister Hardy Religious Experience Research Centre* (Lampeter, UK: University of Wales Trinity Saint David, March 8, 2018; 1979), www.uwtsd.ac.uk/library/alister-hardy-religious-experience-research-centre/online-archive.

[10]"Account No. 003734," in *Archive of the Alister Hardy Religious Experience Research Centre* (Lampeter, UK: University of Wales Trinity Saint David, March 8, 2018; 1977), www.uwtsd.ac.uk/library/alister-hardy-religious-experience-research-centre/online-archive.

[11]"Account No. 002314," in *Archive of the Alister Hardy Religious Experience Research Centre* (Lampeter, UK: University of Wales Trinity Saint David, March 8, 2018; 1971), www.uwtsd.ac.uk/library/alister-hardy-religious-experience-research-centre/online-archive.

[12]Alex Pappademas, "Career Arc: Paul Verhoeven," *Grantland*, February 12, 2014, http://grantland.com/features/career-arc-paul-verhoeven/.

[13]Ross Douthat, "Varieties of Religious Experience," *The New York Times*, December 24, 2016, www.nytimes.com/2016/12/24/opinion/sunday/varieties-of-religious-experience.html.

As I became increasingly interested in the field of theology and film, I was struck by how many people claimed religious, even revelatory, experiences while watching *Magnolia*. I wasn't alone. In both published writings and personal conversations, *Magnolia* was regularly identified as a film worthy of theological engagement.[14] Other movies, too, are regularly cited for their apparent capacity to prompt revelatory experience. This has since led me to wonder, if certain films elicit claims of religious experience more frequently than others, what is it about those films that draws such a response?

Revelation, Emotion, and Film Images

The central argument. One possible answer to this question would be to say that the subject matter of such films is explicitly religious. And, yes, it's true that many films noted for their spiritual power contain religious subject matter. But that's not always the case. Some quite ostensibly "secular" films seem capable of prompting this type of experience. For every *Silence* (Martin Scorsese, 2016)[15] or *Of Gods and Men* (Xavier Beauvois, 2010)[16] there is a *Bicycle Thieves* (Vittorio De Sica, 1948)[17] or indeed *Magnolia*. So the answer can't be that religious experience is contingent *only* on a movie's subject matter.

What, then, are the *stylistic features* of these films? This is an interesting question in part because it aims to identify a correlation between film form and revelation. But such an undertaking is also potentially problematic. Why? Because God's agency has primacy in revelation, and therefore the relationship can't be causative. In other words, no film—nor indeed any other thing except God—can *cause* revelation. Whatever we say on the matter, we mustn't compromise divine agency. In what way, therefore, can these formal components—and images in particular will be a focus of this book—be said to be conducive

[14]For examples of theological engagement with *Magnolia*, see Robert K. Johnston, *Useless Beauty: Ecclesiastes Through the Lens of Contemporary Film* (Grand Rapids, MI: Baker Academic, 2004), 73-92; Callaway, *Scoring Transcendence*; Roy Anker, *Of Pilgrims and Fire: When God Shows Up at the Movies* (Grand Rapids, MI: Eerdmans, 2011); Shane Hipps, "*Magnolia*: The Exodus for Kids," *Metaphilm* (9 May 2003).

[15]Ranked #6, "Top 100 Films—2020," *Arts & Faith*, accessed December 23, 2021, http://artsandfaith.com/index.php?/films/&do=year&id=8.

[16]Ranked #5, "Top 100 Films—2020," *Arts & Faith*, accessed December 23, 2021, http://artsandfaith.com/index.php?/films/&do=year&id=8.

[17]Ranked #38, "Top 100 Films—2020," *Arts & Faith*, accessed December 23, 2021, http://artsandfaith.com/index.php?/films/&do=year&id=8&page=2.

to revelatory experience while still preserving the essential primacy of God's agency? This is the question at the heart of my investigation.

Here, in a nutshell, is what I intend to argue in this book: though God is indeed the primary agent of revelation, certain visual and other stylistic features may invite affective responses that guide viewers to those aspects of reality through which God reveals Godself. Through the artful use of imagery, these movies may usher viewers into a state of heightened awareness of the divine (irrespective of the director's intentions). That means we can identify elements of a film that, though not themselves able to cause revelation, may nevertheless put some viewers in a state of greater receptivity to God. When it comes to film-mediated revelation, form matters.

Why revelation? This project is comprised of three core components: revelation, emotion, and film images.[18] It may be personal experience that has fostered my interest in revelation, but I'm confident I'm not alone here. For some, a trip to the movies may be little more than entertainment, but for others, cinema may also be deeply meaningful, even *spiritually* meaningful. While there is some value in textual analyses that locate the religious meaning of a film in the film itself without much thought given to the audience, I'm mostly interested in movies that really do seem to occasion these sorts of experiences for some viewers. A film that illustrates religious truth may offer food for thought, but a film that occasions what could be interpreted as divine encounter? *That* leaves a mark. Simply put, this book focuses on revelation, because it is what I find most theologically compelling about cinema—more so than other strategies like the presence of Christ figures, cinematic treatments of biblical stories, or explicit theological themes (though, of course, a film containing these may still occasion revelation).

But such an undertaking poses profound challenges. Studying revelation brings with it significant ambiguities. Revelation isn't something that can be demonstrated empirically. William James, the pioneering psychologist and philosopher of religious experience, once said,

> There are moments of sentimental and mystical experience . . . that carry an enormous sense of inner authority and illumination with them when they

[18] Indeed, *Revelation, Emotion, and Film Images* is the subtitle to the original doctoral dissertation of which this volume is an adaptation.

> come. But they come seldom, and they do not come to everyone; and the rest of life makes either no connection with them, or tends to contradict them more than it confirms them. Some persons follow more the voice of the moment in these cases, some prefer to be guided by the average results.[19]

In other words, the same data can be variously interpreted. The same experience can be either embraced as a true insight into the nature of reality or dismissed as an anomaly. I'm inclined toward the former response, but others could equally view such experiences as illusory. While this study is not empirical, it is, I hope, sensitive to experience.

Another ambiguity of revelation rests in the fact that it's difficult to establish from written responses to films whether or not viewers even *claim* revelatory experience. Lay viewers who post film reviews on websites like Internet Movie Database (IMDb) and Rotten Tomatoes, for example, often reach for religious terminology to describe the viewing experience, yet this language may lack precision, making it unclear whether or not they believe the experience to be revelatory.

With this in mind, the study will involve three key steps. First, I'll examine how revelation has been understood in theological tradition. Second, I'll select a number of films that seem frequently to elicit religious experiences and examine the stylistic elements of these films, with a particular focus on images. Third, I'll consider the degree to which these films and their concomitant responses align with what has been said about revelation in theological tradition. Though undertaking this process will still not finally allow definitive claims, it will nevertheless permit us to establish a degree of plausibility regarding the claim that particular films can become the occasion for personal encounter with God and so of revelation.

Why emotion? In Alexander Payne's "14e arrondissement," the final section of the anthology film *Paris, je t'aime* (Bruno Podalydès et al., 2006), a rube-ish, middle-aged American tourist, Carol (Margo Martindale), relates an experience she had while sightseeing around Paris. In her broken French, the lonely woman recounts the highlights of her tour around the City of Love, which culminates in a memorable lunch in a park. Sitting on a park bench, Carol is suddenly struck by the scene around her—children playing on a playground, lovers

[19]William James, *Varieties of Religious Experience: A Study in Human Nature* (n.p.: n.p., 1902), Kindle, 24.

kissing on the grass, a nearby woman waiting for her companion, elderly singles and couples on adjacent benches—and is overcome with a powerful feeling.

As the camera tracks forward, Carol's backlit face comes to occupy most of the frame, giving special prominence to her facial expression, while also intensifying our empathy with her. She describes the singular experience for her French class in voiceover narration (translated into English subtitles):

> Then something happened, something difficult to describe. Sitting there, alone in a foreign country, far from my job and everyone I know, a feeling came over me. It was like remembering something I'd never known before or had always been waiting for, but I didn't know what. Maybe it was something I'd forgotten or something I've been missing all my life. All I can say is that I felt, at the same time, joy and sadness. But not too much sadness, because I felt alive. Yes, alive.

Carol doesn't claim to have had a divine encounter, nor do we know what Payne had in mind when he penned this scene with Nadine Eid. Nevertheless, Carol's description sounds very much like C. S. Lewis's notion of *Sehnsucht* (or "Joy," in his own idiolectic sense), an intense, nostalgia-like yearning for something ineffable and elusive, which is simultaneously pleasurable and painful, "an unsatisfied desire which is itself more desirable than any other satisfaction."[20] As we have already noted, Lewis initially considered these affective experiences merely aesthetic; later, he would consider them divine revelation.[21]

Little if any propositional content is involved in Carol and Lewis's experiences. Carol doesn't come to any fresh insight; she simply feels alive. Lewis doesn't learn any new truth; he simply feels a peculiar sensation to which all other pleasures pale in comparison.[22] Protestant theological traditions, such as my own evangelical heritage, have historically favored propositional forms of revelation, in which the essential component is the information imparted. Feeling is secondary, if not irrelevant entirely.[23] The problem with relying exclusively on this model of revelation when approaching the issue of revelation

---

[20]C. S. Lewis, *Surprised by Joy*, 12.

[21]Lewis, *God in the Dock*, 175. Caroline Franks Davis classes Lewis's *Sehnsucht* as a type of numinous experience. Caroline Franks Davis, "Religious Experience," in *Philosophy of Religion: An Anthology*, ed. Charles Taliaferro and Paul J. Griffiths (Hoboken, NJ: Blackwell, 2003), 180n55.

[22]Lewis, *Surprised by Joy*, 13.

[23]Pentecostalism is a notable exception to this tendency. See, for example, James K. A. Smith, *Thinking in Tongues: Pentecostal Contributions to Christian Philosophy* (Grand Rapids: Eerdmans, 2010), Kindle.

mediated by film or the arts generally is that consideration of revelatory experience in terms of a "moral of the story" is often reductive and, for the recipient, may feel as if it misses the point entirely. Contemporary Christian preachers, to choose just one trivial example, often pepper sermons with references to movies, but ordinarily do so by using the film to merely illustrate a truth already known. This hardly does justice to the experience of being gripped or moved by the presence of God in a movie theater.

We see the revelatory function of affect in Nicole Cliffe's account of her conversion to Christianity. Granted, cinema does not feature in the prominent feminist blogger's story, but her account is relevant to our discussion because it suggests that "meeting Jesus" may sometimes be a matter of feeling, rather than a primarily intellectual affair. An avowed and content atheist, Cliffe stumbled across an obituary for the late Christian philosopher Dallas Willard and unexpectedly burst into tears, kicking off a series of crying episodes over the next few days prompted by the most ordinary activities. "I wasn't sad, I wasn't frightened," she writes. "I just had too many feelings."[24] Inspired by the obituary, Cliffe read various Christian classics authored by Willard and others, all of which drew more tears. So she undertook a process of conscious reflection, probing her sudden emotional sensitivity, which culminated in her conversion to Christianity. Cliffe writes,

> I am occasionally asked by other Christians, "What happened during that hour [of conversion]?" I answer that God did not speak to me. Rather, like the protagonist in *Memento* putting his past together with Polaroids, I figured out what I already knew. What happened during that hour was the natural culmination of my coming to faith: I had been cracked open to the divine, I read books that I would have laughed at before the cracking, and the stars lined up and there was God, and then I knew, and then I said it out loud to a third party, and then I giggled.[25]

Although she describes the process as entailing some "figuring out," clearly the greater part was intuitive and affective rather than cognitive. Tellingly, Cliffe makes a point of saying that God did not *speak*. There seems to be little or no propositional content communicated here. She's simply "cracked open to the divine." This is revelation, but of an affective sort. Crucially, Cliffe concludes,

---

[24]Nicole Cliffe, "Undone: How God Seriously Complicated My Happy Atheist Life," *Christianity Today*, June 1, 2016, www.cbmcint.com/undone-how-god-seriously-complicated-my-happy-atheist-life/.
[25]Cliffe, "Undone."

"This is why apologetics, in my opinion, are hugely unconvincing . . . I had to be tapped on the shoulder. I had to be taken to a place where books about God were something I could experience without distance. It was alchemical."[26]

An important, yet largely overlooked dimension of the "alchemy" of revelatory experience is affect. Religious aesthetician Frank Burch Brown has demonstrated the flaw of purism, in which art is believed to be purely affective and preconceptual, by pointing out that an exact replica of an awe-inspiring ancient cathedral at Disney World would fail to inspire awe if we knew beforehand it was constructed out of fiberglass.[27] Cognition influences emotional response to art. But while I reject purism, I equally reject the opposite impulse to reduce art to mere "text."[28] For Brown, aesthetics are "all those things employing a medium in such a way that its perceptible form and 'felt' qualities become essential to what is appreciable and essential."[29] The felt qualities of film are part of what make it aesthetic. Affect, therefore, warrants closer attention than theologians have sometimes paid it.

Why images? There's a scene in *Raging Bull* (Martin Scorsese, 1980) in which former boxer Jake LaMotta (Robert De Niro) removes the gemstones from an old championship belt for quick cash, only to learn he could have made more money by leaving the championship belt intact. In her *Salvation from Cinema*, Crystal Downing writes,

> Like LaMotta, many theologians and religion scholars extract gems of insight from movies, not realizing that the brilliant objects are more valuable when seen as part of the film's entire visual structure. Ignoring visual artistry, they tend to discuss the implications of cinema in terms of story. But if it's all about the profundity of a carefully crafted story, why not simply read the screenplay?[30]

This is a vital insight. The best theological engagement with film requires we take the visual dimension of cinema seriously, yet theologians have often failed to do so. In the mid-aughts, a dozen prominent scholars in the field of religion and film assembled to identify the primary lacunae in the

---

[26]Cliffe, "Undone."

[27]Frank Burch Brown, *Religious Aesthetics: A Theological Study of Making and Meaning* (Princeton, NJ: Princeton University Press, 1989), 6, 75.

[28]Brown, *Religious Aesthetics*, 9-10.

[29]Brown, *Religious Aesthetics*, 22.

[30]Crystal Downing, *Salvation from Cinema: The Medium Is the Message* (London: Routledge, 2015), ebook, 5.

theology and film conversation. One of the chief of these, as outlined in the resultant book, *Reframing Theology and Film: A New Focus for an Emerging Discipline,* is the tendency for theology to "read" film through literary lenses (*read* thus being the operative word).[31] There's a tendency to treat the meaning or significance of film images, not to mention other stylistic elements, as self-evident. Theological engagement, therefore, often skips ahead to thematic content distilled from plot and character, mostly glossing over formal analysis.

In his introduction to *Reframing Theology and Film,* Robert K. Johnston further clarifies the issue: "It is not story per se but the reduction of film interpretation to literary techniques that is the problem."[32] The book thus issues a call for theology and film to break free from its "literary captivity."[33] In mounting a case for "religious visuality," S. Brent Plate quotes theology and literature specialist David Jasper: "Where it seems to me the cinema comes closest to stimulating theological reflection is not by its themes or specific motifs, but by its very form and nature."[34] There is a dearth of attention paid to that which makes cinema *cinematic,* namely images (among other components), which is why in this book I will pay particular attention to images.

But I'm far from being the only person to have made this sort of attempt. I've already mentioned Downing and Plate, both of whom have called attention to style in their theological engagement with film. In the early 1980s, Michael Bird wrote about the hierophanic capacity of the film medium, particularly as it presents the world to us visually.[35] A decade earlier, Paul Schrader famously devised a form-sensitive treatment of religious cinema.[36] Schrader's work was substantially informed by European theorists stretching back to the 1950s, including Amédée Ayfre, Henri Agel, André Bazin, and Siegfried

[31]Robert K. Johnston, ed., *Reframing Theology and Film: New Focus for an Emerging Discipline* (Grand Rapids, MI: Baker Academic, 2007).

[32]Johnston, *Reframing Theology and Film,* introduction, Kindle.

[33]Johnston, *Reframing Theology and Film,* introduction, Kindle.

[34]David Jasper, "On Systematizing the Unsystematic: A Response," in *Explorations in Theology and Film: Movies and Meaning,* ed. Clive Marsh and Gaye Ortiz (Oxford: Blackwell, 1997), 240; cited in S. Brent Plate, "Religion/Literature/Film: Toward a Religious Visuality of Film," *Literature and Theology* 12, no. 1 (1998): 18.

[35]Michael S. Bird, "Film as Hierophany," in *Religion in Film* (Knoxville: University of Tennessee Press, 1982).

[36]Paul Schrader, *Transcendental Style in Film: Ozu, Bresson, Dreyer* (New York: Da Capo, 1988), http://catdir.loc.gov/catdir/enhancements/fy0830/88015974-d.html.

Kracauer, who all saw spiritual potential in images themselves. Others, too, have championed film form in their religious engagement. So clearly there is a tradition of style in religious and theological engagement with film.

On the whole, however, the prevailing tendency has been to overlook form in favor of "literary" elements: plot, character, and theme. Invoking Marshall McLuhan's famous aphorism "the medium is the message," Downing writes,

> Failure to engage with and assess the visual medium is especially ironic for Christian scholars. Doctrine hammered out in the first five centuries of the church—often in defiance of gnosticism—emphasizes that salvation is mediated not through stories and insights spoken by Jesus, but through his material body hung upon the cross, a medium *seen* after the resurrection.[37]

The fact of Christ's incarnation is essential, as is our own embodiment. The body is where my emphases on form and emotion meet. Perception of images is sensory, and the affective effects are corporeal. We see with sense organs, eyes, but also "feel" what we see with our whole bodies. It's important, therefore, that we attend to the material dimension of film. Images are not the only stylistic component worthy of attention. The choice to home in on images is partly pragmatic, a measure taken to give this project focus and avoid becoming unwieldy. That said, I'll discuss other aspects of film where relevant, since audiences experience films as a unified whole, not as discrete, formal elements.

Furthermore, I'm not "Nestorian" in my approach to images. Downing points out, "Scholars who acknowledge artistry in the cinematic medium tend to be Nestorian about it: separating out discussion about technique from discussion of spiritually enlightening message."[38] Form is informed by subject matter, just as subject matter is shaped by form. Accordingly, my approach is holistic. Nevertheless, form has suffered from neglect—and theology and film as a field of study has suffered as a result. My emphasis here on film images is a modest attempt to redress this neglect.

The Cultural Importance of Revelation Through Film

Christian artist Makoto Fujimura has written about the prescience of Vincent van Gogh's masterpiece *The Starry Night*. The painting features a church

---

[37]Downing, *Salvation from Cinema*, 26.

[38]Downing, *Salvation from Cinema*, 26.

building at the center, but despite its privileged position, the church is dark while surrounding buildings are brightly lit. Fujimura muses,

> What do we do in a culture in which the light of the Spirit has departed church buildings and gone swirling instead into nature, into life's margins? . . . For we are living in the world Vincent depicted. The church has kept the structure of truth, but we have largely lost touch with the Spirit in creating beauty.[39]

The decline of the church's influence in the West is well documented, but it is not the case that Westerners have become wholly uninterested in the metaphysical. Contemporary Anglophone Westerners are often characterized as "spiritual but not religious," a recent form of Romanticism with roots in 1960s counterculture. According to theologian Owen C. Thomas, the current Western spirituality movement has four key characteristics: (1) an emphasis on interiority over exteriority; (2) an orientation toward private, rather than public, faith; (3) an epistemological preference for feeling over rationality; and (4) a pronounced distinction between religion and spirituality, the former being disparaged while the latter is lauded.[40] We see this in the "spiritual but not religious" descriptor: a private, interior, affectively oriented spirituality is construed as antithetical—and far preferable—to a public, exterior, rational religiosity. As in *The Starry Night*, some Westerners believe the light has gone out in the church. Yet, crucially, *there are lights elsewhere.*

One of these lights outside the church is literally comprised of light: cinema. Theology and film scholar Clive Marsh has found that theologians often fail to take film and pop culture seriously, as if such populist fare were unworthy of scholarly attention.[41] But this attitude is out of touch with the *zeitgeist*. A few years ago, I spoke with a scholar at a university in my native New Zealand who shared that, while most of the theology department's classes attract rather modest numbers, their class on theology and pop culture had an enrollment of several hundred students. In the early years of this century, as much as 20 percent of Americans identified "media, arts, and other cultural institutions" as the primary locus of their spirituality, a number predicted to rise to a full

---

[39]Makoto Fujimura, *Culture Care: Reconnecting with Beauty for Our Common Life* (New York: The Fujimura Institute, 2017), chap. 10, Kindle.

[40]Owen C. Thomas, "Spiritual but Not Religious: The Influence of the Current Romantic Movement," *Anglican Theological Review* 88, no. 3 (2006): 397-415.

[41]Clive Marsh, *Cinema and Sentiment: Film's Challenge to Theology*, Studies in Religion and Culture Series (Eugene, OR: Wipf & Stock, 2004), 143-44.

one-third of Americans by 2025.[42] The church must become conversant with the arts, especially populist arts like film, if it is to understand the spirituality of contemporary people. Even more importantly, if it is indeed true that revelation is sometimes mediated by film, Christians must attend to this phenomenon simply to keep step with the Spirit. To return once more to *The Starry Night*, we dare not hunker down in our old (dark?) church and miss the bright light found in the world outside ecclesial walls.

Trailer: Overview of the Book

It's rare to see a movie without first knowing something about the film. Often, we've already seen the film's trailer, which has clued us in to the premise, genre, and (somewhat annoyingly) its best gags. I want this section to serve as a kind of "trailer," giving you some idea of how my argument will unfold.

This book is divided into two parts. Part one, "Lenses on Revelation," lays the theoretical foundations. In it, I examine revelation through several "lenses": filmic, theological, cognitive, and biblical. Initially, I explore film-mediated revelation, starting with empirical research—a rarity in this field—that validates the possibility of revelation through film. That being established, I turn to one of the most influential accounts of film form with respect to religious transcendence, namely transcendental style. This style has genuine explanatory power, but also has significant shortcomings. So I draw also on the model of spiritual realism, a form-sensitive approach to film that is less gnostic and more theologically palatable than transcendental style taken alone.

I then tackle the theological questions undergirding this project, demonstrating how we can account for film-mediated revelation by introducing the doctrine of general revelation, albeit ultimately in a revised form. Protestant theology has historically taken a rather dim view of general revelation or, more precisely, of fallen humanity's capacity to rightly receive it. The revised, pneumatologically oriented version of general revelation offered here takes a more optimistic view of the divine knowledge that general revelation can impart, thus making revelation through film a genuine possibility.

Finally in this section, I consider emotion as it relates to revelation. Humans are not primarily thinking, but rather feeling, beings. At this point, I turn to cognitive film theory, a school of thought within film studies that has focused

[42] George Barna, *Revolution* (Carol Stream, IL: Tyndale House, 2005), 48-49.

largely on audience affect. I also draw on Jacob's divine encounter at Bethel in Genesis 28 as an analogy for thinking about film-mediated revelation. Just as Jacob became suddenly aware of God's presence that was already there, so filmic emotion may guide a viewer's awareness to those aspects of reality in which God reveals Godself. I then outline criteria for discerning genuine revelation from erroneous claims.

Part two, "Pictures of Revelation," puts the theory into practice. It's composed of case studies—examinations of certain films and their stylistic features. These are "*pictures* of revelation" in three senses: (1) these chapters focus on specific motion pictures that frequently occasion claims of revelatory experience; (2) there's a special emphasis on the pictorial facets of cinema (i.e., images); and (3) each of these case studies provides a concrete "picture" of film-mediated revelation.

I begin by analyzing two films together, *Ordet* (Carl Theodor Dreyer, 1955) and *Silent Light* (Carlos Reygadas, 2007), the latter being a quasi-remake of the former. I explore a range of mostly visual devices with a special emphasis on the lighting in both films. These films depict "wonders" and, in turn, elicit wonder, not least through their lighting. As such, I look at the resonances between light and wonder in Scripture, theology, and religion.

I then continue by looking at the seminal sci-fi film *2001: A Space Odyssey*. I offer an analysis of various stylistic devices, visual and aural, that give this ostensibly materialist film its perennial spiritual potency, before concentrating in particular on the mise en scène, specifically the use of celestial bodies in the frame, which inspire awe. I thus round out my analysis of *2001* by looking at biblical and theological perspectives on awe.

I then turn my attention to the film that inspired this scholarly journey: *Magnolia*. Like many other network narratives, *Magnolia*'s editing calls attention to the intersection of strangers' lives, though it further intensifies the effect through creative editing strategies. The film both depicts interconnectedness between characters and elicits a sense of connectedness of the audience with the characters, grounded in a profound sense of our shared humanity. The consideration of *Magnolia* concludes with some reflections on communion as essential to personhood, both divine and human.

Finally, I draw the various threads of this study together and ultimately conclude that film images may affectively predispose viewers to revelation, and that the formal analyses detailed in this study serve as concrete examples of how stylistic devices may function in this way.

A word about my own theological location is in order. I was raised as and continue to identify as an evangelical Christian. Like many evangelicals, I have mixed feelings about the term. *Evangelical* has increasingly become saddled with troubling connotations, especially in the United States. I don't endorse everything that takes place in the name of evangelicalism. Some of it is shameful. But however much I may wish to distance myself from its more disturbing associations, it still more or less names my fundamental theological location.[43] True to my evangelical convictions, therefore, I must state at the outset that I believe God is revealed most definitively in the person and work of Jesus Christ. Though I'm enthusiastic about the possibility that film may mediate revelation, any such claims must ultimately be examined in the light of what God has made known of Godself in and through Jesus.

I also recognize that evangelicalism is just one sliver of the Christian tradition. As such, I'm enthusiastic about the gifts the wider church offers, and I freely interact with and draw on thinkers from the broader Christian tradition, including Catholic (e.g., Avery Dulles) and Eastern Orthodox (e.g., John Zizioulas). These theologians and the traditions they represent do much to address the lacunae and shortcomings of my own. Even as an adolescent, for example, I found the poetry of the Jesuit Gerard Manley Hopkins, brought to my attention by my English teacher, strangely compelling. That this Victorian poet could impress a teenager with precisely zero interest in poetry seemed odd at the time, but I suspect that even then my soul was stirred by the poet's sacramental vision ("The world is charged with the grandeur of God")[44] largely lacking in my own tradition. Thus, I echo Johnston's sentiment: "I am a Protestant deeply influenced in my theology of culture by Catholic sacramentality."[45] Indeed, I am deeply influenced by the wider Christian tradition in myriad other ways.

---

[43]A more helpful understanding is offered by historian David Bebbington, who has identified four key characteristics of evangelicalism: conversionism, activism, biblicism, and crucicentrism. See David W. Bebbington, *Evangelicalism in Modern Britain: A History from the 1730s to the 1980s*, 1st ed. (New York: Taylor and Francis, 2003). For more recent reflections on evangelical identity, see Mark Labberton, ed., *Sill Evangelical?: Insiders Reconsider Political, Social, and Theological Meaning* (Downers Grove, IL: InterVarsity Press, 2018).

[44]Gerard Manley Hopkins and Gardner W. H., *Poems and Prose of Gerard Manley Hopkins*, Penguin Classics (New York: Penguin, 1985), 27.

[45]Johnston, *Reel Spirituality*, 78.

IS SEEING BELIEVING?

After doubting his fellow disciples' reports, Thomas finally confessed Christ as Lord upon seeing the risen Christ. Jesus famously replied, "Because you have seen me, you have believed; blessed are those who have not seen and yet have believed" (Jn 20:29). According to the fourth Gospel, belief that comes *without* seeing is the highest sort of faith.

But in the Old Testament, faith is often predicated on seeing.[46] Take, for example, the result of God's destruction of the Egyptians as they pursued the Hebrews through the Red Sea: "Israel saw the Egyptians lying dead on the shore. And when the Israelites saw the mighty hand of the LORD displayed against the Egyptians, the people feared the LORD and put their trust in him and in Moses his servant" (Ex 14:30-31). Jewish studies scholar Ilana Pardes writes,

> There is a certain immediacy and vitality in revelation through the sight that revelation through the word does not convey. No knowledge, no cognition, can weaken the impact of a wondrous sight (Buber: 75). The visual experience of God's presence has the power to transform (however briefly) the skeptical children of Israel into a community of believers, to lead to a sudden sharp insight.[47]

Like the ancient Israelites, many today are skeptical of the God of Scripture. This contemporary skepticism is captured by Mark Tansey in his painting *Doubting Thomas* (1986), a creative reinterpretation of Caravaggio's *The Incredulity of Saint Thomas* (c. 1601–1602). In Tansey's piece, a man dressed in modern Western attire fingers not the wound in Jesus' side but rather a deep crevasse that has appeared in the ground beneath his parked car. The forces of the modern world have left the earth shaken and the ground beneath our feet has opened up, no longer affording us a sure footing.[48] Jesus' commendation of those whose faith is not based on sight surely remains valid, but in an age where the West's religious foundations are undergoing seismic upheaval, maybe for some people religious faith (or spirituality) once again requires

[46]Ilana Pardes, "Moses Goes Down to Hollywood: Miracles and Special Effects," *Semeia* 74, no. 15 (1996): 14-31.

[47]Pardes, "Moses Goes Down to Hollywood," 26; Martin Buber, *Moses: The Revelation and the Covenant* (Atlantic Highlands, NJ: Humanities Press International, 1988/1946), 75.

[48]I owe this insight into *Doubting Thomas* to Barry Taylor. Barry Taylor, "The State of the Nation" (Fuller Theological Seminary, Pasadena, April 5, 2010).

sight. For some, *seeing* is believing. In fact, it would be more representative of my argument here to say seeing is feeling, and feeling is believing—but even this would be far too simplistic. Much more nuance will need to be added to this formulation. I hope in the following pages to add that nuance and to demonstrate that film images can be religiously powerful and even conducive to revelation. Indeed, we might take our cue from *another* of Jesus' blessings: "Blessed are your eyes because they see" (Mt 13:16).

PART ONE

LENSES ON REVELATION

1

Revelation Through Film

The news sent a shockwave through the film community: Martin Scorsese had labeled Marvel movies as "not cinema." The fêted director of *Raging Bull* (1980) and *The Irishman* (2019) likened Hollywood's most financially successful franchise to the cheap thrills of an amusement park.[1] In a follow-up op-ed for *The New York Times*, he clarified his position; his beef was less with Marvel films themselves than with the industry that has embraced them so wholeheartedly, effectively sounding a death knell for the future of lower budget films in Hollywood.[2] Francis Ford Coppola, Scorsese's fellow American New Wave auteur, was less guarded in his criticism, calling the films "despicable."[3] Coming at the end of a decade in which Marvel dominated the box office, their disapproving remarks sparked a backlash from fans—and the filmmakers behind them.[4] When the critics are as revered as these two elder statesmen, next-generation directors are bound to become defensive about their work.

But what, according to Scorsese, is the quality of "real" cinema that Marvel movies lack? In a word, *revelation*. "For me, for the filmmakers I came to love and respect, for my friends who started making movies around the same time that I did," writes Scorsese, "cinema was about revelation—aesthetic, emotional and spiritual revelation."[5] Scorsese's op-ed may not be emphatically theological, but it does nevertheless seem to imply that he is open to the

---

[1]Nick De Semlyen, "The *Irishman* Week: Empire's Martin Scorsese Interview," *Empire*, November 6, 2019, www.empireonline.com/movies/features/irishman-week-martin-scorsese-interview/.

[2]Martin Scorsese, "Martin Scorsese: I Said Marvel Movies Aren't Cinema. Let Me Explain," *The New York Times*, November 4, 2019, www.nytimes.com/2019/11/04/opinion/martin-scorsese-marvel.html.

[3]Catherine Shoard, "Francis Ford Coppola: Scorsese Was Being Kind—Marvel Movies Are Despicable," *The New York Times*, October 21, 2019, www.theguardian.com/film/2019/oct/21/francis-ford-coppola-scorsese-was-being-kind-marvel-movies-are-despicable.

[4]Shoard, "Francis Ford Coppola."

[5]Scorsese, "I Said Marvel Movies Aren't Cinema."

possibility of divine revelation through film. But not everyone is so enthusiastic about the revelatory possibilities of cinema. Indeed, Scorsese has been on the receiving end of what could be construed as the polar opposite sort of religious engagement with film: boycott. Upon the release of his *The Last Temptation of Christ* (1988), conservative evangelical groups sought to deprive the film of an audience by demanding that the studio cease production, picketing outside the studio, coordinating large-scale mailouts to churches criticizing the film, calling for citywide bans on its screening, and vandalizing cinemas and, in one instance, a film print.[6]

In fact, there is considerable variation in theological responses to film, which Robert K. Johnston has organized into the following typological categories: avoidance, caution, dialogue, appropriation, and divine encounter.[7] *Avoidance* entails a posture of condemnation of film, historically with respect to the medium itself.[8] *Caution* seeks to engage rather than avoid, albeit with a substantial dose of circumspection.

Dialogue charts a *via media*, understanding that arriving at truth is a dialectical process, each side of the dialogue allowed to truly speak and be heard.[9] *Appropriation* pushes beyond dialogue by acknowledging that the film may contribute something unique and positive, and this approach goes hand-in-hand with seeing film viewing as a quasi-religious activity.

Others go further still, holding that seeing a film may be the occasion for *divine encounter*. Theologian Craig Detweiler is a prominent example of this camp: "The best movies are revelatory in nature; they do not just talk about God and ultimate questions but become an occasion for the hidden God to communicate through the big screen. Cinema is a *locus theologicus*, a place for divine revelation."[10]

[6]Tom Pollard, *Sex and Violence: The Hollywood Censorship Wars* (Boulder, CO: Paradigm, 2009), 162.

[7]Robert K. Johnston, *Reel Spirituality: Theology and Film in Dialogue*, 2nd ed. (Grand Rapids, MI: Baker Academic, 2006), 55-79.

[8]The mid-twentieth-century evangelicalism in which my mother was raised, for example, frowned on cinemagoing. But this was not unusual for the time nor limited to New Zealand.

[9]For example, New Testament scholar Robert Jewett employs "dialogue in the prophetic mode" by letting the writings of Paul and the films of American culture mutually inform their respective interpretations. See Robert Jewett, *Saint Paul at the Movies: The Apostle's Dialogue with American Culture*, 1st ed. (Louisville, KY: Westminster John Knox, 1993), 7.

[10]Craig Detweiler, *Into the Dark: Seeing the Sacred in the Top Films of the 21st Century*, Cultural Exegesis (Grand Rapids, MI: Baker Academic, 2008), 42.

Detweiler has no qualms about naming these filmic experiences as general revelation. Gareth Higgins writes, "Film can transport you to . . . a 'thin place,' where the line between harsh reality and the transcendent is so subtly blurred for a moment, or if you're lucky, moments, you find it difficult to tell the difference."[11] Higgins, an Irish writer, explains that the Celtic concept of so-called thin places is possible because, quoting David Dark, "there isn't a secular molecule in the universe."[12] For those of this persuasion, watching a movie—something that others treat cautiously or avoid entirely—may become a moment of revelation, even a conversion experience.[13]

It is with this final category that my interests lie.[14] Other approaches have their merits, and the sheer diversity of movies available probably requires flexibility and the willingness to adopt different approaches as required. But if this assertion that certain movies may actually help usher the viewer into an encounter with the divine is correct, then this is surely the most theologically compelling dimension of cinema—and that is precisely where we will focus our attention.

The Case for Revelation Through Film

But does this *really* happen? Could it be that film-mediated revelation is something dreamed up by ivory tower theologians with little connection to lived experience? The work of Jonathan Brant speaks to this question with something rarely seen in the field of theology and film: empirical data.[15] There are good reasons for the dearth of such data, not least the fact that revelation can be neither proven nor disproven empirically. God can't be observed under a microscope. But Brant's aims are far more modest; he wishes only to demonstrate

[11]Gareth Higgins, *How Movies Helped Save My Soul: Finding Spiritual Fingerprints in Culturally Significant Films* (Lake Mary, FL: Relevant Books, 2003), xviii.

[12]Higgins, *How Movies Helped Save My Soul*, xix.

[13]For example, see Kathie Lee Gifford and Kate Shellnutt, "Kathie Lee Gifford: How Billy Graham Led Me to Christ," *Christianity Today*, 2016, www.christianitytoday.com/ct/2016/march/kathie-lee-gifford-how-billy-graham-led-me-to-christ.html.

[14]I do not expect to adhere to it exclusively, since these typological categories are all highly fluid, with many commentators drawing on several or all types as appropriate. See Johnston, *Reel Spirituality*. The boundaries between divine encounter and appropriation are especially porous. Since divine encounter comes only if and when God wills, advocates of this type often move effortlessly between this and appropriation. So divine encounter could be seen as a kind of "appropriation plus."

[15]For an example of another empirical study, see A. C. Van Hell, "Widening the Screen: Orthodox Protestant Film Viewers in The Netherlands and the Appropriation of Meaning in Relation to Their Religious Identity," Vrije Universiteit, 2016, http://dare.ubvu.vu.nl/handle/1871/54466.

the *possibility* of revelation by analyzing the experiences of nonprofessional viewers.[16] To that end, he undertook qualitative research among Latin American filmgoers, seeking to address "the glaring lack of audience data that undermines the religion-film discourse's efforts to speak meaningfully of the potential religious impact of films upon their viewers."[17]

The genesis of the study lies in Brant's prior experience as a pastoral worker in Uruguay, during which time "a troubling question arose as to whether urban young people, many of whom were almost completely alienated from the natural environment, were left without access to the *general revelation* that Christians normally associate with the beauty of the created order."[18] Brant thus conducted surveys and interviews among film festival attendees and cinema patrons in Montevideo, Uruguay, to determine whether these filmgoers had had revelatory experiences in response to movies like that described by the influential theologian Paul Tillich. Tillich famously claimed an experience of revelation upon seeing the painting *Madonna with Singing Angels* by Sandro Botticelli, one that would profoundly shape his theology of culture:

> Gazing up at it, I felt a state approaching ecstasy. In the beauty of the painting there was Beauty itself. It shone through the colours of the paint as the light of day shines through the stained-glass windows of a medieval church. As I stood there, bathed in the beauty its painter had envisioned so long ago, something of the divine source of all things came through to me. I turned away shaken. That moment has affected my whole life, given me the keys for the interpretation of human existence, brought vital joy and spiritual truth. I compare it with what is usually called revelation in the language of religion.[19]

Brant takes this experience as paradigmatic, adopting it as a yardstick against which to gauge his research subjects' filmgoing experiences. Revelation happens, argued Tillich, when there is a breakthrough from the surface form of an artwork to reveal the religious substance underneath.[20] For Tillich, the subject matter of the piece is irrelevant, since the surface is penetrated,

[16]Jonathan Brant, *Paul Tillich and the Possibility of Revelation Through Film* (Oxford: Oxford University Press, 2012), 8, ebook.

[17]Brant, *Paul Tillich*, 8.

[18]Brant, *Paul Tillich*, 6; emphasis original.

[19]Paul Tillich, *On Art and Architecture*, ed. John Dillenberger and Jane Dillenberger (New York: Crossroad, 1987), 234-35. Cited in Brant, *Paul Tillich*, 52.

[20]Brant, *Paul Tillich*, 56.

enabling encounter with the underlying Absolute. The content of revelation is therefore less important than its impact, its healing or salvific effect. Revelation is not about information, but rather transformation.[21] In describing revelation, Tillich prefers the term *event*, over and against *experience*, because it has both objective and subjective components. The revelation event occurs when elements in objective reality align with elements of the subjective mind.[22]

Brant wants to know if filmgoers recognize their own experience in Tillich's. Brant thus applies six parameters of Tillich's theology of revelation to the experiences of the participants' reported experiences: (1) the individual (i.e., viewer) on a quest for meaning and wholeness; (2) the artwork (i.e., film) that enables access to the substratum of meaning and power undergirding all of life; (3) the "event" of revelation (occasioned by a film viewing) in which the individual's existential quest and the artwork's meaning are united; (4) the revelatory content, comprised of an effable experience of the "ground of being" (God, approximately speaking) in which the artwork serves as the occasion; (5) the effect(s) of healing or "salvation," broadly conceived, in the life of the individual; and (6) the individual's existential involvement with Jesus as Christ, the criterion of all revelation, regardless of whether it is interpreted as such by the individual.[23]

So what were Brant's findings? The study revealed that a number of respondents reported experiences congruent with Tillich's account. This congruence does not *prove* that revelation has occurred, as if such a thing were possible, but it does demonstrate that filmgoers have experiences that could be interpreted as such. For example, one Catholic participant, Augusto, says, "It's not that God speaks through a film but yes, I believe he takes advantage of that opportunity in order to . . . in order to question us and in order to . . . make us see things that . . . or in order to ask us, or in order to . . . I don't know, return things to us. . . . As I said to you, the ways of God are, are strange."[24]

A nonreligious participant, Lucilda, says,

> I have felt those experiences in the cinema. Uhm, well yes, occasionally, I'd say . . . I'd say it's as if the film transmits to me, I'd say, and . . . it's as if I'm completely

---

[21]Brant, *Paul Tillich*, 10, 73.
[22]Brant, *Paul Tillich*, 67-68.
[23]Brant, *Paul Tillich*, 183-205.
[24]Brant, *Paul Tillich*, 203.

> and absolutely immersed and it's something beyond [*mas alla*—which often has superstitious or mystical connotations] that which . . . uhm . . . look, beyond that which I am as pure rationality, no? But it's not something that I can . . . [25]

Lucilda trails off at this point, struggling to articulate the experience. When Samuel, an atheist, recounts similar film-watching experiences, he likewise frequently falls silent and leaves sentences unfinished, "particularly when he is about to name what it is that he encounters in these [possibly revelatory] moments."[26] Despite his initial misgivings, by the interview's end, Samuel is happy to describe these experiences as revelatory, even if he does not elaborate or identify the agent of that revelation.[27] Indeed, Brant explains that Tillich's account of revelation allows for the possibility that an atheist may experience revelation, since the revelation is an ineffable first-order experience, the description of which is merely a second-order activity.[28] In other words, a nonbeliever could have an experience of revelation, yet describe or interpret it without recourse to religious or theistic language.

As a qualitative research project, Brant seeks insights into revelatory experience through thick description, and is thus "not overly concerned with the numbers of respondents contacted, questionnaires completed, or interviews recorded."[29] Instead of figures and statistics, this qualitative approach yields a wealth of data about the nature of alleged revelatory experiences with which Brant was able to substantiate some aspects of Tillich's account and challenge others. An example of the latter is the way his data calls into question Tillich's belief that the subject matter of the artwork is of no consequence. Brant grants that, for some participants, the effect of the event itself was of greater significance than any noetic content communicated. Nevertheless, the data suggests that the subject matter is often crucial to the revelation event (Brant thus suggests that the religious content of Tillich's beloved Botticelli is perhaps not as incidental as he insisted).[30] The data also reveals some aspects of revelation overlooked by Tillich such as, for instance, the fact that revelation is also communal and cumulative. The aggregate impact of cinemagoing over a long

[25]Brant, *Paul Tillich*, 203.

[26]Brant, *Paul Tillich*, 186.

[27]Brant, *Paul Tillich*, 183-88.

[28]Brant, *Paul Tillich*, 202.

[29]Brant, *Paul Tillich*, 219.

[30]Brant, *Paul Tillich*, 231-32.

period of time was for many participants greater than the impact made by any individual film.[31]

One pertinent aspect of Brant's research is the emergence of two categories of revelatory experience: a cognitive type and a mystical type (see table 1.1). The cognitive type is associated with the discursive aspects of the film, gradual onset, effability, and intellectual engagement. The mystical type is associated with the aesthetic aspects of the film, immediate onset, ineffability, and emotional engagement. Tillich's Botticelli experience is clearly of the mystical type, and so one way to read the data is to conclude that the conceptual net cast by Brant's questionnaire has caught not only truly revelatory experience (mystical type), but also nonrevelatory experience (cognitive type). But, instead, Brant reads these cognitive type experiences as also genuinely revelatory, because they have a high level of congruence with Tillich's account, have transformative power, and were identified by some participants as being of divine origin.[32] We needn't sharply distinguish between the two types for the purposes of this book, but instead simply note that both types are potentially revelatory.

Table 1.1. Comparison of cognitive-type and mystical-type experiences

	Cognitive Type	**Mystical Type**
Pertinent filmic aspects	discursive	aesthetic
Speed of onset	gradual	immediate
Effability	effable	ineffable
Type of engagement	intellectual	emotional

An issue of particular importance for this project is whether or not film form has any bearing on revelation. Is there something about the *film itself* that might lend itself to revelatory experience? Theological discussion about cinema has rarely gone down that route, but Brant's research speaks to the matter, as his study bears out the subjective and objective aspects of revelation. For example, participants' individual histories often significantly shaped their experiences of revelation through film. Films were sometimes identified as revelatory insofar as they depicted a historical situation the participant had

[31]Brant, *Paul Tillich*, 211.

[32]Brant, *Paul Tillich*, 171-79, 91-92.

lived through or if they were set in locations familiar to the participant.[33] Tillich's account is illuminating at this point. He holds that revelation happens when "the subjective constellation of revelation" (e.g., an individual's narrative) comes into alignment with "the objective constellation of revelation" (e.g., resources of the artwork).[34] The individual is on a personal quest, even if only unconsciously.[35] What that viewer brings to the encounter, therefore, matters. In a manner of speaking, it could be the making or the breaking of revelation (remembering, of course, that God is the generative agent of revelation). In fact, Brant even observes a correlation between the style of film and the type of experience it typically elicits: realism tends to elicit cognitive-type revelation; formalism tends to elicit mystical-type revelation.[36]

The recognition of an objective component to revelation is important. When it comes to revelation, there *is* something significant about the film itself. This need not always be the case; even kitsch may sometimes be revelatory.[37] Nevertheless, the qualities—and, indeed, *quality*—of a movie usually have some bearing on the outcome. If we set aside film and even the arts for a moment, we see that the same principle applies to revelation through nature. People will sense God's presence more often while watching a sunset than while seeing a decaying possum corpse; more often while pondering the infinities of space than while thinking about a backache; more often while holding a newborn baby than while massaging a slab of raw ribeye. There is no manufacturing of revelation. It strikes whenever and wherever God so chooses. Yet both experience and common sense tell us that certain things are more likely to serve as its occasion.

Brant's research clearly suggests that Tillich is not alone. Several participants related experiences occurring in the context of the cinema that could be described as potentially revelatory.[38] Brant thus concludes his study by saying,

---

[33]Brant, *Paul Tillich*, 179-81.

[34]Brant, *Paul Tillich*, 190.

[35]Brant, *Paul Tillich*, 188.

[36]Brant, *Paul Tillich*, 191.

[37]Sheila J. Nayar, "Reconfiguring the 'Genuinely' Religious Film: The Oral Contours of the Overabundant Epic," *Journal of the American Academy of Religion* 78, no. 1 (2010): 101-2, https://doi.org/10.1093/jaarel/lfp086.

[38]Brant's methodology is rigorous, applying a stringent set of criteria to "weed out" any experiences less likely to be genuinely revelatory. A broader conceptual net would likely have yielded many more purportedly revelatory experiences in response to film.

"It is my hope that the experiences that were so graciously shared by the interview respondents might be recognized as examples of the possibility of revelation through film, that is of the possibility of the inbreaking of the Spirit of God into the human world in healing, shaking, and even saving power."[39]

This conclusion is modest, a reflection of the inherent limitations of this type of data in investigating the mysterious workings of the divine. Although film-mediated revelation is not provable, according to Brant's study, it is *plausible*. The data reveals that experiences akin to Tillich's Botticelli experience are not uncommon. At least one reviewer has noted that this is hardly earth-shattering news,[40] but I think this assessment underestimates the value of the findings. The study adds empirical weight to claims that otherwise tend toward the vague and idiosyncratic. Brant demonstrates that the experience of film-mediated revelation is more than a solipsistic fiction dreamed up by academics or by those possessed by an overzealous mysticism. Experiences regarded as revelatory *actually* happen for ordinary filmgoers.

Transcendental Style in Film

Aesthetics for ascetics. We may be satisfied that, yes, viewers do indeed report film-mediated revelation, making divine encounter through cinema a genuine possibility. And since revelation involves an objective component and not solely a subjective one, we may consider what, if anything, film form contributes to these purportedly revelatory experiences of cinemagoers. My focus in this book will be primarily on images. Is there something about the way a movie is lit, edited, framed, or composed that is especially conducive to revelatory experience?

A similar question, albeit articulated differently, lies behind Paul Schrader's seminal articulation of transcendental style, a cinematic aesthetic he claims "has been used by various artists in diverse cultures to express the Holy."[41] Schrader's theory warrants close examination, not only because of its monumental influence, but also because it is an account of film form with respect to revelation (or, at least, something close to it). My project is more expressly

---

[39]Brant, *Paul Tillich*, 234-35.

[40]Steve Nolan, "Paul Tillich and the Possibility of Revelation Through Film: A Theoretical Account Grounded by Empirical Research into the Experiences of Filmgoers," *Journal of Contemporary Religion* 29, no. 1 (2014): 172, https://doi.org/10.1080/13537903.2014.864834.

[41]Paul Schrader, *Transcendental Style in Film: Ozu, Bresson, Dreyer* (New York: Da Capo, 1988), 3.

theological than Schrader's, yet he is a useful sparring partner through which to explore the stylistic dimensions of films that regularly occasion claims of revelatory experience.

Schrader, a scholar-turned-filmmaker, explains that his interest in transcendental style stemmed from his own experience as a viewer:

> In certain films, I sensed a kind of link between my past [Christian upbringing] and my present [film career], between the sacred and the profane, between the spiritual life of the Christian and the commercial life of a film. But that link was not content; it was style . . . spirituality and art are not connected by the "what"; they're connected by the "how."[42]

The "how" he refers to is cinematic style. For Schrader, truly religious cinema is defined by form. "Although transcendental style . . . strives towards the ineffable and the invisible," he writes, "it is neither ineffable nor invisible itself. Transcendental style uses precise temporal means—camera angles, dialogue, editing—for predetermined transcendental ends."[43]

It might be too much to say that Schrader claims transcendental style mediates *revelation* as such. As a work of film scholarship rather than theology, the theological implications of transcendental style are not spelled out for us. Nevertheless, Schrader seems to envisage a viewer experience akin to revelation, or at the very least, conducive to it. Transcendental style is a cinematic form that "expresses the Transcendent," enables the viewer to "perceive the Transcendent, and then experience transcendence."[44] Schrader acknowledges that transcendence has been understood by other thinkers variously as mere psychological projection and as caused by an external Other, but he doesn't himself take a clear position.[45] The experiences Schrader envisages may be, to use phenomenologist Jean-Luc Marion's concept, a "saturated" phenomenon, in which something is so overwhelmingly rich it defies objectification, in excess of the subject's ability to grasp.[46] Regardless of Schrader's

[42]Paul Schrader and Joseph Kickasola, "Paul Schrader on Revisiting Transcendental Style in Film (TIFF 2017)," in *TIFF Originals* (December 20, 2017), www.youtube.com/watch?v=m4F8I8OVmUU.

[43]Schrader, *Transcendental Style in Film*, 3-4.

[44]Schrader, *Transcendental Style in Film*, 51-52.

[45]Schrader, *Transcendental Style in Film*, 5-6.

[46]Jean-Luc Marion, *In Excess: Studies of Saturated Phenomena* (New York: Fordham University Press, 2002); Christina M. Gschwandtner, "Might Nature Be Interpreted as a 'Saturated Phenomenon'?," in *Interpreting Nature: The Emerging Field of Environmental Hermeneutics* (New York: Fordham University Press, 2014).

precise theology on this point, he clearly has in mind the experiential dimension that often accompanies claims of revelation, or transcendence, which Johnston equates with divine encounter and refers to as "'Transcendence' with a capital T."[47] Indeed, Schrader's theory comes close enough to suggesting revelation that Johnston considers it under the rubric of divine encounter.[48] As film scholar David Desser says, "Transcendental style is not dependent on showing us characters . . . who have achieved grace or transcendence, but rather with letting us *experience* the Transcendent through the film's style."[49]

Before explaining precisely what transcendental style is, let's look at what it is *not*. Transcendental cinema is a world away from the movies that normally grab the attention of the religious mainstream. Biblical movies, for example, often generate excitement—or disappointment—among Christians. There seems to be an underlying assumption that the best way to depict the "spiritual" on film is to adapt scriptural narratives for the screen. This stems from a low view of general revelation; the only way a film may be considered revelatory is to take *special* revelation and turn that into a movie. We'll explore this further in the next chapter.[50]

It's no small irony then that orthodoxy in film studies holds biblical epics to be among the *least* likely films to occasion revelatory experience.[51] Writing at a time when big-budget religious epics were already an established Hollywood staple, Schrader argued that truly religious films are the very antithesis of religious epics. Consider, for example, how Schrader describes a scene of theophany in Cecil B. DeMille's biblical epic *The Ten Commandments* (1956):

> In the title scene Moses is on Mount Sinai and God is off-screen to the right. After some premonitory thundering, God literally pitches the commandments, one by one, onto the screen and the awaiting blank tablets. The commandments first appear as small whirling fireballs accompanied by the sound of a rushing

[47]Johnston, *Reel Spirituality*, 242.

[48]Johnston, *Reel Spirituality*, 76-78.

[49]David Desser, "Transcendental Style in Tender Mercies," *Religious Communication Today* 8 (1985): 22.

[50]So absolute is this belief that these films are apparently granted a "free pass" by the same sensitive Christian viewers who might ordinarily oppose transgressive content—for example, the gory violence of *The Passion of the Christ* (Mel Gibson, 2004), considered to be among the most violent Hollywood films ever made.

[51]Ann Hardy, *Film, Spirituality and Hierophany: The Contemporary Search for Meaning* (Alister Hardy Religious Experience Research Centre, 2002), 7-8.

> wind, and then quickly—building in size all the while—zip across and collide with the blank tablets. Puff! the smoke clears, and the tablet is clearly inscribed.[52]

For Schrader, the scene is bathetic—and pathetic. The problem with these types of movies, he argues, is their reliance on spectacle for their spiritual potency. They may thrill or terrify or emotionally engage an audience, but they lack the ability to facilitate an experience of transcendence. This on-the-nose type of religious film was parodied in the Coen brothers' *Hail, Caesar!* (Ethan Coen, Joel Coen, 2016), a movie set in golden-era Hollywood. In the film, filmmakers watch dailies of a forthcoming biblical epic, in which Saul of Tarsus encounters the risen Christ. It cuts suddenly from the actor Baird Whitlock's (George Clooney) face to a title card that reads "Divine presence to be shot." Later, as he beholds Christ on the cross, Whitlock struggles to alight upon the right awestruck facial expression. This prompts the director to bark, "Squint at the grandeur!" Beneath the trademark Coen brothers' humor is a profound point: using Hollywood spectacle to portray God on screen is absurd.

Enough with the preliminaries—what *is* transcendental style? Transcendentalism takes a minimalist approach, employing plain, unflashy production values, resulting in a decidedly austere look and feel. Religious subject matter is optional; the religious element in transcendental style is a matter of form, not content.[53] It is the very antithesis of the blockbuster Hollywood religious epic, yet a more authentically religious aesthetic. According to Schrader, transcendental films achieve this through a three-stage filmic structure: (1) the everyday, (2) disparity, and (3) stasis.[54]

The everyday. This first stage consists of creating a sense of the everyday, the banal details of ordinary existence. Ostensibly a depiction of "real" life, it is in fact highly stylized. After all, real life *does* have moments of genuine drama—all strenuously avoided by the transcendental filmmaker in her depiction of the everyday. The strategy at this stage is simple: minimize the dramatic and maximize the mundane. To that end, the camera is kept static and a narrow range of camera angles employed. Editing is functional, repetitive, predictable. Pacing is slow, if not downright ponderous. Story beats are subtle, lacking the drama of more conventional cinema. Music is minimal, if not absent entirely.

---

[52]Schrader, *Transcendental Style in Film*, 163.
[53]Schrader, *Transcendental Style in Film*, 4.
[54]Schrader, *Transcendental Style in Film*, 39-53.

Performances are subdued to the point that "acting" becomes almost a misnomer. The aggregate effect of these techniques is an ascetic aesthetic.[55] The everyday is, however, only a means, not an end. Were it an end in itself, it would be essentially nihilistic.[56] Instead, the everyday is preparatory, a quasi-ritualistic way of priming "reality for the intrusion of the Transcendent."[57]

Disparity. The second stage involves tampering with the rigorously constructed everyday, thereby creating "a crack in the dull surface of the everyday."[58] Specifically, it involves inserting a moment of emotional expression into what is otherwise an unemotional environment. In classical style, such a demonstrative display would be unremarkable. But in transcendental style, virtually any emotional expression is thrown into sharp relief by its drab context. And so there's a disparity between the cold, indifferent environment of the film and the sensitive, impassioned character(s), prompting us to wonder, "If the environment is unfeeling, where do man's feelings come from?"[59]—cognitive dissonance that demands resolution. As moments of disparity accumulate throughout the film, what starts out as solely affective gradually takes on a spiritual dimension.[60] Disparity gradually chips away at the everyday façade, and the resulting tension culminates in a climactic moment of disparity, which Schrader terms *decisive action.*[61]

Stasis. This ultimate instance of disparity leads immediately into the third step of transcendental style, in which the tension between the everyday and disparity is finally resolved. But I use "resolved" only loosely, since resolution in transcendental style doesn't entail either side of the tension triumphing over the other. Instead, both the everyday and disparity are simply accepted, yet seen, somewhat ineffably, as complementary and interconnected. In other words, their incongruity is *transcended.* How? Most typically by ending the film with a static shot, though no ordinary static shot will do. The image must somehow place the film's conflict into a wider context: a well-chosen still life; a static coda of nature; intercutting a still shot with something more dynamic;

---

[55]Schrader, *Transcendental Style in Film*, 39-42.
[56]Schrader, *Transcendental Style in Film*, 42.
[57]Schrader, *Transcendental Style in Film*, 39.
[58]Schrader, *Transcendental Style in Film*, 42.
[59]Schrader, *Transcendental Style in Film*, 43.
[60]Schrader, *Transcendental Style in Film*, 43.
[61]Schrader, *Transcendental Style in Film*, 46.

zooming or tracking back to reveal the subject against its broader backdrop—techniques that convey an attitude of quiescence.[62] "Frozen motion . . . establishes an image of a second reality which can stand beside the ordinary reality; it represents the Wholly Other."[63]

Abundant and sparse means. At a more fundamental level, transcendental style can be understood as a particular handling of what Schrader, borrowing language first used by Jacques Maritain, calls *abundant means* and *sparse means*.[64] Abundant means in art are those techniques that are "sensual, emotional, humanistic, individualistic . . . characterized by soft lines, realistic portraiture, three-dimensionality, experimentation; they encourage empathy." Sparse means, on the other hand, are those techniques that are "cold, formalistic, hieratic. They are characterized by abstraction, stylized portraiture, two-dimensionality, rigidity; they encourage respect and appreciation."[65] Abundant means are inherently interesting and thus tend to grab and hold the viewer's attention, whereas sparse means are comparatively dull.

Transcendental style may use both abundant and sparse means, but in terms of spirituality, Schrader argues the latter is superior: "Sparse means . . . are necessarily closer to the Holy."[66] Similarly, he writes, "The ratio of abundant and sparse means can be a measure of the 'spirituality' of a work of art. The more a work of art can successfully incorporate sparse means within an abundant society, the nearer it approaches its transcendental 'end.'"[67] Elsewhere, Schrader has described sparse means as "withholding techniques," because the director withholds expected and desired features.[68] Conventional films rely on abundance for their appeal; indeed, the Hollywood blockbuster has become synonymous with hyperabundance, as each new mega-budget popcorn movie seeks to out-Hollywood earlier efforts by turning the dial way up on special effects, computer-generated imagery, dramatic plotlines, fast cuts, a star-studded cast, and so on. This type of film may thrill, intrigue, amuse, frighten, and titillate. But like its baptized cousin, the biblical epic, it is not

---

[62]Schrader, *Transcendental Style in Film*, 49-52.
[63]Schrader, *Transcendental Style in Film*, 49.
[64]Schrader, *Transcendental Style in Film*, 154-55.
[65]Schrader, *Transcendental Style in Film*, 155.
[66]Schrader, *Transcendental Style in Film*, 154.
[67]Schrader, *Transcendental Style in Film*, 155.
[68]Schrader and Kickasola, "Paul Schrader on Revisiting Transcendental Style."

ordinarily expected to be spiritually resonant. And, unlike other art forms, cinema has been steeped in abundance since its inception. Abundance is its "mother tongue," while it has had to learn sparseness.[69] Crafting a film in transcendental style requires not only striking the right balance between abundant and sparse means, but also progressively tipping the scales toward sparseness as the film progresses.[70] By the transcendental film's end, abundant means have been dispensed with entirely, leaving only sparse means—so sparse we are left with total stillness (stasis).

Getting the balance of abundance and sparseness right is important. For Schrader, religious epics are "overabundant" and some experimental films are "oversparse," and thus fall short of being transcendental.[71] That said, films may effectively use elements of the transcendental style without committing to it exclusively.[72] In fact, Schrader chose Dreyer as one of his three principal subjects precisely because he used transcendentalism only partially. That transcendental style can be employed to varying degrees has allowed critics to argue, for instance, that *Tender Mercies* (Bruce Beresford, 1983)[73] is more transcendental than *Places in the Heart* (Robert Benton, 1984),[74] though the latter too demonstrates modest use of transcendental elements.[75] Componential use of transcendental style means that the style is more operative in the cinema of today than might initially appear to be the case.

Transcendental style in contemporary film: Tamasese, Dardenne, Reygadas. After starting out as a film scholar, Schrader went on to become a celebrated screenwriter and director. As such, some scholars have sought to interpret Schrader's own films through the lens of transcendental style.[76] While Schrader acknowledges the influence of transcendentalists like Bresson

---

69 Schrader, *Transcendental Style in Film*, 158-59.

70 Schrader, *Transcendental Style in Film*, 159.

71 Schrader, *Transcendental Style in Film*, 162-67.

72 Schrader, *Transcendental Style in Film*, 10.

73 Ranked #49, "Top 100 Films—2020," *Arts & Faith*, 2020, accessed January 3, 2022, http://artsandfaith.com/index.php?/films/&do=year&id=8&page=2.

74 Ranked #95, "Top 100 Films—2020," *Arts & Faith*, 2020, accessed January 3, 2022, http://artsandfaith.com/index.php?/films/&do=year&id=8&page=4.

75 Richard Engnell, "The Spiritual Potential of Otherness in Film: The Interplay of Scene and Narrative," *Critical Studies in Mass Communication* 12, no. 3 (1995): 258, https://doi.org/10.1080/15295039509366936.

76 For example, see Bill Nichols. "American Gigolo: Transcendental Style and Narrative Form," *Film Quarterly* 34 (1981): 8-13.

and admits the possibility of having employed transcendental style subconsciously,[77] he claims to never have consciously sought to use in his own films the aesthetic he identified and made famous—that is, until he released *First Reformed* (Paul Schrader, 2017).[78] For the first time in his storied career, Schrader intentionally employed transcendental style in one of his own films.[79]

But we need not look only to *First Reformed* to find recent examples of transcendental style. Though Schrader wrote *Transcendental Style in Film* in the 1970s, transcendental style is alive and well in contemporary film even outside his own work. Indeed, Schrader wrote an updated introduction for an anniversary edition of his book in which he equates transcendental style with the contemporary genre of slow cinema.[80] When Schrader originally penned his work on transcendental style, he concentrated on its chief exponents at the time: Yasujirō Ozu, Robert Bresson, and, to a lesser extent, Carl Theodor Dreyer. All three are undisputed master auteurs, their films still essential viewing for modern-day cinéastes. But appreciating these films in terms of their transcendental qualities is a challenge for some contemporary viewers, since the hierophanous effect is potentially undermined by techniques that feel foreign and alienating. Granted, feeling foreign and alienating is the point. Distancing is partly how transcendental style apparently works, but it seems to me that these techniques may be less spiritually potent for modern audiences. Rather than repeat Schrader's analyses of the classical transcendentalists then, let's examine more recent films that employ and update the style, like *The Orator* (Tusi Tamasese, 2011), *The Son* (Jean-Pierre Dardenne and Luc Dardenne, 2002),[81] and *Silent Light* (Carlos Reygadas, 2007). Note, therefore, that the following films are my examples, not Schrader's.[82] We have much to learn from Ozu, Bresson, and Dreyer, but also much from this contemporary transcendental triumvirate of Tamasese, the Dardenne brothers, and Reygadas.

[77]Schrader provides a brief response to Nichols's transcendental analysis in Nichols, "American Gigolo," 13.

[78]Ranked #11, "Top 100 Films—2020," *Arts & Faith*, 2020, accessed January 3, 2022, http://artsandfaith.com/index.php?/films/&do=year&id=8.

[79]Schrader and Kickasola, "Paul Schrader on Revisiting Transcendental Style."

[80]Paul Schrader, *Transcendental Style in Film: Ozu, Bresson, Dreyer*, vol. 1 (Oakland: University of California Press, 2018), chap. 1, ebook.

[81]Ranked #8, "Top 100 Films," *Arts & Faith*, 2011, accessed January 3, 2022, https://imagejournal.org/top-100-films/.

[82]Schrader has, however, subsequently cited *Silent Light* as an example of transcendental style. Schrader and Kickasola, "Paul Schrader on Revisiting Transcendental Style."

Examining how these films both adhere to and deviate from classical transcendentalism will give greater insight into how the style is meant to work.

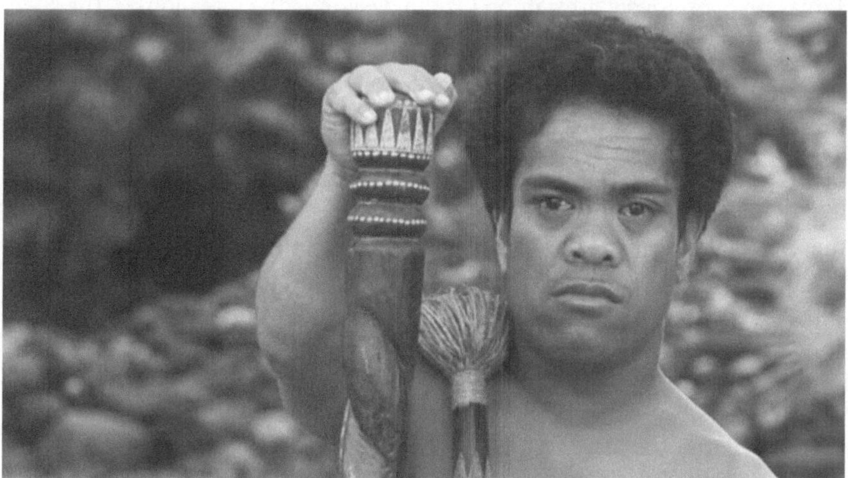

Figure 1.1. A rare display of emotion in *The Orator* marks this moment as the decisive action

The first ever Samoan-language feature film (a Samoa-New Zealand coproduction), written and directed by the Samoan Tamasese and set entirely in Samoa, *The Orator* tells the story of a taro farmer, Saili (Fa'afiaula Sagote), stigmatized for his dwarfism, who finds his voice and reclaims his late father's chiefly status through an oratorical *tour de force* that secures his right to bury his deceased wife, Vaaiga (Tausili Pushparaj), on family land. Schrader's concept of the everyday is operative here, and is created through languid pacing, unmotivated shots, and muted performances. Disparity too is apparent, culminating at the film's climax in Saili's decisive action of exhorting Vaaiga's family to return her body to him and bestow forgiveness upon her—and, in his only bluntly expressive moment, he cries (fig. 1.1). The film's penultimate scene is one of stasis, as Saili's tearful plea cuts to a shot of Saili and Vaaiga's daughter, Litia (Salamasina Mataia), sitting on a bus with Vaaiga's wrapped body on the floor. Saili's request is granted, but the juxtaposition in a single image of polar opposites—life and death, happiness and sadness—elicits the transcendental effect identified by Schrader.[83]

[83]Historian Valerie Bichard's observation that "Tamasese does not appear to be interested in delivering an answer or solution to everyday problems" suggests a complexity to the film's ending that goes beyond a simple happy/sad binary. Valerie Bichard, "O Le Tulafale/The Orator," review of *The Orator*,

Critics have noted *The Orator*'s similarities to the work of transcendental master Ozu, with both, for instance, sharing a predilection for long-takes.[84] Tamasese consciously drew upon Ozu in designing the film's look: "The style that I was most attracted to was Japanese, like [that of Yasujirō] Ozu. . . . It's very similar to the master, Ozu. I was trying to find a style that would suit how I wanted to tell the story."[85] Nowhere is Ozu's influence on the *The Orator* more apparent than in the interior *fale* (house) shots. These evoke Ozu's *tatami* mat shots and interior scenes, which give Ozu's films the feeling that "the ends of the earth are no more distant than outside the house."[86] Tamasese's debt to Ozu is also apparent in the acting. Ozu (and Bresson) employed what Schrader calls *nonexpressive* performances,[87] which Tamasese too has sought. Though Sagote is a nonprofessional actor—taro farming is his day job[88]—his nondemonstrative performance isn't due to a lack of skill;[89] it's simply consistent with transcendental style.

Despite Ozu's influence, *The Orator* breaks with transcendental style in a number of ways. Far from creating the dull surface required by the everyday, the spare visual techniques accentuate the beauty, natural and cultural, of the film's setting. There are enough cinematic flourishes, such as the "un-Ozu" use of dollies and pans, to suggest that Tamasese is seeking to maintain viewer interest rather than frustrate it as rigorous transcendentalism would dictate.[90] The final scene, too, ever so slightly deviates from the style, with Saili sitting peacefully on Vaaiga's grave on his own land while holding her newborn granddaughter as her daughter sweeps. The shot tracks back into the *fale* to show the characters in their larger natural context—a transcendental technique[91]—but the ending is moderately uplifting. Saili has found his voice, Vaaiga has been

Journal of Pacific History 48, February 19, 2013, https://dx.doi.org/10.1080/00223344.2013.769291.

[84]Martin Rumsby, "The Ocean Is Our Prairie," *Millennium Film Journal*, no. 61 (2015).

[85]Richard Gray, "The Other Side of Paradise: Tusi Tamasese on 'The Orator,'" *Metro Magazine: Media & Education Magazine*, 2012, 32.

[86]Joseph L. Anderson and Donald Richie, *The Japanese Film*, ed. Donald Richie (New York: Grove Press, 1960), 359; cited in Schrader, *Transcendental Style in Film*, 19.

[87]Schrader, *Transcendental Style in Film*, 66.

[88]Helen Barlow, "Tusi Tamasese: A Voice from Samoa," *NZ Herald* (New Zealand), September 8, 2011, www.nzherald.co.nz/entertainment/news/article.cfm?c_id=1501119&objectid=10750044.

[89]Sagote was a finalist for the top acting award at the Asia Pacific Screen Awards. *New Zealand Film Commission Annual Report 2011–2012*, 9, www.nzfilm.co.nz/sites/default/files/NZFC_Annual_Report_2011-2012.pdf.

[90]Schrader, *Transcendental Style in Film*, 63-64.

[91]Schrader, *Transcendental Style in Film*, 52.

forgiven, her body buried on his land, and the next generation is thriving. In the final analysis, the commonalities between *The Orator* and transcendental style boil down mostly to emotional restraint and an unhurried pace.

While *The Orator* is far more picturesque than classic transcendental films, the same can't be said of *The Son,* a film of "almost punishing restraint."[92] The bleak aesthetic that earned directors and brothers Jean-Pierre and Luc Dardenne the moniker "the brothers Grim" is fully realized in this story of a carpentry teacher of at-risk youth who accepts into his class the adolescent murderer of his young son, keeping his identity as the victim's father a secret from the apprentice.[93] The Dardenne brothers are frequently likened to the transcendentalist *par excellence* Bresson, and his influence is plain to see. Their Palme d'Or-winning *The Child* (2005)[94] draws heavily on Bresson's *Pickpocket* (1959), particularly in its final prison visitation scene. Nevertheless, they differ substantially from their fellow Francophone in other respects.[95] While Bresson's camerawork is static,[96] the Dardennes' is mobile, "frantic, desperate, vertiginous."[97] They have carried the use of handheld cameras over from documentary, on which they cut their teeth, to their fictional films, using closeup, tightly framed shots.[98] Reviewers have made much of the fact that we spend an inordinate amount of screen time looking at the nape of protagonist Olivier's (Olivier Gourmet) neck, shot as it is largely over his shoulder.[99] The film is set entirely in unphotogenic locations using naturalistic lighting (fig. 1.2). Exterior scenes are shot in grimy, decaying urban environments against uniformly overcast skies. Despite its departure from Bresson's stillness, however, it more effectively constructs the everyday for modern viewers reared on *cinéma vérité,* not to mention "am-cam" news footage and YouTube videos. Contemporary audiences equate handheld photography with documentary realism.

---

[92]Erica Abeel, "The Son (Le Fils)," review of *The Son,* Buying & Booking Guide, 2003.

[93]Justin Chang, "Nothing but the Truth," *Variety,* 2014, 63.

[94]Ranked #46, "Top 100 Films," *Arts & Faith,* 2011, accessed January 3, 2022, https://imagejournal.org/top-100-films/.

[95]Chang, "Nothing but the Truth," 62.

[96]Schrader, *Transcendental Style in Film,* 67.

[97]Richard Locke, "Realism with a Heart: The Dardenne Brothers Bring an Idiosyncratic Sympathy to Their Portrayals of Belgian Lowlifes," *The American Scholar* 83, no. 2 (2014): 90.

[98]Locke, "Realism with a Heart," 90-91.

[99]Abeel, "The Son (Le Fils)."

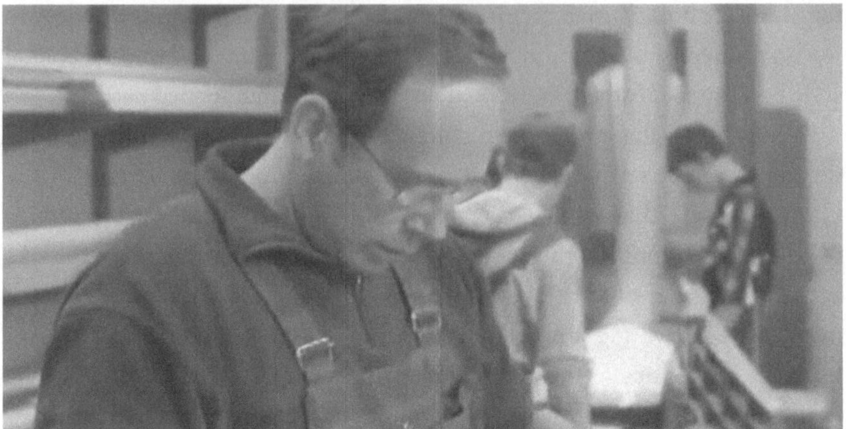

Figure 1.2. The bleak naturalism of *The Son* is an example of the everyday

Like Bresson, the Dardennes employ nonexpressive acting:[100] "We don't ask [our actors] to express, we don't want them to emote, we don't want them to act."[101] Critic Erica Abeel quips that Gourmet's performance is "remarkable for its complete absence of, well, acting."[102] (Like *The Orator*'s Sagote, Gourmet's poker-faced performance nevertheless earned industry accolades, including the supreme acting award at Cannes.)[103] What we know of Olivier, we know by what he *does*—sprinting, hiding, spying. The look and the performances of the film consistently thwart typical audience strategies of engagement, precisely as transcendental style dictates.[104] The ambience is thus so affectively stifling that when moments of disparity occur—such as when Olivier's ex-wife, Magali (Isabella Soupart) rages and then faints on learning of his acquaintance with their son's killer—the contrast between the film's superficial indifference and the characters' depth of pain is striking. This is exactly the sort of tension for which Schrader lauded Bresson, but which may be lost on many present-day viewers of Bresson's films.

The film's decisive action comes when Olivier pins his apprentice Francis (Morgan Marinne) to the ground with his hand around his throat, about to

---

[100]Schrader, *Transcendental Style in Film*, 65-67.

[101]Robert Sklar, "The Terrible Lightness of Social Marginality: An Interview with Jean-Pierre and Luc Dardenne," *Cineaste* 31, no. 2 (2006): 20.

[102]Abeel, "The Son (Le Fils)."

[103]Joan M. West and Dennis West, "Taking the Measure of Human Relationships: An Interview with Jean-Pierre Dardenne and Luc Dardenne," *Cineaste* 28, no. 3 (2003): 14.

[104]Schrader, *Transcendental Style in Film*, 63-64.

snuff out his life the way this boy had done to Olivier's son five years prior. But he allows his fury to subside and, in a poignant act of mercy, releases Francis. The final scene has Francis return to Olivier and, without either uttering a word, resume assisting Olivier in loading a trailer with timber. Stasis is achieved since the film's tension is "resolved" more by acceptance than by triumph. Yet it is a more hopeful form of stasis than Schrader expects of transcendental films; Olivier has forgiven the unforgiveable.

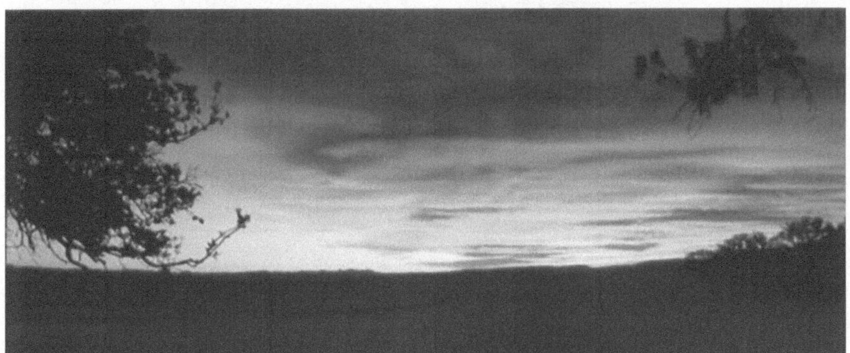

Figure 1.3. The opening image of the sunrise in *Silent Light* is frequently cited for its dazzling beauty

Pacing is the first thing the viewer notices about *Silent Light,* a film about an adulterous relationship in a Mennonite community in Mexico. The opening shot, a pan from the sky to the horizon as night turns to day, is well over five minutes in duration (fig. 1.3). After the opening shot, the languid pace continues. Indeed, that the very next image immediately following the sunrise is of a ticking clock suggests that this film is well aware of its unconventional relationship with time. We then watch a Mennonite family in silent prayer for several minutes, presented as a series of long-takes. Breakfast follows and, once finished, the family vacates, leaving husband and father, Johan (Cornelio Wall), alone. Johan is framed in a midshot that lasts over three minutes, still and expressionless until he begins to sob uncontrollably. A sudden expression of buried emotion interrupts the quotidian façade, disparity amid the everyday as transcendental style stipulates.

Reygadas consciously draws extensively and overtly from Dreyer's *Ordet* (1955),[105] which Schrader considers to be the Danish auteur's most transcendental

[105]Jonathan Romney, "Carlos Reygadas: Silent Light," *Sight and Sound* 17, no. 7 (2007).

film. *Silent Light*'s debt to *Ordet* is seen most clearly in the decisive action wherein Johan's deceased wife Esther (Miriam Toews) is brought back to life. For Schrader, the resurrection moment in *Ordet* is the perfect example of decisive action, yet he argues that the ending falls short of true stasis.[106] *Silent Light*'s ending is a purer expression of stasis, because of the remarkable lack of celebration in response to the miracle, as if this were an ordinary event (fig. 1.4). This imbues the moment with a pronounced air of mystery, truer to the spirit of transcendental style. From here, the camera begins its movement away from the room where the resurrected Esther lies, across landscapes until it comes to the place where the film began. The final shot is a long-take of the sunset, a mirror image of the opening, bringing the film full circle. Like Ozu, Reygadas contrasts the vicissitudes of human life with the constancy of the setting sun and the natural world.

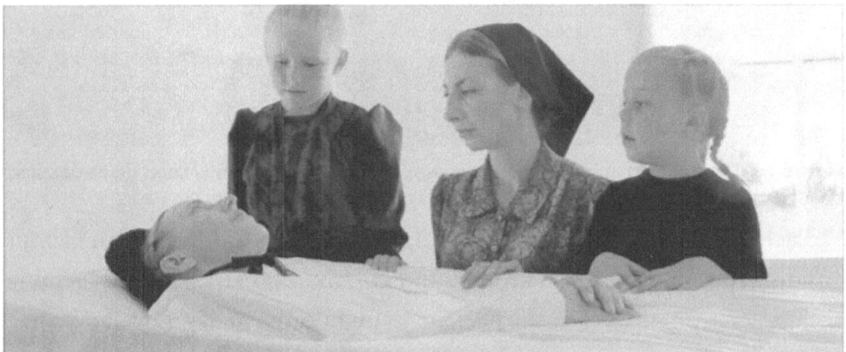

Figure 1.4. The stoic response to Esther's resurrection contributes to stasis in *Silent Light*

Other transcendental elements are on display in *Silent Light.* "Actors are coached to stare into space for long moments before delivering stiff dialogue with unnatural solemnity," says reviewer Kirk Honeycutt.[107] Like Bresson and the Dardenne brothers, Reygadas favors amateur actors, casting actual Chihuahuense Mennonites.[108] The film also employs a staple technique of transcendental cinema: frontality, in which subjects are framed front-on in symmetrical composition, evocative of religious iconography. Schrader himself has identified *Silent Light* as transcendental.[109] But for all its transcendental

[106]Schrader, *Transcendental Style in Film*, 132-38.

[107]Kirk Honeycutt, "Silent Light," *Hollywood Reporter* 399 (2007).

[108]William Johnson, "Between Daylight and Darkness: *Forever* and *Silent Light*," *Film Quarterly* 61, no. 3 (2008): 21, https://doi.org/10.1525/fq.2008.61.3.18.

[109]Schrader and Kickasola, "Paul Schrader on Revisiting Transcendental Style."

credentials, the film defies neat categorization. Critics have rightly noted its austerity, yet, paradoxically, it has an inescapably sumptuous quality.[110] Those long, lingering takes seem calculated to let us *drink in* the scene, inviting us to luxuriate in the undeniably lovely images. The camera tracks toward Johan as he weeps, visually eliciting our sympathy. Lens flare dances across the screen as Johan and Marianne kiss passionately in closeup (fig. 1.5), making palpable the sunshine and warmth of the moment. Delightful children bathe in a pool, actual Mennonite youngsters who do not need to "act" to convey joy. The dawn-dusk bookends are breathtaking. Simply put, it's too beautiful to be transcendental in the strict classical sense. Though literally an everyday occurrence, the rising and setting sun is anything but mundane when viewed through Reygadas's camera. Like his muse Dreyer, Reygadas has blended transcendental style with more expressive approaches.[111] We will explore *Silent Light,* and its cinematic predecessor, *Ordet,* in far greater detail in chapter four.

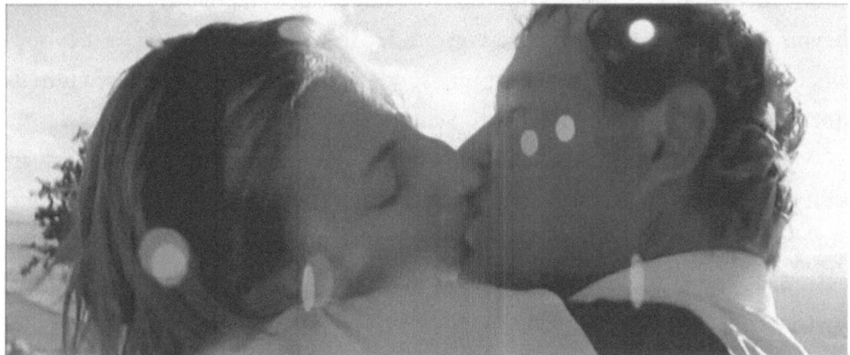

Figure 1.5. Backlighting and lens flare call attention to the presence of sunlight, as if the illicit union were divinely blessed

Critique of transcendental style. As these contemporary films demonstrate, transcendental style has enjoyed remarkable staying power. *Transcendental Style in Film* remains an important exploration of film form with respect to the Transcendent. But it has at least two limitations. First, transcendental style is not nearly as universal as Schrader claims, being just one of a number of possible cinematic styles potentially capable of facilitating transcendence. Though Schrader grants that some partially transcendental films may be successful, he

[110]Honeycutt, "Silent Light."

[111]Schrader, *Transcendental Style in Film,* 113-14.

apparently considers them successful only to the extent they employ the style.[112] Dreyer's films, for instance, are always an alloy of transcendental and other styles, which Schrader claims is why they are only ever partially successful at the transcendental level. Dreyer himself thought the religious power of his films stemmed from their expressionist elements. Schrader disagrees. He believes expressionism is incapable of rising above the psychological; only transcendental style is up to the task.[113]

But transcendental style does not have the monopoly on transcendence. *Tender Mercies*, with its Ozuesque narrative ellipses and "retrospectivity" (chronologically ambiguous scene transitions), looks in many ways to be a clear-cut example of transcendental filmmaking.[114] But communication scholar Richard Engnell argues that it tinkers with the transcendental formula by giving us an ending that expands and indeed *improves* upon mere stasis: "*Tender Mercies* goes beyond the frozen, largely empty unity of transcendental stasis. . . . This form of transcendence is not frozen or static, but dynamic. The viewer goes beyond acceptance to a hope that is grounded in something certain yet beyond what can be known."[115] Engnell's point suggests the spiritual weight of a film is not determined purely by fidelity to Schrader's approach.

Much of what animates Schrader's theory then is his belief in the universality of transcendental style, an aesthetic supposedly versatile enough to encompass the symbolism of diverse religious and cultural traditions, thereby acting as a kind of cinematic *lingua franca* with respect to the spiritual potential of film. Indeed, the very first lines of the book read,

> In recent years film has developed a transcendental style, a style which has been used by various artists in diverse cultures to express the Holy. Just as anthropologists at the turn of the century discovered that artisans in unrelated cultures had found similar ways to express similar spiritual emotions, so, in cinema, unrelated film-makers have created a consensus of transcendental style.[116]

Later, he writes, "Transcendental style, like Byzantine art, is a universal form because it can accommodate different artists and different cultures within a

---

112 Schrader, *Transcendental Style in Film*, 112.
113 Schrader, *Transcendental Style in Film*, 118.
114 Desser, "Transcendental Style in Tender Mercies," 25-26.
115 Engnell, "Spiritual Potential," 258.
116 Schrader, *Transcendental Style in Film*, 3.

common structure . . . transcendental style can adapt to both cultures because it expresses the Transcendent, which knows no culture."[117] The style may be found across various cultural boundaries, but Schrader seems to think it somehow stands above culture.

The persistent claims of universality strike me as improbable. What he takes to be universal is in fact every bit as culturally conditioned as any other. The most persuasive voice on this front is film and literature scholar Sheila Nayar. Nayar has convincingly argued that the scholarly preference for sparse means in cinema stems from the unconscious cultural privileging of literacy over orality. Despite the critical tendency to treat abundance as kitsch—recall the negative assessments of Hollywood's religious epics above—films of this type often serve for lay audiences as the occasion for hierophany. Nayar cites, for example, a widely attested incident at a 1975 screening of a low-budget Indian movie depicting various Hindu deities in which audiences prostrated themselves in the theater, showering the screen with flower petals.[118] One man's trash really is another man's treasure.

But the difference in reception cannot simply be chalked up to good taste versus bad. According to Nayar, a viewer's reception is rooted partly in her episteme, the way of knowing osmosed from the cultural context. Orality fosters a predilection for abundant means, the kind embraced by both Bollywood and Hollywood. Such means are not restricted to the spoken word *per se* but extend to characteristics that tend to accompany speech as opposed to writing, namely techniques and traits that aid comprehension and that have a collective orientation: spectacle, repetition, narrative closure, agonistic action, and a nonpsychological disposition, to name just a few. Plus, storytelling in oral cultures tends toward upholding, not challenging, the status quo:

> In the epistemically oral realm, where story functions largely to *conserve* cultural meaning accumulated over the ages, participants are less inclined to "play" indiscriminately with that meaning. For similar reasons, we find that iconography amplified; amplification mitigates any chance of misinterpretation in the transmission of meaning, which a culture that relies on communication as a form of safeguarded memory cannot tolerate.[119]

[117]Schrader, *Transcendental Style in Film*, 107-8.
[118]Nayar, "Reconfiguring the 'Genuinely' Religious Film," 102-3.
[119]Nayar, "Reconfiguring the 'Genuinely' Religious Film," 108; emphasis original.

Not only so, but the spectacle typical of religious epics flows out of the epistemic context in which their source material was birthed. Films based on the Old Testament, for instance, tend toward overabundance precisely because the Old Testament itself does likewise, incubated as it was in an oral culture.[120] So when film scholars dismiss overabundant religious films as kitsch, they betray their bias toward high literacy. They associate divine encounter with silence and solitude because those are precisely the conditions in which they usually read and write.[121] We must conclude then, against Schrader, that there is not a transcendental style, but *styles*. As Nayar points out, "Surely the ineffably mysterious is mysterious enough to be ineffable in multiple ways."[122]

Critiques of transcendental style have come from other quarters too, which brings me to the second major shortcoming of Schrader's analysis of transcendental style. According to Terry Lindvall, W. O. Williams, and Artie Terry, there is a gnostic strain in Schrader, informed by his Calvinist heritage, that is "unduly weighted toward denial of the sensate."[123] For Schrader, the "enemy of transcendence is immanence."[124] Addressing Bresson's prison motif, Schrader writes, "On the theological level, the prison metaphor is linked to the fundamental body/soul dichotomy, a linkage which is made by the wellsprings of Western thought: both Plato *and the scriptures*. To St. Paul the body of sin is prison."[125] Such a dualism is certainly Platonic, but it is not biblical. At the center of the Christian Scriptures stands the divine incarnation and bodily resurrection. Orthodox Christianity is inescapably corporeal. Granted, Schrader's dualistic interpretation is a common reading of the Bible—but it is a regrettable *mis*reading. He writes, "Disparity is the paradox of the spiritual existing within the physical."[126] The fact he sees the coexistence of the spiritual and physical as a paradox—indeed, a paradox crying out for resolution—betrays his implicit gnosticism. Without the assumption that the physical and spiritual are fundamentally incompatible, there is no disparity, and

[120]Nayar, "Reconfiguring the 'Genuinely' Religious Film," 111.

[121]Nayar, "Reconfiguring the 'Genuinely' Religious Film," 121.

[122]Nayar, "Reconfiguring the 'Genuinely' Religious Film," 103.

[123]Terry R. Lindvall, W. O. Williams, and Artie Terry, "Spectacular Transcendence: Abundant Means in the Cinematic Representation of African American Christianity," *Howard Journal of Communications* 7, no. 3 (1996): 206.

[124]Schrader, *Transcendental Style in Film*, 11.

[125]Schrader, *Transcendental Style in Film*, 88; emphasis mine.

[126]Schrader, *Transcendental Style in Film*, 82.

transcendental style falls flat. Schrader's theological lenses lead him to misconstrue how transcendental style actually "works," at least some of the time.

It may be, therefore, that the transcendental style functions according to Schrader's explanation only when the viewer shares his dualistic assumptions. If you see the physical world as somehow at odds with the spiritual, then you'll be looking for a film to transcend its materiality in order to attain the spiritual. Those who embrace human embodiment, on the other hand, are less inclined to perceive disparity, because they reject the notion that only negation of the physical can pave the way for the spiritual. Lindvall, Williams, and Terry look to African American expressions of Christianity as a counterexample. In answer to Schrader's everyday-disparity-stasis model, they suggest that cinematic representations of famously exuberant African American religion evidence a spectacular-charisma-renewal pattern. The result is hierophany via abundant means, a "spectacular transcendence." But while this pattern is evident in Black cinema, Lindvall et al. argue that Schrader's blindspot is essentially anthropological and theological, rather than cultural: "A persuasive case should be made that Schrader's neglect is not even about race—it is about the expression of the Body."[127]

As the studies of Nayar and Lindvall et al. demonstrate, there are multiple ways to mediate transcendence through cinema. This isn't to say that the transcendental style is entirely wrongheaded. On the contrary, it remains an illuminating account of the spiritual in film. Contemporary transcendentalists, like the Dardenne brothers, show there is genuine power in sparse means. The problem I see in Schrader's account is less in the what as in the why. *Why* do transcendental films have a religious quality? For Schrader, the answer lies in the transcendence of the mundane material world, which is antithetical to the spiritual. The everyday is nothing more than a mere foil for disparity, at which point a sense of the sacred is first intimated. This implicit denigration of the physical is not only theologically unpalatable, it doesn't do justice to how a good many films realize their spiritual power.

The everyday and spiritual realism. According to Schrader, genuinely religious cinema portrays "real" life as a flat, mundane reality requiring transcendence. But, as countless mystics and ordinary saints have discovered, quotidian

---

[127]Lindvall, Williams, and Terry, "Spectacular Transcendence," 18.

life can be the locus for divine encounter. Could it be that rather than being relegated to the role of mere foil, the everyday may itself mediate the divine? This seems to me to be closer to how transcendental films often actually function religiously. In his essay *Film as Hierophany*, religious studies scholar Michael Bird detailed a cinematic style he terms *spiritual realism*. For Bird, cinema may become the occasion for hierophany, a "disclosure of the transcendent or sacred precisely through the material of reality."[128] For this reason, hierophany is "particularly valuable for those explorations that begin with the everyday raw material of existence," the same raw material from which film is fashioned.[129] First, Bird uses the work of Tillich and phenomenologist Mikel Dufrenne to detail the relationship between material reality as embodied by culture and the transcendent. As discussed above, Tillich argued that reality may become transparent to ultimate reality that undergirds it, which he termed *belief-ful realism*.[130] In this view, we perceive the reality of God not by looking away from our earthly existence, but rather *at* it. Material reality thus becomes a window onto the holy. Bird draws a comparison between belief-ful realism and Dufrenne's notion of "sensuous realism," in which an aesthetic object enables the spectator to advance beyond mere reflection to corporeal feeling, enabled to perceive "a *Real* that underlies the *real*."[131] For Tillich and Dufrenne, close examination of the physical yields the depth that lies beneath.

Second, Bird examines the work of influential film theorists André Bazin and Siegfried Kracauer, who independently argued that the true strength of cinema lies in its relationship to reality.[132] Bazin was influenced by French phenomenologists.[133] Against the previously dominant "formative" school of thought, which held that a film attains the status of art only insofar as it transforms reality, Bazin championed realism as cinema's true strength.[134] He noted that painting is inescapably subjective. The viewer knows that the painting has been reproduced by human hand. Photography, by contrast, is

[128]Michael S. Bird, "Film as Hierophany," in *Religion in Film* (Knoxville: University of Tennessee Press, 1982), 3.
[129]Bird, "Film as Hierophany," 3.
[130]Bird, "Film as Hierophany," 5-7.
[131]Bird, "Film as Hierophany," 8; emphasis original.
[132]Bird, "Film as Hierophany," 9-13.
[133]Andrew Quicke, "Phenomenology and Film: An Examination of a Religious Approach to Film Theory by Henri Agel and Amédée Ayfre," *Journal of Media and Religion* 4, no. 4 (2005).
[134]Bird, "Film as Hierophany," 9-14.

mechanically reproduced, untainted by human intervention, lending it an air of objectivity.[135] Thus, Bazin creatively contrasts the frame of a painting with the border of a film image. The ornate frame of a painting establishes the painting's discontinuity with reality, whereas the edge of a film frame is akin to "a piece of masking" that suggests the cinematic image is continuous with reality itself: "The frame is centripetal, the screen centrifugal."[136] Similarly, film scholar Siegfried Kracauer posited that film's essence is its ability to capture physical reality, "to explore this texture of everyday life":[137]

> Film renders visible what we did not, or perhaps even could not, see before its advent. It effectively assists us in discovering the material world with its psychophysical correspondences. We literally redeem this world from its dormant state, its state of virtual nonexistence, by endeavoring to experience it through the camera. . . . The cinema can be defined as a medium particularly equipped to promote the redemption of physical reality. Its imagery permits us, for the first time, to take away with us the objects and occurrences that comprise the flow of life.[138]

For Kracauer, the problem with the modern world is that it has fallen prey to abstraction. The solution is film.[139] It is no coincidence that Kracauer resorts to religious language to describe cinema's peculiar power, namely physicality's "redemption." For him, film is a microscope on daily life and thus he finds the world not void, but rather infused with the sacred.

Third, Bird turns to two of Bazin's disciples: Amédée Ayfre and Henri Agel. Ayfre and Agel, both devout Christians, used Bazin's spiritually inflected thought to focus specifically on cinema as the vehicle for transcendence. Bird explains:

> Ayfre suggests that there is a cinematic approach to the sacred that discloses not only at surface appearances but also its inner strivings that point to its depth. "Genuinely" religious films . . . are those in which the cinematographic recording of reality does not exhaust reality but rather evokes in the viewer the sense of its ineffable mystery.[140]

---

[135]André Bazin, *What Is Cinema?*, ed. Hugh Gray, Jean Renoir, and François Truffaut (Berkeley: University of California Press, 2005), 12-13.

[136]Bazin, *What Is Cinema?*, 165-66.

[137]Siegfried Kracauer, *Theory of Film: The Redemption of Physical Reality* (Princeton, NJ: Princeton University Press, 1997), 304.

[138]Kracauer, *Theory of Film*, 300.

[139]Kracauer, *Theory of Film*, 285-96.

[140]Bird, "Film as Hierophany," 14.

For thinkers like Ayfre and Agel, cinema may help us perceive the "holy within the real," which happens when cinema turns its attention to reality in such a way that the sacred is perceptible therein.[141]

Religious film scholar Andrew Quicke notes that, because these Francophone theorists' work remains untranslated into English, they are known to Anglophone audiences mostly through their influence on Schrader.[142] Quicke thus draws a close association between Schrader and these earlier French thinkers. But there is a significant difference between transcendental style and spiritual realism, at least as it is articulated by Bird. While Schrader views ordinary physical life as being at cross-purposes with spiritual existence, Bird sees materiality as a portal to the sacred. In spiritual realism, "cinema becomes not so much a voice of the artist but rather a diaphragm which is sensitive to the speech of the cosmos waiting to be heard."[143] The difference between transcendental style and spiritual realism is, in part, theological. And perhaps this difference is the reason Agel could find the experience of watching *The Passion of Joan of Arc* (Carl Theodor Dreyer, 1928)[144] transcendent, while Schrader could only dismiss it as being too expressionist to be capable of such.[145]

Bird seems to imply that cinema may achieve transcendence through a quasi-documentary approach to reality. I am less convinced on this particular point, since contemporary cinema has yielded spiritually resonant works that depart from realism to some extent and yet, in doing so, accentuate the sacred quality of reality. *The Tree of Life* (Terrence Malick, 2011),[146] for example, features computer-generated imagery of dinosaurs and protozoa (not to mention a levitating person and a highly symbolic birth sequence), but seems capable of revealing a sense of the holy by virtue of its sensuousness. We might call this *sacramental style*, since it is an aesthetic in which the physical need not be transcended; rather, here creation may be the mediator of divine sacramentality (it's surely no coincidence that Schrader has expressed puzzlement about the

---

[141]Bird, "Film as Hierophany," 13.

[142]Quicke, "Phenomenology and Film," 247.

[143]Bird, "Film as Hierophany," 13, 20.

[144]Ranked #1, "Top 100 Films," *Arts & Faith*, 2011, accessed January 3, 2022, https://imagejournal.org/top-100-films/.

[145]Bird, "Film as Hierophany," 15.

[146]Ranked #3, "Top 100 Films—2020," *Arts & Faith*, accessed January 3, 2022, http://artsandfaith.com/index.php?/films/&do=year&id=8&page=2.

religious appeal of Malick, dismissing it as "pantheist mumbo-jumbo").[147] Again, Nayar is helpful in helping us understand how it is that such an abundant film, which explicitly departs from reality at times, may still hold religious power for some audiences. Apart from this minor quibble with Bird, his notion of spiritual realism may often be a more accurate and theologically robust account of how certain films function religiously than transcendental style. The close scrutiny of our world afforded us by this sort of cinema may lead us to exclaim, like Jacob, that "surely the LORD is in this place . . . How awesome is this place!" (Gen 28:16-17).

Spiritual realism often takes the form of a focus on the quotidian. Film scholar Ann Hardy has called this type of filmic representation of daily life *meditative style*, which lacks any gnostic sense that mundane existence must be transcended in order to be religiously meaningful.[148] This sort of slow-paced, closely shot film mesmerizes and entrances, opening us to a sense of the sacred. On screen, the ordinary objects, settings, and actions that make up our unremarkable lives are "redeemed," taking on a beauty and meaning mostly invisible to us in the warp and woof of lived experience. Despite the directors' respective debts to the classical transcendentalists, perhaps the dazzling *Silent Light* and even the grim *The Son* owe their spiritual power as much to meditative style as they do to transcendental style. Indeed, Reygadas takes an expressly Kracauerian position, stating that

> cinema is the art of reality, the medium in which reality's beauty is captured, where you can film marble or a face, or record someone's voice, a sunset, the innate beauty of what you're contemplating . . . take Cornelio Wall's wrinkles, his tone of voice in *Silent Light*. These are things I didn't imagine before, I only allowed my camera to absorb them. . . . The camera is a funnel taking in reality.[149]

Though superficially a textbook example of transcendental style, the opening sequence of *Silent Light* that culminates in Johan's tears is in actuality deep perception and deep contemplation of the world. It isn't just disparity that strikes us as sacred here—it is the everyday too. Perhaps the power of the everyday that Schrader highlights is due not to its being mundane, but rather its capacity to reveal the extraordinary quality of ordinary reality. This is why

---

[147] Schrader and Kickasola, "Paul Schrader on Revisiting Transcendental Style."

[148] Hardy, *Film, Spirituality and Hierophany*, 12.

[149] Carlos Reygadas, José Castillo, and Camino Detorrela, "Carlos Reygadas," *BOMB*, no. 111 (2010): 74-75.

Silent Light opens with a long-take of a sunrise so rhapsodic that, as film and literature scholar Roy Anker notes, what on paper would seem unbearably pretentious in fact won over a good many reviewers.[150] The film is austere, yet also abundant. The camera reveals the abundance of ordinary existence that we routinely overlook. Transcendentalism is not entirely absent, as even here we find traces of it, particularly in its narrative structure and acting. Roy Anker notes how the nonexpressive acting prods viewers to "ponder the mysteries of the soul and its embodiedness, and especially the depths that lie beyond expression."[151] Elements of transcendental style coexist with meditative style.

Even *American Beauty* (Sam Mendes, 1999) similarly blends such styles.[152] Ricky obsessively films his life as a form of meditation, tapping into film's hierophanous potential, his grainy footage of real life paradoxically more authentically beautiful than the luxuriant imagery of Lester's sexual fantasies.[153] Meanwhile, the film's ending exhibits stasis, in which the contented expression on the face of the freshly murdered Lester is met by Ricky's quizzical gaze, paradoxically uniting death and beauty. Hardy concludes that

> the ambiguous resonance of this sequence suggests that Schrader's theory of transcendental style as a description of the means by [which] hierophany can be melded with a parable-like form of narrative retains considerable explanatory power. But at the same time, the fact that *American Beauty* is, relatively speaking, embedded in abundance and irony, reinforces claims that there is more work to be done on examining the nature of representations of transcendence in popular, post-modern, as opposed to elitist and modernist film.[154]

Hardy is right: transcendental style does indeed have explanatory power. But, taken alone, it does not explain enough, because many films that resonate spiritually with audiences are steeped in abundance. For many viewers, abundance holds more potential for transcendence than sparseness. Transcendental style works to frustrate viewer affect and thwart emotional identification with characters—quite the opposite aim to that of mainstream styles.

---

[150]Roy Anker, "Dazzle Gradually," *Books & Culture*, 2009, 22.
[151]Anker, "Dazzle Gradually."
[152]Hardy, *Film, Spirituality and Hierophany*, 19-20.
[153]Johnston, *Useless Beauty*, 66-68.
[154]Hardy, *Film, Spirituality and Hierophany*, 19-20.

Schrader writes, "For the many who require no more from sacred art than emotional experience, [religious epic] films are sufficient."[155] The implication is clear: there is little room for emotion in transcendental style.

The problem is that affect is often closely intertwined with revelatory experience. Recall that Brant identified two types of potentially revelatory experience: cognitive type and mystical type. The type of experience reported by the participants in Brant's study sometimes correlated with the degree of immediacy of the experience. Those participants who described the onset of the purportedly revelatory experience as gradual had a tendency to emphasize its intellectual component, whereas those who described it as immediate were slightly more likely to emphasize its emotional component.[156] Nevertheless, most participants interpreted their experiences as significantly engaging intellect *and* emotion.

We cannot, therefore, think of revelatory experience solely in terms of reason, as if it were always simply a cognitive process. Allegedly revelatory experience is often bound up with intense emotion. We see this, for example, in Kutter Callaway's analysis of lay viewers' online responses to *Moulin Rouge!* (Baz Luhrmann, 2001), specifically its music. Callaway identifies a three-stage pattern in which these viewers relate their affective responses to spirituality: (1) They describe the intensely emotional quality of the experience; (2) they recognize their affective response in terms of the physiological changes they experience (e.g., crying, tingling); and (3) they often use religiously inflected language to describe the significance of the experience.[157] It seems there is a profound connection between affect and experiences we interpret as revelatory. You would be hard-pressed to find a film more abundant than *Moulin Rouge!*, but it is precisely its abundance that gives it its power to facilitate "'Transcendence' with a capital *T*."[158] As the work of Nayar and Lindvall et al. have shown, there are ways to mediate the transcendent through cinema that diverge from Schrader's transcendental style, styles that embrace abundance.

For that reason, this book covers a diverse range of films, both sparse and abundant. We'll look at *Ordet*, which Schrader identifies as *almost* exemplary

---

[155]Schrader, *Transcendental Style in Film*, 163-64.

[156]Brant, *Paul Tillich*, 172.

[157]Callaway, *Scoring Transcendence*, chap. 4.

[158]Johnston, *Reel Spirituality*, 242.

of the style, and *Silent Light,* which as we have already discussed, mixes elements of transcendental but also meditative (or sacramental) style. We'll analyze *2001: A Space Odyssey,* a far cry from transcendental style yet employing sparse amid abundant means. And we'll explore *Magnolia* too, which is "hyperabundant," to co-opt Nayar's term. This selection of films reflects my conviction that a range of film styles may elicit claims of revelatory experience. I will invoke transcendental style where appropriate, because of its enduring explanatory power, but only with the qualifier that I reject any implied spirit-matter dualism. As such, my understanding of how the style functions (at least some of the time) differs from that of Schrader and aligns more neatly with the spiritual realism of Michael Bird.

Scorsese is not alone in finding cinema to be a haven of revelation. Claims of divine revelation are indeed elicited by films—and, I have been arguing, by a more diverse array of films than has sometimes been accounted for by scholars. Sparse means remain important in the discussion of religious cinema, but abundant means are just as relevant. Ironically—though, in the light of our discussion above, not surprisingly—the evidence suggests even Scorsese's disfavored Marvel movies may function in this capacity for some viewers.[159] Perhaps it is the revelatory possibilities of cinema that have led Scorsese to remark elsewhere, "I believe there is a spirituality in films, even if it's not one which can supplant faith. . . . They fulfill a spiritual need that people have to share a common memory."[160] The "spirituality" he speaks of is not reducible to religious subject matter; it is inextricably linked to form and to the experience of film viewing itself.

---

[159]For example, some audiences have understood their response to Marvel's *Black Panther* (Ryan Coogler, 2018) as a religious experience. See Laurel Zwissler, "Black Panther as Spirit Trip," *Journal of Religion & Film* 22, no. 1 (2018).

[160]Martin Scorsese and Michael Henry Wilson, *A Personal Journey with Martin Scorsese Through American Movies* (Hyperion Books, 1997), 166. Cited in the epigraph of Clive Marsh and Gaye Ortiz, eds., *Explorations in Theology and Film: Movies and Meaning* (Malden, MA: Blackwell, 1998).

2

Revelation Reconsidered

It's just a plastic bag circling about in the wind. But when Ricky Fitts (Wes Bentley) shows girlfriend Jane Burnham (Thora Birch) the footage of the discarded bag in *American Beauty* (Sam Mendes, 1999), he says it's the most beautiful thing he has ever filmed. The sight is ostensibly mundane, but it's clear from how Ricky watches, transfixed, that the moment was anything but mundane. Eyes brimming with tears, he waxes poetic about the experience: "That's the day I realized there's this entire life behind things and this incredibly benevolent force that wanted me to know that there was no reason to be afraid—ever. . . . Sometimes there's just so much beauty in the world I feel like I can't take it and my heart is just going to cave in."

It was an experience of transcendence, even revelation. Watching it is Ricky's quasi-religious ritual, a potent reminder of the sacred presence that undergirds life. The scene was inspired by a real incident. Screenwriter Alan Ball had an experience of watching a plastic bag circle him several times. Ball recalls, "I started to feel weird. And then, I don't know, there was something striking about the experience, and I really did feel like I was in the presence of something."[1] A routine sight became the occasion for divine encounter.

Though later allegations of sexual misconduct against lead actor Kevin Spacey have retrospectively cast a sinister shadow over the Oscar-winning film,[2] this scene nevertheless prompts a fundamental theological question: Where does divine knowledge come from? Few would take issue with evangelical theologian Bruce Demarest's claim that "only God can make God

[1]Russ Spencer, "Where You Find It," *Salon*, March 25, 2000, www.salon.com/2000/03/25/ball_2/.
[2]Maria Puente, "Kevin Spacey Scandal: A Complete List of the 15 Accusers," *USA Today*, November 7, 2017, www.usatoday.com/story/life/2017/11/07/kevin-spacey-scandal-complete-list-13-accusers/835739001/.

known."[3] To the extent that we know God, we do so due to divine self-disclosure. But how? What are the means? How is divine revelation mediated? On this matter, there has been far less consensus. Indeed, the question has lain at the heart of theological disputes as epochal as Rome versus the Reformation and as acrimonious as Barth versus Brunner.

Nevertheless, most Christian traditions at most times have given revelatory priority to certain redemptive divine actions throughout history that ultimately reach their climax in the person of Jesus Christ, as recounted and interpreted by Scripture (and, for some, by ecclesiastical tradition too). But revelation appears also to take place outside of the Christian sphere, mediated by means not directly related to Christ, a phenomenon often referred to in the Reformed tradition as *general revelation*. By observing and reflecting on nature, for instance, a person may come to some knowledge of the divine. While such reflection has usually been understood in terms of reason, it has occasionally been construed affectively, such as we find in Romanticism. Poet William Wordsworth, for example, famously wrote,

> And I have felt
> A presence that disturbs me with the joy
> Of elevated thoughts; a sense sublime
> Of something far more deeply interfused,
> Whose dwelling is the light of setting suns,
> And the round ocean and the living air,
> And the blue sky, and in the mind of man:
> A motion and a spirit, that impels
> All thinking things, all objects of all thought,
> And rolls through all things . . . [4]

The great Romantic is eloquently expressing a sentiment similar to that articulated by Ricky Fitts. Rarely, however, has divine knowledge that comes by way of these more particular and primarily affective experiences been incorporated into accounts of general revelation. Is there room in a Christian theology of revelation for such experiences, like that of Ricky Fitts (and Alan

---

[3]Bruce A. Demarest, *General Revelation: Historical Views and Contemporary Issues* (Grand Rapids, MI: Zondervan, 1982), 13.

[4]William Wordsworth, *The Collected Poems of William Wordsworth* (Ware, Herfordshire: Wordsworth Editions, 1994), 243.

Ball)? Dare we consider knowledge of a benevolent presence mediated by something as areligious, particular, idiosyncratic, and ordinary as a plastic bag caught in an updraft as being potentially authentic, as indeed *revelation*?

Surveying the Revelation Landscape

Before examining general revelation more closely, we ought first to take a step back and consider the notion of revelation more generally. Jesuit theologian Avery Dulles has divided Christian revelation into five types:[5]

1. *Propositional Type (Revelation as Doctrine).* Revelation comes by way of propositions expressed in words. The almost total identification of revelation with written language leads in this view to the special prominence of Scripture, usually held to be inerrant.
2. *Historical Type (Revelation as History).* Revelation is centered on the acts of God in history, thus leading this model to emphasize narrative and "salvation history."
3. *Experiential Type (Revelation as Inner Experience).* Revelation takes place as an inner, oftentimes affective experience. Such experience is immediate, that is to say revelation does not require mediation. Revelation is not primarily disclosure of truths *about* but rather disclosure *of* the divine itself.
4. *Dialectical Type (Revelation as Dialectical Presence).* Revelation is restricted to Jesus Christ; he alone is revelation, the Word of God. In this model, the Bible "'becomes' the Word of God insofar as it is the means God uses to witness to Jesus Christ, God's Word."[6]
5. *Consciousness Type (Revelation as New Awareness).* Revelation takes the form of breakthrough to more advanced states of consciousness empowered by the divine. The content of revelation is nonpropositional and God is the horizon rather than object of revelation.[7]

---

[5]Avery Dulles, *Models of Revelation* (Dublin: Gill and Macmillan, 1983).

[6]D. K. McKim and P. S. Chung, "Revelation and Scripture," in *Global Dictionary of Theology: A Resource for the Worldwide Church*, ed. William A. Dyrness and Veli-Matti Kärkkäinen (Downers Grove, IL: InterVarsity Press, 2008), 759.

[7]Dulles dedicates the second half to outlining his own position, which could be called the *symbolic type (revelation as symbol)*. Since it is peripheral to our purposes here, I've included only those five Dulles himself initially identifies. For a paragraph summary of Dulles's position, see McKim and Chung, "Revelation and Scripture," 759.

At points, these types represent radically different views of revelation and consequently radically different expressions of Christianity. As such, general revelation is more closely associated with particular models, namely the propositional and historical. With respect to how these various types view the possibility of revelation outside the biblical religions, the first two models adhere to exclusivist views of revelation except insofar as they invoke general revelation as preparatory to special grace. The remaining three conceptions of revelation, however, either do not require general revelation or oppose it entirely.[8] Evangelical and Reformed theology, historically most closely aligned with the propositional type and sometimes also the historical type,[9] have made particular use of the general-special distinction with regard to revelation.

Evangelical Dictionary of Theology defines general revelation as the "divine disclosure to all persons at all times and in all places by which humans come to know that God is and what he is like."[10] It's the knowledge of God that is universal, accessible to virtually all through ordinary channels without explicit reference to the christological—most archetypically, nature—and is therefore not particular to any given religion. Such knowledge is often seen as being both internal, grounded in moral conscience and an innate sense of the divine, and external, arising from reflection on nature and history.[11] Special revelation, on the other hand, is the saving knowledge via acts and words "crowned by the incarnation of the living Word and the inscripturation of the spoken word."[12] In other words, special revelation is the knowledge of God's redemptive acts in history culminating in the person of Jesus Christ, especially as expressed in the sacred writings of the Bible. It's a form of divine self-disclosure in which "God reveals specific things to specific people at specific times," imparting knowledge that can't be gained simply by, say, contemplating nature.[13]

---

[8]Although, as we will discuss below, the dialectical model may not be as diametrically opposed as is sometimes thought, at least as it is expressed by its most influential exponent, Karl Barth. See Dulles, *Models of Revelation*, 121.

[9]Certain strands of evangelicalism have also been significantly influenced by the dialectical type via Barth.

[10]Walter A. Elwell, *Evangelical Dictionary of Theology*, 2nd ed. (Grand Rapids, MI: Baker Academic, 2001), 1019.

[11]Elwell, *Evangelical Dictionary of Theology*, 1019.

[12]Elwell, *Evangelical Dictionary of Theology*, 1021.

[13]Carisa A. Ash, *A Critical Examination of the Doctrine of Revelation in Evangelical Theology* (Eugene, OR: Wipf & Stock, 2015), Kindle, 79.

The validity or weight granted general revelation varies between theological traditions. Demarest notes that liberal theology tends to exaggerate the value of general revelation, while conservative theology tends to minimize it.[14] Reformed theologian G. C. Berkouwer chronicled the pendulum swinging between general revelation and special revelation that has taken place, a perennial tendency among theologians to treat the two categories as being in competition rather than as complementary.[15] The Bible doesn't always see it that way. The psalmist of Psalm 19, a classic so-called nature psalm, clearly adheres to what medieval theologians might have described as a *two-book theory* (where one "book" is that of nature and the other, the literal book of Scripture).[16] The psalm opens with divine knowledge mediated by nature (general revelation):

> The heavens declare the glory of God;
> the skies proclaim the work of his hands.
> Day after day they pour forth speech;
> night after night they reveal knowledge.
> They have no speech, they use no words;
> no sound is heard from them.
> Yet their voice goes out into all the earth,
> their words to the ends of the world. (Ps 19:1-4)

The latter half of the psalm shifts its focus to divine knowledge mediated by the law, the sacred writings and teachings of Israelite religion (special revelation):

> The law of the LORD is perfect,
> refreshing the soul.
> The statutes of the LORD are trustworthy,
> making wise the simple.
> The precepts of the LORD are right,
> giving joy to the heart.
> The commands of the LORD are radiant,
> giving light to the eyes. (Ps 19:7-8)

The first half refers to the divine by the more generic designation *El* ("God"), while the second half uses the Israel-specific *Yahweh* ("LORD"); the one deity

---

[14]Demarest, *General Revelation*, 15.
[15]G. C. Berkouwer, *General Revelation* (Grand Rapids, MI: Eerdmans, 1955), 10-16.
[16]Demarest, *General Revelation*, 235.

is identified with the other. The psalmist thus evidently understands knowledge mediated by nature and the law respectively to stand in a complementary relationship, each in their own way an articulate and dependable witness to the character of the one true God.

Despite the ease with which the psalmist moves between these two sources of revelation, a good many theologians have been far less nimble, if not downright skeptical. In her analysis of approximately eighty evangelical systematic theologies, theologian Carisa A. Ash found that evangelical theologians often pay lip service to general revelation, but rarely use the doctrine substantially or consistently.[17] The most influential skeptic of general revelation has been Swiss theologian Karl Barth. Against the backdrop of the Nazis' rise to power, Barth clashed with fellow dialectical theologian and countryman Emil Brunner over revelation. Their disagreement centered on a cluster of interconnected theological issues related to natural theology, which posits the possibility of genuine knowledge of God sans revelation, arrived at by way of human reason alone. Natural theology is thus distinct from general revelation, though the two doctrines are related. Brunner argued that the image of God in humans remains partly intact despite sin, leaving a "point of contact" between God and humanity.[18] Barth opposed Brunner sharply, giving his response the terse title *Nein!* Clinging to some residual element of the image of God that would give humanity access to God, he argued, is tantamount to claiming that humans contribute to their own salvation. For Barth, revelation begins and ends with Christ. His concern was that, apart from Christ, sinful humanity is doomed to misconstrue divine knowledge mediated by nature, leading to knowledge only of *false* gods, "those principalities and powers of the world of ideas and demons."[19] Contrast this bleak conclusion with that of Psalm 19, which holds the "God" revealed through creation to be one and the same as the "LORD" revealed in the law.

Barth was uncompromising in his opposition to Brunner's mildly optimistic perspective on natural theology and related doctrines. His vehemence was motivated by an unrelenting insistence that revelation is in Christ alone, a

---

[17]Ash, *Critical Examination.*

[18]Karl Barth and Emil Brunner, *Natural Theology: Comprising "Nature and Grace" by Emil Brunner and the Reply "No!" by Karl Barth*, trans. Peter Fraenkel (Eugene, OR: Wipf & Stock, 2002), 23, 31.

[19]Barth and Brunner, *Natural Theology*, 81.

position Berkouwer called *Christomonism*.[20] Note, however, that Barth's thoroughgoing opposition was *not* due primarily to a belief that divine knowledge cannot be mediated through creation, as is supposed in one common misreading of Barth. Such an interpretation seems untenable in the light of his emphatic claim that "God may speak to us through Russian Communism, a flute concerto, a blossoming shrub, or a dead dog."[21] So Barth did not dismiss divine disclosure through creation out of hand. The problem is not that creation is incapable of mediating divine knowledge as such, but that *apart from Christ* fallen humans are liable to misconstrue that knowledge. Thus, the tenor of Barth's polemic against Brunner is one of skepticism, to put it mildly.[22]

Later in his career, however, Barth would speak of the "lesser lights" of the created world that do provide some illumination. That Barth acknowledged these lesser lights, phenomena that others have been content to group under the banner of revelation, suggests that his desire to reserve the word "revelation" for Christ alone is at least partly a semantic choice. But, to the extent that it is a linguistic decision, it is a significant and telling one. It speaks to how absolute Barth's opposition was to any doctrine of revelation that would relegate Christ to the margins. Standing as a bulwark against the tide of ecclesiastical support for the Nazis, Barth's dogged insistence that revelation is found in Christ alone (not Hitler!) is admirable, even heroic, and contextually necessary. But no matter how it is parsed—whether *revelation* or *lesser lights*—there is something illuminating about the created world that ultimately even Barth did not deny completely. We'll return to the debate between Barth and Brunner in the next chapter when we examine criteria for discernment.

General revelation, by definition, is distinguished from natural theology in its encompassing knowledge that *God* discloses, rather than knowledge that humans gain by unaided reason. Many forms of natural theology assert the adequacy of human faculties alone to discern divine truth from creation. While Augustine believed in a general intuition of the divine partially preserved by common grace, Thomas Aquinas considered naked human reason sufficient to establish some knowledge of God's existence, greatness, goodness,

---

[20]Berkouwer, *General Revelation*, 25.

[21]Karl Barth, *Church Dogmatics*, ed. G. W. Bromiley and Thomas F. Torrance (Peabody, MA: Hendrickson, 2010), I.1: 55.

[22]I owe insight into this nuanced reading of Barth to Murray Rae. Murray Rae, November 11, 2015.

and universal providence, thereby creating a more fully developed natural theology that would profoundly shape Roman Catholic thought on the matter.[23] General revelation is similar insofar as it focuses on knowledge drawn from creation, but insists on its being an act of divine disclosure. This is not to say that adherents of general revelation deny that divine knowledge may come about through use of human reason—on the contrary, reasoned deductions from creation are supposed to be a, or even *the*, primary way it operates[24]—but simply that human reason must be divinely assisted.

But evangelical theology has kept general revelation on a short leash. There are at least two reasons for its being accorded relatively little value. First, conservative Protestants have taken a dim view of humankind's ability to receive revelation. The argument goes that while God does indeed speak through creation, humans' ability to hear and rightly interpret that speech has been muffled by sin, if not eliminated completely. On this point, it helps to distinguish between the ontic and the noetic: there is real revelation mediated by creation (ontic), but sinful humans are incapable of rightly receiving that revelation (noetic). As Berkouwer puts it, "Knowledge and revelation are *not* identical."[25] John Calvin, who set the scene for the Protestant discussion about general revelation, explained that sinful humanity requires Scripture in order to rightly perceive general revelation, just as the vision-impaired require glasses to be able to read a book.[26] Various theologians have therefore interpreted Calvin as claiming that general revelation results in no *actual* knowledge of God mediated by creation, due to sin's noetic implications. Demarest, however, argues that despite Calvin's misgivings, he still held general revelation as capable of giving rise to authentic knowledge in practice.[27] Whether or not Demarest's reading of Calvin is accurate, there can be little doubt that the overriding attitude of nonliberal Protestants about general revelation has been pessimistic.

[23]Demarest, *General Revelation*, 20, 37.

[24]Demarest, *General Revelation*, 233.

[25]Berkouwer, *General Revelation*, 314; emphasis original.

[26]John Calvin, *Institutes of the Christian Religion*, trans. Henry Beveridge (1845) (n.p.: Digireads, 2014), Kindle, I.vi.1, www.amazon.com/Institutes-Christian-Religion-John-Calvin-ebook/dp/B00KJ39IHO/.

[27]Demarest defends his reading of Calvin by classifying Calvin's pessimistic statements regarding what may be known through the world into three groups. These statements were made in order to either (1) oppose the hubris of scholastic natural theology, (2) oppose those who claim such knowledge may be salvific, or (3) strengthen the rhetorical force by overstating his case. Demarest, *General Revelation*, 244.

Second, and relatedly, the conversation has been limited to the soteriological, the knowledge at issue restricted to that which may or may not lead to salvation. Evangelical theologian Robert K. Johnston, whose work on general revelation profoundly informs this chapter (and book), makes much of this point. General revelation, he notes, has been poorly defined, focused on that knowledge of God communicated to everyone everywhere at all times. But such a generic communication is powerless to convey much of substance about the divine, achieving nothing more than to render human beings culpable for sin.[28] That the Bible identifies at least nineteen propositions about God that are revealed via creation is usually given short shrift.[29] While the nature psalms demonstrate no discomfort in acknowledging both the cosmic and soteriological types of creationally mediated knowledge,[30] the same cannot be said of vast swathes of Protestantism. Berkouwer's approach is typical: he concludes that the nature psalms are written through eyes of faith and are not indicative of what can be known through nature without true faith. In other words, special revelation is the necessary prerequisite to appreciating general revelation; general revelation alone does not impart anything positive to the unbeliever.

The focus on saving knowledge has squeezed out the possibility of nonsalvific knowledge conveyed through nature, history, and experience. That leaves general revelation with just one actual function: rendering us inexcusable. Certain streams of theology have thus assigned general revelation only a negative function, latching onto and absolutizing Paul's claim that "since the creation of the world God's invisible qualities—his eternal power and divine nature—have been clearly seen, being understood from what has been made, so that people are without excuse" (Rom 1:20). This viewpoint makes "it sound as though God is covering his bases," writes Ash, since it implies that original sin alone is not sufficient to leave us condemned.[31] By being so closely bound to the soteriological, what may be known of the divine through creation has been reduced to judgment. General revelation renders us guilty before God, but nothing more.

---

[28]Robert K. Johnston, *God's Wider Presence: Reconsidering General Revelation* (Grand Rapids, MI: Baker Academic, 2014), chap. 1, 8, Kindle.

[29]Demarest, *General Revelation*, 242-43.

[30]Berkouwer, *General Revelation*, 128-29.

[31]Ash, *Critical Examination*, 140.

When oriented around the question of salvation, the debate takes on higher stakes and thus becomes an all-or-nothing matter. If general revelation cannot impart salvific knowledge, the thinking goes, then it is of negligible worth, if not downright dangerous. But what if the possibility of nonsalvific knowledge is taken into consideration? Then the picture becomes more complex. Even as conservative a scholar as Demarest concedes that some nonsalvific truth and goodness may be found in non-Christian religions. Any apparent value he sees in them, however, is dwarfed by these faiths' almost total impotence with regard to salvation.[32] Soteriology has loomed large in the discussion, casting a long shadow of pessimism over the question. Dutch theologian Theodoor L. Haitjema claimed that nature reveals only "the dark bass-tone of the angry justice of God."[33] This may be even more pessimistic than the prevailing Protestant perspective—but only just. For most nonliberal Protestants, when it comes to authentic knowledge of God mediated by creation, the outlook is bleak.

Reconsidering General Revelation

General revelation: Neglected, yet needed. But not all are satisfied with how general revelation has traditionally been understood. In his book *God's Wider Presence: Reconsidering General Revelation*, Johnston has issued a challenge to the way the doctrine has typically been formulated.[34] He notes the paucity of writing on the topic in recent decades, a reflection of the relatively low value placed on general revelation that we discussed above. General revelation has been relegated to the margins and, as a result, the doctrine has ossified. At the same time as the conversation about general revelation has come to a standstill, seismic cultural shifts have made the question of how God may be active

---

[32]Demarest, *General Revelation*, 254-61. Demarest allows for the outside possibility that on rare occasions a Muslim could receive saving knowledge through Islam but this claim is based on Islam's partial inclusion of special revelation and esteem for Jesus Christ. Similarly, he recognizes that in very rare instances a pagan might come to saving faith through unusual acts of supernatural revelation. But Demarest quickly reverts to downplaying the possibility, a response symptomatic of the skittishness with which evangelical and Reformed theology has handled general revelation. In both cases salvation is possible only to the extent that there is special revelation. Moreover, it should be stressed that in both cases, Demarest imagines the numbers of such beneficiaries of salvific knowledge to be "small at best."

[33]Th. L. Haitjema, "Het 'Barthiaanse' Bezwaar Tegen Artikel II der Nederlandse Geloofsbelijdenis," *Onder Eigen Vaandel* (1938): 211; quoted in Berkouwer, *General Revelation*, 272.

[34]Johnston, *God's Wider Presence*, chap. 7.

outside of the traditional Christian sphere more pressing than ever. Johnston highlights two such shifts. Aesthetic experience through the arts and media is increasingly being cited as an arena—and for growing numbers, *the* arena—in which spiritual meaning is made. Another significant change that demands a revisioning of general revelation is the unprecedented level of religious pluralism in modern life.[35] Thus, our experience in the modern world has changed in important ways. Johnston believes it's important we attend to that experience in our theological reflection. "What are we as Christians to make of those occasional encounters with God in our everyday lives that seem more real than everyday reality, more fundamental than everything else?" Examples Johnston gives include those overwhelming experiences we may associate with seeing a sunset, witnessing the birth of your child, participating in a communal act of justice, or encountering a powerful work of art. Crucially, such experiences often occur in places other than those ordinarily considered religious; rather, God's revelatory presence meets us in "creation, culture and conscience."[36]

Historically, such experiences have been largely neglected or dismissed by the majority of theologians, yet they demand our attention not least because of our culture's recent turn to the spiritual. Experience of God in the West is becoming both *less centralized* and *more important* than our theological positions; less centralized insofar as institutions that were in times past the primary sites of religious meaning are being abandoned for private, individualized religious practices; more important insofar as transcendent experience frequently trumps traditional doctrine for religious authority in the individual's life.[37] Of course, this is not to say that experience is the exclusive domain of the *non*religious. Indeed, of those theologians who have written about revelation, many have done so inspired by their own revelatory experiences. Avery Dulles wrote about his experience of seeing a budding tree at Harvard; Paul Tillich famously had a transformative experience when viewing a Botticelli painting in Berlin; and even Barth spoke similarly about hearing Mozart as a child, though he was predictably unwilling to name it as revelation.[38]

---

[35]Johnston, *God's Wider Presence*, chap. 1.
[36]Johnston, *God's Wider Presence*, preface.
[37]Johnston, *God's Wider Presence*, chap. 2.
[38]Johnston, *God's Wider Presence*, chap. 6.

Our understanding of general revelation must be reconfigured in order to account for these experiences. "Rather than merely flowing from the *cultural* memory of God's past Presence, or being an inference from God's past *creational* activity, or being understood as the outworking of humankind's *conscience*, general revelation should be understood as referring to present, particular experience(s) of the Transcendent in life."[39] Such experiences, Johnston explains elsewhere, "are more than mere deductions based on the footprint of God's act of creation. They are more than mere echoes or traces of his handiwork, though that is sometimes how they are described by Christian theologians. Those who experience the Numinous speak instead of a transformative moment, something illumining, even if precritical and hard to adequately name."[40] It is in those quotidian moments where the ordinary becomes suddenly, fleetingly, and ineffably extraordinary that we are confronted with God's wider presence. It is time, Johnston argues, that we revisited general revelation.

Against the "footprint" model. What about this doctrine specifically needs rethinking? Simply put, Johnston believes often what is identified as general revelation is not revelation at all. Traditional formulations of general revelation tend to restrict its purview to knowledge inferred from creation, usually by way of human reason. In this view, revelation discloses a knowledge grounded in God's past activity rather than in ongoing, present-day encounters with God. Johnston likens this to a divine "footprint" stamped on creation, as if God was active at some point in the distant past but is now no longer present. The footprint model is merely a recollection or human projection based on a kind of primordial revelation. Restricted as it is to the past, Johnston argues that it falls short of being revelation at all.[41]

The so-called footprint model arises from the traditional interpretation of Romans 1–2, historically the scriptural focal point in the discussion around general revelation (especially Rom 1:18-22; 2:14-15). Taking their cues from this text, early Christian theologians understood general revelation as being tied to salvation and judgment, based on an echo of God's initial creation and rooted in human reason. Thus, almost since the outset, the footprint model

---

[39]Johnston, *God's Wider Presence*, chap. 8; emphasis original.
[40]Johnston, *God's Wider Presence*, preface.
[41]Johnston, *God's Wider Presence*, chap. 8.

has been the default way of thinking about revelation that takes place outside of the church and without direct reference to Christ. Johnston sees at least three major problems with this view. First, what it defines as revelation is in fact not revelation at all. In making this point, Johnston draws on the work of Barth, who was unwavering in his stance that revelation is only such when it is the direct result of God's action, not some innate human capacity. Johnston holds that, though possibly insufficiently trinitarian, Barth rightly safeguards the "Godness of God":[42] "To speak of general revelation, as many do, as the footprint of God in creation, or as an echo, the remainder after God has completed his creation (and departed? surely not), is to make revelation one step removed from the event of God's presence. And that is one step too many. . . . It is not the footprint of God that reveals God to us, but the *Spirit speaking in and through the footprint.*"[43]

Second, the footprint model understands revelation as entailing knowledge deduced by reason. Johnston looks to the great Romantic theologian Friedrich Schleiermacher as his ally in challenging the tradition on this point.[44] Writing in the shadow of, and in reaction to, the Enlightenment, Schleiermacher wanted to place felt experience of God, not reason, at the heart of theology. For him, revelation does not consist of propositions about God rationally apprehended; the divine is rather intuited precritically, in what he famously described as "the feeling of absolute dependence." The flaws in Schleiermacher's thought were that he largely abandoned reason altogether, and generally deviated from some core tenets of orthodoxy. But Johnston argues that these do not invalidate his giving primacy to the experiential precritical intuition of the divine.[45] "Thus, though his larger theological system might be found wanting,"

---

[42]Johnston, *God's Wider Presence*, chap. 6.

[43]Johnston, *God's Wider Presence*, chap. 6; emphasis mine.

[44]This is perhaps a surprising move given that, as Johnston puts it, Schleiermacher is the "obverse of Barth" and Barth's "respected nemesis." Considering Johnston's optimism about the possibility of revelation outside of explicit reference to Christ, however, that he leans heavily on Barth might strike some as the bigger surprise. See Johnston, *God's Wider Presence*, preface, chap. 6.

[45]Johnston asks if Schleiermacher's departure from orthodoxy is an inevitable consequence of his methodology, namely "his movement from Spirit to Word." Is starting with the pneumatological a recipe for an eventual rejection of historic doctrine? According to Johnston, no. The problem rather arises from Schleiermacher's anthropology. Humans are simultaneously feeling, thinking, and doing beings. But because this unity was for Schleiermacher at the level of the precritical, when it came to moving to the level of consciousness, reason was abandoned. His fatal flaw lay in his anthropology, not his methodology. Johnston, *God's Wider Presence*, chap. 6.

writes Johnston, "his understanding of the dynamics of our experience of revelation remains fundamental."[46]

Third, there has traditionally been a tendency to view general revelation as being of value only insofar as it is preparatory for special revelation. To make his point, Johnston looks to scholar and novelist C. S. Lewis, who has had a monumental impact on popular Christian thought. Lewis's contribution to the discussion comes mostly through his memoir, *Surprised By Joy,* which recounts his journey to Christian faith. His conversion came as the culmination of a series of highly affective revelatory experiences throughout his life up to that point stretching back into childhood, experiences which he called simply *Joy* (though defined idiosyncratically; elsewhere, he calls it *Sehnsucht*).[47] But in the final analysis Lewis serves as a negative example for Johnston, because upon conversion to Christianity Lewis treated these experiences as relatively worthless.[48] For Johnston, it's not worthless; rather, "this revelation is foundational and directional, providing precritical knowledge of the Divine that not only proves 'prevenient' but also continues to illumine even those who have experienced the Light of Life—Jesus Christ."[49]

Interpreters of Romans 1–2 have historically held that general revelation mediates a knowledge grounded in the residual effects of God's original

---

[46]Johnston, *God's Wider Presence,* chap. 6.

[47]Paul Brazier, *C. S. Lewis—Revelation, Conversion, and Apologetics* (Eugene, OR: Pickwick, 2012), 30.

[48]Lewis writes,

> But what, in conclusion, of Joy? . . . I now know that the experience, considered as a state of my own mind, had never had the kind of importance I once gave it. It was valuable only as a pointer to something other and outer. While that other was in doubt, the pointer naturally loomed large in my thoughts. When we are lost in the woods the sight of a signpost is a great matter. He who first sees it cries "Look!" The whole party gathers round and stares. But when we have the road and are passing signposts every few miles, we shall not stop and stare. They will encourage us and we shall be grateful to the authority that set them up. But we shall not stop and stare, or not much; not on this road, though their pillars are of silver and their lettering of gold. "We would be at Jerusalem." (Lewis, *Surprised by Joy* [London: Fount, 1998], 185)

Lewis's conviction that "we shall not stop and stare" indeed suggests that he no longer ascribed the same importance to Joy that he had once done. Though important in pointing the way, these experiences were mere signposts, largely rendered superfluous upon arrival at his destination: conversion. Lewis does concede that Joy may still serve as an encouragement in the life of the believer, and his modest qualification, "or not much," betrays the lingering attraction such experiences still held for Lewis. The line immediately following the above quotation (the final line of the book) reads, "Not, of course, that I don't often catch myself stopping to stare at roadside objects of even less importance." Lewis, *Surprised by Joy,* 185.

[49]Johnston, *God's Wider Presence,* chap. 6.

creation and deduced by human reason. Counter to this interpretation, Johnston argues that revelation depends on divine action, not innate human capacity (Barth); revelation is felt, not apprehended by reason (Schleiermacher); and general revelation has ongoing value even for the believer (Lewis, albeit negatively). He concludes that the opening of Romans, therefore, "cannot serve as the *locus classicus* for our understanding of general revelation."[50]

But if this won't act as the primary biblical basis for general revelation, what will? Johnston argues the church has overlooked many of those parts of the Bible that speak to the topic. Yes, Scripture is primarily interested in God's particular redemptive acts in history culminating in the ultimate revelation of God through Jesus Christ—that is to say, special revelation. But the primacy of special revelation in Scripture has blinded most readers to those passages where God reveals Godself to those outside the covenant community. The bulk of the biblical discussion about general revelation has thus centered on a small handful of well-worn passages, making it easy to dismiss the phenomenon as anomalous or insignificant. Yet there are other texts relevant to the topic.[51]

God's wider testimony. These overlooked passages fall roughly into two categories. The first are texts depicting characters outside the covenant community who are nevertheless portrayed as recipients of genuine divine revelation. An example is 2 Chronicles 35:20-27, which relates an incident in which King Josiah and his Israelite army confront King Necho of Egypt as he leads his army. Necho urges peace: "It is not you I am attacking at this time, but the house with which I am at war. God [*elohim*] has told me to hurry; so stop opposing God, who is with me, or he will destroy you" (1 Chron 35:21). The normally exemplary Josiah "would not listen to what Necho had said at God's command but went to fight him on the plain of Megiddo" (1 Chron 35:22). As a result, archers shoot Josiah dead. Johnston concludes:

> What is telling in this recounting of Josiah's actions is the theological failure of Josiah to recognize that Yahweh might also be revealing himself to and through an Egyptian pharaoh, perhaps even through an Egyptian pharaoh's "false" religion. Neco's description of a "generic" spirituality—his reference to *elohim*—or, worse, his reference to his own Egyptian god, seemed paltry and surely mistaken, given Josiah's lifetime of covenantal faithfulness. It was the people of

[50] Johnston, *God's Wider Presence*, chap. 6.
[51] Johnston, *God's Wider Presence*, chap. 1.

> God who should be telling this pharaoh what it was that the Lord (Yahweh) desired, not vice versa. After all, Israel read the law. After all, it was they who worshiped God aright in Jerusalem.[52]

Yet the implication of the story is clear: though Josiah could not accept it, Necho's message was genuinely from God. Josiah's theological assumptions blinded him to true revelation when it occurred in an unexpected place—and the consequences were fatal.

Another instance of divine revelation granted to an outsider occurs in the story of Melchizedek found in Genesis 14:17-20. In this short account, Abram is greeted by Melchizedek, King of Salem and priest of "God Most High," who then bestows a blessing on Abram in the name of God Most High (*'el 'elyon*). Abram apparently considers the blessing legitimate. He offers Melchizedek a tithe in return for the blessing, and later uses Melchizedek's appellation "God Most High" (Gen 14:22), despite appearing only once elsewhere in the Old Testament by an Israelite (cf. Ps 78:35). This Canaanite priest has evidently had a revelation from God that he bless Abram and has acted accordingly, which Abram, and the text itself, recognizes as valid. This story tacitly affirms, or at least condones, Melchizedek's religious rites, which presumably reflect the contemporaneous practices of Canaanite religion: "There is in this small vignette the transfer of pre-Israelite religious traditions into Israel. . . . God embraced this priesthood and built on it. This is to say that all theology emerges out of indigenous religious traditions that are embraced, purified, and extended."[53] That aspects of Israelite religion are a palimpsest, informed by pagan practices, implies that general revelation played a role in the cultic development of the covenant community.

The second category of neglected Scriptures are those texts that are themselves taken from outside the covenant community, yet have been incorporated into the special revelation of Scripture. For example, Proverbs 22:20-21 refers to "thirty sayings" though it's not clear there are actually thirty sayings in the passage. This puzzled biblical scholars until 1922, when Egyptologist Sir Ernest Budge was working with a papyrus containing the Instruction of Amenemope. He noticed its similarities to this passage in Proverbs, yet the Egyptian text clearly had thirty sayings. Later scholarship has confirmed that

[52]Johnston, *God's Wider Presence*, chap. 4.
[53]Johnston, *God's Wider Presence*, chap. 5.

Proverbs has borrowed from Amenemope. Interestingly—perhaps even scandalously—with its incongruous reference to thirty sayings, little effort has been made to disguise the text's external origins.[54] Something similar appears to be at play in Psalm 29, which scholars believe is based on a Canaanite hymn about a storm deity. The only change has been the introduction of the Israelite name for God, Yahweh. The inclusion of these foreign texts in the canon of Scripture, often with minimal redaction, is strong evidence that a divine word may be spoken and heard outside of the people of God. Special revelation includes and, in some instances is built upon, general revelation. This exact process in which pagan writings are appropriated by the covenant community as Scripture is in fact depicted in Acts 17:16-34, one of the few relevant Scriptures that has enjoyed ample attention. At the invitation of local Athenian philosophers, Paul publicly presents his "strange ideas" (Acts 17:20) to them. Troubled by their idolatry, Paul preaches about the "unknown god" to whom one of their idols is dedicated. Thus, Paul is simply building upon what they had already correctly perceived in part.[55] Of particular interest is Paul's quotation of two classical writers: Epimenides and Aratus. These quotations, in their original contexts, are references to Zeus, not Yahweh. Paul co-opted the theological claims of Greek thinkers and applied them to the God of Israel. As in Psalm 29, pagan words have become part of inspired Scripture.

The examples abound. Johnston identifies a broad range of relevant texts from Proverbs, 1 and 2 Chronicles, Psalms, Genesis, various prophetic books, and Acts. Johnston dedicates a full two chapters to these mostly neglected texts. Having been long subjected to myopic readings, it turns out that Scripture yields a relative wealth of data relevant to the topic of general revelation. Though still only a minor theme in Scripture, relatively speaking, the biblical evidence for general revelation is nevertheless considerable. And, crucially, the knowledge it imparts may be greater and of more beneficial than traditional readings of Romans 1–2 have supposed.

[54]Johnston, *God's Wider Presence*, chap. 4.

[55]Johnston writes, "Rather than simply criticize the Athenians for their idolatry, an idolatry that Luke has already indicated was deeply distressing to Paul, Paul chooses to recognize that in their groping after God, the Athenians have evidenced a genuine sensitivity to God 'who made the world and everything in it, he . . . is Lord of heaven and earth' (Acts 17:24). That is, these Greeks had received in truth God's revelation to them." Johnston, *God's Wider Presence*, chap. 5. That a number of Paul's audience came to faith in Jesus Christ is proof his strategy of starting with general revelation and moving to special revelation was successful.

An enlarged pneumatology. Johnston attributes much of the neglect of general revelation to a deficient pneumatology. For much of its history, the Western church has subordinated the Holy Spirit to Christ, giving Christology primacy over pneumatology.[56] "What is needed as an antidote is to treat the pneumatological as a parallel and helpful perspective to the christological as we seek a fuller understanding of God."[57] This leads Johnston to echo Protestant theologian Jürgen Moltmann's contention that the *filioque* clause be removed from the Western Nicene Creed. The unilateral addition of this Latin word (meaning "and the Son") to the creed has had the effect in the Western church of relegating the Spirit to "third place" in the Trinity.[58] Scripturally, however, the Spirit's activity is broad—quite literally cosmic. The Spirit is creator and sustainer of the cosmos, yet "when this universal perspective is applied to humankind generally, too often the Spirit's work among and in all people is wrongly reduced to the Spirit's work in the Christian community."[59] But, according to Moltmann, that the Spirit is on equal footing with the Son means that we must acknowledge the Spirit's "relative independence."[60]

Moltmann does not treat God's immanence and transcendence as irreconcilable polarities; rather, he describes the Spirit's presence as "immanent transcendence." Because of the Spirit of Life, every experience has a transcendent side and transcendence can therefore be experienced in all parts of life; God is "in, with and beneath" all our daily experiences.[61] Moltmann thus embraces "the panentheism of a pneumatologically charged creation theology."[62] Johnston also employs the work of Catholic theologian Elisabeth Johnson, whose panentheism resembles Moltmann's. In her view, "The universe is encompassed by the Matrix of the living God. . . . The relationship created by this mutual indwelling, while nonhierarchical and reciprocal, is not strictly

[56]Johnston, *God's Wider Presence*, chap. 7.

[57]Johnston, *God's Wider Presence*, chap. 7.

[58]Jürgen Moltmann, *The Spirit of Life: A Universal Affirmation* (Minneapolis: Fortress, 1992), 293; cited in Johnston, *God's Wider Presence*, chap. 7. Johnston also cites evangelical scholar Amos Yong in support of the idea of abandoning the *filioque*. Yong suggests instead that we embrace the metaphor first used by second-century theologian Irenaeus: the Spirit and the Son as the two hands of the Father. Amos Yong, *Beyond the Impasse* (Grand Rapids, MI: Baker Academic, 2003), 186; cited in Johnston, *God's Wider Presence*, chap. 8.

[59]Johnston, *God's Wider Presence*, chap. 7.

[60]Moltmann, *Spirit of Life*, xi; cited in Johnston, *God's Wider Presence*, chap. 7.

[61]Moltmann, *Spirit of Life*, 17; cited in Johnston, *God's Wider Presence*, chap. 7.

[62]Johnston, *God's Wider Presence*, chap. 7.

symmetrical, for the world is dependent on God in a way that God is not on the world."[63] This mutual abiding of Spirit and world—for which an apt metaphor is the pregnant female body—leads her to a sacramental view of creation, where all and any experience is potentially the location for divine encounter.[64] As Moltmann puts it, "We sense in everything that God is waiting for us."[65] Johnston's expansive pneumatology, deeply informed by those of Moltmann and Johnson, opens up the possibility that we might experience the divine in creation, culture, and conscience.

Critiquing God's Wider Presence

Analysis of Johnston's account. Johnston offers an invigorating reconsideration of a doctrine desperately in need of such. More pertinently for this book, his account gives us the theological framework we need to consider revelation through cinema. According to Johnston, those highly affective, particular experiences of *apparent* revelation in response to a movie may be *actual* revelation. For that reason, the broad strokes of his perspective significantly shape my work in this book. I say *broad* strokes, however, because I do feel compelled to challenge Johnston's account at a key point, and thus ultimately amend it slightly. I hope to alight upon a modified version of the theory, one I think is not only more theologically robust, but also capacious enough to encapsulate a broader range of viewer experiences.

As we have already seen, Johnston takes aim at the so-called footprint view of general revelation, wherein creation mediates knowledge of God through traces of God's creation. My issue with Johnston's view centers around his interpretation and eventual dismissal of these "footprints." Contrary to Johnston, I think these traces of God's handiwork *also* qualify as genuinely revelatory. Johnston construes God's creative activity as anchored in the past:

> The problem with traditional notions of general revelation that have been based in God's past revelatory action, not his present revelatory Presence, is that nothing fresh is seemingly "communicated"; rather, the knowledge that is garnered is simply "derived." But that is to say that such knowledge is not really revelation at all. It is rather the recollection of or human projection from God's

---

[63]Johnston, *God's Wider Presence*, chap. 7.
[64]Johnston, *God's Wider Presence*, chap. 7.
[65]Johnston, *God's Wider Presence*, chap. 7.

> past actions—God's past revelation. . . . General revelation is not a universal, second-order reflection derived from the human capacity for transcending one's self (conscience)—the image of God (imago Dei) in men and women—nor is it a human inference from creation's "glory" that there is something greater than humankind. General revelation is not to be confused with human culture's residual memory of God's prior relationship with humankind. For each of these common descriptors fails the test of revelation, remaining rooted in creature and not Creator.[66]

The metaphor of a footprint suggests an act confined to history, hinting at a presence long since departed. But I suggest this understanding of creation is too static. Even if we were to reject the patristic understanding of creation (or preservation) as requiring the continuous agency of God,[67] we ought still to affirm a more dynamic view of creation, not only as a one-time act taking place in the primordial past but also as a process culminating in the eschatological future. In other words, God's creative activity is ongoing. Even the creation account of Genesis 1 has been interpreted along these lines in both early and modern Christian thought (e.g., *The Epistle of Barnabas*, Gerhard von Rad);[68] we are living in the sixth day awaiting the seventh day when God's creative activity will come to completion.[69] To claim that knowledge inferred from creation qualifies as genuine, therefore, is not necessarily to insist on the original act as such. If God not only creat*ed*, but is creat*ing*, then insight that comes via creation may be anchored just as much in the present as in the past.

An example of the footprint that it seems Johnston would reject is the "religious *a priori*" that many of the theological giants upon whose shoulders we stand—Paul, Augustine, and the Reformers—have held to. This school of thought claims we are each endowed with innate capacities upon which (very limited) divine knowledge is founded.[70] Calvin postulated the existence "by

[66]Johnston, *God's Wider Presence*.

[67]See, for example, Athanasius, *On the Incarnation of the Word* (n.p.: Amazon Digital Services, 2010), 1.1-4, Kindle, www.amazon.com/St-Athanasius-Incarnation-Word-ebook/dp/B003ELPVJM.

[68]Joseph Barber Lightfoot, John Reginald Harmer, and Michael William Holmes, *The Apostolic Fathers: Greek Texts and English Translations of Their Writings* (Grand Rapids, MI: Baker, 1992), 182-83; Gerhard von Rad, *Genesis: A Commentary* (Philadelphia: Westminster, 1972), 60-61; cited in Stanley J. Grenz, *Theology for the Community of God* (Grand Rapids, MI: Eerdmans, 2000), chap. 4, Kindle.

[69]Grenz, *Theology for the Community of God*, chap. 4.

[70]Demarest, *General Revelation*, 42.

natural instinct" of a "sense of Deity" in the human heart and mind.[71] Recent psychological theory suggests this theological hypothesis also has a psychological basis.[72] According to psychologist Justin Barrett, we exhibit proclivities and capabilities from infancy that incline us to believe in deities. Barrett goes so far as to suggest that we are born predisposed to "natural religion," the skeleton of natural beliefs upon which grows the flesh of the parents' particular religious tradition.[73] Psychology then is uncovering evidence for what theologians have already claimed: humans are born believers.

Regardless of what we may make of the born believers hypothesis, this religious impulse, the sense of deity, is itself a type of knowledge. Dulles, drawing upon philosopher of science Michael Polanyi, highlights an ostensibly paradoxical claim: the first stage of discovery, seeing the question, actually requires an ineffable *prior awareness* of the answer being sought: "To see a problem is itself an act of tacit knowledge—a knowledge going beyond what we can put into words."[74] About the theological quest, Dulles writes, "Our search for God, viewed retrospectively after the finding, was accompanied by a certain prior awareness that directed the entire question."[75] To my mind then, the intuitive, innate sense of deity, the *sensus divinitatis*, is itself a kind of genuine knowledge, yet it would seem to flunk Johnston's test for revelation, due largely to his dependence on Barth:[76]

> Barth's critique of Brunner also remains foundational to all else, his argument that revelation must always be understood as "event," as encounter with the living God through the Spirit. Revelation is never rooted somehow independent of God in creation's footprint. It is here that the voice of Barth remains necessary for us to hear again today. . . . Revelation is never the result of creation independent of the Presence of the Spirit in and through it.[77]

---

71 Calvin uses both the heart and mind as the location of the *sensus divinitatis*.

72 Justin L. Barrett, *Born Believers: The Science of Children's Religious Belief* (New York: Atria Books, 2014), Kindle.

73 Barrett, *Born Believers*, 154.

74 Avery Dulles, "Revelation and Discovery," in *Theology and Discovery: Essays in Honor of Karl Rahner, SJ*, ed. William J. Kelly (Milwaukee: Marquette University Press, 1980), 5.

75 Dulles, "Revelation and Discovery," 10-11.

76 Johnston, *God's Wider Presence*, chap. 6. Johnston does not address the *sensus divinitatis* directly but, given his siding with Barth over Brunner on the related issue of the point of contact in the *imago Dei* and his wider argument against the footprint model, it seems reasonable to assume that he would not class it as revelation.

77 Johnston, *God's Wider Presence*, chap. 6.

An instance in which somebody makes a reasoned deduction about God from creation would not meet this "event" criterion—at least as Johnston parses it—and is therefore not authentic revelation. For Johnston, transcendent experience qualifies as genuine revelation; *knowledge universally mediated by creation does not.* This insistence on the event nature of revelation is surely correct as far as it goes, a needed corrective to the notion that divine knowledge can be ascertained from the natural world by *unaided* reason. But is it not true that wherever somebody is discerning something of God, the Spirit is at work? Paul's insistence that "no one can say, 'Jesus is Lord,' except by the Holy Spirit" (1 Cor 12:3) may be applied to any divine truth about God someone asserts.[78]

A general theology of revelation. Johnston would have us discard the traditional understanding of general knowledge as universal and see it solely as particular. I, however, suggest that we view general revelation as encompassing both the particular and the universal. Let's momentarily put aside divine knowledge specifically, and consider knowledge more generally. How is it that we can know anything at all? The answer is revelation. Think about the many ordinary, nontheological ways we use the word *revelation.* News media recount the revelations of an eyewitness's testimony; sports reporters describe an outstanding rookie as a revelation; TV critics describe the drama of a soap opera in terms of its revelations; and spouses grow closer or are driven further apart through revelations of their past. This is just the tip of the iceberg; we're continually participating in revelation—in a broad sense, rather than a narrow theological sense—even when we do not explicitly name it as such.[79] As theologian Colin Gunton argues, revelation is woven into the fabric of ordinary life. Gunton, therefore, writes not just about general revelation, but about a general theology of revelation.[80]

What is a general theology of revelation? Gunton's explanation appeals to the words of poet Samuel Taylor Coleridge: "All Truth is a species of Revelation."[81] The fact that revelation happens in interpersonal relationships—that is to say, we as beings in relation reveal ourselves to one another—is probably self-evident.

---

[78]I owe this insight to William A. Dyrness, August 5, 2015.

[79]Of course, not all self-revelation is intentional; we may reveal inadvertently through, say, body language. Colin E. Gunton, *A Brief Theology of Revelation: The 1993 Warfield Lectures* (Edinburgh: T&T Clark, 1995), 23.

[80]Gunton, *Brief Theology of Revelation,* 20.

[81]Gunton, *Brief Theology of Revelation,* 22.

Less obvious, however, is the fact that our knowledge of nature also hinges on revelation. This claim might be counterintuitive. This is perhaps especially so, writes Gunton, since the medieval synthesis of reason and revelation dissolved, leading to the separation of secular and religious reason such that "these [secular] forms of knowledge do not appear to depend on revelation at all."[82] But despite appearances, science, too, is dependent on revelation.

There is a revelatory dimension to even scientific endeavor. Dulles notes how scientific discovery comes in a "Eureka!" moment inevitably described in the language of revelation.[83] Thus, according to Gunton, there is a sense in which we must be taught by and wait on nature to reveal her secrets. Our scientific understanding of the natural world, albeit provisional and faltering, is genuinely advancing: "It seems to be beyond serious question that there is a process of unfolding taking place before our eyes, and indeed a kind of intellectual progress. We simply know more about how the world is than did earlier generations. Our wisdom may often be less than theirs, but our knowledge is incomparably greater."[84] Granted, there are differences between nature's self-revelation and our own. For instance, we cannot ascribe agency to nature, which is "relatively passive under our enquiry." Nevertheless, "it remains true that knowledge of her comes as a gift, and is therefore a species of revelation."[85]

The central thesis of Gunton's *A Brief Theology of Revelation* is that all revelation is mediated. In the case of the natural world, it is mediated to us through, for instance, scientific theories and through the arts.[86] This may be jarring to those accustomed to seeing the world as essentially nonrevelatory. Projectionist perspectives hold that our knowledge arises solely from our own subjectivity imposed ("projected") outward with no necessary correlation with the objective world. But such views fail to account for the consistency of our experience, particularly when we bump up against the brute facts of concrete reality. That prolonged submersion in water will result in drowning, for example, is no mere projection. We've seen this truth play out in our own age with tragic consequences. No matter how much Donald Trump might have tried to simply wish away Covid-19 by spouting a triumphalistic narrative, the

[82]Gunton, *Brief Theology of Revelation*, 32.
[83]Dulles, "Revelation and Discovery," 5.
[84]Gunton, *Brief Theology of Revelation*, 26-27.
[85]Gunton, *Brief Theology of Revelation*, 25, 35.
[86]Gunton, *Brief Theology of Revelation*, 28-30.

virus still ravaged the US with utter indifference to the president's counterfactual rhetoric.[87] There is something in the structure of the human mind, in our subjectivity, that accords with the objective cosmos. No less a luminary than Albert Einstein recognized this correspondence as the miracle that makes science possible.[88] All this is to say that all knowledge is fundamentally revelatory. "All Truth is a species of Revelation."[89]

If it is true, it is revealed. But by what—or by whom? For the likes of Calvin, the agent of all knowledge, divine or otherwise, is the Holy Spirit.[90] Gunton agrees:

> If there is revelation of the truth of the world, it is because the Spirit of truth enables it to take place. To put it another way, the creator Spirit brings it about that human rationality is able, within the limits set to it, to encompass the truth of the creation. We therefore neither control nor create our knowledge, even though the concepts by which we express it are in part the free creations of our minds.[91]

The ramifications of this are significant. Evangelical theologian David Diehl has argued that evangelical theology's failure to recognize the pneumatological basis of knowledge has resulted in an inability to consistently engage with modern knowledge, particularly scientific advancements. More specifically, the fault lies in an underdeveloped concept of general revelation, deployed *ad hoc*, that limits general revelation's worth to its ability to establish humanity's guilt; that is to say, it conveys only a *religious* truth and a negative one at that. But, writes Diehl, general revelation pertains not merely to knowledge *of God*, but indeed genuine knowledge of all things.[92] Psalm 19:1 bears this out: "The heavens declare the glory of God; the skies proclaim the work of his hands." Creation communicates knowledge not only of God, but also of that which God has created. Regardless of whether we wish to call that general revelation or not, the point is the same: Revelation does not "just

---

[87]Stephen Collinson. "Trump's Wish for an End to the Pandemic Contradicts Reality," CNN, June 16, 2020, https://edition.cnn.com/2020/06/16/politics/donald-trump-coronavirus-politics-oklahoma-election-2020/index.html.

[88]Gunton, *Brief Theology of Revelation*, 34-37.

[89]Gunton, *Brief Theology of Revelation*, 22.

[90]Calvin, *Institutes of the Christian Religion* 2.2.15.

[91]Gunton, *Brief Theology of Revelation*, 34-35.

[92]David W. Diehl, "Evangelicalism and General Revelation: An Unfinished Agenda," *Journal of the Evangelical Theological Society* 30, no. 4 (1987), www.etsjets.org/files/JETS-PDFs/30/30-4/30-4-pp441-455-JETS.pdf.

happen"; rather, the Holy Spirit discloses it. Our theology of general revelation must be undergirded by a robust general theology of revelation.

And this is what Johnston's argument lacks. It doesn't sufficiently account for the fact that *all* knowledge is revealed by the Spirit, and therefore the universal, too, may qualify as genuine revelation. As mentioned above, Johnston's Barthian insistence on revelation as event is right; we don't gain divine knowledge by unaided reason. But the event of revelation encompasses more than Johnston allows. In his laudable zeal to gain a hearing for those indelible experiences that come to us through creation, culture, and conscience, Johnston marginalizes other means by which authentic divine knowledge is imparted. As he himself so forcefully argues, the Spirit is the Spirit of creation. Surely then, all knowledge mediated by creation is grounded in the Spirit. The footprint is never only a footprint, as if once upon a time the Spirit created and has since departed, leaving only vestiges. Rather, the Spirit conveys knowledge through creation in myriad ways, including that which comes by way of reason and by imagination. All knowledge has a pneumatological basis. For this reason, I suggest Johnston's useful notion of God's wider presence be nested within Gunton's general theology of revelation.

General revelation, universal and particular. At the risk of oversimplification, we might put it this way: Tradition has said general revelation is universal; Johnston says it's particular; I'm saying it's both. A major weakness of the propositional model of revelation is its inadequacy to experience, requiring assent to propositions that may not necessarily speak to her situation.[93] On the other hand, a weakness of the experiential model is that it breaks significantly with the mainstream of the biblical and Christian tradition.[94] Johnston gives us the best of both worlds: resonance with lived experience *and* the affirmation of the supremacy of the revelation through Jesus Christ.

The Puritans believed knowledge imparted by general revelation to be coolly intellectual, while that of special revelation is warmly practical.[95] But Johnston shows that general revelation has "warmth" too. Think of those

[93]Dulles, *Models of Revelation*, 50-51.

[94]Dulles, *Models of Revelation*, 77-83. As a result, the experiential approach has often devolved into theological liberalism, an instance of what Berkouwer identifies as the "suction power" of full-fledged natural theology that often seems to be at work whenever there is a move away from Christomonism. Berkouwer, *General Revelation*, 56.

[95]Demarest, *General Revelation*, 71.

profoundly moving experiences you've had, experiences that may also have been transformative in your life. *Those* are part of God's wider presence. They communicate not that God *was* here, like some faded divine graffiti scrawled across a decaying cosmos from long ago. They communicate that God *is* here, still present and still speaking. Though not always reducible to propositional content, this "speech" imparts genuine knowledge, knowledge that wields significant transformative power precisely *because* of its felt quality.

Understood this way, general revelation sounds a note of optimism. It is a far more positive understanding of this doctrine than has been characteristic of evangelical or Reformed theology in the past. In a time when evangelicalism is often seen as reactionary and judgmental, such a hopeful paradigm for cultural engagement ought to be welcomed. By opening up the discussion beyond the confines of soteriology, we can affirm that such revelation is not only the basis of condemnation, but also the source of genuine enlightenment for all, regardless of faith. We can, therefore, open ourselves to the possibility—nay, probability—of divine encounter through creation, culture, and conscience.[96]

Recall Ricky Fitts's experience of being entranced by a swirling, twirling plastic bag, overwhelmed by the sudden awareness of a benevolent presence in an otherwise unremarkable moment. Could such an ostensibly mundane experience, one that occurs outside the church and without direct reference to Christ, still be genuinely revelatory? We can now answer this question in the affirmative. Yes, revelation may indeed occur through highly particular, affective experience, whether it be occasioned by a plastic bag—or, crucially for our purposes, by a film.

[96]Since providential history has historically been held as a site of general revelation, we might like to add history to Johnston's list of revelatory loci: creation, culture, conscience, and "chronicles" (just to maintain the alliteration!).

3

Revelation and Emotion

When Pete Docter, from Pixar's stable of directors, sought to make a movie about emotions, he turned to Disney's animated short *Reason and Emotion* (Bill Roberts, 1943) for inspiration. This war-time short imaginatively presents the inner workings of its characters' minds as a battleground between personifications of Reason and Emotion. Reason is depicted as a civilized, eminently sensible fuddy-duddy; Emotion, an uncouth, hotheaded Cro-Magnon. At the climax, no less a villain than Hitler appears (!), grandstanding and gesticulating wildly. Within moments, Reason is bound and gagged, while Emotion is goosestepping and shouting "*Sieg heil*!" The message is hardly subtle: emotion is crude, atavistic, and dangerous—with only our highly evolved reason to keep it in check. Docter wanted his film to present a less denigrating view of emotion,[1] and thus was born *Inside Out* (2015), praised by psychologists for depicting emotion as a vital part of healthy human functioning.[2]

I see my task in this book, and especially this chapter, as being analogous to Docter's. As we saw in the previous chapter, revelation has often been understood as closely tethered to reason, as if emotion were either irrelevant to the matter or perhaps even at odds with it. Evangelicalism has tended toward a propositional model of revelation, smuggling in with it the notion that religious knowledge is mostly an intellectual affair. But to class as potentially revelatory only those instances that involve propositional content is to ignore vast swathes of transcendent experience. The sorts of film-viewing experiences we are considering are often highly, sometimes *primarily* affective. To rightly understand them then, we need to develop a paradigm of revelation

[1]Daniel Smith, "Pixar's Mood Master: Can Pete Docter's New Movie Change the Way We Think About Our Emotions?," *The Atlantic*, June, 2015, 20.
[2]Smith, "Pixar's Mood Master," 21.

that grants emotion its rightful place at the center of some revelatory experience. That's what I seek to do in this chapter. My work here is less *Reason and Emotion*, and more *Inside Out*.

Writing about affect casts me in the role of "romantic theologian," which according to Lewis, isn't "one who is romantic about theology, but one who is theological about romance, one who considers the theological implications of those experiences that are called romantic."[3] Being theological about romance is a worthy enterprise when exploring film-mediated revelation. Why? Because the romantic, by which I mean chiefly something like *feeling*, is inextricably entwined with religious experience, not least that facilitated by art. The close association between emotion and revelation is observed by Callaway in his reception-oriented study of film music. He writes that

> these moments of "transcendence" do not always contain discernibly religious content. Indeed, for many, the words "transcendent" or "revelatory" function as catchwords to describe the mysterious, the ineffable, and the inexpressible quality of their musical-aesthetic experience. Thus, the larger significance of these films and the music therein is rooted *not in what is revealed but in the intensely affective experience itself*. In other words, it is the filmgoing experience that is revelatory.[4]

What Callaway claims for film music, I extend to cinema generally and film images specifically. Though ineffability seems to be a particular quality of music,[5] film *viewing* too can be a somewhat ineffable, affective experience, which strikes certain viewers as spiritual.[6] As such, purported experiences of film-mediated revelation may carry a significantly emotional dimension.

Before going any further, a qualification. Part one, including this chapter, is intended to lay a foundation for part two, in which we'll analyze particular

---

[3]C. S. Lewis, "Essays Presented to Charles Williams," ed. Charles Williams and Dorothy L. Sayers (London: Oxford University Press, 1947), vi. It may be more accurate to speak of being "post-romantic." Callaway points to the work of philosopher Charles Taylor in identifying the following traits as indicative of our present post-romantic culture: (1) judgment and meaning are subjectively grounded; (2) meaning is discovered affectively; and (3) art is revelatory or "epiphanic." Kutter Callaway, *Scoring Transcendence: Contemporary Film Music as Religious Experience* (Waco, TX: Baylor University Press, 2013), chap. 4n57.

[4]Callaway, *Scoring Transcendence*, chap. 6; emphasis mine.

[5]See, for example, the association between music and mystical-type revelatory experience in Jonathan Brant, *Paul Tillich and the Possibility of Revelation Through Film* (Oxford: Oxford University Press, 2012), 194-95.

[6]Callaway, *Scoring Transcendence*, chap. 4.

films and explore how various formal devices may become instruments of divine revelation. At face value, this might seem to be a theologically risky and futile endeavor. It might seem as if I'm claiming that revelation is simply a matter of technique. Just use this visual device and—hey presto!—revelation results. Theologian David Brown writes,

> Yet, however argued, it is that step from God active in the natural world to human creativity also mediating the divine to which exception is most likely to be taken. It will be said that God is now subject to human manipulation. Put crudely, it looks as though the divine can now be summoned at will, simply by artists obeying the right set of rules to evoke the corresponding divine attribute or feature of revelation.[7]

But to make such a claim would not only be erroneous, it'd be preposterous. No filmmaker can force God's hand into self-disclosure. Revelation depends solely on the initiative and action of God. It has no other basis than the divine will, and certainly has no basis in any creaturely device. Yet revelation through film does not appear to be purely random, arbitrary, or haphazard. Any movie *may* serve as the occasion for revelation, but some movies commonly and consistently elicit claims of a theological nature more than others. My purpose is to investigate the formal, especially visual, features of those films that generate such responses without compromising divine agency. On the one hand, we must insist that God is the primary and essential agent of revelation; on the other hand, film form does not appear to be inconsequential to claims of revelation, apparently having some bearing on such experiences. How can that be? That's the puzzle at the heart of this chapter.

The Effect of Affect

Because of the (conservative) Protestant preference for the propositional model, equating revelation with doctrine, religious knowledge has been seen as the cognitive apprehension of those truths. At best, affect has been treated as inconsequential and, at worst, misleading. The Cartesian assumptions here are plain to see: I *think* Christian thoughts, therefore I am Christian. But what if knowledge comes through the affective as much as it does through the cognitive? If that were true, our understanding of revelation would have to flex to

[7]Brown, *Divine Generosity and Human Creativity,* chap. 1.

better accommodate affect—and that is precisely where certain recent theological developments point us.

In his Cultural Liturgies trilogy, theologian James K. A. Smith demonstrates that knowledge is affective as well as cognitive; indeed, it is affective *before* it is cognitive.[8] His project is well known, so I won't rehash its intricacies here, but simply offer a brief summary. Smith writes that for too long Christian institutions have operated with an intellectualist anthropology, construing humans as primarily *thinking* creatures. By contrast, the most influential cultural institutions—paradigmatically, the shopping mall—(de)form us not through intellectual argumentation, but through embodied habituation. Thus, Smith advocates a "liturgical anthropology" in which our hearts, specifically our desires, are most critical in shaping the people we become.[9] In explaining *how* our desires shape us, he focuses in particular on affect and art, two of our principal concerns in this book. More fundamental than our intellect is our imagination, by which he means not the capacity to make-believe but rather "a quasi-faculty whereby we construe the world on a precognitive level, on a register that is fundamentally *aesthetic* precisely because it is so closely tied to the body."[10] The things with the greatest power to shape us, therefore, are those that most effectively tap into our corporeality. This is why affect, which involves the body at least as much as it does the mind, is so important. A certain type of knowledge is fundamentally affective, rather than cognitive.

Smith turns to seminal phenomenologist Maurice Merleau-Ponty for a closer-to-the-ground account of knowledge. Traditional epistemologies privilege conceptual knowledge and treat it as more or less consciously housed in the mind. But these standard accounts are woefully inadequate. They are, Smith says, like the *X*s and *O*s on a coach's chalkboard, which, taken alone, won't impart the knowledge you need to succeed on the field. *That* knowledge can only be acquired in the thick of the action during game-time. Merleau-Ponty calls this latter, more concrete type of knowledge *perception*. Perception

---

[8]In order to distinguish him from another scholar who appears in this chapter, Greg Smith, I will sometimes refer to James K. A. Smith by the less cumbersome "Jamie Smith."

[9]James K. A. Smith, *Imagining the Kingdom: How Worship Works*, Cultural Liturgies (Grand Rapids, MI: Baker Academic, 2013), introduction, Kindle.

[10]Smith, *Imagining the Kingdom*, introduction. It seems to me theologian Friedrich Schleiermacher's elusive "feeling of absolute dependence" is a phenomenon (though not figment!) of the imagination as Smith defines it. Friedrich Schleiermacher, *On Religion: Speeches to Its Cultured Despisers*, trans. John Oman (n.p.: Beloved Publishing, 2015).

is not a processing of environmental stimuli in an entirely neutral way; rather, perception is *already* shaded with prereflective evaluations before it is actively thought about. In a sense, the body has already made judgments about the world before the mind has had a chance to evaluate the data for itself. This *is* knowledge, but not as we ordinarily conceive of it. It is, to use Merleau-Ponty's term, *preconscious knowledge*. Our body "knows" how to inhabit and find its way through the world, and does so mostly without conscious thought. How is preconscious knowledge acquired? Through habits.[11] Thus, Smith argues, personal transformation requires the alteration of habits, not merely beliefs. And the efficacy of habits, which put our bodies through particular motions and performances, is grounded in the power of narrative: "The way to the heart is through the body, and the way into the body is through story."[12] Rituals are simply stories in microcosm.

So far, Smith proves a helpful ally. By locating preconscious knowledge in the body and highlighting the importance of affect, he opens the way for consideration of narrative and aesthetics—and, therefore, movies—as significantly formative. But, at this point, our dependence on Smith will require some qualification. Despite the power of story—in fact, *because* of it—Smith doesn't seem to hold out much hope for what he terms *secular liturgies*. Liturgies, whether religious or secular, tell the body a formative story. But the story told by, say, the mall is inescapably *de*formative, invariably molding shoppers into obedient consumers with all the concomitant character flaws. Presumably then, going to the cineplex *within* that mall is every bit as unhealthy.

That said, I don't think Smith is opposed to Christian engagement with cinema. On the contrary, he is deeply conversant with and indeed profoundly appreciative of the arts and pop culture, including film. Yet, as Callaway notes, "it would be almost impossible using his categories to identify a secular liturgy that functions in constructive ways."[13] So while Smith gives us an account of human knowing that significantly bolsters the apparent value of aesthetic experience, wholesale adoption of his theory may lead some to write film-watching off as irredeemably deformative.

---

[11]Smith, *Imagining the Kingdom*, chap. 2.

[12]Smith, *Imagining the Kingdom*, introduction.

[13]Kutter Callaway and Dean Batali, *Watching TV Religiously: Television and Theology in Dialogue*, Engaging Culture (Grand Rapids, MI: Baker Academic, 2016), 148-49.

Smith sees (a particular form of) Christian liturgy as being the antidote to the deformative practices of secular liturgies. But his sharp distinction between Christian and secular liturgies is shaky, operating as if the meanings of cultural practices are fixed.[14] They're not. Theologians Cory Willson and Robert Covolo counter: "Cultural practices have multiple meanings operating simultaneously."[15] A practice may entail official, public, and private meanings all at once. This, they write, is the intuition behind Paul's conciliatory treatment of the then-controversial matter of eating meat sacrificed to idols (1 Cor 10:14–11:1), which took place in the markets, the Greco-Roman equivalent of the contemporary shopping mall. Pagan priests assigned one meaning to the practice (official), yet the church could collectively construct an alternative meaning (public), while the practice could hold yet other meanings for individual believers (private). In his epistle to the Corinthian church, Paul was happy to reject the official meaning and promote an oppositional meaning, while remaining mindful of the possible private meanings held by fellow Christians. Paul is sensitive to the deformative potential this consumption practice holds for some, yet doesn't see this meaning as wholly determinative. As always for Paul, love must be the overriding principle governing Christian behavior (1 Cor 10:24, 31-33). Nevertheless, he affirms the practice by appealing to the goodness of and God's sovereignty over creation (1 Cor 10:26).[16] For Paul, this "secular liturgy" needn't be secular at all, even if considered so by fellow believers. Thus, Willson and Covolo write, "cultural liturgies do *not* need to have the final say on the significance and purpose of our engagement."[17] As theologian William Dyrness says of "symbolic practices," similar to Smith's notion of liturgies, "They are places where, because of God's continuing presence in creation and God's redemptive work in Christ and by the Spirit, God is also active,

[14]Callaway and Batali, *Watching T.V. Religiously*, 148-54.

[15]Robert Covolo and Cory Willson, "When Is a Mall Just a Mall? The Complexity of Reading Cultural Practices," *The Other Journal*, February 2, 2012, http://theotherjournal.com/2012/02/02/when-is-a-mall-just-a-mall-the-complexity-of-reading-cultural-practices/.

[16]Smith himself implicitly acknowledges the importance of the meanings attached to a cultural practice. To function formatively, Smith holds that Christian liturgy requires concordant belief. Though affect is fundamental, clearly cognition still plays a vital role. Conversely, secular liturgies are presumably at their deformative "best" when paired with compatible ways of thinking. Thus, conscious awareness of how secular practices can deform us may in fact counteract that deformation. Smith, *Imagining the Kingdom*, chap. 4.

[17]Covolo and Willson, "When Is a Mall Just a Mall?"; emphasis original.

nurturing, calling, and drawing persons—and indeed, all creation—toward the perfection God intends for them."[18]

Qualifications aside, Smith gives us an account of knowledge that accords affect an essential place.[19] But can it be *revelation*? Recall Colin Gunton's general theology of revelation that, following Coleridge, posits "all Truth is a species of Revelation."[20] Contrary to the impulses of Christian fundamentalism with its tendency to reduce truth to the brute "facts," truth is complex. Smith writes,

> A story or poem does not merely communicate "a truth" that I can also "get" in some other way. Rather, the truth of a story or poem is carried in its form, in the unique affect generated by its cadences and rhythm, in the interplay and resonances of the imaginative world it invokes, in the metaphorical inferences that I "get" on a gut level.[21]

The arts communicate truth that reverberates and resides in the gut, a form of knowledge that comports with human embodiment. Indeed, if we take a Tillichian view of revelation as transformative,[22] we might say that revelation *must* enlist the imagination, must be *felt*, lest it take up residence in the mind as nothing more than an intellectual curio lacking transformative power. Others, too, have written about the revelatory power of imagination. According to David Brown, for example, "One of the principal ways in which God speaks to humanity is through the imagination, and, as we might have expected, the human imagination has not stood still over a further two thousand years of Christianity."[23] He has argued that revelation has frequently occurred throughout Christian tradition, mediated via the arts, which are "imaginative and innovative."[24] Brown's viewpoint will be too strong for some,

[18]William A. Dyrness, *Poetic Theology: God and the Poetics of Everyday Life* (Grand Rapids, MI: Eerdmans, 2011), chap. 1, Kindle.

[19]Admittedly, Smith sometimes describes this know-how as *knowledge* only with some qualification. Smith says that, for Bourdieu, *habitus* is "enough like knowledge to still be named in that ballpark." Smith, *Imagining the Kingdom*, chap. 2. So is it knowledge or not? The issue is semantic. Smith occasionally puts the word *knowledge* in scare quotes simply to highlight the fact this it is a nonconceptual mode of knowing.

[20]Gunton, *Brief Theology of Revelation*, 22.

[21]Smith, *Imagining the Kingdom*, chap. 3.

[22]Brant, *Paul Tillich*, 247.

[23]David Brown, *Tradition and Imagination: Revelation and Change* (Oxford: Oxford University Press, 1999), part 1, Kindle.

[24]Brown, *Tradition and Imagination*, chap. 1.

but the fundamental point stands regardless: imagination is a crucial component of revelation. And if, to push the argument further, imagination has primacy, then we have every reason to expect revelation to be *primarily* affective some of the time. Of course, revelation may be cognitive, but it can equally be affective—or both simultaneously.

FILM, AFFECT, AND REVELATION

The emergence of cognitive film theory. Given the central role that narrative and aesthetics play in formation, the connection with film is obvious. Most films are narrative; all are aesthetic. But when intellectualist assumptions hold sway, the fundamentally aesthetic character of cinema is minimized. If we take revelation to be exclusively propositional, then the indispensable part of a film will likewise be propositional. Film form becomes little more than the "container" for a didactic "message." Indeed, this has been the prevailing tendency of Christian commentary on film, whether popular or scholarly. Rather than being seen as inextricably bound up in the form, the meaning of a film has been treated as distillable, as though it could be boiled down to its essential message. In other words, in order for a film to impart religious knowledge, it must do so discursively. It is, in Smith's words, "relentlessly thematic" and affect, therefore, is accorded little value.[25] Theme is the medicine; affect (and aesthetic), the proverbial spoonful of sugar.

But, in actuality, there is an irreducibility to art and its effect that defies neat propositional summation. Smith writes, "There is a synergy between stories and bodies, between poems and our physiology. There is an irreducible materiality to both that makes a difference. Materiality matters. So the poem is not just a disembodied idea or a distilled content."[26] Failure to recognize this is, in literary critic Cleanth Brooks's famous phrase, to commit the "heresy of paraphrase."[27] In *that* sense, much Christian engagement with film has been "heretical."

There have been calls from within the theology-film dialogue too for more affect-sensitive approaches to film. Theologian Clive Marsh, for example, holds that theological engagement with cinema has erred in its inattention to audience reception, and has neglected *actual* viewer experience. For most

---

[25]Smith, *Imagining the Kingdom*, chap. 3.
[26]Smith, *Imagining the Kingdom*, chap. 1.
[27]Smith, *Imagining the Kingdom*, chap. 4.

viewers, that experience is significantly affective.[28] Marsh thus launches a defense of sentiment and sentimentality (though sentimentality is often a negative, Marsh uses the term in a mostly neutral sense). Though often derided, sentimentality deserves our close attention, because of its prominence in popular film, not to mention that sentimentality points to the deepest human concerns and is therefore of intrinsic theological interest.[29] Theology's role then, among other things, is to structure viewers' emotional responses to films, though Marsh doesn't elaborate much on how this structuring happens.[30]

Though useful, Smith's account only takes us so far. Though affective, the sort of formation he envisages largely works "invisibly," shaping us over time through routine and repetition. Many film-mediated revelatory experiences, however, are acute, keenly felt by the viewer, and thrust into the center of awareness. This is especially true of Brant's mystical-type experiences, which are characterized by sudden onset and therefore may be quite arresting.[31] In order to better understand the role of affect in these more conspicuous experiences, it will be fruitful to engage with film studies, which theology has historically failed to do.[32] More specifically, we'll look to cognitive film theory, which has often focused on affect and emotion.

Cognitive film theory emerged as a reaction to the dominant paradigms that preceded it. Just as the theology-film dialogue has taken a discursive, thematic approach to cinema, film studies has often done the same. Film studies has often been dominated by ideological criticism seeking to expose the mechanisms by which cinema indoctrinates spectators ideologically. This stream of thought has thus held the crucial aspect of film to be the thematic, albeit accessed using significantly different critical tools. Despite ostensibly affective phenomena like pleasure, desire, and fantasy being cornerstone concepts in the conversation, these concepts have been freighted with technical meanings quite divergent from ordinary usage, shackled to psychoanalytic assumptions about the unconscious that are significantly counterintuitive.[33]

---

[28]Marsh, *Cinema and Sentiment*, 89.

[29]Marsh, *Cinema and Sentiment*, 69, 110-11.

[30]Marsh, *Cinema and Sentiment*.

[31]Brant, *Paul Tillich*, 172.

[32]Johnston, *Reframing Theology and Film*, 254-76.

[33]Carl R. Plantinga, *Moving Viewers: American Film and the Spectator's Experience* (Berkeley: University of California Press, 2009), 8.

Affect has occupied only a marginal place until relatively recently. One of my undergraduate film studies professors bemoaned feeling emotionally manipulated by some films. I recall being mystified: Is not *feeling*, I wondered, precisely why we watch films in the first place? (Indeed, it is.)[34] I suspect this scholar's attitudes were a reflection of the low view of emotion that has sometimes characterized the discipline, yet is a far cry from how most viewers experience film.

Film scholar Carl Plantinga challenges film studies' customary description of film viewing as "reading" a "text" and the underlying intellectualist assumptions therein:

> Film and media scholars sometimes use the tired literary metaphor of "a reading" to describe the viewer's encounter with a film. Not only does this terminology deny the essential differences between viewing images and reading words, it implies that film viewing is a cool, intellectual experience. Perhaps for some audiences, and in relation to some films, the experience *is* cool and intellectual. A "reading" is what some academics do in a classroom, days after the screening. Audiences at the movies, however, are often thrilled, excited, or exhilirated; moved to tears, laughter, scorn, or disgust; made fearful, expectant, curious, or suspenseful; absorbed or focused; outraged, angered, placated, or satisfied; given elevated heartbeats, sweaty brows, and galvanic skin responses; made to scream, yell, and excoriate the bad guys; and usually relieved and calmed at the film's end.[35]

This appreciation for the affective nature of film viewing is evident in cognitive film theory. Don't let the name fool you. "Cognitive" often strikes us as antithetical to emotion (recall the battle depicted in *Reason and Emotion*). To assess a situation unemotionally is to be "clearheaded." Emotions are thought to "cloud" judgment. In this view, an emotionless person would be the ultimate decision-maker, able to analyze a situation rationally without interference from pesky human emotions. But as cognitive science has progressed, earlier Cartesian assumptions that would have us pit mind against body, thinking against feeling, have become awfully shaky. Plantinga and fellow cognitivist Greg M. Smith explain:

---

[34]Ed S. Tan, *Emotion and the Structure of Narrative Film: Film as an Emotion Machine*, Routledge Companion Series (New York: Routledge, 1995), 32-35.

[35]Plantinga, *Moving Viewers*.

> A cognitive understanding of emotions asserts . . . that emotions and cognitions tend to work together. Putting Western prejudices against the messy emotions aside, cognitivists emphasize the way that emotions and cognitions cooperate to orient us in our environment and to make certain objects more salient. Emotions help us evaluate our world and react to it more quickly. Fear or love provides a motive force that more often than not works in tandem with thought processes.[36]

As the boundary between thought and emotion has blurred, so the cognitive perspective has become increasingly affectively and emotionally oriented. Thus, cognitivism has emerged as an alternative to the psychoanalytic paradigm that previously monopolized film studies, an approach that has tended to lack specificity with regard to, or indeed even interest in, emotion.

Cognitivism has come under fire for being overly scientific, and indeed the sub-discipline encompasses a diverse array of research methods and interests, including the particularly scientific-sounding eye-tracking studies and neurocognitive research, much of which emerged only in the 2000s.[37] But my interest is primarily in the "nonempirical" cognitivists, who emerged earlier (and continue to the present day). Their primary interest has been in viewer affect and emotion.

Nonempirical cognitivism. Cognitive film theory relies, in large part, on psychological models. Psychologists of emotion have traditionally stood in one of four broad, sometimes overlapping traditions: (1) peripheral theory, in which emotional experience is believed to depend on feedback from peripheral bodily systems, especially the face; (2) central nervous system theory, which situates the center of emotional experience in the central nervous system concentrated in the thalamus; (3) appraisal theory, in which cognitive assessment, and not merely bodily response, shapes emotional experience; and (4) social constructivism, which posits that emotions are primarily a social phenomenon, shaped through socialization and performing a social role.[38]

---

[36]Carl R. Plantinga and Greg M. Smith, eds., introduction to *Passionate Views: Film, Cognition, and Emotion* (Baltimore: Johns Hopkins University Press, 1999), 2.

[37]Ted Nannicelli and Paul Taberham, *Cognitive Media Theory*, AFI Film Readers (New York: Routledge, 2014), 2, 87. A comparison of the cognitivist anthologies *Passionate Views: Film, Cognition, and Emotion*, published in 1999, and *Cognitive Media Theory*, published in 2014, shows this quite clearly. The earlier volume is comprised of essays concerned solely with emotion, while the later one covers a much more diverse range of foci. Nannicelli and Taberham, *Cognitive Media Theory*; Plantinga and Smith, *Passionate Views*.

[38]Greg M. Smith, *Film Structure and the Emotion System* (Cambridge: Cambridge University Press, 2003), chap. 2, Kindle.

Most film scholars, in applying the psychological theory to film viewing, have emphasized cognitive appraisal (model 3) as being essential to emotion. Cognitivist pioneer Noël Carroll takes this view. For him, cognitive appraisal precedes bodily sensation, and together they form emotion. If applied to a shark attack, for example, an appraisal of imminent danger as the great white beelines toward you in the water might result in increased heart rate, surging adrenaline, and so on, generating a sense of fear.[39] This perspective makes intuitive sense, but, if correct, presents us with something of a problem. After all, Jamie Smith's focus in the discussion above has placed heavy emphasis on the *non*cognitive. Other cognitivists disagree somewhat with Carroll, preferring instead to assign cognition a diminished role. Greg Smith identifies studies in which at least some emotion (or emotion-like) activity occurs even when cognitive processing is impossible (e.g., decorticated animals still exhibit play behaviors, albeit to a lesser degree). For Greg Smith, cognition is an important facet of emotion, but not essential.[40] I suggest we take a *via media* following Plantinga, who charts a sensible path between the extremes of cognitive fundamentalism, in which emotion is reduced to deliberate cognition only, and cognitive inessentialism, in which emotion is wholly unconscious. His cognitive-perceptual approach sees cognition as a necessary component of emotion, but allows that this cognition may be largely or wholly unconscious. As such, this model incorporates the unconscious more plausibly than does the psychoanalytic model traditionally favored by film scholars.

What is emotion? Plantinga explains, "At the core, an emotion is a mental state that is accompanied by physiological arousal."[41] Moreover, he defines an emotion as a "'concern-based construal' that is often accompanied by various sorts of feelings, physiological arousal, and action tendencies."[42] Returning to our shark scenario, you have a *concern* for your survival which gives the *construal* that your life is under threat—a certain quality that includes various bodily changes and the impulse toward particular actions. Emotions are notoriously difficult to boil down to an essence, however, given their considerable diversity. For Plantinga, intentionality is an almost essential characteristic of

[39]Noël Carroll, *The Philosophy of Horror, or Paradoxes of the Heart* (New York: Routledge, 1990), 24-27.

[40]Smith, *Film Structure and the Emotion System*, chap. 2.

[41]Plantinga, *Moving Viewers*, 54.

[42]Plantinga, *Moving Viewers*, 54.

emotion; emotions are *about* something. Like others (e.g., Greg Smith), Plantinga distinguishes between affect and emotion. The former is a bodily state, while the latter *also* involves cognitive appraisal. Emotion is, therefore, a subset of affect. But the line between the two is blurry and distinguishing between them is of little importance for our purposes.[43] Of more importance to us is what all cognitivists agree on, namely that *emotion necessarily involves a significant bodily component.* The physiological arousal of an emotion may be subtle, barely registering at the level of consciousness (e.g., breathing slowing) or not at all (e.g., pupils dilating), and yet it is this somatic aspect that separates feeling from mere thinking. Film is "the sensual medium," directly appealing to the senses, an obvious fact that has nevertheless been regularly overlooked in favor of a more intellectual, less corporeal mode of engagement. Much of what is involved in film viewing is prereflective: nonconscious, nonlinguistic, even noncultural.[44] Watching a film, therefore, is an exercise in feeling, not solely in thinking.

The bodily basis of affect. In considering the role of the body in film, we need to venture beyond the cognitivist camp. Film theorist Vivian Sobchack puts embodiment at the front and center of the film-viewing experience. While film reviewers frequently discuss films in terms of their physical impact, using visceral, sensual, and tactile language, film theorists have traditionally avoided such bodily descriptions.[45] The physical dimension of film viewing has sometimes been treated by scholars as inconsequential, on a par with the thrills of a theme park, or even as a source of embarrassment.[46]

So, like Jamie Smith, Sobchack looks to Merleau-Ponty to "flesh out" a theory grounded in human embodiment.[47] Sobchack claims that "the film experience is meaningful *not to the side of our bodies but because of our bodies.* Which is to say that movies provoke in us the 'carnal thoughts' that ground and inform more conscious analysis."[48] A central tenet of Sobchack's theory is the

[43]Plantinga, *Moving Viewers*, 131-32.

[44]Plantinga, *Moving Viewers*, 113-14.

[45]Vivian Sobchack, "What My Fingers Knew: The Cinesthetic Subject, or Vision in the Flesh," in *Carnal Thoughts: Embodiment and Moving Image Culture* (Berkeley: University of California Press, 2004), 47-48.

[46]Sobchack, "What My Fingers Knew," 48-49.

[47]Sobchack, *The Address of the Eye: A Phenomenology of Film Experience* (Princeton, NJ: Princeton University Press, 1992), 29.

[48]Sobchack, "What My Fingers Knew," 50-51; emphasis original.

dialogical nature of the relationship between viewer and film. It is an encounter between two physical entities; physical, because of the notion of the "film's body," which she insists is *not* metaphorical.[49] This "nonmetaphor" of film's body possibly obfuscates more than it illuminates,[50] but Sobchack's thoroughgoing emphasis on the physical, sensuous, and bodily dimension of film viewing yields useful insights, such as her discussion of viewer transcendence. Transcendence begins in immanence, in our bodies, writes Sobchack, and is in fact experienced somewhat counterintuitively as an amplified sensuality:

> The structure of this experience [of transcendence] is paradoxical in that it emerges from our sensual embodiment even as it seems to release us from our bodies' ontic constraints and demands. Thus, in its most heightened state as at the movies, our sense of transcendence in immanence not only relocates us "beyond" the *presentness* of our flesh to dwell in the on-screen world but also refers us reflexively (and without a thought) back to our own fleshly *presence*—this in a mediating structure that, as it vacillates between our intentional relocation "elsewhere" on the screen and our fleshly presence "here" and "now" in the theater, simultaneously *intensifies* and *diffuses* both our senses and our sensual location. There is, then, a paradoxical bodily character to a heightened sense of *ex-static* transcendence: a sensual (and affective) enhancement in which our body's "here" and "now"—in something like a feedback loop and without conscious thought—reflexively refracts its own sensuality in a process of *mimetic exchange* with both the general perceptive and expressive sensuality of cinema as a medium and the specific figurations (both visual and acoustic) that constitute the "elsewhere" on the screen.[51]

This is a dense, challenging passage. Put simply, however, Sobchack is describing the paradoxical nature of transcendent experience in response to film: the viewer is both immersed in the film's story world, as if *less* present physically, yet also *more* physically stimulated.

This process happens in *any* film-viewing experience, and is thus a kind of "ordinary transcendence," but this same process is at work "*explicitly* in a film with manifestly 'spiritual' or 'religious' subject matter."[52] Sobchack thus sorts

---

[49]Sobchack, *Address of the Eye*, 22-23, 162.

[50]For a more detailed critique of Sobchack's notion of the "film body," see Plantinga, *Moving Viewers*, 115-16.

[51]Vivian Sobchack, "Embodying Transcendence: On the Literal, the Material, and the Cinematic Sublime," *Material Religion* 4, no. 2 (2008): 197, https://doi.org/10.2752/175183408X328307.

[52]Sobchack, "Embodying Transcendence," 198.

religious films into three categories: (1) Figural Literalism, in which the content of transcendence is portrayed literally and materially; (2) Transcendence in Immanence, in which the depiction of material reality becomes a kind of opening to the "more" that lies beyond; and (3) Ungraspable, in which transcendence is presented as an absence or ellipsis, thus functioning apophatically.[53] That at least two of these categories roughly correspond to those found in Paul Schrader's work discussed in the previous chapter, namely religious epics ("Figural Literalism") and transcendental style ("Transcendence in Immanence"), respectively, makes Sobchack's theory a valuable complement to Schrader's. Sobchack serves as a strong corrective and a compelling reminder of the centrality of embodiment to the film-viewing experience. Plantinga appreciates and appropriates some of her thinking on prereflexive responses, though he still grants primacy to reflective, conscious experience.[54] Approximately speaking, we might say that Sobchack gives an account of affect, while Plantinga et al. give an account of emotion proper.

The Bethel paradigm of revelation. Through our discussion of Jamie Smith's work, we concluded that revelation can have an affective quality. But despite operating on an affective, imaginative register, the knowledge conveyed through our practices might not *feel* especially revelatory. Habits are routine by definition, and so may seem rather humdrum, whirring away in the background beneath the level of awareness. That doesn't mean it's not genuine revelation. After all, all knowledge, conceptual or nonconceptual, is revealed. But what can we say about the highly conspicuous, highly memorable moments of film-mediated revelation? What, if any, is the significance of affect in those singular revelatory moments like Tillich's Botticelli experience, in which we become powerfully conscious of God? To return to our earlier example of *American Beauty*, how is Ricky's emotion—eyes brimming with tears, lump in his throat—related to his realization of "this entire life behind things . . . this incredibly benevolent force"?

In the biblical account of Jacob's dream at Bethel we find a powerful revelatory experience that sheds light on our consideration of revelation in response to film (Gen 28:10-22). Fleeing from his avenging brother, Esau, Jacob stops on his way to Harran, spends the night under the stars, and has a dream

[53]Sobchack, "Embodying Transcendence," 199-202.
[54]Plantinga, *Moving Viewers*, 116.

in which he has a revelation of God's abiding presence. Jacob's actions only bear a very superficial similarity to an ancient incubation ritual in which revelation was actively sought by sleeping in a sacred place (cf. 1 Kings 3:4-5).[55] Jacob is apparently not seeking revelation; he wouldn't expect to encounter God in this place.[56] Jacob is a frightened "home-loving boy,"[57] no doubt eager to get to civilization (and away from Esau), only stopping here because the sun has set (Gen 28:11).[58] He is "between places," forced to bed down in the middle of nowhere. And yet it is here in the most unlikely of places that God's self-revelation comes to Jacob in the form of a dream.

In this dream, Jacob sees a staircase (traditionally, "ladder"), probably resembling a ramp-like structure typical of Babylonian temple ziggurats,[59] on which God's messengers climb up and down, thus forming a "temple through which earth touches heaven."[60] This is consistent with the ancient Near Eastern worldview in which heaven and earth were understood to be separate, and temples being the place wherein a god deigns to appear. Jacob subsequently pronounces this place "the gate of heaven" (Gen 28:17), the point at which heaven and earth meet.[61] This is a "thin place." In the dream, Yahweh promises to continue to be with Jacob and reiterates the promise of global blessing made to his grandfather, Abram (cf. Gen 12:2-3). Jacob awakens from the dream, literally and figuratively. He has awoken to reality, perceiving it anew, seeing the world as it truly is. Old Testament scholar Walter Brueggemann writes, "He finds the world of the dream more convincing than his old world of fear and guilt. In his wakefulness, he resolves to embrace the new reality of the dream. . . . Jacob comes to understand that his undefended sleep in a lonely place has been the entry way for God's awesome power."[62] Thus, Brueggemann also writes that "a 'non-place' is transformed by the coming of God into a crucial place."[63]

[55]Bruce K. Waltke, *Genesis: A Commentary*, ed. Cathi J. Fredricks (Grand Rapids, MI: Zondervan, 2001), 389.

[56]Walter Brueggemann, *Genesis* (Atlanta: John Knox, 1982), 241.

[57]Gordon J. Wenham, *Genesis* (Waco, TX: Word Books, 1987), 225.

[58]Kevin Anthony Walton, *Thou Traveller Unknown: The Presence and Absence of God in the Jacob Narrative* (Carlisle, UK: Paternoster, 2003), 44.

[59]Von Rad, *Genesis*, 279.

[60]Brueggemann, *Genesis*, 243.

[61]Von Rad, *Genesis*, 279.

[62]Brueggemann, *Genesis*, 246.

[63]Brueggemann, *Genesis*, 242.

This is a transformative encounter. According to Waltke, there is chronos time, everyday routine, and crisis time, "life-changing and defining moments."[64] Jacob's experience takes place in crisis time. This isn't simply the ordinary, imperceptible preconscious knowledge discussed above. It's an earthshattering, transformative, revelatory moment, a "theophonic encounter."[65] So Jacob names this backwater *Bethel,* "House-of-God."[66] "The news is that there is traffic between heaven and earth," writes Brueggemann. "'I am with you.' That, of course, is the intent of the ramp-ladder. Heaven has come to be on earth. This promise presents a central thrust of biblical faith."[67] It is essential to recognize the fact that revelation came to Jacob unexpectedly, hence his announcement, uttered with palpable awe, "Surely the LORD is in this place, and *I was not aware of it*" (Gen 28:16, emphasis mine). These are "the words of one who comes from afar,"[68] and so God's presence here comes as a shock. Jacob is not expecting to meet his God in a foreign land, yet the narrative "insists the world is a place of such meetings."[69] It's not that God was absent and then, to use popular evangelical parlance, "God showed up"; rather, God was already present, and Jacob only now perceives it. What changes is Jacob's *awareness.*

There are differences between this narrative and film-mediated revelation. For one thing, a strictly exegetical reading of the narrative yields a more complex picture of God's presence. According to Kevin Walton, "The passage touches on the tension between the particular and the universal: God's presence focused in one place versus God not restricted to one place, with both sides of the polarity finding a place in the passage."[70] Plus, Jacob's awareness shifts in *response* to revelation, rather than preceding it. So, I'm not claiming that the revelatory experience in this story exactly mirrors what we typically find in response to cinema. What I *am* suggesting is that this narrative is analogous, albeit imperfectly, to some film-mediated revelation. This text clearly shows that it is possible to be oblivious to divine presence initially, and then to become aware of it. I have in mind here something similar to what

---

[64]Waltke, *Genesis,* 395.
[65]Brueggemann, *Genesis,* 241.
[66]John Goldingay, *Genesis for Everyone—Part 2* (Louisville, KY: Westminster John Knox, 2010), 90.
[67]Brueggemann, *Genesis,* 244.
[68]Claus Westermann, *Genesis 12–36: A Commentary* (London: SPCK, 1986), 456.
[69]Brueggemann, *Genesis,* 242.
[70]Walton, *Thou Traveller Unknown,* 62.

David Brown posits when he writes that "in Augustine's familiar analogy, God is already everywhere in the world like the water in a sponge, and so it is more a case of tapping into that presence than it having to be brought directly to bear upon the world."[71] Affect in response to film viewing may help us "tap into" God's presence. Sometimes divine self-disclosure requires sensitivity and receptivity. The Bethel narrative therefore provides a lens for understanding how the most unlikely places may become a Bethel, a "House-of-God," if only we become aware of it.

A shift in awareness, therefore, may open the door for revelation to take place. Often there's something objective that triggers that awareness. In the Tillichian language of Brant's study, there is something in the objective constellation of revelation that, in that moment, lines up with the subjective constellation, becoming transparent and allowing the divine light behind it to come bursting through. And this is where cognitive film theory comes in. According to the cognitivists, viewer affect works by shifting awareness. A key characteristic of affect and emotion is how they shape behavior, specifically by injecting a sense of urgency into action and information gathering. Psychologist Nico Frijda, whose work on emotion provides the basis for cognitivist Ed Tan's theory of filmic emotion, speaks of *action tendencies*, the particular sorts of action that various emotions typically prompt. As we have already noted, emotions are oriented toward concerns, helping us ascertain whether or not the situation before us is relevant to those concerns and, if so, urge us to take appropriate action.[72] Simply put, emotions compel action. Fear compels me to flee the scene; anger compels me to insult my foe. Emotions not only shape action, however, but also perception, influencing how we process environmental stimuli. Greg Smith writes, "The orienting function of emotions highlights those portions of our situation that are emotion-congruent. . . . The orienting function of emotion encourages us to seek out environmental cues that confirm our internal state."[73]

Carroll thus likens emotions to searchlights, directing our attention to relevant aspects of the environment.[74] We are constantly flooded with a massive

[71]Brown, *Divine Generosity and Human Creativity*, chap. 1.

[72]Tan, *Emotion and the Structure of Narrative Film*, 44.

[73]Smith, *Film Structure and the Emotion System*, chap. 2.

[74]Noël Carroll, "Film, Emotion, and Genre," in Plantinga and Smith, *Passionate Views*, 28.

array of stimuli, much of which we necessarily ignore. Think back to our earlier shark attack scenario. Upon sighting the great white, you are suddenly no longer cognizant of the unseasonable warmth of the water or the sting of the sea salt in your grazed knee; your attention is immediately and completely directed toward things like the shark's location, the direction of the beach—things germane to your safety. This "searchlight function" of emotions prioritizes data, rendering some details inconsequential while making others pressing. There is a feedback mechanism at work here too, as we search out environmental data that accords with our initial assessment, "prompting us to form expectations about the kinds of things that we should watch for as the situation evolves."[75] Our awareness is guided to particular parts of the situation, and that awareness is thus sustained and even heightened.

Unlike real life, films are, to use Plantinga's phrase, *emotively prefocused*.[76] That is to say, implicit in any film's narration—its lighting, plot, editing, characterization, and so on—is a certain affective flavor, a gestalt, that guides us to understand the film in a particular manner. In a sense then, film too has an inbuilt searchlight function, doing some of the work of emotion. Filmmakers, therefore, may influence viewers' emotional response. Though they cannot *dictate* emotion, they do issue what Greg Smith calls an "invitation to feel."[77] This brings us to the possibly surprising point that formal qualities may act as a catalyst to revelation. I suggest—and this is one of my core contentions—that in some instances *a film may use formal devices that invite particular affective and emotional responses from the viewer, which in turn may direct the viewer's attention to those aspects of the environment through which God "speaks."* The particular way a film is constructed may prompt an emotional response that paves the way for the viewer's sudden awareness of God's presence.

My emphasis throughout has been on feeling, but I suspect that such experiences of revelation usually entail a cognitive component. Bear in mind that cognitivists distinguish between affect and emotion by appealing to cognitive appraisal, which is necessary for the latter. And the searchlight function of emotion requires appraisal. The complexity of transcendent feeling suggests a cognitive element too. Critiquing his own mood-cue approach, which makes

---

[75]Carroll, "Film, Emotion, and Genre," 28.

[76]Plantinga, *Moving Viewers*, 77.

[77]Smith, *Film Structure*, chap. 2.

use of lower-level affective, noncognitive processes, Greg Smith admits that his approach is "limited in its ability to explain more complex emotional phenomena . . . [nostalgia] is probably about as high level an emotion as the mood-cue approach can examine with any degree of confidence."[78] The more complex the emotion, the more likely it is to involve a significant cognitive element. Feelings of transcendence cannot simply be lower-level bodily responses, like the startle reflex. Appraisal is required. But let me be clear: we are not returning to the narrow "proposition only" view of revelation. How so? Because the cognitive aspects of the experience are balanced out by the affective aspects. The cognitive may even be largely unconscious or dwarfed by the affective. Thus, revelatory experiences may still be experienced as primarily affective, propositional content being secondary or lacking entirely. Callaway recommends we "broaden our understanding of revelation, picturing it in terms of God's inspiriting presence rather than simply the disclosure of knowledge about God."[79] After all, it was God's *presence*, not only his message, that left Jacob awestruck.

Let's see how this could play out by imagining a hypothetical scenario involving the film *The Tree of Life* (Terrence Malick, 2011). Many viewers have remarked on its religious power, with lay critics describing it variously as a "profoundly religious experience,"[80] "an overwhelming experience of color, visuals, emotion, and spirituality [that] verges on the transcendent,"[81] "[a] movie [that] connects on a deeply emotional and spiritual level,"[82] and "the most spiritual movie I have EVER SEEN. There is a 20 minute passage of images and music that made me want to believe in God."[83] Imagine a viewer delighted by Malick's formal devices: the way his camera strays from faces,

---

[78]Smith, *Film Structure*, chap. 10.

[79]Callaway, *Scoring Transcendence*, chap. 6.

[80]M. J. Arocena, "The Tree of Life Is a Miracle," review of *The Tree of Life*, by Terrence Malick, 2011, www.imdb.com/review/rw2451503/.

[81]Jonathan L., "User Review of 'The Tree of Life' (Rotten Tomatoes)," 2013, https://web.archive.org/web/20180224163314/https://www.rottentomatoes.com/m/the_tree_of_life_2011/reviews/?page=28&type=user&sort=.

[82]Aaron H., "User Review of 'The Tree of Life' (Rotten Tomatoes)," 2013, https://web.archive.org/web/20180314235855/https://www.rottentomatoes.com/m/the_tree_of_life_2011/reviews/?page=50&type=user&sort=.

[83]Jeffrey G., "User Review of 'The Tree of Life' (Rotten Tomatoes)," 2012, https://web.archive.org/web/20180314235859/https://www.rottentomatoes.com/m/the_tree_of_life_2011/reviews/?page=49&type=user&sort=.

framing appendages and even objects in lingering takes, thereby prompting wonder at the beauty of the quotidian (fig. 3.1); or struck by the stunning imagery of the creation sequence, evoking awe at the temporal magnitude of the evolutionary process (fig. 3.2); or moved by the impression of memory conveyed through editing, arousing a sense of nostalgia or *Sehnsucht* (fig. 3.3). This viewer experiences an emotion—wonder, awe, *Sehnsucht*—in response to these stylistic devices mentioned above, usually working in concert with others. This emotion then guides the viewer's attention, like a searchlight, to particular aspects of the environment, either the film itself or the wider world outside the film ("life") where divine presence may become discernible should God choose to reveal Godself.

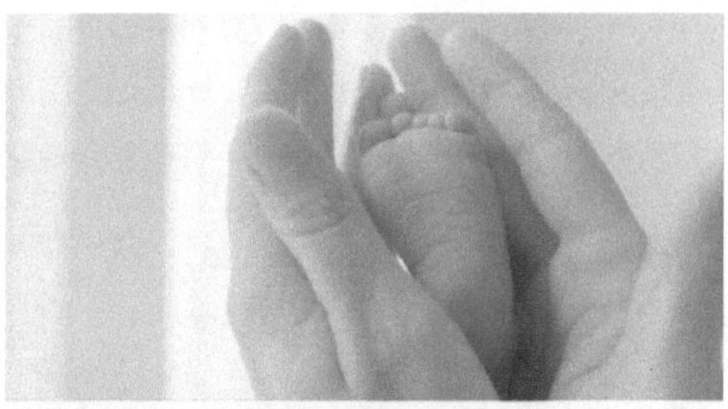

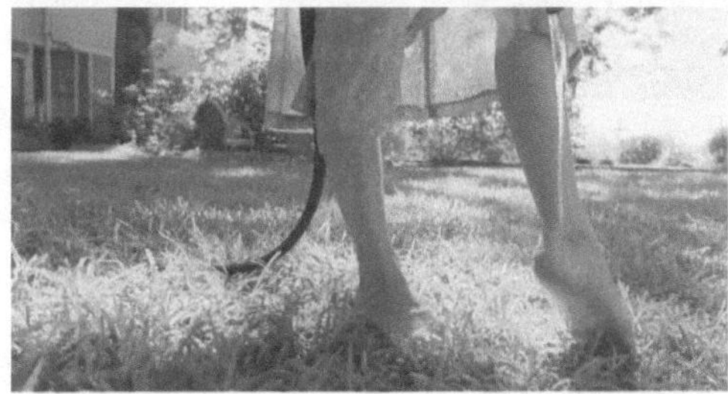

Figure 3.1. Framing in *The Tree of Life* often calls attention to nonfacial body parts and other objects

Not only that, but a sudden awareness of God may prompt further congruent affective responses that help sustain and intensify the experience. Just as Jacob awoke from his dream newly attuned to the presence of God that had in fact been there all along, so our hypothetical viewer emerges from this film—so frequently likened to dreams—with a new awareness of the divine.[84] It is a revelatory moment, yes, but one facilitated by formal characteristics, *The Tree of Life*'s emotive prefocusing. The viewer has become *affectively disposed* to revelation through film form, its narration opening the viewer up to the "voiceless speech" of creation (cf. Ps 19:1-4). Films, through their affective power, may shift our awareness so that we are enabled, however fleetingly, to perceive the divine. Even a cinema may become a "Bethel."

[84]For a history of the dream metaphor in film studies, see Laura Rascaroli, "Like a Dream: A Critical History of the Oneiric Metaphor in Film Theory," *Kinema*, Fall 2002, https://openjournals.uwaterloo.ca/index.php/kinema/article/view/982/1053.

CRITERIA FOR DISCERNMENT

But is it really *God* who is in this cinema? Might there be nothing but an overactive human imagination? Or worse, the demonic? Although revelatory experiences are widely attested, transcending religious divides and spanning millennia, authenticity is far from assured. For some, it seems far too nebulous a phenomenon to be taken seriously. How are we to discern between genuine revelation and its counterfeit?

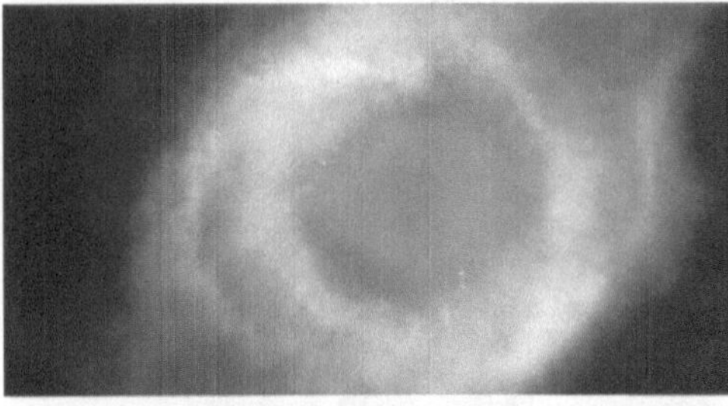

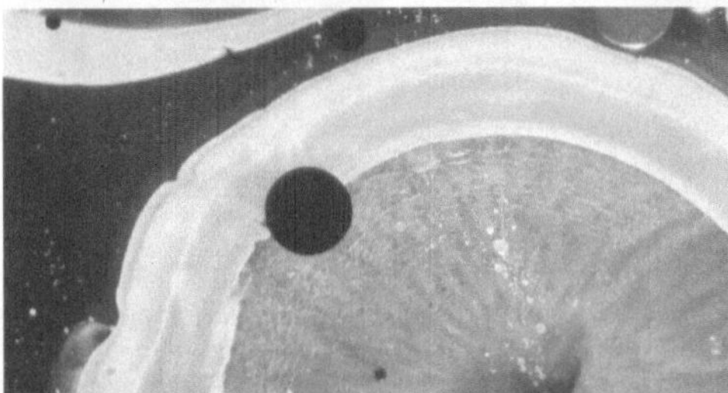

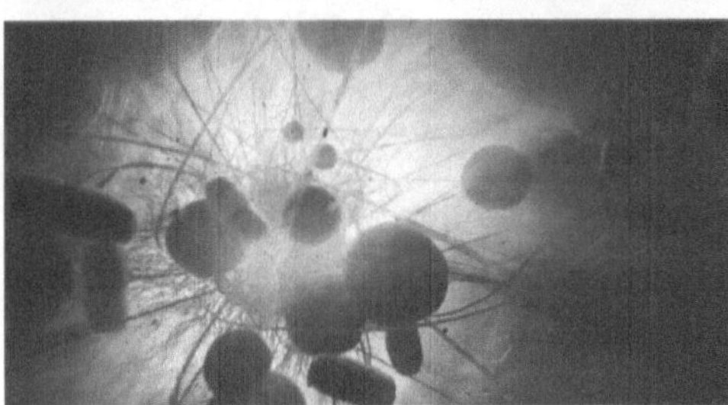

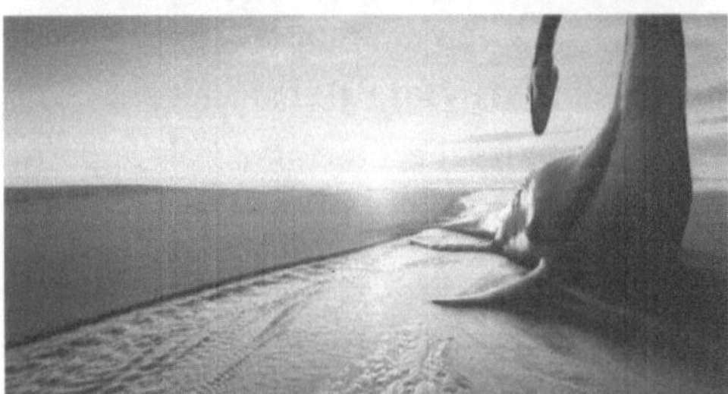

Figure 3.2. The vast timescale depicted in the creation sequence in *The Tree of Life* invites a sense of awe

Take the work of Nazi-sympathizing filmmaker Leni Riefenstahl, for example. Aesthetically, the Nazis trafficked in the grandiose, the monumental, and the sublime.[85] Riefenstahl, Nazism's foremost documentarian, made films with those same sensibilities. Her *Triumph of the Will* (1935) chronicles the Nazi Party Congress of 1934, featuring massive swastika banners, illuminated imperial eagles, a "sea of flags" carried by legions of followers, and the grandiloquent theatricality of the *Führer* himself, pontificating from an enormous stone rostrum framed against vast, clear skies. The imagery is dramatic, designed to evoke a sense of awe and other

[85]Melissa Raphael, *Rudolf Otto and the Concept of Holiness* (Oxford: Clarendon, 1997), ebook, 76-80.

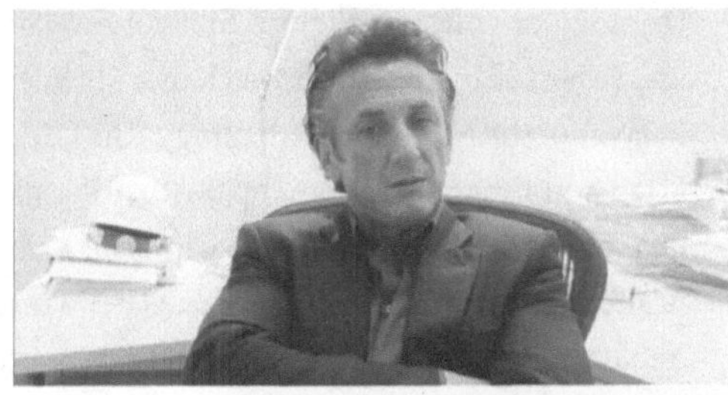

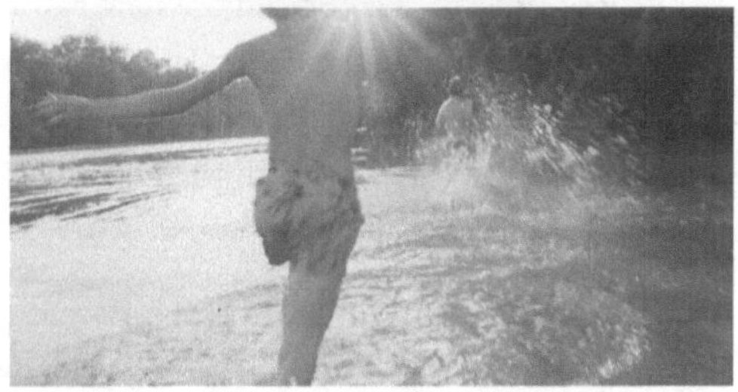

Figure 3.3. Cutting from the present to the past evokes a sense of nostalgia in *The Tree of Life*

congruent emotions. But, of course, the emotion here is not benign. For all the cartoonish excesses of *Reason and Emotion*, its claim that Hitler "controlled" Germans through emotional appeal has real merit. Likewise, Riefenstahl invites an emotional response intended to inspire devotion to the Nazi cause. It is utterly conceivable then that this propaganda film could have had the type of "revelatory" effect on some of its original viewers that we have been discussing, yet toward evil ends, and therefore not of God. By granting the possibility of revelation "outside of the church and its Scripture, and without direct reference to Jesus Christ,"[86] are we not opening ourselves up to being misled, potentially seduced by affectively powerful art that is nevertheless antithetical to God's purposes—like *Triumph of the Will*?

It was in precisely this context that Barth vehemently opposed the notion of any revelation apart from Christ. According to Barth, the "knowledge" of God gleaned from creation that theological friend-turned-foe Brunner asserted is, in actuality, knowledge of "those principalities and powers of the world of ideas and demons."[87] Similarly for Barth, far from exhibiting "preserving grace," the world, considered on its own, might just as well be called an "antechamber of hell"![88] Barth's rhetoric was strong—and rightly so, considering how dire the situation in Germany was, as Bruce Demarest explains:

> Hitler's National Socialist propagandists appealed to the revelation of God in reason, conscience, and the orders of Creation as justification for the Nazi state

[86]Robert K. Johnston, *God's Wider Presence: Reconsidering General Revelation* (Grand Rapids, MI: Baker Academic, 2014), preface.

[87]Karl Barth and Emil Brunner, *Natural Theology: Comprising "Nature and Grace" by Emil Brunner and the Reply "No!" by Karl Barth*, trans. Peter Fraenkel (Eugene, OR: Wipf & Stock, 2002), 81.

[88]Barth and Brunner, *Natural Theology*, 84.

> theology or cultural religion. Biblical revelation in Old and New Testaments was regarded by the Third Reich as a "Jewish swindle" and thus was set aside in favor of the Nazi natural theology. The Göttingen theologians Friedrich Gogarten and Emanuel Hirsch, by postulating the primacy of conscience and the flow of history as the chief modalities of revelation, provided theoretical justification for the Nazi ideology, which later wreaked havoc in Europe and beyond. A majority within the state church (known as the "German Christians") unwittingly or otherwise embraced the new national religion, founded not on the Word of God but on the divine will allegedly embedded in the natural order. Emerging from this fatal exchange came a semi-Christian natural religion (some would say a new paganism) in which the church became a servile instrument of Nazi policy.[89]

Barth was witnessing in real time how natural theology may serve as justification for an evil regime, when divorced from a christological criterion.

But we must be careful not to misunderstand Barth on this point, as has sometimes been the case. Barth insists that the Word of God is Christ alone—not Scripture, church, history, or the world—yet other "words" (or "lights") may nevertheless be found in all parts of life:

> We recognise that the fact that Jesus Christ is the one Word of God does not mean that in the Bible, the Church and the world there are not other words which are quite notable in their way, other lights which are quite clear and other revelations which are quite real. We may think of the prophets in the Old Testament and the apostles in the New. We may think of the genuine prophecy and apostolate of the Church. And why should not the world have its varied prophets and apostles in different degrees? As the Bible attests the one Word of God, and to the extent that the Church adopts and repeats this testimony, important human words are spoken, bright lights are set up in the human sphere and great and little revelations occur. Nor does it follow . . . that every word spoken outside the circle of the Bible and the Church is a word of false prophecy and therefore valueless, empty and corrupt, that all the lights which rise are necessarily untrue. . . . We live by the fact that we may continually hear good words of this kind in the Bible, the Church and the world. What we have to contest, however, is that any one of such words in itself and as such is the Word of God, or can be set beside the Word spoken by God

[89]Bruce A. Demarest, *General Revelation: Historical Views and Contemporary Issues* (Grand Rapids, MI: Zondervan, 1982), 15.

> Himself, i.e., Jesus Christ, either by way of supplement or even to crowd Him out and replace Him.[90]

Christ is the criterion of revelation, but this fact does not preclude that revelation may be mediated by all manner of things. God may enlist anything, whether inside or outside the church—even a "dead dog"[91]—to serve as instruments of divine self-disclosure, but in all such cases, this revelatory significance is derived wholly from Christ.[92]

We'd be foolish to ignore Barth's insistence on the christological criterion and the lessons learned from the horrors of Nazi Germany, in which Riefenstahl's films were arguably complicit. We must tread carefully. If, however, we overcompensate for these dangers, we may end up concluding—in practice, if not in theory—that *no* film, nor any cultural artifact, can be authentically revelatory. Granted, this would conveniently allow us to summarily dismiss the likes of *Triumph of the Will*, but surely we would lose more than we would gain, closing our eyes and stopping our ears to many of the occasions in which the third person of the Trinity appears and speaks. Rather than reject the possibility entirely, therefore, we instead must do the difficult work of exercising discernment.

Fittingly, given his work on general revelation, Johnston has tackled this matter of discernment. In his case study of discernment between religions, he argues that we need to look beyond soteriology, which tends to foster an all-or-nothing mentality. He quotes theologian Clark Pinnock's very Barthian formulation that Christ "is our norm and criterion."[93] Nevertheless, writes Johnston, there "are degrees of truth and falsehood in every religion. A middle way is called for, one that 'allows us to be positive as well as discerning.'"[94] Against those who would have the relationship between theology and world be unidirectional, Johnston insists that our discernment take a dialogical shape, a dynamic back and forth between "hearing God's story" and "telling our stories."

---

[90]Karl Barth, *Church Dogmatics*, ed. G. W. Bromiley and Thomas F. Torrance (Peabody, MA: Hendrickson, 2010), IV.3:97-98.

[91]Barth, *Church Dogmatics*, I.1:55.

[92]Barth, *Church Dogmatics*, IV.3:96-98. This insight into how Barth is commonly misread comes from Rae.

[93]Clark H. Pinnock, *A Wideness in God's Mercy: The Finality of Jesus Christ in a World of Religions* (Grand Rapids, MI: Zondervan, 1992), 109; cited in Johnston, *God's Wider Presence*, chap. 8.

[94]Johnston, *God's Wider Presence*, chap. 8.

The famous Wesleyan Quadrilateral, a fourfold-source model, is more elaborate, involving the Bible, tradition, reason, and experience (fig. 3.4). Even so, it retains its underlying dialogical structure: Bible and tradition as ways of hearing God's story; reason and experience as ways of telling our stories. Johnston's own fivefold-source model is an extension of the Quadrilateral. It entails the Bible, tradition, and experience, but also the local church and culture (fig. 3.5).

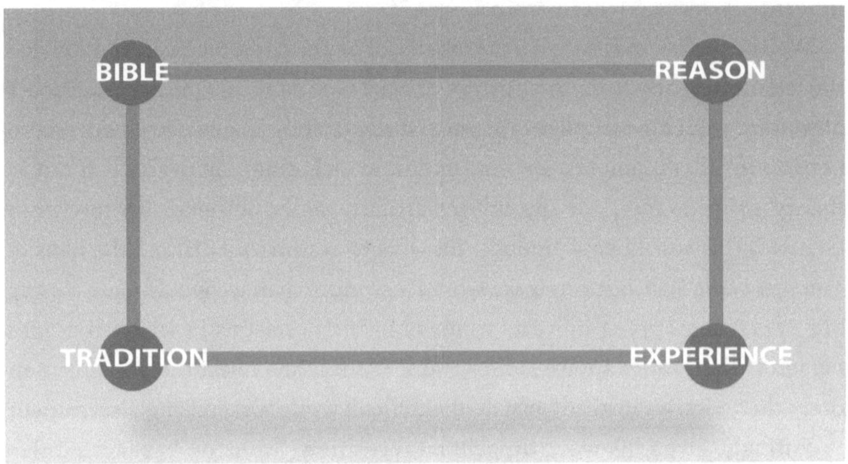

Figure 3.4. Fourfold-source model (Wesleyan Quadrilateral[95]

Inclusion of the local church as a source in this scheme reminds us of the importance of community in the discernment process, especially the particular community that knows and is known by the would-be recipient of revelation. Tradition too is a form of community, one that draws on the wisdom of history. Community in discernment is crucial, helping weed out highly idiosyncratic and dangerous claims (though admittedly not foolproof, to which Nazi Germany stands as a testament). Culture is the most novel aspect of the fivefold-source model (though it has some overlap with Wesley's reason). "Fearing to put our cultural situation on a par with scripture, we have ignored it altogether. We have failed to see culture as both a source of theological reflection and a framework within which our theological understanding takes place."[96] Notice, too, that Johnston places the Bible at the center of the diagram.

[95]Robert K. Johnston, *Reel Spirituality: Theology and Film in Dialogue*, 2nd ed. (Grand Rapids, MI: Baker Academic, 2006), 113.

[96]Robert K. Johnston, "Becoming Theologically Mature: The Task of Theological Education Today for American Evangelical Seminaries," *Ministerial Formation* 73 (April 1996): 48.

Scripture occupies this central position for two reasons. First, it is the "norming norm," the primary authority. Second, we come to Scripture *through* one or more of the other sources: "We read the authoritative biblical text from out of a worshiping community, in light of centuries of Christian thought and practice, as people embedded in a particular culture, who have a unique set of experiences."[97] The shape here is still essentially dialogical. We hear God's story through the Bible, the local church, and tradition; we tell our stories through experience and culture.[98]

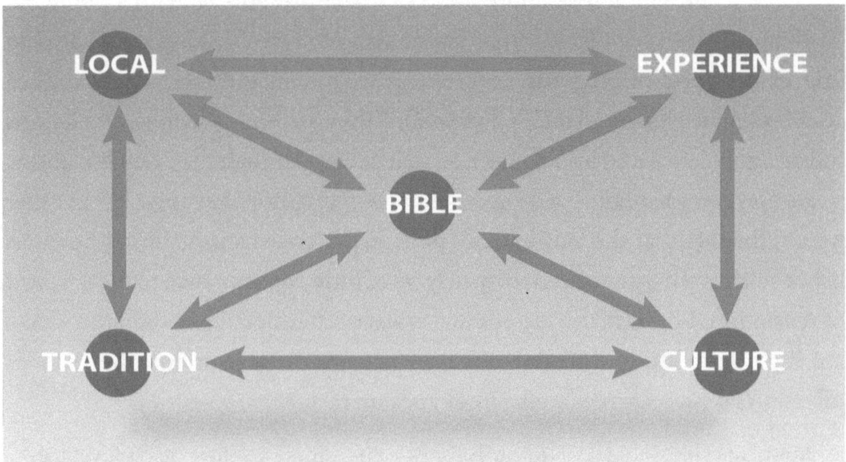

Figure 3.5. Fivefold-source model[99]

So far, however, this leaves the discernment process somewhat abstract. What about more concrete criteria? According to Moltmann, the true test of authentic revelation is "all that affirms Life." One of Pinnock's criteria is "Do people pursue righteousness in their behavior?"[100] He also suggests love of God and neighbor as an important yardstick.[101] Pinnock touches on something crucial here. Revelation ought to be discerned not only in terms of belief. After all, if some knowledge shows up not in our conscious minds but rather in our bodies, then simply testing propositional beliefs will be inadequate. Speaking

---

[97]Robert K. Johnston, *Reel Spirituality: Theology and Film in Dialogue*, 2nd ed. (Grand Rapids, MI: Baker Academic, 2006), 114.

[98]Johnston, *Reel Spirituality*, 114.

[99]Johnston, *Reel Spirituality*, 113.

[100]Pinnock, *Wideness in God's Mercy*, 109. Cited in Johnston, *God's Wider Presence*, chap. 8.

[101]Johnston, *God's Wider Presence*, chap. 8.

about those who obsess over the source of religious experiences, psychologist William James said, "By their fruits ye shall know them, not by their roots."[102]

Make no mistake: the task of discernment is not easy. And *individual* instances of revelation may be difficult to "verify" conclusively. There is no proving revelation. But robust methodologies, like Johnston's fivefold-source model, will usually be able to expose highly irregular and harmful claims as false (the German Christians' methodology was flimsy, therefore necessitating the vociferous Barthian reaction). While it may not always yield *definitive* evidence of authentic revelation—and that fact presents us with a perennial challenge—this is not fatal. What James says of mystical states could also be said of the sorts of religious experiences we're considering (which indeed could often be characterized as mystical): "They are illuminations, revelations, full of significance and importance, all inarticulate though they remain; and as a rule *they carry with them a curious sense of authority* for after-time."[103] In other words, the fact that the authenticity of an experience cannot always be established with any degree of certainty may be of little consequence to the *recipient* of revelation. For him, the experience is self-authenticating. When the stakes are higher, creating a greater onus on accurate discernment, the likes of Johnston's scheme serves well. James goes on to say,

> Mystical states indeed wield no authority due simply to their being mystical states. But the higher ones among them point in directions to which the religious sentiments even of non-mystical men incline. They tell of the supremacy of the ideal, of vastness, of union, of safety, and of rest. They offer us *hypotheses,* hypotheses which we may voluntarily ignore, but which as thinkers we cannot possibly upset. The supernaturalism and optimism to which they would persuade us may, interpreted in one way or another, be after all the truest of insights into the meaning of this life.[104]

So while individual instances of possible revelation may be less than convincing (for third parties), the *cumulative* witness of such experiences is compelling. In *The Evidential Force of Religious Experience,* religious philosopher Caroline Franks Davis argues that while religious experience alone does not make a convincing case for theism, it takes on its own evidential force when

[102]William James, *Varieties of Religious Experience: A Study in Human Nature* (n.p.: n.p., 1902), 27.
[103]James, *Varieties of Religious Experience,* 331; emphasis mine.
[104]James, *Varieties of Religious Experience,* 374; emphasis original.

combined with other nonexperiential evidence.[105] Nevertheless, for many people, the cumulative power of religious experiences remains compelling even when considered alone. This was the case for C. S. Lewis. His spiritual development was a journey of religious experiences he called Joy. I doubt as sharp an intellect as Lewis's would have been convinced by a single unique experience of this sort (keep in mind that he did not identify the source as divine until much later in life), but the gradual accumulation of those experiences eventually led him to embrace theism and ultimately Christianity.[106]

Since the human emotion system grows in complexity over the course of a life, accumulating various associations along the way,[107] it's possible that certain emotions trigger the memory of earlier genuinely revelatory experiences. Thus, an emotion like awe may increasingly hold revelatory associations, starting to "feel" like divine encounter, whether that happens to be the case or not. The emotion itself becomes a kind of reminder. Plus, a lifetime of transcendent experiences may collectively prove more revelatory than discrete occurrences taken individually. This is precisely what Brant's empirical research hints at: "The analysis is now tending towards seeing the potentially revelatory power of film not in individual and momentary terms but in relation to community and to *long-term life-practices.*"[108]

Is discernment a challenge? Absolutely. It's such a challenge, in fact, that we may be tempted to retreat into a safe corner where the line between revelatory and nonrevelatory seems clear-cut, even if impoverishing. But we have been gifted the resources necessary to rise to the challenge. Humankind is, in Brueggemann's phrase, "the trusted creature," entrusted with freedom and responsibility.[109] Discerning the spirit/Spirit is therefore our task and privilege.

Theological aesthetician Frank Burch Brown writes, "One cannot find something—and especially something like 'life'—to be meaningful without feeling it to be so . . . apart from feeling, there is no 'mattering.'"[110] Similarly,

---

[105]Caroline Franks Davis, *The Evidential Force of Religious Experience* (Oxford: Oxford University Press, 1989).

[106]C. S. Lewis, *Surprised by Joy* (London: Fount, 1998).

[107]Smith, *Film Structure*, chap. 2.

[108]Brant, *Paul Tillich*, 212; emphasis mine.

[109]Walter Brueggemann, *In Man We Trust: The Neglected Side of Biblical Faith* (Richmond, VA: John Knox, 1973), 29-47.

[110]Frank Burch Brown, *Religious Aesthetics: A Theological Study of Making and Meaning* (Princeton, NJ: Princeton University Press, 1989), 98-99.

psychiatrist Iain McGilchrist writes, "The essential core of being is subcortical. . . . Emotion and the body are at the irreducible core of experience: they are not there merely to help out with cognition. Feeling is not just an add-on, a flavoured coating for thought: it is at the heart of our being."[111]

Far from being an optional extra then, feeling takes us to the core of reality, to what ultimately matters. Affect stands at the center of my theory. On the one side is revelation with its significant affective dimension. On the other side is film form, designed to elicit affect and emotion. With revelation on the one side and film form on the other, affect is the hinge.

It's important to be reminded that God's agency has primacy in revelation. No human nor humanmade device can generate revelation. Nevertheless, certain formal strategies and structures may help create the "right" affective conditions to render the viewer more receptive to revelation. In this way, some films may become conducive to revelatory experience. That, I suggest, is one reason some movies enjoy a disproportionate amount of attention from religious cinephiles, whether that's in the academic literature or simply in conversations over coffee. As I've already mentioned, this was precisely my own experience with *Magnolia.* This claim may seem unremarkable, common sense even. But it's significant, because if certain films appear to elicit claims of revelatory experience more than others, it follows that certain qualities of a film, even its form, appear to be especially conducive to revelatory experience. The theory I've articulated in this chapter, constructed around the Bethel paradigm of revelation, thus opens up new possibilities for the theology-film dialogue. Rather than being restricted to theme conveyed through discursive elements like plot—which misses what is most compelling about film—theological interaction can branch out into consideration of formal techniques that invite spiritually inflected emotions, knowing that those emotions may at times leave the viewer sensitized to the divine. Such is the power of *truly* moving pictures.[112]

---

[111]Iain McGilchrist, *The Master and His Emissary: The Divided Brain and the Making of the Western World* (New Haven, CT: Yale University Press, 2009), 185; cited in Smith, *Imagining the Kingdom*, chap. 1.

[112]I have borrowed this clever phrase "truly moving pictures" from Heartland International Film Festival, http://heartlandfilm.org/festival/.

PART TWO

PICTURES OF REVELATION

4

Ordet and *Silent Light*

Miracles, Wonder, and Lighting

It's not easy to make a film when your actors are drawn from a religious sect that forbids photographic representation. That's precisely the challenge Mexican auteur Carlos Reygadas faced as he sought to make *Silent Light* (2007),[1] a film about and starring conservative Mennonites in Chihuahua. An elder from the sect, who in his long life had never been photographed let alone filmed, eventually consented to appearing in the film only as a way of documenting their vanishing way of life for posterity. "He had this almost theological question for himself, [about] which value was more important," explains Reygadas. "He thought it was more important to help fix this moment in my culture." Despite their misgivings, Reygadas was granted access to the closed community, resulting in a fresh take on a classic of religious cinema, *Ordet* (Carl Theodor Dreyer, 1955),[2] to which Reygadas's film is significantly and explicitly indebted. In this chapter, we will explore how these two related films function religiously, demonstrating how various formal devices, especially lighting, may invite feelings of wonder, thereby possibly even opening up the viewer to divine encounter.

Methodology: An Overview

Before going any further, I want to further clarify my aims for this chapter and indeed for the entirety of part two. This latter half of the book is composed of

[1]Ranked #84, "Top 100 Films—2020," *Arts & Faith*, accessed January 3, 2022, http://artsandfaith.com/index.php?/films/&do=year&id=8&page=4.

[2]Ranked #1, "Top 100 Films—2020," *Arts & Faith*, accessed December 23, 2021, http://artsandfaith.com/index.php?/films/&do=year&id=8&page=2.

case studies applying the theoretical ground covered in part one to specific films. It's important I briefly outline how I will approach the task both in this chapter and those that remain (except the conclusion).

Chapter structure. Each chapter follows a similar format (the current chapter deviates insofar as it examines two films).

1. *The religious reception of the chosen film.* We'll consider the responses of film scholars, film critics, and lay viewers by accessing academic writings, published film reviews, and user reviews on film websites (i.e., Internet Movie Database [IMDb], Rotten Tomatoes, and film blogs). I'm not just looking for explicit claims of revelatory experience; viewers are rarely so theologically precise. Instead, I cast my net wider, looking for instances in which viewers invoke religious concepts and language in their descriptions. Not all such instances will be revelatory of course, but it seems plausible to suggest that at least some of the time religious language is used, it is used because the viewer has experienced divine encounter, even if interpreted otherwise. And while not strictly "reception," I also discuss the director's religious intentions, or lack thereof, inferred from interviews with the filmmaker(s).

2. *General narrative and formal analysis.* The goal is to identify narrative and formal structures that appear to contribute to the religious response of some viewers without limiting ourselves to (though certainly including) images. Besides images, therefore, we'll also give some attention to plot, character, dialogue, music, sound—anything that seems to invite religious engagement.

3. *Analysis of a religiously potent visual characteristic.* We'll then zero in on a particular *visual* strategy significant to the movie's spiritual power, such as lighting, mise en scène, or editing. This section is a continuation of the previous one, only more exclusively image-oriented. Importantly, we consider a single major emotional response these structures invite.

4. *Theological reflection.* Then we'll change gears, exploring resonances between the chapter's chosen stylistic device, emotion, and theology to assess how this accords (or not) with what theology has said about revelation.

Film selection. How did I select which films to examine in part two? Partly because they all appear on the *Arts & Faith* Top 100 Films, a list of the greatest spiritually significant films according to the *Arts & Faith* community, an online forum focused on the arts from a Christian perspective and now sponsored by Christian arts journal *Image*.[3] Some have explicitly religious subject matter while others don't. But all have been judged by the *Arts & Faith* community as the best films to "experiment with recurring spiritual motifs and questions presented throughout human experience."[4]

Like any such list, it has limitations. It is of course subjective, a reflection of what Frank Burch Brown calls a *community of taste*.[5] As a result, the list skews toward films some might regard as elite with relatively few mainstream films included. Nevertheless, the list is useful, because it mitigates slightly against my personal biases regarding the films chosen for analysis. The movies I've picked are of course still my own choice, but limiting the selection to films included on the list at least ensures that the religious significance of the films has been recognized by others and is not simply a matter of my own judgment.

Directorial intent. Into the discussion of religious reception I also factor in the intentions of the filmmaker(s). The so-called death of the author in film criticism has meant that directorial intentions have often been minimized, if not overlooked completely. But to ignore the role of the auteur is a misstep. "In my view," writes film scholar Alistair Fox, "to diminish the role of the author in the creative process in this way [by unduly emphasizing the *reader's* construction of meaning] flies in the face of all that we now know about the brain and its procedures . . . An understanding of brain processes

---

[3]I have worked with two interations of this list throughout this book, 2011 and 2020. When a film appears on the 2020 list, I have included its 2020 ranking due to its being more recent. When, however, a film appears in the 2011 list but not also the 2020 list, then I have cited the 2011 list. "Arts & Faith Top 100 Films," *Arts & Faith*, 2011, http://artsandfaith.com/top-100. For an updated list, released in 2020, see "Top 100 Films – 2020," *Arts & Faith*, http://artsandfaith.com/index.php?/films/&do=year&id=8. The 2011 poll involved sixty-five participants representing a range of professions and religious affiliations. The criteria for selection are not made explicit and may vary among different respondents. Steven D. Greydanus, "Reading the Eternities," *Image* (2011), https://imagejournal.org/2011/02/14/reading-the-eternities-the-2011-arts-faith-top-100-films/. The 2020 list is significantly different, due in large part to the implementation of a one-entry-per-director rule, as an attempt to foster greater diversity in the list. Kenneth R. Moreland, "Crawling Towards Diversity: Reflections on the Arts & Faith Top 100 Spiritually Significant Films," *The Porch Magazine* (2020), www.theporchmagazine.com/essays/2020/6/3/crawling-towards-diversity-ken-morefield.

[4]"Arts & Faith Top 100 Films."

[5]Frank Burch Brown, *Good Taste, Bad Taste, and Christian Taste: Aesthetics in Religious Life* (Oxford: Oxford University Press on Demand, 2000).

from a neuropsychoanalytic perspective restores the author to his or her proper place."[6] For this reason, I think it's important to consider what a filmmaker intends to convey. That the Holy Spirit may use any film for divine ends, regardless of the directorial intent, necessitates that we remain attentive to the audience's construction of meaning. I only suggest we balance that with an openness to what the director is hoping to communicate.[7]

Image and narrative. Since I'm particularly interested in assessing the impact of cinematic images, it'd be nice if it were possible to "isolate" the effects of those images from other facets of cinema—but it's not. Lighting, acting, editing, writing, music, framing—these and other components of cinema all work in concert to give the movie its affective impact. Not surprisingly, discursive elements, like narrative and message, are judged to be more essential than cinematography when asked what film characteristics *viewers* think most pertinent to revelatory experience (table 4.1).[8] So my focus on images shouldn't be taken as an argument for the priority of image over narrative nor indeed over any other dimension of cinema. I'm not saying images are the component *most* relevant to revelatory experience; just that they are of *some* relevance. Viewers' own judgments appear to support this claim: almost all viewers in Brant's study cited cinematography as being of at least "some" importance.

Table 4.1. Film characteristic by importance as judged by participants

Film Characteristic	Great Importance	Some or Great Importance
Narrative	86%	100%
Message	78%	98%
Cinematography	56%	96%
Music	40%	82%
Setting	68%	96%
Particular Scene	60%	74%

[6]Alistair Fox, *Speaking Pictures: Neuropsychoanalysis and Authorship in Film and Literature* (Bloomington, IN: Indiana University Press, 2016), 111.

[7]Not that a director will always necessarily even be aware of her intentions. Fox's neuropsychoanalytic approach allows for analysis of intentions that may remain opaque to the filmmaker. He demonstrates, for example, the way certain recurring motifs such as bushland and water in Jane Campion's films are symbols of fears housed in her unconscious. Fox, *Speaking Pictures*, 118-20.

[8]Jonathan Brant, *Paul Tillich and the Possibility of Revelation Through Film* (Oxford: Oxford University Press, 2012), 171.

Besides, we can't neatly disentangle image from narrative. Images derive much of their meaning and impact from the surrounding narrative. Film scholar Barbara Klinger has argued for the affective force of "the arresting image," such as the image of Ada (Holly Hunter) descending underwater while tethered to her beloved piano as it sinks in *The Piano* (Jane Campion, 1993). But while lauding Klinger for calling attention to the affective importance of visual elements, Plantinga convincingly argues that an audience's emotional response to this "highly aestheticized, ambiguous, and affectively powerful" image derives in large part from the narrative context, rather than solely from formal properties. "The spectator's initial reaction to these images fundamentally depends on concern-based construals that arise from a familiarity with the character in [her] situation."[9] That's why my analyses of cinematic images factor in narrative content. The two are largely inseparable.

That said, it's worth noting Brant's tentative suggestion that different film characteristics tend to give rise to distinct types of revelatory experience. His data suggests that mystical-type experiences generally lack reference to plot or message, tend to be immediate in onset, are usually described as primarily spiritual or emotional, and are often ineffable.[10] So while images and content are inextricably entwined, it appears they each tend to correlate with distinct types of experience. Nondiscursive components are correlated more strongly with primarily affective experience than they are with primarily cognitive experience. This suggestion must be held in tension with Plantinga's assertion about the affective primacy of narrative. The key point is to note the relationship between style and affect, even if narrative also has profound affective implications.

God's agency has primacy. Finally, I need to be explicit about what I am—and am not—claiming in part two. Though this study concerns itself with the question of revelation through film, I am *not* claiming that these films or stylistic devices necessarily result in revelatory experience. God's agency has primacy in revelation. Revelation cannot be orchestrated by anyone other than God. Recall that certain emotions may function as "searchlights," guiding our attention to those facets of reality in which God may choose to reveal Godself. In that vein, I will suggest ways in which the films that follow may

[9]Carl R. Plantinga, *Moving Viewers: American Film and the Spectator's Experience* (Berkeley: University of California Press, 2009), 145.

[10]Brant, *Paul Tillich*, 191.

sometimes stimulate particular emotions in some viewers, leaving them with a heightened sensitivity to the divine—but whether or not revelation results is God's prerogative. A filmmaker may issue an invitation to feel, but revelation is the work of the divine.

Ordet

Religious reception.[11] We'll return to *Silent Light* shortly, but first let's take a look at its predecessor. In the canon of religious cinema, few films have been more celebrated for their spiritual power than *Ordet*. Nordic cinema scholar C. Claire Thomsen notes a "persistent strand of Dreyer criticism: the metaphysical dimension of his films."[12] Bordwell writes that Dreyer's films "commit themselves to a single project: the revelation of the spiritual."[13] In Schrader's opinion, *Ordet* is his most transcendental work,[14] ahead of his other religious classic, *The Passion of Joan of Arc* (1928).[15] Although not *quite* a textbook example of Schrader's theory, he argues that *Ordet* "has a spiritual depth it normally would not have" were it purely a psychological drama.[16] Film historian P. Adams Sitney sees it as "truly religious in motive and theme."[17] For *Time Out*'s Dave Calhoun, it is a "deeply spiritual, mysterious, and wonderfully odd and bold work . . . what Terrence Malick's 'Tree of Life' might have been if filmed by Ingmar Bergman."[18] Timothy Brayton, scholar and critic, describes it as "the greatest movie about religion."[19] But it's not merely *about* religion. For some viewers, the viewing experience itself is religious. The late film critic Roger Ebert wrote, "When the film was over, I had plans. I could not carry

---

[11]This section is adapted from an article I published previously. See Richard V. Goodwin, "An Old Film in a New Light: Lighting as the Key to Johannine Identity in 'Ordet'," *Journal of Religion & Film* 22.2 (2018): https://digitalcommons.unomaha.edu/jrf/vol22/iss2/2. Used by permission.

[12]C. Claire Thomsen, "The Slow Pulse of the Era: Carl Th. Dreyer's Film Style," in *Slow Cinema*, ed. Tiago De Luca and Nuno Barradas Jorge (Edinburgh: Edinburgh University Press, 2016), 50.

[13]David Bordwell, *The Films of Carl-Theodor Dreyer* (Berkeley: University of California Press, 1981), 1.

[14]Paul Schrader, *Transcendental Style in Film: Ozu, Bresson, Dreyer* (Oakland: University of California Press, 2018), 1:132.

[15]Ranked #1, "Top 100 Films," *Arts & Faith*, 2011, accessed January 3, 2022, https://imagejournal.org/top-100-films/.

[16]Schrader, *Transcendental Style*, 136.

[17]P. Adams Sitney, *Modernist Montage: The Obscurity of Vision in Cinema and Literature* (New York: Columbia University Press, 1990), 55.

[18]Dave Calhoun, "Ordet," *Time Out*, 2016, www.timeout.com/london/film/ordet.

[19]Tim Brayton, "The Bright and Happy Christians," *Alternate Ending*, April 16, 2012, www.alternateending.com/2012/04/the-bright-and-happy-christians.html.

them out. I went to bed. Not to sleep. To feel. To puzzle about what had happened to me. I had started by viewing a film that initially bored me. It had found its way into my soul."[20]

Its religious resonance is no accident. Speaking about *Ordet,* Dreyer said,

> The aim of the film must be to induce in the audience a tacit acceptance of the author's idea, as expressed in the closing stages of the film, namely that *a sufficiently strong faith confers on its possessor the power of performing miracles.* . . . The audience must be made to forget they are seeing a film, and must be persuaded (or, if you prefer, hypnotized) into thinking they are witnessing a divine intervention, so that they go away gripped and silent.[21]

The "author" Dreyer refers to here is probably the playwright Kaj Munk, upon whose play the film is based. Dreyer was explicit that this was to be a film about religious faith strong enough to effect the miraculous.

And indeed for a good many viewers *Ordet* has genuine spiritual force. One lay critic writes, "*Ordet,* for me, is a truly religious experience."[22] "It may be the most breathtaking exploration of religious experience ever filmed," writes another. Explaining his choice to avoid any spoilers, that same reviewer writes, "You should have the same experience of wonder and gratitude I—and probably most moviegoers who've ever seen it—had as it ended."[23] A self-described atheist comments, "I generally have very little patience with people who really believe in God and other such nonsense and fairy tales. But this film left me breathless, and I don't know why."[24] Another reviewer writes, "By the conclusion of 'Ordet' you can believe that miracles can happen. . . . I may not be sure about God, but this film made you think about the possibilities."[25] Hence, one reviewer "seriously recommends this film to

[20]Roger Ebert, "A Hard Winter Worth Braving," March 8, 2008, www.rogerebert.com/reviews/great-movie-ordet-1955.

[21]Carl Theodor Dreyer and Oliver Stallybrass, *Four Screenplays* (London: Thames & Hudson, 1970), 20; emphasis mine; quoted in Sitney, *Modernist Montage,* 58.

[22]Howard Schumann, "A Totally Sincere, Deeply Moving, and Unforgettable Work of Art," May 6, 2002, www.imdb.com/review/rw0055896/?ref_=tt_urv.

[23]Terry Moran, "A Harrowing Excursion into the Miraculous," February 22, 1999, www.imdb.com/title/tt0048452/reviews?start=0.

[24]Arothis, "Sublimely Affecting Film," September 24, 2006, https://m.imdb.com/user/ur4031038/.

[25]Andrew Nerger, "A Haunting and Beautiful Film," March 28, 2006, www.imdb.com/title/tt0048452/reviews?start=3.

those truly searching for meaning in life."[26] Its position in first place on the 2020 iteration of the *Arts & Faith* Top 100 list is reflective of its status as a masterpiece of spiritually inflected cinema.[27]

General narrative and formal analysis. How does *Ordet* succeed in achieving its spiritual ends? Certainly, the narrative, which centers wholly around matters of faith, is essential. It is based on a play by Kaj Munk, a Danish playwright and Lutheran pastor celebrated for his martyrdom at the hands of Nazi occupying forces.[28] The film tells the story of the Borgens, an early-twentieth-century Danish family straining under the weight of religious doubts amid tragedy. One Borgen son, Johannes (Preben Lerdorff Rye), is under the delusion that he is Jesus Christ. Once a promising theology student, Johannes has been driven to insanity by his studies, particularly his reading in Søren Kierkegaard, rendering him a distant, pathetic figure. Inger (Birgitte Federspiel), the wife of another Borgen son, Mikkel (Emil Hass Christensen), dies in childbirth. At the finale, however, she's miraculously resurrected by Johannes, now cured of his messianic fantasy. All rifts in the Borgen family are thus healed and all religious doubts vanquished.

Many cast members had previously acted in the stage version of *Ordet*, and thus came to the production with an intimate knowledge of the play.[29] That the cast succeeds in making the characters convincing coheres with Dreyer's larger program of realism.[30] His commitment to realism was strong, even accompanying Federspiel (Inger) as she went into labor in real life in order to record her screams—these are the labor pains we hear in the film.[31] Actors were coached in the Jutland accent to convey linguistic authenticity.[32] Aural realism is a particular feature. Though almost all action takes place indoors,

[26]Karl_consiglio, "Magical to Say the Least," August 9, 2008, www.imdb.com/title/tt0048452/reviews?start=7.

[27]"Arts & Faith Top 100 Films."

[28]Sören von Dosenrode and Sören Zibrandt von Dosenrode-Lynge, *Christianity and Resistance in the 20th Century: From Kaj Munk and Dietrich Bonhoeffer to Desmond Tutu* (Leiden: Brill, 2009), 8:81-118.

[29]Sitney, *Modernist Montage*, 62.

[30]Preben Lerdorff Rye patterned his Johannes on a real-life man with schizophrenia. Peter L. Doebler, "Jest in Time: The Problems and Promises of the Holy Fool in *Francesco, Giullare Di Dio, Ordet*, and *Ikiru*," *Journal of Religion & Film* 17, no. 1 (2013): 17, 22-23.

[31]Sitney, *Modernist Montage*, 61-62.

[32]Jonathan Rosenbaum, "Mise en Scène as Miracle in Dreyer's *Ordet*," Jonathanrosenbaum.net, 2008, www.jonathanrosenbaum.net/2022/03/mise-en-scene-as-miracle-in-dreyers-ordet/.

noises from farm animals and passing carts are allowed occasionally to intrude as a reminder of the larger world that exists outside the Borgen home. According to Sitney, the film shifts from pastoral comedy to sober-minded tragedy during the abortion scene ("the most brutal scene I know in the history of art").[33] Sitney attributes the grim potency of the scene to its sound design, the entire incident conveyed mostly through the sound of cutting over Inger's anguished cries.[34] The film's realism makes the resurrection all the more startling, a fantastical event grounded in a realistic cinematic world.

The film's success turns on this miracle. It's the most stylized sequence in the film, marking its significance visually. Lighting becomes prominent in the finale, creating a luminous stark white background against which Inger lies in her coffin, giving the film its most enduring image. The various plotlines find their resolution in this scene: The wrangling patriarchs Morten (Henrik Malberg) and Peter (Ejner Federspiel) are reconciled,[35] their children Anne (Gerda Nielsen) and Anders (Cay Kristiansen) are betrothed to each other, Johannes returns home *and* has recovered mentally (an outcome so unlikely that earlier, when Morton imagines his recovery, he calls this hypothetical possibility a miracle), Mikkel finds faith and, most remarkably, Inger is raised back to life. The resurrection serves as the catalyst for most other resolutions. In one fell swoop fractious faiths are reconciled, unbelievers believe, true love prevails, and a miracle occurs. Schrader calls this miracle the "decisive action par excellence."[36]

All sorts of wonders are depicted in films, but usually they comply with the "rules" of that specific film. But, by definition, a miracle breaks the rules, and thus poses a vexing question to the filmmaker: How do you film a miracle such that it is *taken as miraculous*, yet still remains coherent? This question is made even trickier since *Ordet* "militates *against* a religious worldview by suggesting

---

[33]Sitney, *Modernist Montage*, 56.

[34]Sitney, *Modernist Montage*, 56-57.

[35]Morten represents Grundtvigianism, a life-affirming stream of Danish Lutheranism, while Peter represents the Inner Mission, a strict, conservative missional movement directed at winning nominal Lutherans to genuine faith. Caroline Vander Stichele, "Reframing Jesus: Dreyer's Lifelong Passion," in *The Bible in Motion: A Handbook of the Bible and Its Reception in Film*, ed. Rhonda Burnette-Bletsch, Handbooks of the Bible and Its Reception (Berlin: De Gruyter, 2016), 591; Gene Edward Veith, "How Inner Mission Evangelizes," *Patheos: Cranach; The Blog of Veith*, March 15, 2016, www.patheos.com/blogs/geneveith/2016/03/how-inner-mission-evangelizes/.

[36]Schrader, *Transcendental Style*, 134.

despair and dogmatism as its inevitable conditions."[37] To find an answer, we will need to explore the film's camerawork. The camera is moving in almost every shot, something no other film had done prior.[38] As Brayton puts it, "If Dreyer's . . . *The Passion of Joan of Arc* is his film 'about' close-ups, *Ordet* is 'about' camera movement."[39] This strategy allows for conveying narrative information with minimal cutting, resulting in long-takes, which is why Dreyer's work has been cited as presaging the emergence of so-called slow cinema.[40] With an average shot length of about one minute,[41] it comes as no surprise that some find the pacing slow.[42] But Thomsen notes that Dreyer preferred to discuss his pacing not in terms of slowness, but *rhythm*.[43] "Characteristic of all good film," he once wrote, "is a certain rhythm-bound restlessness," an amalgam of camera movement, actor movement, and crosscutting.[44] Ebert wrote that *Ordet*'s long-takes "have an almost godlike quality . . . [panning] back and forth slowly, relentlessly, hypnotically."[45]

Ebert's word choice is apt. According to film critic Jonathan Rosenbaum, the audience's acceptance of the final miracle depends on their being "hypnotized" by the distinctive camerawork in one particular scene.[46] Johannes is sitting alone in the drawing room when young Maren enters and approaches, positioning herself close behind his chair, both facing the camera. After an establishing shot, the camera begins a rotational tracking shot (semi)circling the pair, a shot with a leisurely duration of two minutes. When watching the background, the camera appears to do a full 360-degree movement, and yet somehow the characters are always more or less facing the camera. The effect

---

[37]Rick Warner, "Filming a Miracle: Ordet, Silent Light, and the Spirit of Contemplative Cinema," *Critical Quarterly* 57, no. 2 (2015): 50.

[38]Sitney, *Modernist Montage*, 62.

[39]Brayton, "Bright and Happy Christians."

[40]Tiago De Luca and Nuno Barradas Jorge, *Slow Cinema* (Edinburgh: Edinburgh University Press, 2016), 9-10. In an anthology on slow cinema, Thomsen remarks that "Dreyer's late films are constructed as ahead of their time." Thomsen, "Slow Pulse," 51. Dreyer is quoted as saying, "I believe that long takes represent the film of the future. . . . Short scenes, quick cuts in my view mark the silent film, but the smooth medium shot—with continual camera movement—belongs to the sound film." Ebbe Neergaard, Beate Neergaard, and Vibeke Steinthal, *Ebbe Neergaards bog om Dreyer* (Dansk Videnskabs Forlag, 1963), 98; quoted in Bordwell, *Films of Carl-Theodor Dreyer*, 225.

[41]Thomsen, "Slow Pulse," 48.

[42]For example, see Ebert, "Hard Winter Worth Braving."

[43]Thomsen, "Slow Pulse," 52.

[44]Sitney, *Modernist Montage*, 55-56.

[45]Ebert, "Hard Winter Worth Braving."

[46]Rosenbaum, "Mise en Scène as Miracle in Dreyer's *Ordet*."

is so striking and unusual that critics have proffered various, often incorrect, explanations for how the scene was filmed.[47] Cinematographer Henning Bendtsen explained that the camera crab dollied in an arc shape one way, while the camera panned in the other. This distorts the perception of space, such that the background and foreground appear out of synch, as if inhabiting different spatial and temporal planes.[48] The effect is so odd that, despite knowing of the arc-and-pan, Sitney still wonders if the actors were possibly *on* the dolly.[49] Rosenbaum's larger point is that "we become so entranced by the actors and their delivery as well as by the camera's movement that in effect we become hypnotized."[50] This was apparently Dreyer's intention: "The audience must be . . . must be persuaded (or, if you prefer, *hypnotized*) into thinking that they are witnessing divine intervention."[51] According to Rosenbaum, the "miracle" of mise en scène and camerawork in Johannes and Maren's scene primes us to accept the miracle of the finale, a two-stage process. "Dreyer essentially gulls us into accepting one kind of miracle as a way of preparing us to accept another kind somewhat later."[52]

Granted, this scene is pivotal and its stylization flags it as such. But I think the scene is too isolated and too subtle to do all the heavy lifting of rendering the climactic miracle plausible. Bordwell offers a more convincing account. "A

---

[47]Rosenbaum wonders if the unusual effect was achieved through the camera tracking and panning in opposite directions or by having the actors sit on a rotating surface. But, drawing on comments made by cinematographer Henning Bendtsen, film scholar David Bordwell explains it was executed using the arc-and-pan technique. Bordwell, *Films of Carl-Theodor Dreyer*, 155-56. But, interestingly, Doebler rightly points out that, on closer inspection, the camera actually makes only a 180° movement. Peter L. Doebler, "Jest in Time: The Problems and Promises of the Holy Fool in *Francesco, Giullare di Dio, Ordet*, and *Ikiru*," *Journal of Religion & Film* 17, no. 1 (2013): 21.

[48]Bordwell, *Films of Carl-Theodor Dreyer*, 155-56.

[49]Sitney, *Modernist Montage*, 68.

[50]Rosenbaum, "Mise en Scène as Miracle in Dreyer's *Ordet*." Lennard Højbjerg has argued circular camera movements tend to suggest disorientation or the dissolution of reality. Lennard Højbjerg, "The Circular Camera Movement: Style, Narration, and Embodiment," *Projections* 8, no. 2 (2014): 84-86.

[51]The full quote reads,

> The aim of the film must be to induce in the audience a tacit acceptance of the author's idea . . . that a sufficiently strong faith confers on its possessor the power of performing miracles. With this aim in mind the audience must be gradually prepared, beguiled, inveigled into a mood of religious mysticism. To make them receptive to the miracle they must be led to that special sense of grief and melancholy which people experience at a funeral . . . so, unconsciously, they hope for the miracle and therefore jettison their normal attitude of skepticism. The audience must be made to forget that they are seeing a film, and must be persuaded (or, if you prefer, hypnotized) into thinking that they are witnessing divine intervention, so that they go away gripped and silent. (Dreyer and Stallybrass, *Four Screenplays*, 20; quoted in Sitney, *Modernist Montage*, 58)

[52]Rosenbaum, "Mise en Scène."

miracle must violate natural or scientific laws," writes Bordwell. "Thus it cannot be motivated 'realistically' as verisimilitude. So the miracle must be motivated compositionally—by functioning within a system of motifs."[53] According to Bordwell, Dreyer manages the difficult task of representing such an astonishing miracle by aesthetic minimalism ("sparseness") and by employing camera movement that is neither motivated completely by character movement nor roaming wholly independently of the characters ("theatricalization"), its "spatio-temporal systems relatively independent of narrative logic."[54] Until this point, most scenes have been shot in a single long-take. In the resurrection sequence, however, Dreyer changes tack, reverting to classical style. Instead of being at odds with the narrative, the camerawork and editing now harmonize with it. Bordwell writes:

> It is not just that the miracle resolves the last of the plot difficulties, returning to narrative stability. The miracle is *represented on film* as a return to cinematic intelligibility, to a space and time responsive to narrative demands, to stylistic figures immediately meaningful. In Inger's resurrection, verisimilitude is violated in the name of narrative order, and the sense of order is justified by the return of conventional filmic comprehension.[55]

Religious aesthetics scholar Peter L. Doebler argues that viewers have dismissed Johannes as a holy fool for most of the film, but now the film itself becomes a holy fool, confronting the audience with a conundrum: whether to believe or not.[56]

***Light as a feature and theme in* Ordet.** Sitney makes a fascinating observation regarding the identity of Johannes. Sitney's insight pertains to the scene in which Johannes flees his home after spectacularly failing to raise Inger back to life. Johannes leaves a handwritten note, quoting the book of John, which the English subtitles translate from the Danish as, "Yet a little while I am with you. Ye shall seek me. Whither I go, ye cannot come."[57] This is a quotation of Jesus. No surprise there, since up until now Johannes has consistently co-opted

---

[53]Bordwell, *Films of Carl-Theodor Dreyer*, 147.

[54]Bordwell, *Films of Carl-Theodor Dreyer*, 158-64, 69.

[55]Bordwell, *Films of Carl-Theodor Dreyer*, 170; emphasis original.

[56]Doebler, "Jest in Time," 1-2.

[57]The NIV translation of the Bible renders the verse, unabridged, as follows: "My children, I will be with you only a little longer. You will look for me, and just as I told the Jews, so I tell you now: Where I am going, you cannot come" (Jn 13:33).

Christ's words as his own. But Sitney seizes on an important detail, namely Johannes's inclusion in the note of the scriptural location of the quotation, John 13:33. Sitney writes, "In giving the location of the text Dreyer introduces a subtle note: here, for the first time, Johannes makes reference to the evangelical authority rather than quoting the words of Christ in his own voice. By quoting the fourth Gospel, he recovers his own name, Johannes."[58] This development in the story thus marks a change in Johannes's self-understanding, shifting from erroneously believing himself to be Jesus to instead seeing himself as a *witness to* Jesus. When deluded into believing himself to be Jesus, Johannes's attempts at the miraculous fall flat. But when he realizes he is John, not Jesus, a miracle happens. "Johannes" is thus his true identity, both because this is his actual name *and* because he is following in the vocational footsteps of his biblical namesake, that is, Johannes or John.

But *which* John is Johannes patterned after? For Sitney, it's John the Evangelist, author of the fourth Gospel. His observation, outlined above, is compelling. That there is a shift in Johannes's self-understanding pertaining to the name's referent, thereby establishing a biblical antecedent for the character, is a profound insight. But I think Sitney is only half-right. Yes, understanding Johannes in the light of his Johannine antecedent is important, but I believe that his character makes more sense when understood as modeled not on John the Evangelist, but rather on John the *Baptist*. In order to arrive at this conclusion, however, we must pay close attention to an aspect of the film that has often been overlooked: lighting.

"Lighting was [Dreyer's] great gift and he did it with expertise," remarked actress Birgitte Federspiel. "He shaped light artistically like a sculptor or painter would."[59] Though it is Dreyer's camerawork that has received the lion's share of critical attention, his lighting design was every bit as meticulous. Bendtsen recalls the exactitude of Dreyer's lighting scheme:

> Dreyer's basic rule was to arrange people for the sake of photography and lighting rather than acting. Normally you work with a much simpler lighting plot in which the actors are not tied to a specific area because they must have the opportunity to act freely. In Ordet, their positions were so carefully planned that they had to count their steps at the same time as they said their lines. A

[58]Sitney, *Modernist Montage*, 68.

[59]Torben Skjødt Jensen, "Carl Th. Dreyer—My Metier," December 28, 1995.

> single step too much to one side or the other would mean that we would miss a certain predetermined light effect and the scene would have to be reshot.[60]

The rigor of Dreyer and Bendtsen's lighting was largely in service of realism. Speaking to film historian Jan Wahl, who as a young man serendipitously landed a job working on set during the filming of *Ordet,* Dreyer said, "Because *The Word* [*Ordet*] is a realistic film, shadows, tones, lighting all must give characters a rounded and plastic appearance. It could not be done in the style, for example, of Murnau's beautiful *Faust,* where the lighting had to originate from a single source in order to be allegorical, romantic."[61] Though the influence of German expressionism is apparent in Dreyer's earlier work,[62] the lighting in *Ordet* is more naturalistic. Naturalism notwithstanding, the lighting has been painstakingly stylized to very particular ends.

This is partly due, I think, to the fact that light is not only a significant stylistic feature but also a major *theme,* each informing the other. For example, light crops up intermittently in dialogue. Early on, the delusional Johannes declares, "I am the light of the world, but the darkness does not comprehend it," carrying candles so that, according to his screwy reasoning, "my light may shine in the darkness," a paraphrased amalgam of John 1:5; 8:12; 9:5. Visually, too, light symbolism is prominent. One particularly sophisticated instance comes as the doctor's (Henry Skjær) car leaves, its headlights shining through the window onto the interior wall, which Johannes interprets as a vision of Death come for Inger. Though Johannes is ostensibly mistaken, the fact that Inger indeed dies at that moment creates ambiguity about the validity of his prophecies. Sitney makes a scintillating observation: this episode is a self-reflexive microcosm of how the film itself confronts us. After all, this film, too, is nothing but light projected on a wall, one that will ultimately invite a metaphysical explanation but that we may be tempted to explain away rationally, thereby confirming in ourselves the faithlessness against which Johannes has been preaching all along.[63] We are, therefore, complicit in the unbelief of the film's skeptical characters. For these reasons, light is an important aesthetic and thematic motif.

---

[60]Bordwell, *Films of Carl-Theodor Dreyer*, 224.

[61]Jan Wahl, *Carl Theodor Dreyer and Ordet: My Summer with the Danish Filmmaker*, Screen Classics Series (Lexington: University Press of Kentucky, 2012).

[62]See especially *The Passion of Joan of Arc* (1928), *Vampyr* (1932), and *Day of Wrath* (1943).

[63]Sitney, *Modernist Montage*, 70-71.

It's important, too, that we pay attention to the lighting of faces. Bendtsen has pointed out that, when insane, Johannes's face is mostly lit relatively dimly.[64] Of the eleven distinct scenes in which Johannes features, he is in predominantly dim light in all but the first and last (the former is explicable as a result of being set and filmed outside in the full light of day). While other characters are fully, even ethereally lit, Johannes is often confined to the shadows (fig. 4.1). When, however, Johannes returns to the homestead after a long disappearance, his face is fully illuminated (fig. 4.2). Dreyer and Bendtsen went to extraordinary lengths to achieve this effect:

> Another of the lighting effects of the film created almost insoluble problems. While Johannes is insane, he is walking around in darkness all the time, whereas all the other characters have light on their faces. It created great difficulties when the characters moved around among each other, and the electricians had constantly to turn lamps on and off without this being noticed on the screen.[65]

Evidently, this laborious approach to lighting faces was important to what Dreyer hoped to achieve (for his part, Bendtsen won a Bodil Award, Denmark's highest film accolade).[66] But what does it mean? There is a snippet of dialogue earlier in the film that might offer us a clue. Johannes pronounces a blessing over Maren (Ann Elisabeth Groth) and Little Inger (Susanne Rud): "The Lord be with you. The Lord bless you and keep you. The Lord let the light of His countenance shine upon you and give you grace. The Lord let the light of His countenance shine upon you and give you peace." This is a loose quotation of Numbers 6:24-26, one in which Dreyer has made explicit the notion of light that is only implied by the language of "shine" used in the Bible.[67] According to this benediction, spiritual light issues forth from *God's* face, but that

---

[64]Bordwell, *Films of Carl-Theodor Dreyer*, 224.

[65]Bordwell, *Films of Carl-Theodor Dreyer*, 224-25. As another example of the exactitude of Dreyer's lighting, Bendtsen wrote, "Each image is composed like a painting in which the background and the lighting are carefully prepared. As an example, I might mention the prayer-meeting at Peter the tailor's with twenty people sitting around. Normally we would have used one lamp for throwing light on all of them. Here we used twenty lamps so that each face in fact became an individual portrait study." Bordwell, *Films of Carl-Theodor Dreyer*, 224-25.

[66]Wahl, *Carl Theodor Dreyer and Ordet*, ix-x.

[67]The NRSV translates Numbers 6:24-26 as follows: "The Lord bless you and keep you; the Lord make his face to shine upon you, and be gracious to you; the Lord lift up his countenance upon you, and give you peace."

divine light may shine upon humans. Pictorially speaking, very little light shines upon Johannes until the climax.

Once Johannes has regained his sanity, marked visually by appearing in bright light, he then prays for "the Word that can make the dead come to life." This takes us back, once again, to the book of John, which famously opens with the designation of Jesus Christ as "the Word" (Jn 1:1). The title *Ordet*, Danish for "the Word," suggests this is thematically crucial.[68] Indeed, the entire book of John serves as an important touchstone for *Ordet*, a fact underscored by Johannes's own name. Furthermore, John 1 draws a connection between light and Christ: "In [Jesus] was life, and that life was the light of all mankind. The light shines in the darkness, but the darkness has not overcome it" (Jn 1:4-5). As mentioned above, Sitney draws a parallel between Johannes and John the Evangelist. But as we read on, John the Evangelist introduces us to *another* John: "There was a man sent from God whose name was John. He came as a witness to testify concerning that light, so that through him all might believe. *He himself was not the light; he came only as a witness to the light*" (Jn 1:6-8, emphasis mine). These verses, which refer to John the Baptist, are an interpretive key, one we wouldn't arrive at if we had not attended to the light motif. Until this point in the film, Johannes has erroneously believed *he* is the light, a problem since, to quote Sitney, "so long as he believes he is the Savior, rather than an agent of the Word, and so far as he acts alone, rather than bolstered by the faith of a child, he is powerless . . . his transformation has been around a subtle theological axis, . . . he has recognized his role as a vehicle for the Word, rather than as the Word Incarnate."[69] Now he understands that, like John the Baptist, he is to be a *witness* to the light. In Sitney, therefore, we have a case of mistaken identity. Johannes's biblical archetype is not John the Evangelist, author of the fourth Gospel, but rather John the Baptist.

John the Baptist's function as a witness to the light unlocks the meaning of the lighting. In the finale, Johannes has for the first time understood that, like the Baptist, he is merely a witness to the light—this realization reflected in a lighting change. In his delusional state, Johannes's face was dim and shadowy, but now that he has been restored to his true vocation, his face is fully illuminated, reflecting the light of God and, more specifically, of Christ. For instance,

[68]Dreyer himself implied that the title was taken from John 1:1. Wahl, *Carl Theodor Dreyer and Ordet*, 14.
[69]Sitney, *Modernist Montage*, 70-71.

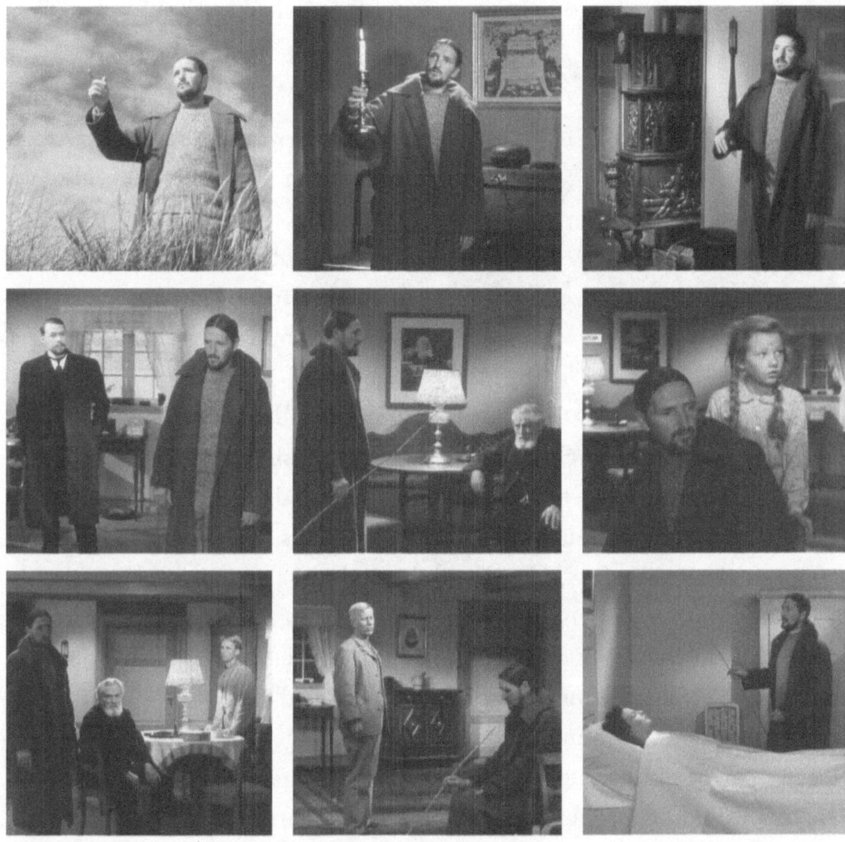

Figure 4.1. In all of Johannes's nine scenes prior to the finale, except the first (outdoors), he is lit dimly, an especially conspicuous strategy when contrasted with how others are lit in *Ordet*

when the still-delusional Johannes initially tries to resurrect Inger but fails, the lighting on his face is weak, especially in comparison to Mikkel (Emil Hass Christensen) and Inger (fig. 4.1, bottom right). But his second attempt, performed once back to full mental and spiritual health, is successful, and his face is strongly lit (fig. 4.2). Earlier, Johannes prophesies, "God has summoned me to prophesy before his face." Now that summons has been fulfilled and the proof is in his radiant visage. If we overlook light as a stylistic device and theme we miss the allusion to John 1:6-8 and thus also miss John the Baptist as the interpretive key to unlocking the identity of Johannes.[70] Dreyer himself

[70]Wahl witnessed the shooting of a scene, in which Johannes returns to sanity, that never made the final cut. He describes it thus: "After this prayer, [Johannes] closes his eyes. Then there is a blinding light—made by manoeuvering the gold and silver screens to *reflect on his face*. The sun emerges

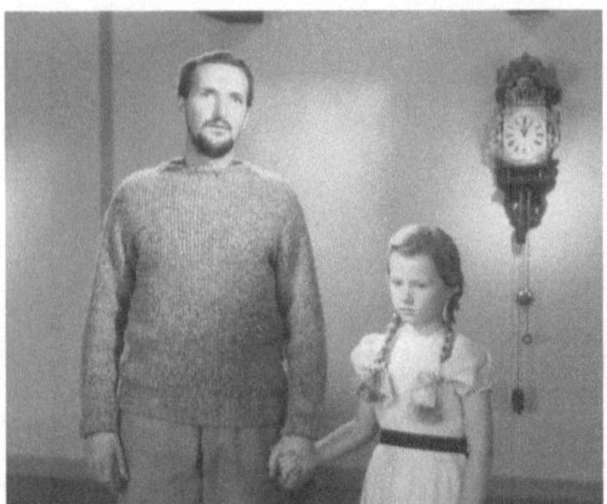
Figure 4.2. At last, in the finale, Johannes appears brightly lit

confirmed the identification of Johannes with the Baptist, saying, "You will recall that John, when he was not preaching, was sometimes mistaken for Jesus. In Danish, John is called Johannes. [Kaj] Munk's story in *The Word* tells of a divinity student who, in that period of intense study just before examinations, has suffered a mental collapse. He thereupon assumes the identity of Jesus."[71]

Dreyer is apparently referring here to the confusion of Jesus and John the Baptist's identities, widely reported in the Gospels (e.g., Mt 16:13-14; Mk 8:27-28; Lk 9:18-19). Though the Baptist took pains to show that he was not the awaited Messiah (e.g., Lk 3:15-17), he and Jesus are nevertheless closely associated in the Gospels, which serves as Dreyer's justification for his depicting Johannes as an *ersatz* John the Baptist figure who mistakenly believes himself to be Jesus. Johannes is apparently modeled after the Baptist, particularly as described in John 1, rather than the Evangelist. We find further evidence in favor of this interpretation in the screenplay for *Jesus of Nazareth*, Dreyer's would-be magnum opus that sadly went unrealized. The first words of the script read, "There was a man sent from GOD, whose name was John. He was not the Light, but was sent to bear witness of [*sic*] the light, the true Light"—a near-verbatim quotation of John 1:8-9.[72] This particular vocation of the Baptist clearly loomed large in Dreyer's thinking.

Of course, both biblical Johns, the Baptist and the Evangelist, are witnesses to the light of Christ—so what difference does this distinction make? The identification of Johannes with the Baptist (1) casts Johannes in a more strictly prophetic role, (2) depicts Morten's prayers that Johannes recover his prophetic vocation as being answered, and, most interestingly, (3) acts as indirect

from the clouds; he accepts this as proof and says, 'The sign. The sign!'" This "deleted" scene suggests interpreting the light on Johannes's face as symbolic of reflected divine light is correct. Wahl, *Carl Theodor Dreyer and Ordet*, 77-78; emphasis mine.

[71]Wahl, *Carl Theodor Dreyer and Ordet*, 14.

[72]Carl Theodor Dreyer, "Jesus of Nazareth—The Script," accessed October 13, 2017, https://issuu.com/dreyer/docs/jesus_dreyer_dfi.

tribute to the playwright Kaj Munk, whose prophetic critique of the occupying German forces in World War II led to his execution at the hands of the Nazis.[73] Dreyer even told Wahl, "Kaj Munk described John the Baptist as being a man who was not extremely cautious, a man who spoke out the truth no matter the cost." I have outlined these implications in greater detail elsewhere,[74] but the important point for our purposes is that attending to a visual motif affects interpretation and lays the groundwork for its spiritual descendant, *Silent Light*, to likewise lean heavily on light for its meaning.

Silent Light

Religious reception. Writing in 1990, Sitney remarked on the surprising lack of influence *Ordet* had had on later films.[75] If that hadn't already started to shift with the arrival of slow cinema, it certainly had with the arrival in 2007 of *Silent Light*, a film that openly and persistently "quotes" *Ordet*. *Silent Light* made a big splash, picking up the Cannes Jury prize and critical accolades. As *Variety*'s Scott Foundas put it, "Shades—and, by the end, big, unmistakable splotches—of Carl Dreyer's 'Ordet' color 'Silent Light.'"[76] Director Carlos Reygadas makes no bones about the influence of Dreyer's film, calling *Silent Light* "*Ordet*'s little brother."[77] Besides Dreyer, Reygadas's other cinematic heroes, like Robert Bresson and his personal favorite, Andrei Tarkovsky, are widely known for their transcendentalist credentials.[78] But does Reygadas share their religious sensibilities? The resurrection of the finale certainly echoes the events of the New Testament, though only indirectly, since Reygadas himself names *Ordet*, and even *Sleeping Beauty*, as the inspiration.[79] So it could be that the film is simply a haphazard, postmodern mishmash of sources. The Mexican auteur says that the thematic "engine" behind *Silent Light* is "the idea of death by emotional pain"—a weighty idea, certainly, but

---

[73]Wahl, *Carl Theodor Dreyer and Ordet*, 14.

[74]Richard V. Goodwin, "An Old Film in a New Light: Lighting as the Key to Johannine Identity in 'Ordet,'" *Journal of Religion & Film* 22, no. 2 (2018), https://digitalcommons.unomaha.edu/cgi/viewcontent.cgi?article=1995&context=jrf.

[75]Sitney, *Modernist Montage*, 55.

[76]Scott Foundas, "Silent Light (Stellet Lichte)," *Variety*, 2007.

[77]José Teodoro, "On Earth as It Is in Heaven," *Film Comment* 45, no. 1 (2009): 51.

[78]Tiago De Luca, *Realism of the Senses in World Cinema: The Experience of Physical Reality*, Tauris World Cinema Series (London: I. B. Tauris, 2014), 32-33.

[79]José Teodoro, "Silent Light: An Interview with Carlos Reygadas," *Cineaste* 34, no. 2 (2009), www.cineaste.com/spring2009/carlos-reygadas-interview/.

not necessarily religious.[80] Reygadas's approach to film is informed by a commitment to photographically capturing reality, not merely mimicking it. The raw material of Reygadas's art is reality itself. "I do not believe in miracles," he says. "But I think reality is a miracle."[81]

This "miraculous" quality of reality shapes Reygadas's religious sensibility. He may be the quintessential "cross-pressured" individual that philosopher Charles Taylor describes, inclined toward disenchanted materialism yet unable to deny the possibility of transcendent reality:[82] "As a boy, I asked my mother all the time about death, and what happens afterwards," he says. "Sometimes I wanted to be an atheist, I managed, but I didn't really believe. I wanted to be an atheist, but I believed despite myself."[83] In terms of trying to establish a religious cinematic vision, this is hardly a smoking gun. But neither should we expect one. Reygadas is not prescriptive about his films' meanings, preferring instead that his audience bring their own perspective to the viewing experience.[84]

Even if the director's intentions are not unambiguously religious, the critical and scholarly response is more unified. J. Hoberman, critic for *The Village Voice*, says that in contrast to his earlier films, *Silent Light* "is willing to assume that all is sacred—or at least God's will. This is not only a factor of the plainspoken protagonist's faith but the movie's contemplative (or what Paul Schrader would call 'transcendental') style."[85] Although, as he points out, the film "oscillates between the sacred and profane,"[86] a certain spiritual element is widely acknowledged. Hoberman writes, "Reygadas manages to imbue every moment with spiritual weight—or what one character calls 'the pure feeling of being alive.'"[87] Writing for *Film Comment*, critic José Teodoro says of Reygadas, to whom he ascribes

---

[80]Carlos Reygadas, José Castillo, and Camino Detorrela, "Carlos Reygadas," *BOMB*, no. 111 (2010): 73.

[81]Karin Luisa Badt, "*Silent Light* or Absolute Miracle: An Interview with Carlos Reygadas at Cannes 2007," August 1, 2007, http://brightlightsfilm.com/silent-light-absolute-miracle-interview-carlos-reygadas-cannes-2007/.

[82]Charles Taylor, *A Secular Age* (Cambridge, MA: Harvard University Press, 2009).

[83]Badt, "*Silent Light*."

[84]Reygadas says, "People have to be involved in what they are looking at, you know. Art, if you like, or just powerful things are nothing by themselves. Someone has to be there to experience them, and then things become meaningful . . . [the viewer] has to contribute." Carlos Reygadas, "Interview by Cinematographos," June 20, 2017, www.youtube.com/watch?v=lDUnG_d4ytY.

[85]J. Hoberman, "Divine Light," *The Village Voice* (New York), September 24-30, 2008.

[86]Hoberman, "Divine Light." Here, he echoes film scholar Jonathan Foltz's observation of how the story "pivots from the sacred to the profane." Jonathan Foltz, "Betraying Oneself: Silent Light and the World of Emotion," *Screen* 52, no. 2 (2011): 159.

[87]Hoberman, "Divine Light."

"unusually earnest transcendentalism," that he "seems to embrace the notion that the two films [*Silent Light* and *Ordet*] are having a dialogue across time, space, and culture . . . on the potency of true faith, the fulfilled promise of redemption for all, and the cinematic power of wondering, waiting, and awakening."[88]

Film scholar Rick Warner locates *Silent Light* within a filmic tradition centered on the miraculous, which "links up in significant ways with what might be called an inclination toward the 'spiritual' in today's contemplative cinema."[89] His study of *Silent Light* and *Ordet* argues that "these two innovative films work to attune the viewer to a certain manner of seeing the world, a contemplative form of thought and vision, and that they undertake this project through an aesthetics of the miraculous that is radically immanent in its effects and implications." Film scholar Tiago de Luca is a somewhat dissenting voice, arguing that the intense focus on material reality in Reygadas's oeuvre is so excessively carnal that it does not permit transcendence.[90] But even his disagreement is predicated on the fact that "the critical reception of Reygadas's work seems to agree that his is a cinema informed by a metaphysical impulse."[91] Most critics place Reygadas in the tradition of "transcendental realism" populated by spiritually minded auteurs.[92]

The rapturous critical reception is echoed by some viewers, described by lay critics variously as "one of the most beautiful and meaningful movies I've ever seen"[93] and "magic and captivating," the latter reviewer writing, "I doubt I will ever see a better one than this."[94] But does it inspire *religious* engagement? That depends on the viewer. One reviewer writes, "Depending on your point of view, 'Silent Light' is either a masterpiece of great social, psychological and theological importance or a load of pseudo-intellectual twaddle."[95] While some viewers take the latter, unimpressed stance,[96] many others stand in the

---

[88]Teodoro, "On Earth as It Is in Heaven," 51.

[89]Warner, "Filming a Miracle," 49.

[90]De Luca, *Realism of the Senses,* 59.

[91]De Luca, *Realism of the Senses,* 32.

[92]De Luca, *Realism of the Senses,* 32-33.

[93]Eleclipse, "One of the Most Beautiful and Meaningful Movies I've Ever Seen," January 14, 2008, www.imdb.com/user/ur7191694/reviews.

[94]Greymumster, "Surrender to the Veracity and Have Your Vitals Pulped," March 13, 2008, www.imdb.com/review/rw1839234/.

[95]Martin Bradley, "Trusting Your Audience," April 15, 2008, www.imdb.com/title/tt0841925/reviews?start=46.

[96]For example, "[The miracle] felt more like a provocation or a special effect . . . than a moment of real transcendence." The_late_Buddy_Ryan, "Anyone Know How to Say 'I Just Cain't Quit You!' in Plautdietsch?," August 25, 2012, www.imdb.com/review/rw2664110/.

more enthusiastic camp. One calls it "a spiritual film worth seeing that stays with you,"[97] and another "a spiritually luminous film which achieves a poetry through its deeply felt and stunningly beautiful images."[98] The latter posits that "the story is told through impressions, giving it an almost spiritual quality," and that "the film turns the relatively straightforward story of a love triangle into something approaching spiritual through its meditative rhythm and painterly visuals."[99] Another writes, "The beautiful way Reygadas uses mysticism [is such that] the film inherently floats in that transcendent, spiritual space."[100] The film "nudges the viewer to perceive a mystical, cosmic world, a world beyond the earth we live in, which is enveloped in love."[101] Though set in a Christian sect, the film resonates with some viewers in a more general spiritual sense, with one viewer remarking, "This all has its meditative sense. . . . From now on, whenever it happens that I have to try and illustrate the Buddhist notion of emptiness, or shunyata, I will reach for this one scene. Something to meditate upon."[102] With its arthouse sensibility and narrative austerity, *Silent Light* is not to all viewers' taste, but clearly for some it occasions a powerful, religiously meaningful experience.

General narrative and formal analysis. So what it is about *Silent Light* that often prompts religious and even theological engagement? One possible factor is its use of transcendental style. The narrative is spare and understated, and arranged according to the pattern identified by Schrader. Early on, we watch Johan (Cornelio Wall), his wife Esther (Miriam Toews), and his "quiver full" of children in sustained silent prayer before tucking into breakfast in relative silence, all unfolding at a leisurely pace. Afterward, Johan, now alone, suddenly bursts into uncontrollable sobs. A scrupulously measured portrayal of quotidian (in)activity suddenly interrupted by the eruption of repressed emotion—this is textbook transcendentalism. We eventually learn the reason for Johan's despair: he is torn between loyalty to his wife and his desire for his

[97]Moviespot, "Intriguing," April 8, 2009, www.imdb.com/user/ur15738722/reviews.

[98]Cmccann-2, "Amongst the Best of the Naughties," May 21, 2013, www.imdb.com/user/ur5239981/.

[99]Cmccann-2, "Amongst the Best of the Naughties."

[100]Zacknabo, "Mexican Ordet-Modern Masterpiece," September 18, 2017, www.imdb.com/user/ur61523435/.

[101]Jugu Abraham, "Visually and Aurally Breathtaking Cinema," January 2, 2008, www.imdb.com/title/tt0841925/reviews?start=0.

[102]Chaos-rampant, "Concealed Unconcealment," November 22, 2013, www.imdb.com/review/rw2909738/.

paramour, Marianne (Maria Pankratz). Moments of despair, usually in which characters shed tears with restraint, are peppered throughout. Eventually, Johan's infidelities, about which he is staggeringly honest with his wife, prove too heavy a burden for her. One day, she flees Johan, collapsing and dying in a field. Johan is grief-stricken.

The story's decisive action comes when Marianne turns up at Esther's wake and, in an obvious nod to *Ordet*, raises Esther back to life with a kiss. Schrader critiqued *Ordet* as eschewing stasis in its denouement.[103] *Silent Light*'s ending, however, is more stasis-like, and thus truer to the transcendental spirit. First, it is more ambiguous, less perceptibly exultant at the miracle. Second, and more significantly, we finish with a long-take of the horizon and sky at sunset that mirrors the opening shot and nearly matches its duration. This not only provides the film with bookends—a Reygadas trademark—but mimics Ozu's nature codas, which juxtapose human transience with the permanence of nature, thereby affirming the paradox of life.[104] Like *Ordet*, the film's success hinges largely on the efficacy of the miracle at the finale. Both films situate that miracle within a plot structure that, with some variation, is characteristic of transcendental style.

But that's only part of the equation. Equally as crucial to the film's religious impact is its *contemplative beauty*, grounded in realism. The contemplative tone is tied to how the film handles time, while its beauty derives from the rich, sensory quality of the images. And this tone is deliberate: "The whole point of great painting, of great moments of music is not information so you can be entertained," says Reygadas. "I really think cinema, unfortunately, has been too close to the circus . . . but just contemplating is one of the most human activities."[105]

The first thing the viewer notices is the film's pacing: its shots are long. The opening image, a time-lapse pan from the sky to the horizon as night turns to day, is approaching six minutes in duration. As such, Latin American film scholar Sheldon Penn notes how the film "diverts emphasis away from movement through space towards time as movement."[106]

---

[103]Schrader, *Transcendental Style*, 132-38.

[104]Schrader, *Transcendental Style*, 49.

[105]Reygadas, "Interview by Cinematographos."

[106]S. Penn, "The Time-Image in Carlos Reygadas' Stellet Licht: A Cinema of Immanence," *Bulletin of Spanish Studies* 90, no. 7 (2013): 1167, https://doi.org/10.1080/14753820.2013.839147.

Teodoro writes that "duration itself becomes a corporeal experience."[107] Long, lingering takes are used throughout the film, and thus Reygadas "emphatically presents the spectator with the experience of time, with the knowledge of time spent in the mechanical processes of filming and viewing deliberately underscored."[108] The sheer length of time images are on screen invites contemplation.

Another factor in the film's impact is the style of composition, images crafted with an eye for beauty. The Chihuahuense landscapes have their own natural beauty, but it is how this world is shot that is crucial. Reygadas's debut feature, *Japón* (2002) depicts the Mexican landscape as drab and unforgiving. For *Silent Light,* Reygadas had a new director of photography, Alexis Zabé, resulting in a film that, compared to the director's earlier work, "depicts nature in a manner more akin to conventional notions of beauty in the transcendental sense of this term."[109] Indeed, the primary motivation for many images seems to be sheer beauty. One closeup of Esther has her move out of frame, which in classical cinema would ordinarily be where the editor cuts. But here the camera holds on the blurry "Monet thicket"[110] of flowers, imperceptibly inching forward until the blossom finally, after almost a full minute, comes into focus. It's delicate, dewy, and seems to exist solely for our aesthetic pleasure.

The most unapologetically beautiful images of the film are the aforementioned bookends of sunrise and sunset. The opening frames are uniformly ink-black until swirling pinpoints of light appear: stars in the night sky. The faintest wisp of cloud comes into view and, against it, the leaves of a tree are silhouetted. The spinning stops and the near-total blackness is broken by a patch of orange light that pulses into view before expanding into a horizontal band of color—red, then also blue, then also yellow—like a single variegated streak of paint on a black canvas. This, the rising sun, sets alight the entire sky, dappled red above the black ground, before illuminating the grain fields below, at last leaving the entire landscape awash in light (fig. 1.3).[111] The image is exquisitely

---

[107]Teodoro, "On Earth as It Is in Heaven," 51.

[108]Penn, "Time-Image," 1165.

[109]De Luca, *Realism of the Senses,* 72.

[110]Teodoro, "On Earth as It Is in Heaven," 50.

[111]Catholic film blogger Victor Morton interprets the shot as a visual retelling of Gen 1, starting with a void, then stars, then light, then nature, then cultivation, etc. V. J. Morton, "TIFF Capsules—Day 4," *Rightwing Film Geek,* 2007, https://vjmorton.wordpress.com/2007/09/12/tiff-capsules-day-4/.

crafted, described by Hoberman as "pantheist ecstasy."[112] De Luca attributes the film's religious reception to its presentation of nature's beauty.[113]

Reygadas also composes his images according to what Schrader has called *frontality*, evocative of religious iconography.[114] People, buildings, and landscapes are framed front-on, centered in symmetrical composition. By depriving us of depth cues, the frontality renders the images flat, while the symmetrical composition lends the images a deliberately formal quality. De Luca writes that "the recurring shots of flat green fields under portentous blue skies, framed in geometric and precise arrangements, evoke painterly compositions."[115] Dreyer himself once described this type of imagery as "pure surface effect," suggesting in a lecture that "instead [of the illusion of depth and distance], one could work toward an entirely new image construct of color surfaces, all on the same plane, forming one great, aggregated surface of many colors from which the notion of foreground, middleground, and background would be completely dropped."[116] The consistent geometry, frontality, and symmetry gives *Silent Light* a distinctive visual style marked by formal elegance.

Despite this formalism, *Silent Light* is also marked by realism, albeit of Reygadas's own particular sort. De Luca describes Reygadas's early work as "cinema of the impossible" in which the "implausibility of fictions" coexists with "realist modes of production."[117] Here "the impossible" means implausible unions, sexual relationships that transgress socially imposed boundaries of age, class, and physical attractiveness. And yet, paradoxically, Reygadas is doggedly committed to realism in other respects, such as his preference for nonprofessional actors. Thus, writes de Luca, "Reygadas appropriates the film medium so as to indeed produce the impossible in reality."[118] Reygadas espouses a Kracauerian approach to film in which the focus is on reality itself:

> In this sense, cinema is the art of reality, the medium in which reality's beauty is captured, where you can film marble or a face, or record someone's voice, a sunset, the innate beauty of what you're contemplating. . . . Often directors talk

[112]Hoberman, "Divine Light."

[113]De Luca, *Realism of the Senses*, 73.

[114]Schrader, *Transcendental Style*, 52-53.

[115]De Luca, *Realism of the Senses*, 73.

[116]Carl Theodor Dreyer, *Dreyer in Double Reflection*, vol. 458 (Perseus Books, 1973), 185; quoted in Sitney, *Modernist Montage*, 64.

[117]De Luca, *Realism of the Senses*, 31.

[118]De Luca, *Realism of the Senses*, 32.

> about how in their films they managed to achieve about 60 percent of what they had envisioned. . . . I always say the contrary; my films are always so much better than I could have ever dreamed of . . . because they utilize things that were unthinkable to me before making them: take Cornelio Wall's wrinkles, his tone of voice in *Silent Light*. These are things I didn't imagine before, I only allowed my camera to absorb them. . . . The camera is a funnel taking in reality.[119]

The camera's ontological relationship to reality means that any artifice in Reygadas's films is somehow "made real." The impossible *actually* transpires before the camera lens. It seems to me that "the impossible" of *Silent Light* has less to do with implausible relationships than with the unprecedented access to the Mennonite community that the film affords us. That photographic reproduction is largely forbidden in this Mennonite sect, coupled with its being a rather sympathetic portrayal of adultery, and this film does indeed seem to be an impossibility. After three years of trying, Reygadas was ready to give up.[120] It was only after meeting Cornelio Wall, who would play Johan, that doors began to open for Reygadas.[121] This is a film about true Mennonites filmed in authentic Mennonite locations spoken in actual Mennonite vernacular. Reygadas is therefore justified in his claim that "*Silent Light* could be seen as a better documentary on Mennonites in Mexico than one produced by National Geographic," despite its fictional and fantastical elements.[122] Penn's description of *Silent Light* as "paradoxical naturalism" seems fitting.[123]

The film's realism is tempered by a strangeness that goes well beyond the novelty of its Mennonite setting. For example, sudden seasonal shifts are handled with so few stylistic cues that it "plunges diegetic chronology into uncertain waters."[124] Darkness is used to evoke mystery, such as the shot of a washroom, in which the camera tracks slowly toward an open door in which someone—who? Johan?—takes a shower. Chiaroscuro typically creates an air of mystery, the play of light and shadow illuminating only a portion of the picture and preventing understanding of the whole.[125] Strangest of all is the

---

[119]Reygadas, Castillo, and Detorrela, "Carlos Reygadas," 74-75.

[120]Carlos Reygadas, "Interview by FILMINKMagazine," June 20, 2017, www.youtube.com/watch?v=pPfjDBFk44A.

[121]Reygadas, "Interview by Cinematographos."

[122]Reygadas, Castillo, and Detorrela, "Carlos Reygadas," 77.

[123]Penn, "Time-Image," 1160.

[124]De Luca, *Realism of the Senses*, 83.

[125]Fox, *Speaking Pictures*, 85-86.

cedar leaf that inexplicably (and portentously) falls from the ceiling after Marianne has announced that this lovemaking session will be their last. Our characters accept this trivial miracle matter-of-factly, as they will the major miracle that is to come. Such enigmatic elements seem to be instances of, to use communication scholar Richard Engnell's phrase, "the somehow credible inclusion of the bizarre" that injects a degree of mysterious otherness into a film, thereby lending it a spiritual quality.[126]

Reygadas likes to dispense with acting entirely and allow his cast to just *be* before the camera, manifesting in Bressonian performances and in scenes that barely seem staged. One celebrated sequence sees Johan's children swimming in an irrigation reservoir. That these children are not performing for the camera, instead simply being "themselves," is apparent from their occasional looks-to-camera.[127] The scene is charming and utterly free of pretense. As we watch, we realize what a rarity it is to see children *being children* on screen. And because these images serve almost no narrative function, they are freed from the need to *narrate* and are allowed instead to *enchant*. The same could be said for a scene inside a milking shed, where the daily morning ritual of a dairy farm, complete with a large cast of cows with no regard for the presence of a film crew, is allowed to unfold in front of the camera in documentary realism. Even Reygadas's preference for direct sound is borne of an uncompromising desire to use the camera to capture, not merely mimic reality.[128]

The realist aesthetic and ethos has religious implications. For Kracauer, this approach to cinema was the "redemption of physical reality,"[129] "with all the spiritual overtones which the word 'redemption' carries."[130] Cinema allows us to properly see that which we usually overlook, giving us a heightened sense of the mystery of the physical.[131] For de Luca, however, Reygadas's close scrutiny of material reality does not translate to a spiritual sensibility, but only "affirms a purely carnal world. Here, the material often ceases to be the means

[126]Richard Engnell, "The Spiritual Potential of Otherness in Film: The Interplay of Scene and Narrative," *Critical Studies in Mass Communication* 12, no. 3 (1995): 258.

[127]Warner, "Filming a Miracle," 63.

[128]De Luca, *Realism of the Senses*, 72.

[129]Siegfried Kracauer, *Theory of Film: The Redemption of Physical Reality* (Princeton, NJ: Princeton University Press, 1997).

[130]Hardy, *Film, Spirituality and Hierophany*, 10-11.

[131]Hardy, *Film, Spirituality and Hierophany*, 10-11.

for reaching a spiritual dimension so as to become an end in itself."[132] He argues that the graphic sexual content of his first two films, which depict "grotesque" bodies not normally seen on film, gives rise to "an extreme carnality that resists transcendence."[133] To the extent that this material is transgressive, which indeed his first two films are, de Luca is correct. But *Silent Light* is a totally different sort of film. The relative restraint of the material invites a type of religious engagement that the shock tactics of his early work precludes. *Silent Light* thus represents an auteur maturing in the direction of his influences who make up the pantheon of religious cinema.

Sunlight as a symbol of time and divine presence. In the hands of Zabé, Reygadas's camera pays close and loving attention to the natural world. But, as the film's title suggests, it is the light that is of particular importance, light that both illuminates that natural world and is itself a part of it. Though it may go unnoticed in many other films, the light here has been noted by scholars and critics. For Hoberman, "it's the quality of the light that really holds you."[134] Critic Mahnola Dargis writes, "There are a handful of ways to understand the meaning of 'Silent Light,' words that I read as an allusion to love, but this is also very much a film about that ordinary light that sometimes still passes through a camera and creates something divine."[135] Likewise, film and literature scholar Roy Anker comments that "Reygadas displays the whole of his tale within an effulgent, circumambient radiance whose quiet majesty seems to bestow meaningfulness of some kind on all that happens. Call it, if you wish, the loving eye of God, which goes everywhere, attending and transfiguring, even into the dankest corners of woe and evil."[136] He goes on to say that the consistent "purity and whiteness of light in which there is hardly shadow at all adorns people, young and old alike."[137] Almost the entire film takes place in daylight, with very little artificial light within the film's diegesis. Thus, most light in *Silent Light* is (ostensibly) sunlight. Rarely has the sun enjoyed such lavish cinematic attention, especially in the opening sunrise and closing sunset.

---

[132]De Luca, *Realism of the Senses*, 37-38.

[133]De Luca, *Realism of the Senses*, 52.

[134]Hoberman, "Divine Light."

[135]Manohla Dargis, "Into the Mennonite World to Explore One Man's Test of Faith (Silent Light)," review of *Silent Light*, by Carlos Reygadas, September 23, 2008.

[136]Roy Anker, "Dazzle Gradually," *Books & Culture*, 2009.

[137]Anker, "Dazzle Gradually."

The sun is the literal star of the show, and the five-minute sunrise establishes it as such. I suggest the sun and sunlight serve two complementary functions: (1) as the primary source and marker of temporal rhythms, and (2) as an intuitive symbol of divine presence.

That the film starts and ends with the sun's coming and going foregrounds its role as the foundation of our temporal rhythms. Time itself is a major motif. After the sunrise, Johan gets up from the table and, in a cryptic action, stops the clock. It is restarted again only after Esther's resurrection. This is an allusion to *Ordet*,[138] where it serves a narrative function: in some cultures, stopping the clock is a customary way to mark the time of death.[139] But in *Silent Light*, there is no obvious reason for Johan to stop the clock. Johan's father (Peter Wall) restarts the clock after Esther's resurrection, despite being unaware of the miracle. The clock motif is suffused with mystery. Moments after the clock has been restarted, the film closes with a sunset, thereby explicitly reestablishing the sun's association with time.

But assigning the sun a temporal function doesn't exhaust its meaning. Sunlight is also depicted in a manner that suggests divine presence. The opening sunrise sets the tone. On paper, nothing could be seemingly less daring than filming a sunrise. It is, quite literally, an everyday occurrence and photographed endlessly, relegating it to the lowly status of sentimental cliché. Yet, in the hands of Reygadas and Zabé, it is truly dazzling and, as such, feels utterly fresh, capturing—nay, *amplifying*—the wonder that the real-life sight of the sun hovering on the horizon famously and perennially draws out. Few, if any, reviewers fail to mention the shot, unanimous in their praise. Anker writes, "The long rhapsodic opening shot of the sun rising over the farms of Chihuahua sounds sure-to-be-draggy, clichéd, and artsy, but in fact, it's quite the opposite: it dazzles, as more than a few jaded reviewers have admitted."[140] He also refers to the "palpable radiance of the sun" and enthuses that this is "numinous nature, enough to make the jaded gasp and kneel right there in the theatre."[141] So gratuitous is the scene that it *asks* us to behold, and thus to

[138]In *Ordet*, Mikkel stops the clock at Inger's death, and Anders restarts the clock after her resurrection (although, in fact, it is a different clock in a different room).

[139]Shane McCorristine, *Interdisciplinary Perspectives on Mortality and Its Timings: When Is Death?* (London: Palgrave Macmillan, 2017), 5.

[140]Anker, "Dazzle Gradually."

[141]Anker, "Dazzle Gradually."

respond with wonder. The scripturally inclined may be reminded of the words of David:

> [God] is like the light of morning at sunrise
> on a cloudless morning,
> like the brightness after rain
> that brings grass from the earth. (2 Sam 23:4)

The image inspires wonder, infusing the film's world with a glory that, for reviewers like Anker, speaks to the sacred in nature.

This opening aubade establishes a visual theme carried throughout the film, namely the wonder of light. Expansive, sunny skies are in abundance. Dargis notes, "The sun floods the wide sky in 'Silent Light' like a beacon, spilling over the austere land and illuminating its pale, pale people as if from within."[142] The skies in *Silent Light* are colorful and vibrant, conveying a gentleness of light that contrasts with the overexposed, comparatively harsh skies of *Japón*.[143] While Ozu has been criticized for his uniformly sunny skies, film scholar Kristi McKim argues that the clear skies function as "a screen on which these complex ideas gain a clarity attributable . . . to the gift of cinematic space and time in which to imagine what this character might imagine, or to imagine what we'd think in this open field of reflection."[144] Not only are Reygadas's sunny skies similarly conducive to contemplation, but they take on a certain spiritual resonance thanks to the polysemy of "the heavens." Somewhat against the grain of his larger argument, de Luca notes the "'weight' of the immense sky upon them, which reinforces the film's metaphysical overtones."[145]

The sunlight has a constancy that contrasts starkly with fickle human emotion, a dynamic that is theologically suggestive, if indeed as I am arguing, sunlight intuitively symbolizes divine presence in the film. Consider the depiction of sunlight in a hilltop kiss between Johan and Marianne. In the scene immediately prior, Johan discusses his predicament with his confidant,

[142]Dargis, "Into the Mennonite World."

[143]This despite the fact that Reygadas has commented on his love for the Chihuahuense Mennonites' faces, "being so white and burned by that terrible sun up there." Reygadas, "Interview by Cinematographos."

[144]Kristi McKim, *Cinema as Weather* (Abingdon: Routledge, 2015), 186.

[145]De Luca, *Realism of the Senses*, 73.

Zacarias (Jacobo Klassen). As best I can ascertain, Johan has confessed the affair to Esther (again?) and resolved to break it off, leaving him heartbroken. Zacarias suggests that being with Marianne is Johan's destiny, even if that means hurting Esther. "A brave man makes destiny with what he's got," Johan responds pragmatically. "I have a woman and a family, and my woman is called Esther." But as he ponders it further, Johan admits that his "feeling" is that Marianne is a more suitable partner. Zacarias, evidently a romantic, replies, "And that feeling may be founded in something sacred. Even if we don't understand it." At that point, Johan begins singing along with the song on the radio, "No Volveré" by Country Roland Band, a song about moving on from an old relationship. As Johan sings with increasing gusto, he seems to have alighted on a similar decision. Seeing this change of heart, Zacarias says, "The swine's on for a good lay, huh?" When, in the next scene, he has a hilltop rendezvous with Marianne, we understand that he has gone from deciding to end the affair to resolving to continue it.

At the top of the hill, Johan meets Marianne and they engage in a passionate hilltop kiss. The sunlight is accentuated. The lovers are backlit by the sun, creating a soft halo effect. Several large flare spots appear across the frame (fig. 1.5). The shot's mobile framing accentuates the lens flare: riffing off the trope of lovers kissing in circular camera movement, evoking the giddy feelings of romance,[146] the handheld camera glides back and forth around the couple in a semicircular movement, causing the spots to stretch and flit about the frame. Reygadas takes issue with those who consider lens flare a defect. He and Zabé consciously sought flare throughout the film, finding lenses from the 1960s in order to achieve the effect,[147] which was a feature of 1970s American cinema.[148] Why lens flare? Aside from Reygadas's stated reason—"I just thought that would be beautiful"[149]—the flare and backlighting call attention to the sunlight. Aside from the monumental eighty-second kiss itself, the most conspicuous element of the scene is its light. The overwhelming presence of the sun, manifest in these ethereal pink, orange, and blue orbs dancing across the image, imbue the moment with the sense that Johan's illicit love for Marianne

---

[146]Højbjerg, "Circular Camera Movement."
[147]Reygadas, "Interview by Cinematographos."
[148]McKim, *Cinema as Weather*, 164.
[149]Reygadas, "Interview by Cinematographos."

indeed "may be founded in something sacred." Perhaps Zacarias was right. The union feels positively *blessed*.

This raises an obvious problem: this relationship is adulterous. Plus, there are no compelling reasons to empathize with Johan in his infidelity; we're given no reason to believe Esther has been anything but a devoted, industrious, and apparently long-suffering wife. Is Reygadas implying that the affair is acceptable, even noble? When questioned on this point, Reygadas has said that, for all their value, religious moral codes can diminish our experience of life. "I understand why there are rules regulating human drives, but I'd much rather embrace human nature with caution, setting limits for myself depending on where I'm coming from and what my goals are."[150] He goes on to say, "I've always hated pronouncements, militancy based on slogans, religious dogmas. Ethics are the result of personal decisions; you ask yourself questions and try to solve them at a particular moment."[151] Given the conservative religious context, the characters themselves are surprisingly nonjudgmental. For example, his confession is met with sympathy from his devout father. Though his father says initially that this "is the work of the enemy" ("I think it's God's doing," Johan replies), he has pledged his unconditional support to Johan by the conversation's end. José Castillo rightly notes that Reygadas does not "seem to judge the possibility of being multiamorous in the film."[152] De Luca writes, "*Silent Light* is therefore laden with Christian signifiers that are either twisted or else presented with an indifference to their moral codes."[153] Reygadas is more interested in exploring the emotional textures of a love triangle than in making moral pronouncements.

Endowed with a Christian ethic of marriage, however, how can we reasonably interpret the sunlight in this hilltop rendezvous as being symbolic of the divine when the relationship is morally objectionable? Is the light indifferent to Johan's transgressions? Not necessarily. From the perspective of Christian theology, we need not interpret the light as indifferent, only *indiscriminate*. Jesus said, "Your Father in heaven . . . causes his sun to rise on the evil and the good, and sends rain on the righteous and the unrighteous" (Mt 5:45).

---

[150]Reygadas, Castillo, and Detorrela, "Carlos Reygadas," 73.
[151]Reygadas, Castillo, and Detorrela, "Carlos Reygadas," 73.
[152]Reygadas, Castillo, and Detorrela, "Carlos Reygadas," 73.
[153]De Luca, *Realism of the Senses*, 57-58.

God bestows blessing without partiality. This is common grace, "a kind of non-salvific attitude of divine favor toward all human beings" that includes "the bestowal of natural gifts, such as rain and sunshine, upon creatures in general."[154] Paul appeals to this same principle when he tells the pagans of Lystra, "[God] has shown kindness by giving you rain from heaven and crops in their seasons; he provides you with plenty of food and fills your hearts with joy" (Acts 14:17)—natural phenomena connected, directly or indirectly, to the sun. Thus, Anker can write, "For Reygadas, that transfiguring light falls on everything and everyone, and especially on the ordinary and the unlovely."[155]

Common grace should not, however, be read as tacit approval of sin. Commenting on Matthew 5:45, New Testament scholar R. T. France says, "The impartiality of God's provision in nature does not, of course, indicate that he is indifferent to people's behavior, nor does it obviate the reality of divine judgment."[156] So we can affirm the sunlight pouring down on Johan and Marianne as indicative of divine blessing without confusing that with divine approval. In a later gesture freighted with meaning, Johan draws the curtains over a window through which light pours in before he and Marianne make love. Johan may want to block out the light, concealing the tryst in shadow, but the sun keeps shining regardless.

The sun's two functions, as symbol of time and of the divine, converge in one particular image. At Esther's wake, a grief-stricken Johan meets Marianne in a secluded outdoor spot. He tells her, "I'd give anything to turn back time. Go back to things as they used to be." She replies, "That's the only thing in life that we cannot do, Johan." As she comforts him in an embrace, she holds her hand up to the sky, blocking the sun. Her hand is shown against the sky in a reverse POV shot, outlined with a halo. Moments later, she brings Esther back to life with a kiss, after which Johan's father restarts the clock that was stopped at the start. It's as if time has been suspended for most of the film, hence Johan's stopping the clock at the beginning, allowing Marianne to do precisely what she has just said is impossible: turn back time, undoing the damage Johan's actions have brought upon his family. Blocking the sun with her hand,

[154]Richard J. Mouw, *He Shines in All That's Fair: Culture and Common Grace* (Grand Rapids, MI: Eerdmans, 2001), Kindle, 9.

[155]Anker, "Dazzle Gradually."

[156]R. T. France, *The Gospel of Matthew*, New International Commentary on the New Testament (Grand Rapids, MI: Eerdmans, 2007), Kindle, 226n701.

it's as if she is halting the inexorable march of time. But, paradoxically, it's also as if she is *drawing upon* the sun, aligning herself with the source of all light, inviting divine power to do the impossible. De Luca's helpful observation is that the film frame's capacity to democratically ignore the relative size of objects means the image of Marianne's hand completely covering the sun "has supernatural overtones as it evokes an eclipse, with her human limb standing for a celestial body of gigantic proportions."[157]

The resurrection miracle at *Silent Light*'s climax takes place in an ethereally bright white room, the film's most overt quotation of *Ordet*. Warner argues that Reygadas has co-opted three stylistic features of Dreyer's "that condition the miracle as well as our response to it":[158] (1) "*Generalised dispersion* of the miraculous event," in which the miracle is the culmination of a series of stylistic elements peppered throughout the film; (2) "inscription in the ordinary," the film's insistence that the action takes place in ordinary reality; and (3) "gentle reflexivity," in which the film subtly acknowledges its own status as a created artifact.[159] The first and second of these features are most pertinent for our purposes. With respect to the first, Warner writes, "This build-up consists mainly of sensory details that come to the fore as the narrative slackens," which, I suggest, includes the depiction of light.

Several commentators have identified a connection between the majesty of the natural, exemplified by its light, and the plausibility of the resurrection scene. Teodoro writes, "Everything in *Silent Light* is carefully calibrated so as to earn a bravura finale in which the sense of the miraculous implicit in the opening sunrise is made manifest."[160] Anker agrees that the ending's miracle "seems a logical extension of the irreducible glory already contained in every sort of thing."[161] And, according to Penn, it works in the opposite direction: "The miracle does not contradict the everydayness of the rest of the film; rather it exposes a strangeness that infects the naturalism."[162] The miracle of the everyday, like the sunset that heralds each new day, makes credible the magic realism of the climax, *and vice versa*. Penn writes, "The ordinary in *Stellet Licht*

[157]De Luca, *Realism of the Senses*, 66.
[158]Warner, "Filming a Miracle," 52.
[159]Warner, "Filming a Miracle," 50-64; emphasis original.
[160]Teodoro, "On Earth as It Is in Heaven," 50.
[161]Anker, "Dazzle Gradually," 22.
[162]Penn, "Time-Image," 1165.

[Plautdietsch title] is as magical as the miracle of the resurrection because the film attempts to get to grips with, to use Deleuze's words, 'the thing itself.'"[163] So while *Ordet* finds the miraculous amid the ordinary, *Silent Light* highlights the miraculous *of* the ordinary. As mentioned above, Reygadas, who Anker claims "has a profound wonder and reverence for all that is,"[164] says, "I don't believe in miracles, but I think reality is a miracle."[165]

What are we to make of the title, particularly the inclusion of the word "light"? As we've already discussed, light and word are prominent motifs in *Ordet* and John 1. Perhaps Reygadas finds in the latter a Johannine metaphor that better resonates with his artistic vision. My hunch is that Reygadas has, possibly unconsciously, picked "light" as a counterpoint to *Ordet*, "The Word." Word is didactic—precisely what Reygadas wants to avoid.[166] Consider his comments:

> I hate the idea that film is actually telling a story! The great part of film is to make you feel, not by the narrative. For example, the first shot of my film is cinematic. The light itself is beautiful. In literature, that does not exist. You can just write: "The sun came up." The beauty in my film is the sun itself. You don't have to recreate it. I also like the white light that she sees when she wakes up. Pure white.[167]

Reygadas wants to move away from the didacticism of word toward the feeling of light. *Silent Light* privileges the sensuality of cinema over its discursive aspects. It is "poetic rather than essayistic and echoes the director's conviction that authentic cinema 'doesn't mean anything' but rather similarly to music, 'conveys feeling.'"[168] We might say that Reygadas wants to get away from the preachiness of *word* and embrace the evocativeness of *light*.

But in what sense is the light "silent"? The most conspicuous depiction of light, the opening sunrise, is accompanied by a faunal symphony of cicadas chirping, birds singing, and cattle lowing. If light indeed represents the divine,

---

[163]Penn, "Time-Image," 1178.

[164]Anker, "Dazzle Gradually," 22.

[165]Badt, "*Silent Light*."

[166]"I didn't want to be very didactic about [the depiction of the passing of time]," he says. "We're still learning to feel cinema, to feel the audiovisual language." Reygadas, "Interview by Cinematographos."

[167]Badt, "*Silent Light*."

[168]Penn, "Time-Image," 1162. This is a prominent theme in Reygadas's filmic philosophy. For example, see Reygadas, Castillo, and Detorrela, "Carlos Reygadas," 73-74.

is calling it "silent" an accusation of divine indifference? Or has the light been *silenced* by Johan's turning a deaf ear to the moral demands the uncreated light makes on him (just as he shut out the light by drawing the curtains on his illicit lovemaking)? Both explanations would be, at best, wildly speculative and, at worst, misrepresentative of the film. A more promising path is suggested by paying attention to clues in *Ordet.* As the minister (Ove Rud) officiates at Inger's funeral, he, framed in ethereal light, invites the mourners to pray the Lord's Prayer in *silence,* and they do so. Moments later, Johannes takes an entirely different approach; he prays out loud for "the Word" and commands Inger to "Arise!" In *Silent Light,* we see the former, but not the latter. Johan's family begin their breakfasts, twice, in sustained silent prayer. Even if standard Mennonite practice, it is so unusual and protracted, that it seems unlikely to be coincidence. Rather, it is a conscious echo of the silent communal prayer of *Ordet.*

This suggests that, for Reygadas, the more potent spiritual moment was the silent petitions of the mourners rather than the verbose invocations of Johannes. Thus, the "silent" of the title underscores the nondidactic nature of light according to Reygadas's vision. Dreyer's Johannes is preachy; Reygadas's light is not. The divergent ways the two auteurs' films have handled the resurrection aftermath is telling. In *Ordet,* upon Inger's resurrection the characters discuss the power of God. In *Silent Light,* what little talk is included is inconsequential. Instead of weighty theological discussion, the camera quickly flees the scene to drink in the setting sun. *Ordet* accounts for its miracle with words about the Word; *Silent Light* "explains" its miracle by pointing us to the source of its light.

WONDER AND LIGHT

Miracles and wonder. *Ordet* and *Silent Light* are both notable for featuring a miracle at the climax. Traditional Protestant theology has mostly downplayed the place of miracles after the New Testament era or even denied the possibility outright.[169] John Calvin, for instance, was dismissive of his opponents' criticism of a perceived lack of miracles accompanying the Reformers' gospel, largely attributing contemporary miracles to demonic forces, and used this argument to undercut papal authority.[170] Indeed, the Reformation was partly

[169]J. Ruthven, "Miracle," in *Global Dictionary of Theology: A Resource for the Worldwide Church,* ed. William A. Dyrness and Veli-Matti Kärkkäinen (Downers Grove, IL: InterVarsity Press, 2008), 547.
[170]Calvin, *Institutes of the Christian Religion,* 1, prefatory address.

a reaction against claims of the miraculous.[171] So when the minister in *Ordet* claims that God chooses against performing miracles to avoid violating the laws of nature, he is simply being a good Protestant. Pentecostalism is the major Protestant stream to have bucked this trend, and it is probably not coincidental that this happens to be the form of Christianity that is flourishing the most globally.[172] The Western context of the productions of *Ordet* and *Silent Light* is significant. *Ordet* was made at the height of modernist skepticism about God. Although *Silent Light* was made in the less secularized context of contemporary Mexico, Reygadas identifies as "Western Mexican"[173] and does not believe in miracles.[174] Both films thus depict resurrections against a backdrop of Western skepticism about the miraculous.

The cultural context of the Bible, however, was one far more open to the possibility of miracles, and indeed miracles feature prominently in the Scriptures. In the book of Mark, for example, 65 percent of the space dealing with Jesus' public ministry is focused on miracles (by contrast, one study found that an average of just 0.3 percent of the space in theological references is given to dealing with the theme).[175] *Ordet* makes explicit reference to the miracles in the Bible when Anne's mother (Sylvia Eckhausen) shows Anne and Anders a picture of Jesus raising Lazarus back to life, foreshadowing Inger's resurrection. The New Testament word for *miracle* is *sēmeion*, rendered variously as "sign," "mark," and "expression," and it often appears in conjunction with other words: *dynamis* ("power"), *ērgon* ("action" or "work"), or *teras* ("wonder"). Thus, we often find the phrase in the Gospels translated as "signs and wonders" (Mt 24:24; Mk 13:22; Jn 4:48). Biblically then, *wonder* is a synonym for *miracle*. This makes intuitive sense since a miracle elicits feelings of wonder.

Religious scholar Robert C. Fuller, who has written extensively on wonder, explains wonder in terms of assimilation and accommodation, categories first advanced by psychologist Jean Piaget. When presented with a new experience, we either interpret the experience in terms of existing cognitive structures

---

171 Ruthven, "Miracle," 547.

172 Ruthven, "Miracle," 547.

173 David Barker, "'I've Never Understood a Traditional Screenplay:' Carlos Reygadas on Post Tenebras Lux," *Filmmaker Magazine*, 2013, http://filmmakermagazine.com/66943-ive-never-understood-a-traditional-screenplay-carlos-reygadas-on-post-tenebras-lux/#.Wd8jEIZx1E7.

174 Badt, "*Silent Light*."

175 Ruthven, "Miracle," 549.

(assimilation) or modify those structures to include these novel perceptions into our understanding of the world (accommodation).[176] Wonder requires accommodation, because the existing cognitive structures cannot adequately account for the unfamiliar stimulus.[177] When we describe a wondrous experience as *mind-blowing*, we are intuitively describing the cognitive processes involved in wonder: existing cognitive structures are being stretched beyond their limits, the mind's categories "blown." So wondrous experiences are an opportunity to rebuild cognitive structures that are better able to account for reality. Wonder is, therefore, an "epistemic emotion," affect that has some relationship to knowledge.[178]

The Gospels allude to the cognitive restructuring entailed by wonder. Take, for example, the frequent references to witnesses' amazement at Jesus' miracles (e.g., Mt 8:27; Mk 2:12; Lk 5:26; Jn 7:21). *Ordet* depicts characters struck by wonder, the miraculous resurrection effecting changes in characters that are almost as miraculous. For example, the miracle defies Mikkel's attempts at assimilation, thereby prompting accommodation, which leads to a sudden and dramatic shift from atheism to belief. The characters' response in *Silent Light* may be more muted, yet for certain *viewers* it elicits wonder (as does *Ordet*). For Anker, the resurrection "delivers a first-class jolt of amazement."[179] Speaking of both *Silent Light* and *Ordet*, Warner writes, "The miracle, as it surfaces across these films, is a spectacular and profoundly material happening, a strange irruption that, in the course of narrative events, brings about intense wonder."[180]

Besides the "wonder" performed by Marianne, *Silent Light* also highlights the wondrous in creation generally and light specifically. Anker eloquently draws connections between the natural world, light, and wonder:

> To see the world this way, as if through a pair of Vermeer-tinged eyeglasses is, frankly, startling. Perhaps this is Reygadas' foremost gift: his "eye," his luminous

176 Robert C. Fuller, *Spirituality in the Flesh: Bodily Sources of Religious Experience* (Oxford: Oxford University Press, 2008), ebook, 58.

177 Robert C. Fuller, *Wonder: From Emotion to Spirituality* (Chapel Hill: University of North Carolina Press, 2006), 147.

178 Piercarlo Valdesolo, Andrew Shtulman, and Andrew S. Baron, "Science Is Awe-Some: The Emotional Antecedents of Science Learning," *Emotion Review* 9, no. 3 (2017): 216, https://doi.org/10.1177/1754073916673212.

179 Anker, "Dazzle Gradually."

180 Warner, "Filming a Miracle," 49.

> apprehension of the physical world . . . the palpable radiance of the sun on the high plains of Chihuahua and of the plain people in the plain, white interiors of their simple farmhouses, the full amplitude of being with just enough "whatever" to inspire awe—what he calls "contemplation."[181]

What Anker calls "awe" could equally be described as "wonder"; the two emotions are close cousins. Both involve accommodation, but wonder does not typically entail fear and the submission impulse implied by some types of awe, and is not as closely associated with vastness as awe. There is a dearth of psychological research on wonder, and it has occasionally been subsumed into awe in the literature.[182] As we've already seen, the film encourages us to consider the miraculous in ordinary existence—perhaps this is the reason for the characters' ho-hum reaction to Esther's resurrection. As Old Testament scholar William P. Brown writes, "An ecology of wonder suggests that 'the greatest wonder is not that there is a God, but that there is a world.'"[183]

My contention has been that *Silent Light* presents the natural world as wondrous, especially in its interaction with sunlight. Certain displays of light routinely elicit wonder according to cultural anthropologist Veronica Strang. Her research has focused on people groups' meaning making and engagement with their natural environments, namely with water and, more recently, with light. "The environment is thus full of images of light and water, and many of these elicit affective responses. Some are sufficiently striking that they may be said to produce 'wonder.'"[184] Light manifests itself to our senses, therefore, not on its own but in its interaction with other objects. Think, for instance, of the dazzling light reflected from the golden cornfields harvested by Johan and his family, images reminiscent of the work of Terrence Malick that has made luminous grainfields a staple of spiritually inflected cinema.[185] Strang notes that one of the most compelling ways in which light is "materialized" and in which we perceive

[181]Anker, "Dazzle Gradually."

[182]Valdesolo, Shtulman, and Baron, "Science Is Awe-Some," 216. Fuller, *Spirituality in the Flesh*, 54; D. Keltner and J. Haidt, "Approaching Awe, a Moral, Spiritual, and Aesthetic Emotion," *Cognition and Emotion* 17, no. 2 (2003), https://doi.org/10.1080/02699930302297.

[183]William P. Brown, "Wonder: Stewards of God's Mysteries," *Journal for Preachers* 36, no. 4 (2013): 12. Though the punctuation indicates a quotation, Brown does not indicate from whom the quotation comes.

[184]V. Strang, "Short Wonderful Light: Affect and Transformation in Engagements with Light and Water" (conference paper, ASA Conference, Edinburgh, June 19-23, 2014).

[185]For example, see *Days of Heaven* (Terrence Malick, 1978), ranked #78, "Top 100 Films," *Arts & Faith*, 2011, accessed January 3, 2022, https://imagejournal.org/top-100-films/.

light is in its interactions with water, whether as vapor (e.g., rainbows, aurorae) or as water bodies (e.g., the sunlight glistening on the surface of a stream).[186] Strang points out that the way surfaces shine and shimmer are particularly mesmerizing. Noting the parallels between the aquatic reflection of light and our neurological processes, Strang goes on to say,

> It is not difficult to see why phenomena composed of water and light elicit powerful affective responses. They tick all the boxes: they are bright; highly colourful and often extremely intensive in hue. They shine gloriously, they shimmer with light and animation, resonating with physiological processes of visual perception. And where they are particularly striking, they induce wonder.[187]

The play of light on water explains the powerful affective impact of two of *Silent Light*'s most celebrated scenes: the opening sunrise and the scene of the children swimming. The sunrise derives its vibrant vermilion grandeur from its interaction with the large cloud mass blanketing the earth (fig. 1.3). Likewise, a number of reviewers have cited the images of the children swimming in an irrigation reservoir as among the most enchanting, the light sparkling on the gently turbulent waters, imbuing the scene with an idyllic allure (fig. 4.3). In these and other scenes, light is made an object of beauty and wonder.

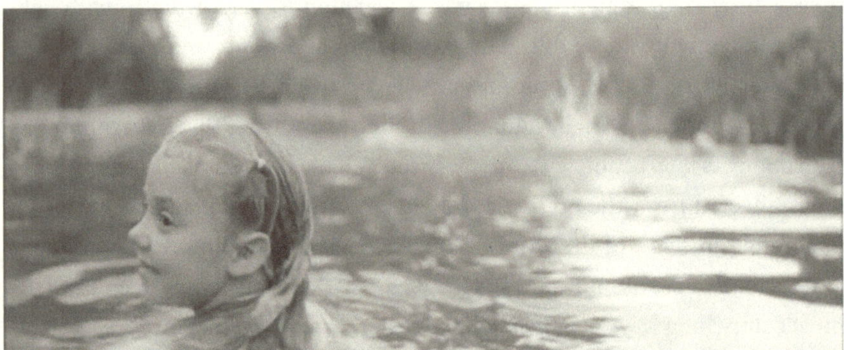

Figure 4.3. Light reflects off the water's surface in *Silent Light*, an example of a phenomenon that commonly elicits wonder

Light symbolism in religious and Christian tradition. Fuller argues that religion exists, in part, to ritualize wonder,[188] for the purpose of religion is to

[186]Strang, "Short Wonderful Light."
[187]Strang, "Short Wonderful Light."
[188]Fuller, *Wonder*, 64-68.

"[hold] us in a state of wonder."[189] Perhaps this is one reason light has been such a pervasive symbol in world religions. Strang says

> It is indubitable that flickering lights—firelight, candlelight, or in more contemporary terms, strobe lights, flickering movie screens—have a compelling effect, and one that is readily exploited crossculturally in (often ritualised) efforts to induce transcendental states of various kinds: religious ecstasy, trances, meditative modes of being etc.[190]

Thus, we find that the head of the ancient Egyptian pantheon was the sun-god Ra, whose very gaze was light, permitting night to come only when he closed his eye. For Zoroastrians, the creator of the world is light, the god Ahura Mazda, opposed by the god of darkness Angra Mainyu.[191] This Persian religion probably informed the Qumran community's heavy emphasis on light imagery, in which they saw themselves as "sons of light" doing battle with "sons of darkness."[192] Gnosticism was a religion in which humans' natural state in darkness could be overcome by freeing the light within the soul.[193] The centrality of light to Buddhism is illustrated by its very name, since "a Buddha is simply one who has become enlightened."[194] Present-day Maya adhere to a syncretistic blend of Catholicism and traditional Mayan religion, their belief in a sun-god persisting to this day, being only slightly subordinate to Diyoos, the Christian God.[195]

Orthodox Christianity, too, has a light metaphorical tradition rooted in Scripture itself. Light "is one of the most important and complex symbols in the Bible."[196] Light figures prominently in creation, in Moses' burning bush theophany and the pillar of fire, the incarnation, Christ's transfiguration, in Jesus' claims to be the "light of the world" (Jn 8:12), and the claim that "God

---

[189]Fuller, *Wonder*, vii.

[190]Strang, "Short Wonderful Light."

[191]Jonathan Keats, "20 Ways to See the Light," *Nautilus*, March 6, 2014, nautil.us/issue/11/light/20-ways-to-see-the-light.

[192]Colin Brown, *The New International Dictionary of New Testament Theology* (Grand Rapids, MI: Zondervan, 1978), 2:492.

[193]Brown, *New International Dictionary*, 2:491.

[194]John Macquarrie, "Symbolism Case Study: Light as a Religious Symbol," in *The Bible in Its Literary Milieu*, ed. John Maier and Vincent Tollers (Grand Rapids, MI: Eerdmans, 1979), 403.

[195]Justin L. Barrett, *Born Believers: The Science of Children's Religious Belief* (New York: Atria Books, 2014), 97.

[196]Leland Ryken and David L. Jeffrey, "Light," in *A Dictionary of Biblical Tradition in English Literature*, ed. David L. Jeffrey (Grand Rapids, MI: Eerdmans, 1992), 451.

is light" (1 Jn 1:5).[197] In Scripture, light variously refers to God, moral goodness, salvation, truth, understanding, and joy.[198]

Christian theology has thus made much of light. It was, for example, a major feature in the thought of Thomas Aquinas.[199] T. F. Torrance, too, has advanced a theology of light. He notes that light may seem visible but, in fact, it is only the things that reflect light that we can perceive (even if only air molecules).[200] So "in a strange way physical light is at once a darkness in itself and yet the source of brightness all around it."[201] Likewise, in Paul's words, God "lives in unapproachable light, whom no one has seen or can see" (1 Tim 6:16), yet it is God who is the "Source of all illumination in the universe."[202] Just as attempts to look at the sun in fact darken our vision, so, too, is it impossible for us to see the light of God except as revealed to us through Jesus Christ.[203] As we've already noted, the book of John presents Jesus as "the light of the world." Christ is not merely the perfect reflection of the light without himself being the light; rather, the "incarnation is the actual embodiment of God's Light within the objective empirical realities of our world in such a way that Jesus Christ is acknowledged as 'God of God and Light of Light,' of one and the same being with the light to which he bears witness."[204]

Torrance also points out light's constancy. It moves at a constant velocity; neither the movement of its source nor the movement or position of any observer will alter its speed.[205] The reliability of light—and, by extension, the cosmos—is rooted in the reliability of God. One aspect of God's constancy is truth and another is grace, the consistently free and unreserved self-giving of God in love to all alike, which is not controlled or conditioned in any way whatsoever by the worth of its object."[206] As noted above, God "causes his sun to rise on the evil and the good" (Mt 5:45). Sunlight, a necessity of life, is equally available to all

[197] A. G. Hebert, *The Bible from Within* (London: Oxford University Press, 1950), 176; cited in Macquarrie, "Symbolism Case Study," 404.

[198] Ryken and Jeffrey, "Light," 451.

[199] David L. Whidden III, *Christ the Light: The Theology of Light and Illumination in Thomas Aquinas*, Emerging Scholars (Minneapolis: Fortress, 2014).

[200] Thomas F. Torrance, *Christian Theology and Scientific Culture* (Eugene, OR: Wipf & Stock, 1998), 94.

[201] Torrance, *Christian Theology*, 87.

[202] Torrance, *Christian Theology*, 90.

[203] Torrance, *Christian Theology*, 93-94.

[204] Torrance, *Christian Theology*, 95.

[205] Torrance, *Christian Theology*, 78.

[206] Torrance, *Christian Theology*, 84.

irrespective of merit. Like Johan in *Silent Light,* even those who would forsake their covenantal vows are beneficiaries of the blessings of a faithful God.[207]

It is no coincidence that "many of the first treatises denying the existence of ghosts and witches came from larger cities in the Netherlands and England, which featured some of the earliest and most extensive street lighting in Europe."[208] Thanks to the light bulb, humans have been able not only to conquer their fear of ghosts and ghouls, but also to master light, making it ubiquitous and "on tap." As a result, light has lost much of the visceral meaning that ancients assigned to it instinctively.[209] Art curator Amnon Barzel writes, "Light as the expression and symbol of the divine . . . could now be substituted by real electrical light elements based on technical, scientific and manufacturing achievement."[210] Catholic theologian David L. Whidden III thus wonders whether the language of light used with respect to God may be a "dead metaphor."[211] John Macquarrie has made the same observation.[212] I believe the films under examination may help rehabilitate the symbolism. Linguists George Lakoff and Mark Johnson have famously demonstrated how metaphors are not merely linguistic, convenient turns of phrase; they are also conceptual and grounded in corporeality.[213] Metaphors are deeply tied to our experiences of embodiment. Thus, as Fox points out, "Metaphors are not always expressed in the words of a language; as cinematic representation amply demonstrates, nonlinguistic metaphors can be manifested in gestures, actions, and rituals."[214] Part of the potential potency of light symbolism stems from its felt, experiential qualities—the feeling of waking up in gentle morning light or the sensation of basking in the warm sun. While technological mastery may have drained some of the potency from light symbolism, *Silent Light,* with its rich sensory depiction of light that taps into embodied experience, might help light recover some of that which has been lost. Light is also a *felt* metaphor.

---

[207]Torrance, *Christian Theology,* 84-85.

[208]Dirk Hanson, "Drowning in Light," *Nautilus,* February 28, 2014, http://nautil.us/issue/11/light/drowning-in-light.

[209]Whidden, *Christ the Light,* 2.

[210]Amnon Barzel, *Light Art: Targetti Light Art Collection* (Milan: Skira, 2005), 8. Cited in Brown, *Divine Generosity and Human Creativity,* chap. 6.

[211]Whidden, *Christ the Light,* 1.

[212]Macquarrie, "Symbolism Case Study," 406.

[213]George Lakoff and Mark Johnson, *Metaphors We Live By* (Chicago: University of Chicago Press, 1980).

[214]Fox, *Speaking Pictures,* 82.

Psalms of wonder. By examining the Psalms, a scriptural repository of wonder, we'll gain insight into the value of wonder for faith and practice. Take, as an example, Psalm 104, in which "rigorous thinking and rapturous wonder find a compelling convergence."[215] It's a psalm about the wonders of creation, not for the purpose of abstract, scientific analysis, but for praise. Of this psalm, Brueggemann writes, "That modernist attempt to compete with science through 'creationism' (or 'intelligent design') misses the point of the theological theme, which on its own terms is never explanatory but is characteristically *doxological*. . . . The psalmist is overwhelmed by the wonder of it all, which is attributed to YHWH."[216] Experiences of wonder are deeply compelling, bringing with them "a sense of the fullness of the present moment, the existential now."[217] We gain a sense of this through the psalm.

According to Fuller, "Wonder often begins as a response to something that strikes us as intensely powerful, real, or beautiful."[218] The psalmist evidently sees these qualities in creation and seeks to evoke this same sense through poetry. Wonder involves an element of surprise, and is thus not unlike the startle response, except that it combines also with interest and joy.[219] Brown writes, "The psalm not only describes joy, it prescribes joy, for us and for God."[220] Creation here is a thing of beauty. Even the fearsome Leviathan—portrayed elsewhere in the Bible as "God's mortal enemy destined for destruction" (cf. Is 27:1)—is presented here as a wondrously playful creature, a beast worthy of marvel.[221] Light is also a significant elicitor of wonder in the psalm: "The Lord wraps himself in light as with a garment; he stretches out the heavens like a tent" (Ps 104:2). Here, as in *Silent Light,* light and sky are objects of wonder.

We've noted that wonder is an epistemic emotion, related to knowledge insofar as it prompts reflection. We see here how wonder works epistemically in Psalm 8:

---

[215]William P. Brown, "The Lion, the Wicked, and the Wonder of It All: Psalm 104 and the Playful God," *Journal for Preachers* 29, no. 3 (2006): 15.

[216]Walter Brueggemann, *Psalms,* ed. W. H. Bellinger (New York: Cambridge University Press, 2014), 447.

[217]Fuller, *Wonder,* 63.

[218]Fuller, *Spirituality in the Flesh,* 54.

[219]Fuller, *Wonder,* 97; Fuller, *Spirituality in the Flesh,* 55.

[220]William P. Brown, *Sacred Sense: Discovering the Wonder of God's Word and World* (Grand Rapids, MI: Eerdmans, 2015), 65.

[221]Brown, *Sacred Sense,* 67.

> When I consider your heavens,
> the work of your fingers,
> the moon and the stars,
> which you have set in place,
> what is mankind that you are mindful of them,
> human beings that you care for them? (Ps 8:3-4)

The psalmist looks up to consider the heavens and its light(s), and as a result is led to ask questions about human purpose, questions that require an ability to imagine dimensions of reality that go beyond what is perceptible through the senses. Wonder fosters contemplation of the metaphysical, and "imbues the world with an alluring quality, fostering increased openness and receptivity rather than immediate utilitarian action."[222] Recall that certain emotions have action tendencies. Wonder, however, is defined more by what we could loosely call an "*in*action tendency," since one of its primary characteristics is that it halts utilitarian behavior and instead promotes sustained contemplation "of a grander scheme of life that strikes us as responsible for life's beauty, order, and vitality."[223]

A fundamental component of this contemplative process is agency detection, the search for the cause(s) behind the surprising stimulus. Curiosity promotes agency detection too, yet it has us look to the component parts of the phenomenon. Wonder, on the other hand, prompts us to search for agency in higher orders of reality, the invisible that lies behind the visible.

> Experiences of wonder respond to uncertainty by alerting us to the possible presence of a more general level of existence that—at least potentially—has causal relevance to our pursuit of wellbeing. Wonder, then, motivates efforts to contemplate—and even adapt to—orders of life that are not "out there" in any straightforward way.[224]

This goes some way toward explaining why wonder is closely associated with religious faith; wondrous phenomena prompt us to look for divine agency.

This is why some scientists treat wonder with ambivalence: it has a propensity for fostering magical thinking.[225] Though fueled by an "appetite for

[222]Fuller, *Spirituality in the Flesh*, 55.
[223]Fuller, *Spirituality in the Flesh*, 69.
[224]Fuller, *Wonder*, 59.
[225]Fuller, *Spirituality in the Flesh*, 68.

wonder," science ultimately subordinates wonder to curiosity.[226] But what do we lose without wonder? Fuller grants that unchecked wonder can be harmful, but wonder-*deprived* thinking is just as dangerous, not least the type found in religious fundamentalism.[227] Psalm 104 takes an unexpected turn at the conclusion when this extravagant celebration of creation abruptly ends on a low note: "But may sinners vanish from the earth and the wicked be no more" (Ps 104:35). Brueggemann explains this sudden change in tone:

> The beauty and wonder of creation are not autonomous realities but are derived from YHWH. This means, in turn that they are not unconditional but belong in the conditionality of Torah requirements. Thus the final verse constitutes a warning against exploitative use of creation that disregards the will and intention of the creation (v. 35). In a quite inchoate way, this verse provides a mandate for care for the environment and a stricture against its careless, destructive use.[228]

Though we must hold this conditionality in tension with the unconditionality of the indiscriminate sunshine of Matthew 5:45, the conclusion of Psalm 104 demonstrates the connection between wonder and creation care. A reverence for the natural world, grounded in wonder, may have little short-term utility but, in the face of the current ecological crises, may in fact be our only hope of survival in the long term.[229] Contrary to those who would caricature wonder as giving rise to religious delusions, it is in fact one of our most useful emotions, nurturing those impulses that elevate us to greater heights. Fuller contends that "wonder can be seen as one of the emotional sources of humanity's highest cognitive achievements," because "the highest conceptions of justice, dignity, and worth all require highly developed notions of a general order of existence that in some fundamental way lies 'beyond' the observed parts of life."[230]

What sets wonder apart from many other emotions is that it encourages an openness to others and the world, nurturing feelings of trust and belonging.[231] It draws us out of ourselves, moving us closer to others and the world, leading

---

[226]Fuller, *Wonder*, 63.
[227]Fuller, *Spirituality in the Flesh*, 71-72.
[228]Brueggemann, *Psalms*, 447-48.
[229]Fuller, *Wonder*, 63-64.
[230]Fuller, *Spirituality in the Flesh*, 71-72.
[231]Fuller, *Spirituality in the Flesh*, 56.

us to empathize with and cherish others for their intrinsic rather than utilitarian value.[232] Wonder is, therefore, one of the primary reasons for human beings' moral sense. "To fail to see the world as God's mystery, as a source of wonder, may well prove disastrous in the end," Brown writes. "We lose our sense of wonder, we lose the world."[233]

Contemplation of higher orders of existence, nonmaterial agency detection, a sense of trust and belonging, a desire to act ethically—it's easy to see how wonder is conducive to religious thought, action, and experience. For some viewers, the wonder of *Ordet* and *Silent Light* takes on a religious quality. We've already mentioned religion's role in ritualizing wonder, but religion is also a *response* to wonder. Indeed, Fuller argues that different religious styles are grounded in divergent emotional experiences. The underlying emotional basis for "apocalypticism," with its emphasis on doctrine, Scriptures, piety, and submission to authority, is fear, shame, and anger. These are the dynamics we see at work between the warring religious factions in *Ordet* until a wonder, the resurrection of Inger, renders such divisions trivial. Wonder, on the other hand, gives rise to "aesthetic spirituality," which emphasizes divine immanence and "being at home in the universe," precisely the feeling *Silent Light* invites through its majestic depiction of nature awash in dazzling light.[234]

Ordet and *Silent Light* are films *about* wonders and films that *elicit* wonder. Though the lighting never works alone, the role of light is crucial in issuing to the audience a call to wonder. Of course, as we've already stated, that these films may invite wonder is no guarantee of revelation. Revelation happens only as God wills it. Nevertheless, it does potentially leave certain viewers in a state of heightened awareness, a posture of openness to the divine. Light has served as such a fruitful, near-universal metaphor in religion that it has, in the modern era, been drained of its force—a dead metaphor. For that reason, Inger and Esther's are not the only resurrections of these two films—through their powerful use of light, a dead metaphor is resurrected too.

[232]Fuller, *Wonder*, 93-100.

[233]Brown, "Wonder: Stewards of God's Mysteries," 12-13.

[234]Fuller, *Wonder*, 145-48; Fuller, *Spirituality in the Flesh*, 52-53.

5

2001: A Space Odyssey

Space, Awe, and Mise en Scène

When Neil Armstrong became the first person to step foot on the moon in 1969, it marked the first of several successful lunar missions that would be the occasion for life-altering religious experiences for a number of Apollo astronauts.[1] One year earlier, however, people were *already* having religious experiences occasioned by space travel, only in the cinematic form of *2001: A Space Odyssey* (Stanley Kubrick, 1968),[2] a groundbreaking science-fiction film that has grown in stature to the point of being widely considered one of the greatest movies of all time.[3] Originally titled *Journey Beyond the Stars*, the film proved for some viewers to be as much a journey beyond the physical into the mysterious metaphysical heart of reality.[4] As a "filmic Rorschach,"[5] the types of spiritual experiences it elicits are diverse—and certainly not exclusively or especially Christian. How is it that such an apparently materialist film perennially serves as a catalyst to religious experience and theological reflection? Many of its stylistic strategies, of which mise en scène—simply, that which

[1]On the return journey, astronaut Edgar Mitchell had an ecstatic epiphany in which he perceived the interconnectedness of all things; while looking at the earth, Gene Cernan came to the sudden realization that there must be a Creator that transcends all religion; and upon returning home, Charlie Duke converted to Christianity as a direct result of his space travel. See *In the Shadow of the Moon* (David Sington, 2007).

[2]Ranked #12, "Top 100 Films—2020," *Arts & Faith*, 2020, accessed January 3, 2022, http://artsandfaith.com/index.php?/films/&do=year&id=8&page=2.

[3]"The 50 Greatest Films of All Time," Sight & Sound, BFI, 2012, www.bfi.org.uk/news/50-greatest-films-all-time.

[4]Jeremy Bernstein, "Beyond the Stars," in *Stanley Kubrick: Interviews*, ed. Stanley Kubrick and Gene D. Phillips, Conversations with Filmmakers Series (Jackson: University Press of Mississippi, 2001), 17.

[5]David W. Patterson, "Music, Structure and Metaphor in Stanley Kubrick's '2001: A Space Odyssey,'" *American Music* 22, no. 3 (2004): 445.

appears within the frame—will be a particular focus, evoke awe, an emotion that has long been associated with religious experience and religion more broadly. Experiences of awe alone do not establish that revelation has occurred, but the common association between awe and religious experience suggests that awe is an emotion with revelatory potential.

2001: A Space Odyssey

Religious reception. There's a paradox at the heart of *2001*: it "has been variously interpreted as both Kubrick's most secular and most religious film."[6] The charge of secularism makes a certain amount of sense. Taken at face value, the film appears to be unconcerned with, perhaps even hostile to religion. After all, it features Richard Strauss's iconic orchestral fanfare *Thus Spoke Zarathustra,* taking its name from the Friedrich Nietzsche novel in which God is famously said to be dead.[7] Religious scholar and film critic James M. Wall sees Stanley Kubrick as presenting "a universe which functions without a metaphysical anchor."[8] Yet he also detects theological ambiguity, as Kubrick "seems to be denying the presence of an ultimate mystery at the core of reality. But his style and the manner in which his film unfolds belie that denial. 'Something' has pulled at man and beast from the beginning of time."[9] English literature scholar Carrol L. Fry mentions the "religious or mystic tone" and "'metaphysical' sense that some critics have found in the film." Similarly, film scholar Anna Powell notes critic Annette Michelson's observation that *2001* has the "ability to stimulate metaphysical speculation."[10] In his early review of the film, film editor and reviewer Robert O'Meara credited the Western interest in Eastern religion at the time for its portrayal of "immortal cosmic consciousness."[11] Another early response from public intellectual Renata Adler complained of the film's

---

[6]Nathan Abrams, "Stanley Kubrick: Midrashic Movie Maker," in *The Bible in Motion: A Handbook of the Bible and Its Reception in Film* (Berlin: De Gruyter, 2016), 668.

[7]Friedrich Nietzsche, *Thus Spoke Zarathustra: A Book for All and None* (Amazon Digital Services, 2012), first part, Kindle.

[8]James M. Wall, "2001: A Space Odyssey and the Search for a Center," in *Image & Likeness: Religious Visions in American Film Classics*, ed. John R. May (New York: Paulist Press, 1992), 40.

[9]Wall, "2001: A Space Odyssey," 41.

[10]Annette Michelson, "Bodies in Space: Film as Carnal Knowledge," *Artforum* 7, no. 6 (1969). Cited in Anna Powell, *Deleuze, Altered States and Film* (Edinburgh: Edinburgh University Press, 2007), 162. It should be noted that Michelson's analysis subordinates any metaphysical relevance to its formal qualities.

[11]Robert O'Meara, "Stanley Kubrick, 2001: A Space Odyssey, 1968," *Screen* 10, no. 1 (January 1, 1969): 110.

"murky implications of theology."[12] The implications may be murky, but they are no less deserving of theological engagement for that.

God is most often invoked in discussions about the identity of the mysterious monolith that appears periodically throughout the film, apparently guiding humankind on their evolutionary journey. The monolith has been explained by various scholars as "pure energy or an integrated immortal consciousness (or perhaps even GOD)";[13] "either a God-like entity . . . [or] a symbol, a metaphor even, for intelligence proper";[14] "alien machines, the presence of God, or visual metaphors for human inspiration";[15] and "extraterrestrial intelligence, a universal totem, or even the image or idea of God."[16] Despite the object's ambiguity, there's remarkable agreement about what it *might* symbolize, namely God. Extending the theological conversation beyond the monolith, Dale E. Williams writes that the film's "central motif . . . is not science technology, but the spiritual future of humanity."[17] Williams concludes that *2001* teaches "self-denial [as] the only way back to God, for by humbly walking with destiny, we can be transformed. We can find communion with God."[18] He thus unapologetically calls *2001* "a religious film."[19] Note, too, the words of UCLA's Howard Suber:

> The paradox of *2001* is that this work, whose story and whose actual making were so dependent upon human technology, itself a concrete manifestation of human logic, should ask us to move beyond logic, beyond concrete realities altogether, that it should take us into the domain hitherto reserved for theology: speculation on human destiny. Like all great films, *2001* takes hold, not merely of the eye and ear, but also of the mind. It is concerned not with the

[12]Renata Adler, "The Screen: '2001' Is Up, Up and Away: Kubrick's Odyssey in Space Begins Run," *The New York Times*, April 4, 1968, www.nytimes.com/movie/review?res=9a04e6da1530ee3bbc4c53dfb2668383679ede.

[13]O'Meara, "Stanley Kubrick," 109-10.

[14]Pedro Blas González, "Stanley Kubrick's '2001': An Existential Odyssey," *Senses of Cinema*, September 2009, http://sensesofcinema.com/2009/feature-articles/stanley-kubricks-2001-an-existential-odyssey/.

[15]Rhonda Burnette-Bletsch, "2001: A Space Odyssey (1968)," in *Bible and Cinema: Fifty Key Films*, ed. Adele Reinhartz (London: Routledge, 2013), 5.

[16]Christopher Rowe, "The Romantic Model of '2001: A Space Odyssey,'" *Canadian Journal of Film Studies* 22, no. 2 (2013): 59, www.jstor.org/stable/24411807.

[17]Dale E. Williams, "2001: A Space Odyssey: A Warning Before Its Time," *Critical Studies in Media Communication* 1, no. 3 (1984): 314.

[18]Williams, "2001: A Space Odyssey," 321.

[19]Williams, "2001: A Space Odyssey," 314.

> evolution of man's body, but with the evolution of man's mind and spirit. It is remarkable not only for its awesome visual effects, which have never been surpassed, but also for the fact that it is, at its core and its conclusion, a sacred drama for a secular society.[20]

Adler called the film a Rorschach test, and indeed one of its defining features is the multiplicity of plausible interpretations it invites.[21] So while there is no scholarly or critical consensus about *2001*'s theological character, the film offers enough to prompt religious engagement from some.

Of *2001*, theologian Gerald Loughlin writes, "It is not evident that Kubrick intended his picture to have any religious resonance, though he is recorded as joking that 'MGM don't know it yet, but they've just footed the bill for the first six-million-dollar religious film.'"[22] But I'm not convinced that Kubrick had no religious intent nor that his comment was entirely facetious. When asked, "Why does *2001* seem so affirmative and religious a film?" Kubrick replied:

> The God concept is at the heart of this film. It's unavoidable that it would be, once you believe that the universe is seething with advanced forms of intelligent life. . . . Once you begin discussing such possibilities, you realize that the religious implications are inevitable, because all the essential attributes of such extraterrestrial intelligences are the attributes we give to God. What we're really dealing with here is, in fact, a scientific definition of God. And if these beings of pure intelligence ever did intervene in the affairs of man, so far removed would their powers be from our own understanding. How would a sentient ant view the foot that crushes his anthill—as the action of another being on a higher evolutionary scale than itself? Or as the divinely terrible intercession of God?[23]

Kubrick made very similar comments elsewhere, again referring to his "scientific definition of God."[24] What, asked journalist Eric Nordern, has alien evolution to do with God? "Everything," replied Kubrick, "because these beings would *be* gods to the billions of less advanced races in the universe . . . if the

[20]Howard Suber, "2001: A Space Odyssey," The Criterion Collection, 1988, updated October 31, 2017, www.criterion.com/current/posts/819-2001-a-space-odyssey.

[21]Adler, "The Screen."

[22]John Baxter, *Stanley Kubrick: A Biography* (London: HarperCollins, 1997), 210; quoted in Gerard Loughlin, *Alien Sex: The Body and Desire in Cinema and Theology* (Hoboken, NJ: Blackwell, 2008), 68.

[23]Joseph Gelmis, "The Film Director as Superstar: Stanley Kubrick," in Kubrick and Phillips, *Stanley Kubrick*, 92-93.

[24]Eric Nordern, "Playboy Interview: Stanley Kubrick," in Kubrick and Phillips, *Stanley Kubrick*, 49-50.

tendrils of their consciousness ever brushed men's minds, it is only the hand of God we could grasp as an explanation."[25] Kubrick rejects the God of classical theology, but believes that alien life could evolve to the point that the boundary between deity and nondeity is blurred.[26] Kubrick even attributed the negative response of a cadre of influential New York critics to their being "so dogmatically atheist and materialist and Earth-bound that [they find] . . . the grandeur of space and the myriad mysteries of cosmic intelligence anathema."[27] What ought we infer from these comments? Was Kubrick truly intending to make a "six-million-dollar *religious* film"? The Kubrick we get in interviews is often at odds with the Kubrick we infer from his work.[28] Maybe, given his penchant for satire, Kubrick is being ironic or even disingenuous. But if Kubrick *is* being sincere in these interviews, the religious character some viewers find in the film may be there by design.

Strictly materialist interpretations may owe more to Arthur C. Clarke's companion novel,[29] which is more explicit about the extraterrestrial element, than the film, which scholars have often failed to sufficiently differentiate from the novel.[30] Science-fiction scholar Suparno Banerjee argues that Clarke's work, published after the film, adheres to hardcore sci-fi literary convention by exploring the possibility of higher intelligence in the universe, while Kubrick employs a minimalist aesthetic "to bring about an ineffable quality that gives the film a quasi-religious air of mystery."[31] Yet even Clarke is aware of the film's religious dimension. "As Kubrick and Clarke both suggested in interviews,"

---

[25]Nordern, "Playboy Interview: Stanley Kubrick," 50.

[26]Nordern, "Playboy Interview: Stanley Kubrick," 49-50.

[27]Nordern, "Playboy Interview: Stanley Kubrick," 49.

[28]For example, against charges of misanthropy, Kubrick said, "You don't stop being concerned with man because you recognize his essential absurdities and frailties and pretensions. . . . I believe in man's potential and in his capacity for progress." Against charges of Ludditism, he said, "I'm not hostile toward machines at all; just the opposite, in fact . . . the interrelationship [between humans and machines]—if intelligently managed by man—could have an immeasurably enriching effect on society." Nordern, "Playboy Interview: Stanley Kubrick," 68, 71. Interestingly, in his audience reception study of *2001*, Peter Krämer found that early audiences interpreted the film as largely optimistic, which "contrasts sharply with what has become the standard interpretation of *2001* in Kubrick criticism, which frames the film through the alleged pessimism of Kubrick's whole oeuvre." Peter Krämer, "'Dear Mr. Kubrick': Audience Responses to 2001: A Space Odyssey in the Late 1960s," *Participations* 6, no. 2 (2009): 254.

[29]Arthur C. Clarke, *2001: A Space Odyssey* (London: Penguin, 1968).

[30]Suparno Banerjee, "2001: A Space Odyssey: A Transcendental Trans-locution," *Journal of the Fantastic in the Arts* 19, no. 1 (2008): 39.

[31]Banerjee, "2001: A Space Odyssey," 40.

writes Fry, "a truly poetic visualisation of this process of death and rebirth would almost certainly have religious connotations."[32] But religious connotations aren't just inevitable, they're intentional. Kubrick once said, "If the film . . . stimulates, however inchoately, [the viewer's] mythological and religious yearnings and impulses, then it has succeeded."[33] Taken at face value, Kubrick's comments reveal that *2001* is apparently *meant* to invoke the divine, though not necessarily as we know it.

The most compelling case for considering *2001* as religiously significant comes from audiences. "While some spectators admittedly left theaters in confusion," writes theologian Rhonda Burnette-Bletsch, "others eulogized the film as a life changing, almost spiritual experience."[34] This claim is borne out by Peter Krämer's audience reception research, based on letters Kubrick received upon its release. He finds that "some equated viewing the film with a spiritual experience . . . the film's admirers quite frequently made extreme claims concerning . . . its spirituality and its life-affirming, life-changing and life-saving powers."[35]

The same is true of more recent responses. A number of IMDb and Rotten Tomatoes users have interpreted the film theologically. One such reviewer describes the monolith as "the ultimate black box containing all the answers to our existence. In other words, 'the monolith' could be God,"[36] while another likewise notes that "replacing the traditional God of world religions is a cosmic intelligence that influences human evolution."[37] HAL is also understood through a theological lens, as one reviewer likens HAL killing his "creator" to the way humans "[kill] the spirit of God that lives in their hearts."[38] Others describe the film-viewing experience itself in reverential, even religious terms. It is "more than just a movie; an incredibly intense, ethereal,

[32]Carrol Fry, "From Technology to Transcendence: Humanity's Evolutionary Journey in 2001: A Space Odyssey," *Extrapolation* 44, no. 3 (2003): 40, https://doi.org/10.3828/extr.2003.44.3.07.

[33]Gelmis, "Film Director as Superstar," 92.

[34]Burnette-Bletsch, "2001: A Space Odyssey," 3.

[35]Krämer, "'Dear Mr. Kubrick,'" 251.

[36]Eternality, "A Meditative Journey into the Nature of Our Existence," 2010, accessed August 31, 2017, www.imdb.com/title/tt0062622/reviews-1558.

[37]Wildduck-1, "Mythological Documentary," 2005, accessed August 29, 2020, www.imdb.com/review/rw1210744/?ref_=tt_urv.

[38]ElMaruecan82, "An Intelligent Masterpiece, Victim of Its Own Greatness," October 4, 2010, www.imdb.com/title/tt0062622/reviews-1574.

mindblowing, near-religious experience."[39] For one viewer, "This movie filled me with a sense of wonder and unknown. . . . This film is impactful and transcendent,"[40] while another writes, "This isn't a film. This is a spiritual journey."[41] We sense the connection between the spiritual, corporeal, and emotional in these user comments: "What make [*sic*] the film so transcendent are its philosophical and spiritual posturings. . . . The overture and opening credits send shivers down my spine every time, and the ending gives me enough energy to fuel a thousand dreams."[42] "This is one of the most complicated and powerful films that have [*sic*] ever been made," enthuses the viewer. "Watching it is an experience equal to being born again. It is enlightenment in film form."[43] As critic Richard Kuipers puts it, "Few works in cinema can prudently and soberly be described as religious experiences: 2001 A Space Odyssey is one of them."[44] For some viewers, *2001* is truly a spiritually meaningful film.

General narrative and formal analysis. This religious resonance of *2001* is owing partly to its mythic quality. As philosopher Irving Singer observes, "*2001: A Space Odyssey* declares its mythic intentions in the subtitle itself."[45] Kubrick was inspired by Homer's *Odyssey*, judging that the sea was as mysterious and unknown to the ancients as space is to moderns.[46] But the journey is not exclusively through space, since Kubrick's "odyssey is, finally, a metaphysical adventure."[47] Kubrick and Clarke were heavily influenced by Joseph Campbell's seminal work on mythology, and thus, according to Clarke, he and

---

39 ShootingShark, "My Mind Is Going," March 15, 2008, www.imdb.com/title/tt0062622/reviews-1359.

40 Christian A, "User Review of '2001: A Space Odyssey' (Rotten Tomatoes)," August 31, 2016, https://web.archive.org/web/20180130032638/https://www.rottentomatoes.com/m/1000085-2001_a_space_odyssey/reviews/?page=8&type=user.

41 Sameen M, "User Review of '2001: A Space Odyssey' (Rotten Tomatoes)," September 7, 2013, web.archive.org/web/20180313083946/https://www.rottentomatoes.com/m/1000085-2001_a_space_odyssey/reviews/?page=46&type=user.

42 WriterDave, "In Space, Everyone Can See You Dream," November 21, 2005, www.imdb.com/user/ur1069062/reviews?sort=submissionDate&dir=asc&ratingFilter=10.

43 Sewaat, "Transcendental. Masterful. Existential," 2017, www.imdb.com/user/ur48192431/.

44 Richard Kuipers, "2001: A SPACE ODYSSEY (1968)," 2001, accessed January 30, 2018, www.urbancinefile.com.au/home/view.asp?a=4657&s=Reviews.

45 Irving Singer, *Cinematic Mythmaking: Philosophy in Film* (Cambridge, MA: MIT Press, 2010), 195.

46 Bernstein, "Beyond the Stars," 18.

47 William R. Robinson and Mary McDermott, "'2001' and the Literary Sensibility," *The Georgia Review* 26, no. 1 (1972): 24.

Kubrick "set out with the deliberate intention of creating a myth."[48] The "myth" they devised is composed of four distinct parts:

1. *The Dawn of Man* (19 mins). Prehistoric hominids battle for survival in a hostile environment, awakening to discover a large black monolith, standing upright in their midst. The hominids enter into a frenzy, both fearful of and strangely attracted to this mysterious entity. Its presence inspires one hominid to use a tapir bone as a weapon, allowing the hominids to kill animals for food and even other hominids for territory.
2. *Journey to the Monolith* (33 mins). Now the setting is outer space on the cusp of the third millennium, and scientist Heywood Floyd (William Sylvester) is on his way to a research station at the Clavius lunar crater to secretly investigate a mysterious discovery: the monolith, now on the moon, buried there four million years prior.[49] As Floyd and his team of scientists visit the site of the monolith, it suddenly emits a piercing sound—a radio signal, as we later learn—that leaves the men staggering.
3. *Jupiter Mission* (60 mins). Eighteen months later, a spaceship controlled by a sophisticated supercomputer, HAL-9000, is making the first ever journey to Jupiter. But the supposedly infallible HAL turns on and kills the crew, forcing the sole surviving astronaut, David Bowman (Keir Dullea), to shut HAL down. Upon doing so, a prerecorded message from Floyd plays, explaining the reason behind the mission: the monolith at Clavius was discovered to be communicating with Jupiter.
4. *Jupiter and Beyond the Infinite* (23 mins). The final section begins with the monolith floating in space, propelling Bowman at terrific speed through the so-called Star Gate, a psychedelic portal through time and space. Bowman mysteriously finds himself in a neoclassical bedroom faced with incarnations of himself at different ages, including himself as a free-floating fetus inside a luminous caul ("Star Child"). The monolith appears again, suddenly launching the fetus into space, as it gazes out over Earth—and at us, the audience.

---

[48]Jerome Agel, *The Making of Kubrick's 2001* (New York: New American Library, 1970), 6.

[49]In fact, according to Kubrick, this is a *second* monolith, but the film leaves this matter ambiguous. Gelmis, "Film Director as Superstar," 91.

The film's mythic quality is surely one reason it has been put into dialogue with Scripture. *Bible and Cinema: Fifty Key Films*, for example, includes an entry on the film, noting its resonances with the biblical narrative.[50] Fry sees echoes of the creation narrative(s) of Genesis in the Dawn of Man sequence, though "a post-Darwinian version: an anti-Eden."[51] Jewish film scholar Nathan Abrams likewise notes parallels between the respective openings of Genesis and *2001*. The film's first "image" is a black frame recalling the "formless void" of Genesis, followed by light so "the very cinema itself moves from darkness, formlessness, and void to light," and next is bare land, before the arrival even of flora.[52]

Fry sees Eastern religious influences, via 1960s counterculture, on the mystical imagery of the Star Gate.[53] Theologian Athena Evelyn O. Gorospe notes that modernity has taken a dim view of traditional mythologies, while arguably replacing these with scientific myths of its own.[54] *2001* is perhaps one such example, the mythological in scientific guise. And such a mythic approach invites religious engagement. Yet the *2001* myth is not overtly or straightforwardly theistic. Indeed, it could be construed as *a*theistic.[55] But, as Wall points out, "something" is pulling at humankind, drawing them forward.[56] Thus, Burnette-Bletsch concludes that the film "affirms the possibility of a guiding force behind human evolution though not necessarily the god of traditional religion."[57]

While the mythic character of the story is conducive to religious reflection, it is the form that provides much of the affective force, thrusting the viewer into an embodied *experience* of this myth. This is achieved partly through the minimization of dialogue. A mere 40 minutes of its 161-minute runtime is dialogue;[58] the first line of dialogue is spoken 25 minutes into the film, and the last comes 23 minutes from the end, excluding credits. Film scholar Robert

---

[50]Burnette-Bletsch, "2001: A Space Odyssey," 3-8.

[51]Fry, "From Technology to Transcendence," 334.

[52]Abrams, "Stanley Kubrick: Midrashic Movie Maker," 669.

[53]Burnette-Bletsch, "2001: A Space Odyssey," 4.

[54]Athena Evelyn O. Gorospe, "Myth," in *Global Dictionary of Theology: A Resource for the Worldwide Church*, ed. William A. Dyrness and Veli-Matti Kärkkäinen (Downers Grove, IL: InterVarsity Press, 2008).

[55]Wall, "2001: A Space Odyssey," 40.

[56]Wall, "2001: A Space Odyssey," 41.

[57]Burnette-Bletsch, "2001: A Space Odyssey," 8.

[58]Mario Falsetto, *Stanley Kubrick: A Narrative and Stylistic Analysis* (Westport, CT: Greenwood, 2001), 52.

Burgoyne astutely observes that as speech disappears from the film, so does narrative linearity.[59]

Though minimally verbal, *2001* is nevertheless considerably aural. The music, writes Ebert, "uplifts. It wants to be sublime; it brings a seriousness and transcendence to the visuals."[60] The musical compositions of the film were preexisting classical works, though some have become practically synonymous with *2001*, especially Richard Strauss's *Also Sprach Zarathustra*.[61] This piece accompanies moments of "becoming," most notably the hominid's epiphany and the appearance of the Star Child, conveying grandeur and momentousness. Johann Strauss's stately *The Blue Danube* plays when the film has transitioned from prehistoric earth to twenty-first-century space, a piece Kubrick chose for its superiority in "depicting grace and beauty in turning."[62] Robert O'Meara found the waltz a surprising choice for a film set in space,[63] which is precisely why Kubrick chose it—in addition to beauty, he wanted to convey how routine space travel would become.[64]

Musicologist David W. Patterson has demonstrated that there are two "mutually exclusive harmonic streams" running throughout the course of the film, the tonal and the atonal.[65] The tonal, comprised of the likes of *Zarathustra* and *The Blue Danube*, expresses the constancy of the universe across epochs despite superficial changes in the *homo* species by virtue of the relationships between the musical structures of these pieces. The atonal, comprised of György Ligeti's *Atmosphères*, *Requiem*, *Lux Aeterna*, and *Aventures*, conveys a sense of the alien "other" by increasingly adding choral elements as the film progresses. Thus, "contrasts in orchestration, texture, text and compositional technique establish gradations between the film's various depictions of the

---

[59]It thus "[dramatizes] the way in which the conventional order of narrative discourse is modeled on the order of the sentence . . . both the 'subject' and the syntax of the narrative action dissolves." Robert Burgoyne, "Narrative Overture and Closure in '2001, A Space Odyssey,'" *Enclitic* V/2, no. 81-82 (Fall-Spring 1981): 172.

[60]Roger Ebert, "Great Movie: 2001: A Space Odyssey Review," March 27, 1997. www.rogerebert.com/reviews/great-movie-2001-a-space-odyssey-1968.

[61]The film's music was initially a "temp track" and controversially was used instead of Alex North's specially commissioned score. Kubrick added insult to injury by failing to break the news to North prior to the film's premiere. Patterson, "Music, Structure and Metaphor,'" 444-48.

[62]Agel, *Making of Kubrick's 2001*, 88.

[63]O'Meara, "Stanley Kubrick, 2001: A Space Odyssey," 109.

[64]Maurice Rapf, "A Talk with Stanley Kubrick About 2001," in Kubrick and Phillips, *Stanley Kubrick*, 78.

[65]Patterson, "Music, Structure and Metaphor," 470.

cosmic 'other,' each individual work adding dimension, definition, and difference to an otherwise shapeless 'unknown.'"[66] Kubrick scholar Mario Falsetto believes the eerie swirl of voices in *Requiem* lends the monolith's appearances a "semireligious quality,"[67] adding a religious layer of meaning to the notion of otherness that the music conveys. During the Jupiter mission, all music ceases and we are confronted with the lonely sound of Bowman's breathing against the crushing silence of space.

As important as the soundtrack is, Kubrick's primary strategies for creating a visceral, affective experience are visual: "I tried to create a *visual* experience," said Kubrick, "one that bypasses verbalized pigeonholing and directly penetrates the subconscious with an emotional and philosophic content."[68] Falsetto has shown how editing techniques do plenty of the narrative heavy lifting. As the hominid pulverizes the skeletal remains of an animal, the sequence is intercut with images of a tapir being slain in slow motion. The precise relationship between the bone-smashing and the tapir-slaying is ambiguous—probably a flashforward to how this bone will be used—but the *impression* it conveys is crystal-clear, using associative editing à la Soviet Montage to suggest the violent turn in the hominid that the monolith has precipitated.[69] This sequence transitions to the next via a celebrated match cut, the bone flung into the air mapping neatly onto the elongated spy satellite in space—a graphical, metaphorical, and thematic match, given the satellite's function as a state-of-the-art weapon.[70]

HAL's murder of the hibernating crew is also narrated purely through editing, a story event that presents the unique challenge of how to implicate an immobile agent in the murders of astronauts in hibernation. An efficient combination of HAL's "red eye" in closeup shots of hibernating crew, and closeups of flashing alerts on a computer monitor creates one of the most chillingly sterile and clinical murders ever realized on screen.[71] The closing bedroom sequence upsets classical point-of-view coding ("the structuring principle of

[66]Patterson, "Music, Structure and Metaphor," 470.
[67]Falsetto, *Stanley Kubrick*, 52.
[68]Nordern, "Playboy Interview: Stanley Kubrick," 47; emphasis mine.
[69]Falsetto, *Stanley Kubrick*, 53.
[70]Falsetto, *Stanley Kubrick*, 54.
[71]Falsetto, *Stanley Kubrick*, 55-57.

[*2001*'s] textual system," according to Burgoyne)[72] by subverting the concomitant shot/reverse-shot pairing, challenging the audience's expectations regarding this most basic of film structures and upsetting their general comprehension of the sequence. The disruption of spatio-temporal continuity toys with filmic subjectivity, suggesting a subjective perspective while also frustrating any effort to clearly assign that perspective to a specific individual.[73] Falsetto contends that the final two sequences, the Star Gate and the neoclassical bedroom, "are constructed around the idea of individual experience. . . . *2001* argues that a different form of communication [than dialogue] may be needed, both by the human species as it moves to exhaustion and by the medium of film."[74] The experiential facets of viewing are thus given primacy, "penetrating the subconscious with an emotional and philosophic content," to use Kubrick's words.[75]

For Burgoyne, there are two "textual operations" at work: "The hermeneutic development of the narrative . . . and the purely formal passages concentrating on motor images, rhythm, and perceptual events."[76] This latter type is why Michelson can state that *2001* "takes for its very subject, theme and dynamics—both narrative and formal—movement itself."[77] As a simple example, take the rotation of the extravehicular activity (EVA) pod as it prepares to dock. A typical approach to this mundane action in another film might be to show the pod at the beginning of its movement, cut away to a shot of the pilot, then return to the pod as it comes to a stop, creating a very short sequence with subtle ellipses in story time. The *point* would be to efficiently convey narrative information. But Kubrick's camera holds on the pod for the duration of the entire maneuver, a single take clocking in at about fifty seconds. Examples like this abound. Burgoyne likens these shots unmotivated by plot to production numbers in a musical, interrupting the narrative development.[78]

Because the plot advances only in fits and starts, the viewer's relationship to the meticulously crafted images is different to those of classical cinema.

---

[72]Burgoyne, "Narrative Overture," 173.
[73]Falsetto, *Stanley Kubrick*, 119-28.
[74]Falsetto, *Stanley Kubrick*, 127.
[75]Nordern, "Playboy Interview: Stanley Kubrick," 47.
[76]Burgoyne, "Narrative Overture," 174-75.
[77]Michelson, "Bodies in Space," 58.
[78]Burgoyne, "Narrative Overture," 174.

Freed to some extent from narrative concerns, these sequences are more easily appreciated for their formal qualities. We are made conscious of time in a way that an action film would typically not permit. We are asked to contemplate time, movement, and materiality—and not merely think about, but indeed *feel* them. Thus, Michelson argues that the film

> solicits, in its overwhelming immediacy, the *relocation of the terrain upon which things happen*. And they happen, ultimately, not on the screen but somewhere between screen and spectator. It is the area defined and constantly traversed by our active restructuring and reconstitution, through an experience of "outer" space, of the "inner" space of the body.[79]

Nowhere is this more apparent than in the Star Gate sequence, which plunges the viewer into a stunning journey through space-time to "beyond the infinite." The planets align, and there hovering in space is the monolith, ushering Bowman into the Star Gate. But, as film scholar Scott C. Richmond notes, at this point movement begins to be unshackled from purpose, its goal-orientation slackening. Filmed as a POV shot, the solid black of space is speckled with tiny dots of light, stars, that begin to stretch and accelerate toward all edges of the frame. These lights become denser and more numerous, changing in color and arrangement, constantly radiating out toward the picture's border in a manner that suggests Bowman—and indeed *we*, by proxy—are being pulled through space at terrific speed. The effect was created using slit-scan photography, in which a flat image is filmed through a slit and then assembled to create mirrored, psychedelic imagery (fig. 5.1). This innovative technique leaves us feeling as if we're passing through vast swathes of space at an unimaginable velocity, "one of the purest examples of the illusion of bodily movement in the history of cinema."[80]

Richmond has already pointed out the widening gap between movement and purpose, thereby calling attention to movement itself. But now in the Star Gate "we have a hyperbole of absolute movement. This movement is movement *through*, but not through any definite space. While there is direction, there is no goal, no *toward*, to explain or anchor such movement. It

[79]Michelson, "Bodies in Space," 59; emphasis original.

[80]Scott C. Richmond, *Cinema's Bodily Illusions: Flying, Floating, and Hallucinating* (Minneapolis: University of Minnesota Press, 2016), 54-55.

becomes pure movement into the depth of the screen."[81] Falsetto likewise suggests that the cerebral nature of the cosmology presented in the Star Gate sequence "has been transformed into the experiential."[82]

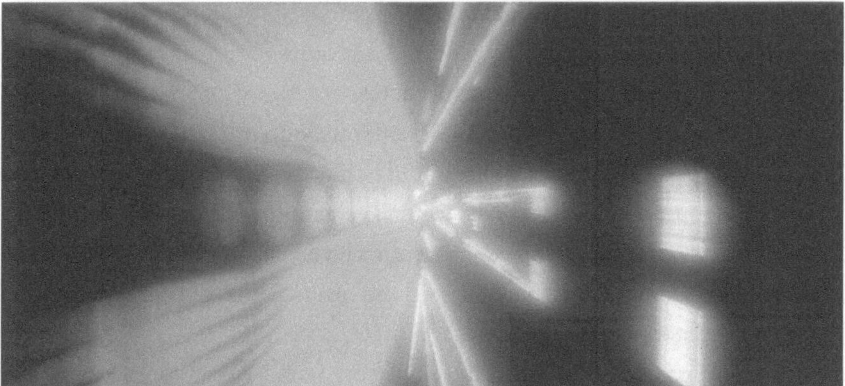

Figure 5.1. The Star Gate sequence in *2001: A Space Odyssey* creates a sense of rapid movement through space-time

In his exploration of *2001*'s affinities with Romanticism, film scholar Christopher Rowe suggests that the Star Gate sequence is an expression of the sublime.[83] Sublimity may reach its zenith in the Star Gate sequence, but it is pervasive throughout *2001*. And it is sublimity not only of space, but also of time. We are first alerted to the importance of time in the Dawn of Man prologue. The first twelve images in this sequence are vast landscapes, rocky and barren. Though we hear the howling wind, there is no discernible motion, not even the rustle of leaves on a tree (there are none). Life is eventually introduced into this inhospitable environment—prehistoric hominids, tapirs, and a leopard—but the sequence is still intercut with images of the empty landscape, as if to reiterate the permanence, even indifference, of the land. Yet, despite its apparent immutability, we know that this landscape has been sculpted by wind over eons. These images are spatially vast, yes, but also temporally vast. Our attention is called to time—geological time, no less.

As we move beyond primeval Earth into space, our awareness of time intensifies. With an average shot length of nearly twelve seconds,[84] *2001* is slow

---

[81]Richmond, *Cinema's Bodily Illusions*, 54; emphasis original.

[82]Falsetto, *Stanley Kubrick*, 51.

[83]Rowe, "Romantic Model of '2001: A Space Odyssey,'" 49-50.

[84]Laura Vaughan-Johnson, "2001: A Space Odyssey," Cinemetrics Database, April 1, 2019, http://cinemetrics.lv/movie.php?movie_ID=23779.

compared to most space films. Movement is smooth and deliberate, with usually just one element moving in the frame at any given moment, imbuing the film with a measured quality. The slow pace is established from the first shot in space. Those images of spacecraft "dancing" with planets are unusually long for imagery unmotivated by plot. But our sense of time is amplified even further during the Jupiter mission section of the film, particularly the spacewalk sequences. Even when Bowman must outwit HAL to gain reentry into the spaceship—a matter of life and death—the action unfolds with a restraint uncommon in classical narration. The acting is defined by an almost Bressonian lack of expressiveness that lends a levelheaded calm to what would ordinarily be dramatic and harried, and the utter silence of these images underscores the static quality of the action.

It all culminates in the Star Gate sequence. True to form, the sequence is far longer in duration than plot considerations require—over nine minutes—so the experience of watching begins to feel unending, yet engrossing. It is intercut with reaction shots of Bowman in freezeframe showing his accelerated aging. The Star Gate breaks down our perception of time, preparing us for the moment when, on the other side, Bowman surrealistically winds up in the neoclassical bedroom, encountering various incarnations of himself at different ages. Indeed, the film, which spans epochs, could justifiably have been titled, "2001: A *Time* Odyssey."

The sublimity of time is also embodied in the monolith. For philosopher Immanuel Kant, conveying the sublime through visual art presented a challenge. Art's job, in Kant's view, was to depict beauty of form, yet the sublime entails formlessness, specifically boundlessness or powerfulness.[85] Philosophers have more commonly associated the sublime with nature than with art,[86] so can art be sublime itself or merely *depict* that which is sublime in nature? Kant believed that it can indeed be sublime, but only indirectly so, smuggling sublimity in under the guise of beauty. Because of its mimetic quality, visual art must employ *indirect* means in order to present the sublime, objects or figures which, though portrayed as beautiful, symbolize the (nonbeautiful) sublime.[87]

---

[85]Robert Doran, *Theory of the Sublime from Longinus to Kant* (Cambridge: Cambridge University Press, 2017), 276.

[86]Doran, *Theory of the Sublime*, 276.

[87]Doran, *Theory of the Sublime*, 278.

While Kubrick uses some direct means, examined below, he also uses indirect means as per Kant. The monolith in *2001* is an object of "geometric perfection" that conjures up thoughts of vast periods of time. The monolith makes four cameos: (1) its appearance amid the hominids; (2) its discovery and visitation by lunar scientists; (3) its appearance in space drawing Bowman into the Star Gate; and (4) its appearance in the neoclassical bedroom. As such, it exists across epochs, transcending ordinary temporal limits. At its first appearance, the hominids approach it with trepidation until one finally works up the courage to touch it. When Floyd likewise extends his hand to touch the monolith, now on the moon, these two gestures connect, traversing millions of years and evoking the vast scale of time, not unlike what you might feel were you to press your own hand against the ancient hand paintings of Cuevas de las Manos in Argentina. The monolith comes to symbolize temporal magnitude, perhaps even eternity. So massive are the timescales embodied by the monolith that it represents the sublime.

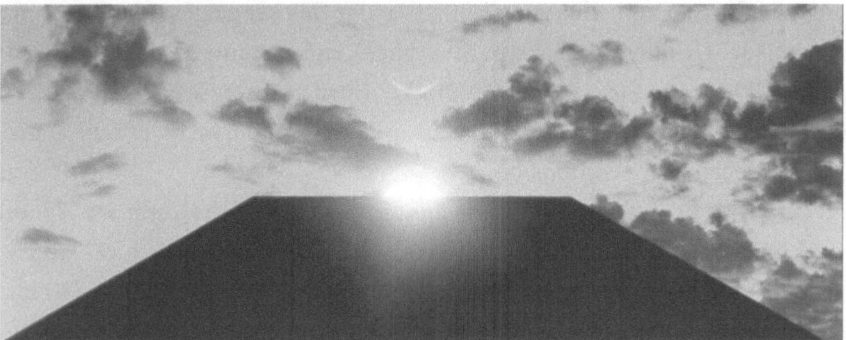

Figure 5.2. This recurring low-angle shot of the monolith in *2001: A Space Odyssey* accentuates its power and thus makes it a sublime object

The way the monolith is photographed, specifically the composition and angle of framing, suggests this sublimity. Initially, it is imposing, but not overwhelming in size (the choice to depict such a powerful entity as just a few meters tall seems to stem from the transcendental impulse to employ sparse means in service of evoking the divine). But a long shot of the monolith, luring the hominids into forming a groping cluster around it, cuts to a very low-angle shot of the monolith, where it appears to truly tower above us (fig. 5.2). The sun peeks over the top of the daunting monolith with a crescent moon immediately above in direct alignment, a moment of portentous syzygy. That the monolith should be in harmony with celestial bodies suggests great *power*; that it looms so large in the frame suggests great *magnitude*—hallmarks of what Kant called the dynamic and mathematical sublime respectively.[88] The image is repeated twice more, this repetition contributing to a sense of sublimity of the monolith.

Celestial bodies in deep-space composition. "This film captures the sublime in ways that few cinematic works ever have," writes philosopher Pedro Blas González.[89] The sublimity González observes stems from, among other things, the fact that its outer space setting has the appearance of the infinite, a crucial element of sublimity as envisaged by the godfather of the philosophy of the sublime, Longinus.[90] Kubrick, along with cinematographer Geoffrey Unsworth and special effects supervisor Douglas Trumbull, used mise en scène to convey the vastness of space, confronting us with the sublime and thus inviting a sense of awe. *Mise en scène* (French for "putting into the scene") refers to what appears within the frame.[91] The term is borrowed from the theater and, as such, refers mostly to elements found also in plays. So while the likes of angle of framing and editing do not fall under this heading, setting, lighting, staging (actors' movement and performance), and costumes do.[92] It is a broad term, but I want to focus on how Kubrick constructs the mise en scène of *outer space* by looking just at certain objects or figures that he includes within the frame in deep-space composition.

Let's consider just the *second and third sections of the film* ("ordinary" space does not feature so prominently in the others). There are five distinct exterior sequences in these sections: (A) Floyd's journey to the space station, (B) his journey to the moon, (C) his journey across the lunar surface to the monolith site, (D) Bowman's spacewalk to retrieve the "faulty" unit, and (E) Bowman's effort to salvage Poole's (Gary Lockwood) body after his spacewalk goes awry. The table (table 5.1) below shows what is included in each shot in each sequence's exterior images, whether spacecraft, people, or celestial bodies (i.e., earth, moon, or sun).[93]

---

[88]Doran, *Theory of the Sublime*, 221-59.

[89]González, "Stanley Kubrick's '2001': An Existential Odyssey."

[90]Doran, *Theory of the Sublime*, 126.

[91]David Bordwell and Kristin Thompson, *Film Art: An Introduction*, 10th ed. (New York: McGraw-Hill, 2012), 113.

[92]Bordwell and Thompson, *Film Art*, 112-40.

[93]Since I'm interested in the composition of outer space, all interior shots have been omitted from the list. I have not documented instances where the *lunar* surface is visible in the frame in the third

Table 5.1. Objects in the mise-en-scène of exterior space sequences (+ indicates the inclusion of the object within the frame; – indicates its exclusion)

Shot #	Shot Description	Celestial Body	Spacecraft	Person(s)
A. Floyd's journey to the space station				
1	Pan from satellite to Earth	+	+	–
2	Satellite orbiting Earth	+	+	–
3	Satellite orbiting Earth with Sun visible	+	+	–
4	Pan from satellite to Earth, then Moon	+	+	–
5	Space station with Earth visible	+	+	–
6	Pan from Earth to spaceplane	+	+	–
7	Spaceplane traveling to space station	+	+	–
8	Space station with Earth visible	+	+	–
9	Spaceplane viewed from space station	–	+	–
10	Spaceplane approaching space station	–	+	–
11	Spaceplane approaching space station	–	+	–
B. Floyd's journey to the moon				
1	Lunar lander traveling to Moon	+	+	–
2	Lunar lander in motion	–	+	–
3	Lunar lander traveling to Moon	+	+	–
4	Lunar lander traveling to Moon	+	+	–
5	Lunar lander descending (low)	–	+	–
6	Lunar lander descending (high)	+	+	–
7	Lunar lander descending (side)	+	+	–
8	Astronauts watch lunar lander's descent	+	+	–
9	Lunar lander's approach to landing pad	–	+	–
10	Landing pad opening	–	–	–
11	Lunar lander touching down	+	+	–
C. Floyd's journey across the lunar surface to Clavius				
1	Moonbus traveling (low)	–	+	–
2	Moonbus traveling	–	+	–
3	Moonbus traveling (high)	–	+	–
4	Moonbus traveling with Earth visible	+	+	–

sequence; at that point the action is on the moon itself, and thus the lunar surface functions simply as the ground rather than as a far-flung celestial body. Also, I've stopped my analysis at the point in which the scientists enter the site of the monolith, when the action becomes more interior-like.

Table 5.1. (continued)

Shot #	Shot Description	Celestial Body	Spacecraft	Person(s)
5	Moonbus above moonscape	–	+	–
6	Medium long shot of moonbus	+	+	–
7	Moonbus traveling across moonscape	–	+	–
8	Moonbus traveling	–	+	–
9	Medium long shot of moonbus	–	+	–
10	Moonbus traveling	–	+	–
11	Moonbus with monolith site in foreground	+	+	–
12	Approaching the monolith site on foot	+	–	+
D. Bowman's spacewalk to retrieve the faulty unit				
1	Spacecraft with meteoroids hurtling past	–	+	–
2	Spaceship launching EVA pod	–	+	–
3	EVA pod emerging from spaceship	–	+	–
4	EVA pod rising above spaceship	–	+	–
5	Spaceship's satellite dishes	–	+	–
6	EVA pod rotating	–	+	–
7	Bowman disembarking EVA pod	–	+	+
8	Bowman spacewalking toward spaceship	–	+	+
9	Bowman spacewalking toward spaceship	–	+	+
10	Closeup of Bowman	–	–	+
11	Bowman taking hold of satellite dishes	–	+	+
12	Bowman circling to satellite dishes' rear	–	+	+
13	Bowman preparing to remove panel	–	+	+
14	Bowman removing panel	–	+	+
15	Bowman removing panel	–	+	+
16	Bowman removing AE-35 unit	–	+	+
E. Bowman's effort to salvage Poole's body				
1	Establishing shot of spaceship	–	+	–
2	EVA pod rising above spaceship	–	+	–
3	Poole spacewalking toward spaceship	–	+	+
4	EVA pod attacks Poole	–	+	–
5	Poole hurtles through space untethered	–	–	+
6	Poole and EVA pod hurtle through space	–	+	+
7	Poole hurtles away from spaceship	–	+	+

Table 5.1. (continued)

Shot #	Shot Description	Celestial Body	Spacecraft	Person(s)
8	Poole "descends" through space	–	–	+
9	Pod bay doors open	–	+	–
10	EVA pod prepares to launch	–	+	–
11	Poole almost disappears from view	–	–	+
12	EVA pod rises up beside spaceship	–	+	–
13	EVA pod rises up beside spaceship	–	+	–
14	Poole "descends" through space	–	–	+
15	EVA pod ventures after Poole	–	+	–
16	EVA pod journeys away from spaceship	–	+	–
17	Poole "descends" through space	–	–	+
18	EVA pod locates Poole	–	+	–
19	EVA pod nears Poole	–	+	+
20	EVA pod grabs hold of Poole	–	+	+
21	EVA pod awaits pod bay doors to open	–	+	+
22	Medium shot of EVA pod waiting	–	+	+
23	EVA pod awaits pod bay doors to open	–	+	+
24	EVA pod awaits pod bay doors to open	–	+	+
25	Medium shot of EVA pod waiting	–	+	+
26	EVA pod awaits pod bay doors to open	–	+	+
27	EVA pod turns toward airlock	–	+	+
28	EVA pod releases Poole	–	+	+
29	EVA pod turns back toward spaceship	–	+	+
30	EVA pod extends arms toward airlock	–	+	–
31	EVA pod rotates locks on airlock	–	+	–
32	EVA pod successfully opens airlock	–	+	–
33	EVA pod rotates	–	+	–

From this table, we can see what Kubrick includes in the frame in outer space images and how they change over the course of the film. The first three sequences (A, B, C) are all from the second part of the film, the journey to see the monolith on the moon, and are unified by some shared characteristics. Likewise, the remaining sequences (D, E), both from the third section of the film, have much in common. We should thus treat sequences A, B, and C as a unit, and sequences D and E as another unit (although C is something of an "in between" sequence, a point to which we shall return). This makes sense in terms of plot: the first three sequences revolve around Floyd's journey to see the monolith, while the last two concern Bowman and Poole's efforts to fix an apparently faulty unit on their spacecraft while on the Jupiter mission eighteen months later.

What can we glean from this shot analysis? Celestial bodies are prevalent initially (A, B, and, to a lesser extent, C), but completely absent in the later sequences (D, E). This could be seen as merely a function of the plot: earlier sequences (A, B, C) are relatively local so that the earth, moon, and sun are never far from view, whereas the Jupiter mission (D, E) takes place in the middle of nowhere, cosmically speaking. But Kubrick could easily have set this part of the story in proximity to Jupiter. Given that Jupiter has at least sixty-nine moons, there'd be no shortage of celestial bodies to populate the frame. Indeed, Jupiter's moons *do* make an appearance eventually, coming into beautiful alignment immediately before Bowman is drawn into the Star Gate. The exclusion of celestial bodies from the mise en scène of the Jupiter mission appears deliberate. Plot alone cannot explain the later absence of celestial bodies.

So why this strategy? And, more importantly, what is its effect? Of course, we're dealing with distances that are mind-bogglingly large. Each exterior shot has us staring out into the infinite. The irony is, however, that this massive setting lacks the points of reference for apprehending depth that terrestrial images offer. Depth cues are an important part of mise en scène.[94] We know that outer space is unimaginably vast, but when gazing out into the undifferentiated black of space, we do not have the usual points of reference to convey its scale. Kubrick's use of planets helps. By putting a planet or moon in the background, Kubrick is able to create the ultimate deep-space compositions.[95] Take, for instance, the image of the lunar lander arriving, the uniformly black background gaining massive depth through the inclusion of Earth (fig. 5.3, top). Or consider the establishing shot of the scientists' arrival at the site of the newly discovered monolith. The depth of the image is enhanced by the positioning of Earth in the background as just a small element of the composition, reminding us of just how far from home we are (fig. 5.3, bottom). This strategy gives us a visual reference point for intuiting the vast expanses of

---

[94]Bordwell and Thompson, *Film Art*, 146.

[95]Bordwell and Thompson define deep-space compositions as those "in which a significant distance seems to separate planes." Bordwell and Thompson, *Film Art*, 148.

space. Deep-space composition is a feature of Kubrick's filmmaking style, but here it is taken to new heights—or new depths, to be precise.[96]

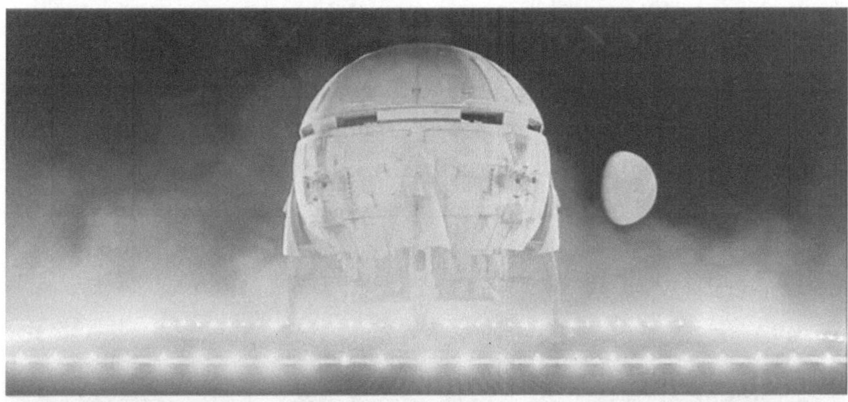

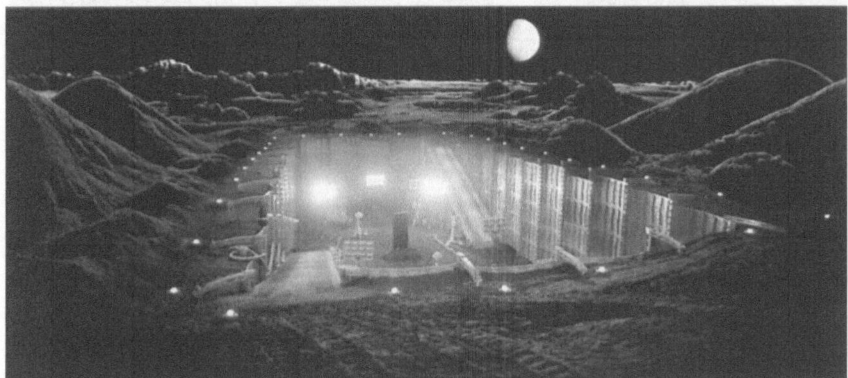

Figure 5.3. The inclusion of a celestial body, namely Earth, in these frames from *2001: A Space Odyssey* acts as a depth cue, conveying the vastness of space

Celestial bodies figure prominently in the first two exterior sequences (A, B), but are omitted completely from the last two exterior sequences (D, E). What about sequence C? It has only a moderate number of images that include celestial bodies. And those images that *do* include planets do so only as a small element of the composition, providing the depth cue to convey vastness that we discussed above without giving the image the same awesome beauty of those images in which the earth or moon dominate the frame. In that sense, sequence C is transitional. It shares with the earlier sequences a sense of proximity to home, yet lacks the majesty of the earlier sequences.

[96]Falsetto, *Stanley Kubrick*, 37.

The table also reveals the reverse happens with human figures: they don't figure in the frame of the earlier sequences, but do in the later sequences. Again, this is partly explicable in terms of plot; the astronauts must leave the safety of the spacecraft and spacewalk to the location of the instrument they believe to be defective. But seeing these characters exposed with nothing but a spacesuit between themselves and the infinite conveys the scale of space with more potency than an image of space with *no* human figure in the frame would. We imagine ourselves in that same position as these human bodies, powerless against the everlasting abyss of space. It conveys isolation in the most visceral way.

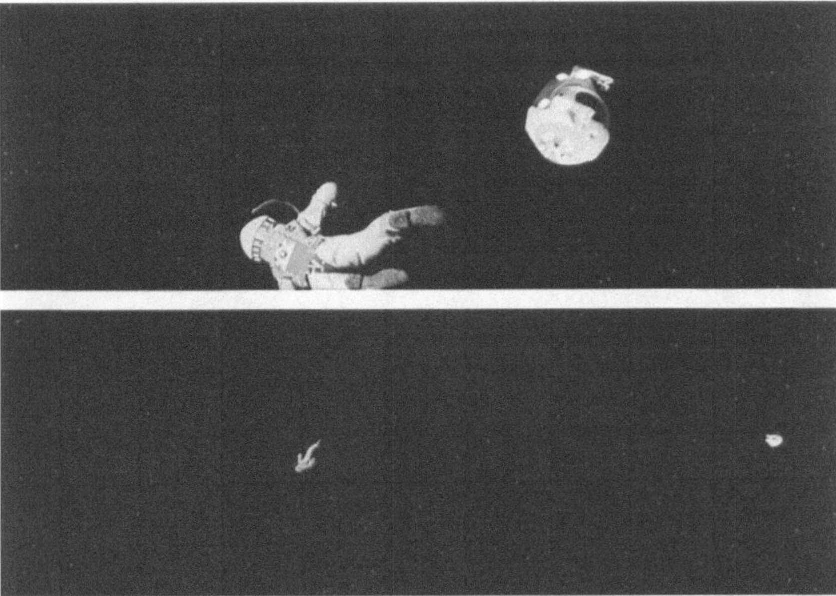

Figure 5.4. In this shot from *2001: A Space Odyssey*, size diminution acts as the only depth cue, depicting space as an abyss

Size diminution, in which the relative size of an object signals its distance, is an important device in this regard.[97] For example, when HAL cuts Poole loose, his body is flung out into space at great speed. The uniformly black background of space deprives us of the ability to pick out planes in the image, so our only depth cue is that his body and the pod decrease in size until they

---

[97]Bordwell and Thompson, *Film Art*, 147.

are little more than specks (fig. 5.4). Here there are no planets, just the black void of space. Ironically, the relative paucity of spatial reference points may convey a greater sense of distance. Space is so utterly empty, an abyss of the highest order, that the horror of his body hurtling through space infinitely and eternally is visceral and crushing. We are made to *feel* the boundlessness of space as an existential threat.

The exterior mise en scène is crafted to accentuate the "intimidating vastness of space,"[98] and the perception of vastness is a necessary facet of awe. According to psychologists Dacher Keltner and Jonathan Haidt, prototypical awe is comprised of two features: vastness and accommodation.[99] "A stimulus may convey vastness in physical space, in time, in number, in complexity of detail, in ability, even in volume of human experience."[100] So while we may be awed by the spatial vastness of the galaxy, we may equally be awed by its temporal vastness. Ebert thus writes that "*2001* is not concerned with thrilling us, but with inspiring our awe."[101] Theologian Bryan Stone writes that it "elicits a sense of awe both visually and in terms of its sound editing and musical composition."[102] One lay viewer rhapsodizes about being struck by "awe, ecstasy, and wonder!"[103]

One curious feature of awe is that it mixes seemingly contradictory feelings, positive and negative. Keltner and Haidt describe awe as being in "the upper reaches of pleasure and on the boundary of fear."[104] Awe is a characteristic response to the sublime, which is also similarly complex. We have already briefly touched on how *2001* conjures the temporal sublime through indirect means, encapsulated by the monolith. But (pace Kant) Kubrick also presents the sublime through direct means, the realistic depiction of outer space. Modern art has disabused us of the notion that art must always be beautiful, and we therefore perhaps do not share Kant's insistence that sublimity be

---

98 González, "Stanley Kubrick's '2001': An Existential Odyssey."

99 Keltner and Haidt, "Approaching Awe, a Moral, Spiritual, and Aesthetic Emotion," 304.

100 Michelle N. Shiota, Dacher Keltner, and Amanda Mossman, "The Nature of Awe: Elicitors, Appraisals, and Effects on Self-Concept," *Cognition & Emotion* 21, no. 5 (2007): 945, https://doi.org/10.1080/02699930600923668.

101 Ebert, "Great Movie: 2001: A Space Odyssey Review."

102 Bryan P. Stone, *Faith and Film: Theological Themes at the Cinema* (Atlanta: Chalice Press, 2000), 42.

103 Krovek, "The Epic of Evolution" (user review), 2008, www.imdb.com/title/tt0062622/reviews?sort=submissionDate&dir=asc&ratingFilter=0.

104 Keltner and Haidt, "Approaching Awe," 297.

represented "within" beauty. The earlier exterior shots (sequences A, B) tend toward awesome beauty, but as the celestial bodies are gradually removed from the frame and exposed human bodies are framed against the expanses of black space (D, E), the balance tips increasingly toward the sublime. Of course, this is not the only means by which awe is elicited. The Star Gate sequence, for example, reconfigures our sense of space, and yet is perhaps for some viewers even more awe-inspiring than the early photorealistic imagery of outer space. But the earlier solicitation of awe prepares us for even more intense experiences later. Thus, for Rowe, the Star Gate offers "a direct expression of the Romantic sublime,"[105] and indeed he even claims that "its narrative is virtually uninterpretable without recourse to the Romantic idea of the sublime image."[106]

Cognitivists Tan and Frijda note that "one stimulus of awesome sentiment is a filmic representation of an object that in reality, too, makes people fall silent."[107] An image that includes awe-inspiring phenomena in the frame often has the potential to be awe-inspiring itself, and few things in life elicit awe as reliably or as consistently as nature. One psychological study in which participants recounted their experiences of awe found that nature was the most common elicitor, ahead of the arts, personal accomplishment, social interaction, or another's accomplishment.[108] Moreover, the researchers found that the natural scenes that most reliably elicited awe were those that evoked a sense of mystery.[109] This makes sense, given that mystery by definition defies assimilation. *2001* is less about the natural world and more about the natural "*out-of-this*-world," yet it seems reasonable to assume that it is every bit as awe-inspiring as terrestrial nature, if not more so. The capacity of outer space to

---

[105]Rowe, "Romantic Model," 43, 49-50.

[106]Thomas, "Spiritual but Not Religious: The Influence of the Current Romantic Movement," 401. Theologian Owen C. Thomas points out that one of the primary similarities between the original Romantics and the "new Romantics" of the 1960s was their shared love of science fiction. It seems the sublime—and its paradigmatic response, awe—are deeply entwined with the genre that *2001* both redefined and exemplifies.

[107]Ed S. H. Tan and Nico H. Frijda, "Sentiment in Film Viewing," in *Passionate Views: Film, Cognition, and Emotion*, ed. Carl R. Plantinga and Greg M. Smith (Baltimore: Johns Hopkins University Press, 1999), 62.

[108]Shiota, Keltner, and Mossman, "Nature of Awe," 949. Although Keltner and Haidt included it in their prototypical study of awe, "encounter with God" as an elicitor was omitted from this study. Keltner and Haidt, "Approaching Awe," 305.

[109]Shiota, Keltner, and Mossman, "Nature of Awe," 951.

inspire awe is well known. The University of Central Florida even has a Space, Science, and Spirituality initiative. Armed only with comparatively rudimentary knowledge of the universe, the psalmist could claim the "heavens declare the glory of God" (Ps 19:1). That said, a celestial setting alone does not guarantee awe. Plenty of space movies fall far short of being awesome, so *2001*'s stylistic strategies are essential. Of course, the images in *2001* are not *actually* of space—filming took place very much on Earth!—but so sophisticated were Kubrick's techniques that verisimilitude is achieved. His exquisite images are not merely a backdrop to the drama. In *2001*, space *is* the drama.

The earlier exteriors (sequences A, B) feature images of elegance and beauty, while the later exteriors (C, D) feature images of emptiness and threat, a formal development that reflects the film's thematic concerns. Consider what in the mise en scène does *not* change: spacecraft, present in almost every frame. Why? Because this is a film about technology and humans' relationship to it. The Dawn of Man section opens with several barren landscapes, devoid of anything that might testify to the presence of (proto)humans. But in the second and third part of the film, gone are any images of *pure* "scenery"; humans or human artifacts feature in all exterior shots.[110] As the title of the first sequence suggests, this is indeed a story about the dawn of *humanity*.

Nevertheless, technology has been an inextricable part of that evolutionary process, the instrument that has propelled humankind to the stars. Yet the film's perspective on technology changes over the course of the film. The journey to the moon represents a technological highpoint, whereas HAL's malevolent turn on the Jupiter mission marks the unraveling of that technological optimism. Early on, spacecraft waltz with planets and glide through space in majestic images. Later, spacecraft grind their way across the vast, black void of space so total it threatens to swallow them up. The music echoes this narrative and thematic development: a lively waltz in the earlier sequences (A, B), exultant in human achievement; utter silence in the later exterior shots (D, E), accentuating isolation (again, sequence C is transitional: its music, *Atmosphères*, is orchestral like the earlier sequences, yet also ominous, anticipating the inhospitable atmosphere of deep space). A paean to technology turns into a lament—and warning—about the same.

---

[110]Although table 5.1 shows shot B.10 as having no spacecraft or human figures in the frame, it is in fact an image of a landing pad and thus includes a human artifact.

Intriguingly, the awe-eliciting potential is sustained throughout both these earlier and later sequences. How can we be awed both by pleasant and threatening images? That it may have either a positive or negative valence—that is to say, either "good" or "bad"—is an important feature of awe. Keltner and Haidt propose that awe is "flavored" by various additional "themes": threat, beauty, ability, virtue, and supernatural causality.[111] While a film like *Interstellar* (Christopher Nolan, 2014) is also an "awe-inspiring spectacle"[112] with "scenes . . . of marvellous beauty and awe,"[113] the type of awe it elicits is qualitatively different to that of *2001*. *Interstellar* scores high in terms of virtue. Characters wax poetic about love, going so far as to suggest that even the evolutionary process is undergirded by love. Threat figures prominently too, with humanity facing extinction, but it is neutered somewhat by the suggestion that the universe is ultimately benevolent, a place in which love acts as a transdimensional force. In *2001*, however, virtue is low and threat is high.

A discussion of the two films in terms of the other valence factors (beauty, ability, and supernatural causation) would be enlightening, but this brief look at virtue and threat will suffice. In *2001*, we can see that different "flavors" of awe may be elicited at different points during the film. The awe evoked by spacecraft moving gracefully between the earth and the moon is flavored by beauty; the awe evoked during the Jupiter mission, flavored by threat. And this may go some way toward explaining why these later exterior sequences seem particularly sublime.

AWE AND THE NUMINOUS

Awe in religious tradition and experience. "*2001: A Space Odyssey* is, for me, primarily about the experience of total awe," writes critic Killian Fox. González was similarly awed at his first viewing at a similar age, leading to a longstanding love affair with the film.[114] Awe seems to me to be crucial to the film's religious reception. Awe isn't always religious, nor is religion always awesome.

---

[111] Keltner and Haidt, "Approaching Awe," 304-5.

[112] Francesca Rudkin, "Movie Review: Interstellar," *NZ Herald*, November 6, 2014, www.nzherald.co.nz/entertainment/news/article.cfm?c_id=1501119&objectid=11353493.

[113] Justin Craig, "'Interstellar' Review: Matthew McConaughey Shines, but Anne Hathaway Is Miscast," Fox News, updated August 31, 2014, www.foxnews.com/entertainment/2014/11/03/interstellar-review-matthew-mcconaughey-shines-but-anne-hathaway-is-miscast.html.

[114] González, "Stanley Kubrick's '2001.'"

But there is a strong connection between awe and religion, a fact to which viewers' response to *2001* testifies.

Awe is a common feature of religion, particularly in response to divine encounter. Scripture is replete with examples of characters awestruck by an experience of God.[115] They typically respond with fear, reverence, and submission, all reactions characteristic of awe. The biblical injunction to "Fear the Lord your God" (Deut 6:13) could be taken as a command to stand in *awe* of Yahweh, the appropriate response to the holiness of God. Indeed, in scriptural instances of theophany, fear seems inevitable, as the recipient is often urged *not* to fear (e.g., Gen 15:1, Judg 6:23).[116] Awe figures prominently in other religious traditions too. In the Hindu Bhagavad-Gita, Arjuna receives a spectacular vision that leaves him "bewildered and astonished, his hair standing on end" (11:14) and says, "I am gladdened, but at the same time my mind is disturbed with fear" (11:45).

Recent psychological research also suggests that feelings of awe often accompany religious experience. Religious psychologist Louise Sundararajan has shown how in mysticism, the divine defies understanding, a hallmark of apophatic theology, meaning that any attempt at assimilation fails and the mystical experience thus requires "radical accommodation."[117] It is during this time of cognitive upheaval that the mystic experiences the oft-reported "dark night of the soul."[118] According to Sundararajan, the willingness to embrace the experience ("avowal") transforms this from a potentially traumatic experience into a healthy one.[119]

Awe may also increase belief in God. A study on the effects of awe on supernatural belief found not only correlation, but causation: experiences of awe were found to have a causal effect on supernatural belief and belief in the divine (mediated by an increase in agency detection, the impulse to look for an agent behind events).[120] And the fact that some psychologists believe "awe-inducing

---

115 Cf. Gen 28:17; Ex 3:6; Is 6:5; Ezek 1:28; Acts 9:3.

116 Samuel Terrien, "Fear," in *The Interpreter's Dictionary of the Bible*, ed. George Arthur Buttrick (New York: Abingdon, 1962), 256-57.

117 Louise Sundararajan, "Religious Awe: Potential Contributions of Negative Theology to Psychology, 'Positive' or Otherwise," *Journal of Theoretical and Philosophical Psychology* 22, no. 2 (2002): 175, https://doi.org/10.1037/h0091221.

118 Sundararajan, "Religious Awe," 175.

119 Sundararajan, "Religious Awe," 181.

120 P. Valdesolo and J. Graham, "Awe, Uncertainty, and Agency Detection," *Psychological Science* 25,

events may be one of the fastest and most powerful methods of personal change and growth" surely holds important ramifications for religious transformation.[121]

Rudolf Otto and the numinous. One of the most seminal thinkers about awe's relationship to religion is German theologian Rudolf Otto. Otto held that at the heart of all religion is the holy,[122] comprised of the numen, an ineffable presence to which the paradigmatic feeling response is numinous experience. Otto wrote in German, but cited the English word *awe* as a close approximation of numinous feeling.[123] C. S. Lewis, himself profoundly influenced by Otto,[124] wrote, "We have in English an exact name for the emotion aroused by the Numinous which Otto, writing in German, lacked; we have the word Awe."[125] It would be fair to say numinous experience is a particular type of awe, one that accompanies certain religious experiences.

There are resonances of numinous experience in the sublime. Religious scholar Lynn Poland writes, "Throughout its history the status of the sublime has hovered between the aesthetic and religious."[126] Numinous feeling is complex, blending the repellent with the attractive. Such "complex pleasure" is a feature also of the sublime, what French literature scholar Robert Doran calls the "dual transcendence-structure of sublimity,"[127] insofar as the sublime paradoxically blends both the feeling of being overwhelmed with that of being exalted, and the sense of inferiority with superiority.[128] The same is true of awe. Though in Keltner and Haidt's model, awe does not *require* fear, it is certainly

---

no. 1 (2014): 9-13, https://doi.org/10.1177/0956797613501884. Increases in agency detection are due, in part, to greater "intolerance of uncertainty," thereby motivating a desire for a causal explanation, that is, an agent. Interestingly, other studies have shown that *dispositionally* awe-prone people—that is, those who tend to experience awe more regularly in life—are *more* comfortable with ambiguity. Michelle N. Shiota, "Comment: The Science of Positive Emotion: You've Come a Long Way, Baby/There's Still a Long Way to Go," *Emotion Review* 9, no. 3 (2017): 236, https://doi.org/10.1177/1754073917692665.

[121] Keltner and Haidt, "Approaching Awe," 312.

[122] Rudolf Otto, *The Idea of the Holy: An Inquiry into the Non-Rational Factor in the Idea of the Divine and Its Relation to the Rational*, trans. John W. Harvey, 2nd ed. (London: Oxford University Press, 1950), 6.

[123] Otto, *Idea of the Holy*, 14.

[124] Andrew Walker, "Scripture, Revelation and Platonism in C. S. Lewis," *Scottish Journal of Theology* 55, no. 1 (2002): 29.

[125] C. S. Lewis, *God in the Dock: Essays on Theology and Ethics* (Grand Rapids, MI: Eerdmans, 1970), 174.

[126] Lynn Poland, "The Idea of the Holy and the History of the Sublime," *The Journal of Religion* 72, no. 2 (1992): 180, https://doi.org/10.1086/488862.

[127] Doran, *Theory of the Sublime*, 11.

[128] Doran, *Theory of the Sublime*, 9-11.

a common feature. This duality is reflected in English vernacular; something that elicits awe may be positive, as in the ubiquitous colloquialism *awesome!*, or negative, as in *awful*. Doran writes that "what unites the key theories of sublimity . . . is a common structure—the paradoxical experience of at once being *overwhelmed* and *exalted*—and a common concern: the preservation of a notion of transcendence in the face of the secularization of modern culture."[129]

Doran's latter point warrants elaboration. It's no coincidence that the sublime enjoyed a renaissance in the eighteenth century just as secularization was on the rise. Like Doran, Poland sees this as a symptom of, and an attempt to "cure" secularization.[130] Thus, Doran calls the sublime a "secular analog of religious transcendence."[131] Otto himself notes the similarity of the sublime to numinous experience, writing that "the sublime exhibits the same peculiar dual character as the numinous."[132] But, for Otto, the sublime is mere *analogy*. The numinous is in a category all its own, distinct from the sublime in nature or everyday awe, though the sublime "is well adapted to excite [the numinous] and be excited by it."[133]

Otto famously characterized the numen as *mysterium tremendum et fascinans*: *mysterium*, because it is wholly other;[134] *tremendum*, because it inspires fear of a distinct sort, namely uncanniness (i.e., "spooky");[135] and *fascinans*, because far from being repellent, it is in fact alluring.[136] This is an opportune moment to return to the question of the monolith's identity. "Is it God? Is it some other cosmic force?" wonders Wall. "Kubrick's film does not provide an answer."[137] Clearly some viewers take the monolith to represent God, but that's far from being the only interpretation. When offering a "lowest level" explanation of the plot, Kubrick refers to the monolith as "an artifact left on earth four million years ago by alien explorers."[138] This matches Clarke's comments and his novelization of the film.[139]

---

[129]Doran, *Theory of the Sublime*, 4; emphasis original.
[130]Poland, "Idea of the Holy," 180-83.
[131]Doran, *Theory of the Sublime*, 12.
[132]Otto, *Idea of the Holy*, 42.
[133]Otto, *Idea of the Holy*, 42.
[134]Otto, *Idea of the Holy*, 25-30.
[135]Otto, *Idea of the Holy*, 13-24.
[136]Otto, *Idea of the Holy*, 31-40.
[137]Wall, "2001: A Space Odyssey," 46.
[138]Gelmis, "Film Director as Superstar."
[139]Bernstein, "Beyond the Stars," 18.

But if it's nothing more than extraterrestrial life, why do so many associate the monolith with God, or at the very least, admit the possibility? The depiction of the monolith suggests more than "mere" aliens. English literature scholar Philip Kuberski reports that Kubrick found representing aliens convincingly impossible, which thus allowed "Kubrick to dispense with aliens as an instrument of human development and to ponder the void itself."[140] It is evident from Kubrick's remarks during interviews that he still envisages extraterrestrial life as an integral part of the film, and yet there is something "more" to his treatment. Contrary to conventional depictions of alien life, the monolith is "an absence"[141] a "*via negativa* . . . marking an unknown [people or characters] can acknowledge but not understand."[142] Though commonly referred to as a *monolith*—"single stone," etymologically—it is radically distinct from the irregular rock of the surrounding landscape; its "geometric perfection marks it as wholly 'Other.'"[143] It is an instance of, or analogous to the *mysterium tremendum et fascinans*.

Consider the hominids' reaction to its sudden appearance. It is mysterious: its arrival, unexpected; its origin, unknown; its purpose, inscrutable. Its impeccable form marks it as wholly other, and thus qualifies as *mysterium*.[144] It is also *tremendum*, hysteria descending immediately upon the frightened protohumans as they encircle it skittishly. But they do indeed encircle it, with one even daring to reach out and touch it in trepidation *and* adoration. It is this alluring quality, the *fascinans*, that is most striking and novel. Although modern humans seem less awed by the monolith than their evolutionary ancestors,[145] the same primal impulse is evident behind the cool façade. The scientists are confused about its identity (*mysterium*); treat it with extreme caution, outfitting the site in elaborate scientific paraphernalia (*tremendum*); and are irresistibly drawn to it (*fascinans*). Floyd is also seduced into reaching out and touching. Despite appearing inert, the monolith has "super agency"; its effect on all who dare approach marks it as an entity of great power—indeed,

---

[140]Philip Kuberski, *Kubrick's Total Cinema: Philosophical Themes and Formal Qualities* (London: A&C Black, 2012), 163.

[141]Kuberski, *Kubrick's Total Cinema*, 166.

[142]Loughlin, *Alien Sex*, 71.

[143]Burnette-Bletsch, "2001: A Space Odyssey," 5.

[144]Burnette-Bletsch, "2001: A Space Odyssey," 5.

[145]Kuberski, *Kubrick's Total Cinema*, 168.

"*numinous* power."[146] That the hominids experience the numinous does not necessarily mean the monolith is divine, and yet the intimation is inescapable. Recall that Kubrick sees the film as offering a "scientific definition of God,"[147] and when challenged about the theological relevance of alien life, he replied that these "beings would *be* gods to the billions of less advanced races."[148] For Kubrick, this is a film about alien life *and* divine life, the two inextricably entwined. However heterodox, in *2001*, Kubrick is presenting a *theology*.

Of course, the theology of *2001* is a far cry from classical theology. As Burnette-Bletsch notes, the film "affirms the possibility of a guiding force behind human evolution though not necessarily the god of traditional religion."[149] Stone observes that the monolith

> bears little resemblance to the "living God" of the Bible. . . . The monolith merely appears and sits there, and though it affects us, we do not, in turn, appear to affect the monolith. The God of the Bible, on the other hand, is lively and dynamic, the one who is present with us and yet always out ahead of us, the one who enjoys and experiences us.[150]

And the impersonal monolith, cold and aloof, apparently lacks God's most fundamental characteristic: love. *2001* therefore invites significant theological critique. Nevertheless, the monolith is a compelling depiction of the numinous, almost singular in its efficacy. Religious studies scholar Jason D. Fuller has noted that some of his students struggle to understand Otto's concepts—until he has them watch the first half-hour of *2001*, at which point the numinous makes sense.[151] The "scientific God" of *2001* may not align neatly with the God of Scripture, but it draws out an aspect of divine encounter that might otherwise remain foreign and inaccessible to some.

Challenges to Otto's concept of the numinous. Otto's account has real theological value, though it has in some senses been underappreciated. I agree with religious studies scholar Philip Almond's assessment, that Otto's is "an insightful [analysis] . . . enormously suggestive as a way of seeing parallels across

[146]Kuberski, *Kubrick's Total Cinema*, 156; emphasis mine.

[147]Gelmis, "Film Director as Superstar," 93.

[148]Nordern, "Playboy Interview: Stanley Kubrick," 50.

[149]Burnette-Bletsch, "2001: A Space Odyssey," 8.

[150]Stone, *Faith and Film*, 43.

[151]Jason D. Fuller, "Dreaded Monoliths: Rudolf Otto's Das Heilige and 2001: A Space Odyssey," *Teaching Theology & Religion* 12, no. 1 (2009).

religious traditions, and the distinction between *tremendum* and *fascinans* captures a polarity that is present in many, especially the Semitic, traditions."[152] In her *Rudolf Otto and the Concept of Holiness*, Jewish theologian Melissa Raphael writes that she has

> chosen to classify and interpret Otto's concept of holiness as a form of philosophical theology, and to show that numinous experience is a useful category of theological analysis. Despite the widespread view among theologians and biblical scholars that Otto's work is of a generalized significance to the history of religious studies, I argue that the object of his research, the holy, is, or should be, at the heart of theology.[153]

In Otto's day, a common view among liberal Protestants was that the primitive Hebrew concept of sacerdotal holiness had been eclipsed by a more refined ethical version of holiness found in the Old Testament prophets and Jesus.[154] But Otto demonstrates that the former so-called primitive view is alive and well in the modern age. Yes, the holy is comprised of rational, moral purity, but also of nonrational, numinous feeling. For Otto, the nonrational numinous plus rational moral goodness equals the holy.[155] He offers us a useful corrective and a valuable, if overlooked, theological resource.[156]

But there are problems too. Otto's legacy has been tarnished by the cultural context in which his thought emerged and, it should be pointed out, in which it proved enormously popular.[157] The concept of the numinous, in which power is separated from morality, fits the post–World War I German milieu, becoming an "*unwitting* preview of the Nazis' divorce of moral values from the exercise of power."[158] There is indeed a "numinosity of great evil," which Raphael herself sensed when visiting Babi Yar, the site of a massacre in which German and Ukrainian forces murdered nearly 34,000 Jews during World War II.[159] This is why Otto's account of the numinous has often been invoked in

[152]Philip C. Almond, *Rudolf Otto, An Introduction to His Philosophical Theology* (Chapel Hill: University of North Carolina Press, 1984), 86-87.

[153]Melissa Raphael, *Rudolf Otto and the Concept of Holiness* (Oxford: Clarendon, 1997), ebook, 17-18; emphasis original.

[154]Raphael, *Rudolf Otto*, 49.

[155]Otto, *Idea of the Holy*, 6-7.

[156]Raphael, *Rudolf Otto*, 83.

[157]Raphael, *Rudolf Otto*, 73-84.

[158]Raphael, *Rudolf Otto*, 76; emphasis original.

[159]Raphael, *Rudolf Otto*, 78.

discussions of horror movies.[160] As a result, some harbor significant misgivings. The concept of the numinous is susceptible to misuse and abuse.[161] Biblical scholar Samuel Terrien warns that any talk of the numinous must be sufficiently qualified, since the God of Scripture is personal and gracious, neither of which are necessary attributes of the numen.[162] To anyone who would champion the concept of the numinous without qualification or nuance, Nazi Germany serves as a cautionary tale. This is especially so in an age in which White supremacists, particularly in the US, have been emboldened (and whose own intimidation tactics have often historically employed "awe-full" aesthetics).[163]

But the association with evil and horror is a gross distortion of Otto's thought (Otto himself was no Nazi sympathizer, having become deeply depressed by the suicide of his Jewish friend Hermann Jacobsohn in 1933 and by being unable to adopt Jacobsohn's son afterward).[164] Those who would appropriate the numinous to evil ends do so highly selectively. Raphael notes that "discussion of the relation of holiness and horror parodies Otto's argument by neglecting his injunction that, despite its nonrational essence, religion is best served when penetrated by rationality. It mistakes Otto's defense of the 'not-yet rational' for promotion of the irrational."[165]

This "rationality" is God's moral perfection. "Otto's concept of holiness holds the rational and nonrational elements of religion in creative tension, and as such it has a corrective function as a *via media* through the contemporary religious situation."[166] In service of evil, the numinous tends to be all *tremendum* and no *fascinans*. Caroline Franks Davis points out that numinous feeling brings with it a strong desire for union with the numen, a painful yearning that is paradoxically blissful,[167] much like Lewis's notion of *Sehnsucht*.[168] Sheer terror thus lacks this indispensable *fascinans* element of the

[160]Noël Carroll, *The Philosophy of Horror, or Paradoxes of the Heart* (New York: Routledge, 1990), 165.
[161]Raphael, *Rudolf Otto*, 80-81.
[162]Terrien, "Fear," 258.
[163]Maggie Astor, "A Guide to the Charlottesville Aftermath," *The New York Times*, August 13, 2017, www.nytimes.com/2017/08/13/us/charlottesville-virginia-overview.html?mcubz=1.
[164]Almond, *Rudolf Otto*, 25, 147n85.
[165]Raphael, *Rudolf Otto*, 78.
[166]Raphael, *Rudolf Otto*, 22.
[167]Caroline Franks Davis, *The Evidential Force of Religious Experience* (Oxford: Oxford University Press, 1989), 173.
[168]Walker, "Scripture, Revelation and Platonism in C. S. Lewis," 30-31.

numinous. If we overemphasize *tremendum* at the expense of *fascinans*, we're in dangerous territory.

Ecological theologians, too, have objected to Otto's thought in regard to the sacred-profane distinction implied by the concept of holiness. According to this line of thought, holiness desacralizes creation, leaving it vulnerable to human exploitation. A feminist theologian, Raphael is sympathetic to this critique, yet maintains the distinction, recasting the profane as a way of naming oppression. Exploitation profanes an otherwise sacred creation. As such, the concept of holiness may play a prophetic role.[169] *2001* may be understood to be similarly prophetic. A celebration of technology turns into a warning about technology. Our technological hubris may be our undoing, and by it we may profane creation.[170]

Critiques notwithstanding, Raphael wants to preserve the notion of holiness, "the essence of divine being."[171] Yet despite her claim that in both "Jewish and Christian theology God is, above all other gods, worthy of worship because he alone is holy," Christian theology posits a different divine essence.[172] Granted, some Christian theologians have claimed holiness as the fundamental divine attribute,[173] but others, like Stanley Grenz, argue that "love is the eternal essence of the one God. But this means that trinitarian love is not merely one attribute of God among many. Rather, love is the fundamental 'attribute' of God. 'God is love' is the foundational ontological statement we can declare concerning the divine essence."[174]

The uniquely Christian doctrine of the Trinity is the basis for this claim. Strictly speaking, love is not an *attribute*; it describes the very being of God. Holiness, on the other hand, is an attribute of God, a function of divine love.[175] Hebrew thought likewise understands God's holiness in relation to God's love. For example, Jacob's exclamation, "How awesome is this place!" is coupled with "This is none other than the house of God; this is the gate of heaven"

[169]Raphael, *Rudolf Otto*, 177-85.

[170]Even here, however, the divine in *2001*, however understood, remains "sovereign," guiding humanity to its next evolutionary stage despite our technological hubris.

[171]Raphael, *Rudolf Otto*, 86.

[172]Raphael, *Rudolf Otto*, 86.

[173]For example, see James Muilenburg, "Holiness," in *The Interpreter's Dictionary of the Bible*, ed. George Arthur Buttrick (New York: Abingdon, 1962).

[174]Stanley J. Grenz, *Theology for the Community of God* (Grand Rapids, MI: Eerdmans, 2000), chap. 2.

[175]Murray Rae, August 28, 2017.

(Gen 28:17), demonstrating that his "experience of dread is inseparable from the reaffirmed sense of his destiny and the acceptance of a 'tremendous' promise of land."[176] The Trinity, however, offers a more robust foundation for situating holiness within God's love, allowing us to speak of divine holiness without allowing it to be co-opted by evil.

While Otto talks about awe with respect to experience, for Jewish theologian Abraham Heschel, it names an entire way of life: "Awe is a way of being in rapport with the mystery of all reality."[177] Indeed, it is the supreme way of life, Judaism's cardinal virtue being not faith, but awe.[178] Thus, the faithful Jew is *yare hashem*,[179] "one who holds God in awe."[180] Even in the New Testament, the faithful are occasionally described as "those who fear him" (Lk 1:50; 18:2, 4).[181] That the women to first hear of Jesus' resurrection left "afraid yet filled with joy" (Mt 28:8) again points to a complexity of feeling that suggests awe rather than sheer terror.[182] Thus, Heschel's words are as applicable to the Christian as they are to the Jew: "The beginning of awe is wonder, and the beginning of wisdom is awe."[183]

Jerome Agel's pastiche book *The Making of Kubrick's* 2001, includes a section titled, "Interviews with Scientists and Theologians"—an unlikely, but telling pairing.[184] This is sci-fi with exceptional capacity to prompt theological reflection. And the *type* of theological reflection it invites may be especially challenging to views of God that are overly chummy. Raphael rightly notes that certain "forms of Christian fundamentalism . . . domesticate the numen."[185] *2001* posits a God-like presence at work in the cosmos, eliciting awe and depicting numinous experience in a manner that may impart a richer theological understanding to those who would tame God.

---

[176]Terrien, "Fear," 258.

[177]Abraham Joshua Heschel, *God in Search of Man: A Philosophy of Judaism* (New York: Octagon Books, 1972), 74.

[178]The Hebrew *yirah* can mean "fear" but is more fundamentally "awe." Heschel, *God in Search of Man*, 76-77.

[179]Heschel, *God in Search of Man*, 77.

[180]Eugene B. Borowitz and Frances Weinman Schwartz, *The Jewish Moral Virtues* (Philadelphia: Jewish Publication Society, 1999), 312.

[181]Terrien, "Fear," 259.

[182]Terrien, "Fear," 259.

[183]Heschel, *God in Search of Man*, 74.

[184]Agel, *Making of Kubrick's* 2001.

[185]Raphael, *Rudolf Otto*, 22.

None of this is meant to imply that revelation is inevitable. When viewers report a heightened sense of spiritual or divine reality, this can't be taken as "proof" of revelation. But what *2001* may do is to invite an experience of awe, which may in turn prompt a greater receptivity to the divine. The most famous line of dialogue from Clarke's concurrent *2001* novel has become synonymous with awe, as the gobsmacked astronaut utters, "Oh my God!—*it's full of stars!*"[186] We're accustomed to hearing God's name uttered in this way without the least thought being given to God. But, for some viewers, *2001* stands in a long tradition, evident for instance in Psalm 8, in which contemplation of the vast expanse of the heavens leads precisely to the confession of God.

[186]Clarke, *2001: A Space Odyssey*, 202.

6

Magnolia

Divine Action, Connectedness, and Editing

Magnolia (Paul Thomas Anderson, 1999)[1] was released on the cusp of the new millennium, a time when apocalyptic concerns were at the forefront of popular consciousness. *Entertainment Weekly* had already christened 1999 "The Year That Changed Movies" in recognition of the sudden spate of films that dispensed with the old rules and enthusiastically embraced exciting and original styles of filmmaking.[2] *Magnolia* was named among that crop, yet just as this film rushed headlong into this supposed new era of filmmaking, it also called viewers' attention to the ancient past, specifically to an ancient text. In ways both subtle and overt, the film referenced, quoted, and echoed the Bible, thereby embodying the film's own repeated adage that "we may be through with the past, but the past is not through with us." The scriptural allusions, along with a diverse range of formal qualities and narrative components, worked together to evoke for some viewers a sense of divine presence in a context of millennial uncertainty. One distinctive of *Magnolia*'s religious quality is its collective orientation, a feature of network narratives generally but one that is consistently underscored and amplified through various other strategies specific to *Magnolia*. For that reason, this chapter has a special emphasis on editing, which weaves together disparate characters and lives into a larger tapestry.

---

[1]Ranked #82, "Top 100 Films—2020," *Arts & Faith*, accessed January 3, 2022, http://artsandfaith.com/index.php?/films/&do=year&id=8&page=2. Previously ranked #16, "Top 100 Films," *Arts & Faith*, accessed January 3, 2022, https://imagejournal.org/top-100-films/.

[2]Jeff Gordinier, "1999: The Year That Changed Movies," *Entertainment Weekly*, November 26, 1999, www.ew.com/ew/article/0,,271806,00.html.

MAGNOLIA

Religious reception. *Magnolia* might seem an unlikely choice of film for a project like this one. Little about the film is overtly religious; indeed, much is unabashedly "profane." Much of the academic literature on it has therefore been nonreligious, often taking the form of ideological criticism, especially feminist critiques of patriarchy.[3] Nevertheless, a sizable number of religiously minded scholars have engaged with it along theological lines. The biblical allusions, buried deep in the mise en scène or heard as a mumbled aside, are subtle yet unambiguous, and have thus opened the film up to a range of theological interpretations. Many film scholars have noted the scriptural motif,[4] but the more sustained religious treatments have come from theologians. Callaway has interacted theologically with *Magnolia*'s music.[5] Johnston has put the film into dialogue with Ecclesiastes as mutually illuminating sources of wisdom, also with a special emphasis on the music.[6] The analysis proffered by Catholic Theodora Hawksley details a Barthian take on the film's aural dimensions with a focus on nonmusical sound. A liberationist perspective has been adopted by theologian and filmmaker Mario DeGiglio-Bellemare.[7] In a less scholarly treatment, pastor Shane Hipps has similarly used the exodus as a lens for viewing the film.[8] Biblical scholar Erin Runions and theologian David Congdon have both separately advanced apocalyptic analyses.[9] Meanwhile, Old Testament scholar Jason M. Silverman has countered these apocalyptic approaches by taking a prophetic angle.[10]

---

[3]For example, see Joanne Clarke Dillman, "Twelve Characters in Search of a Televisual Text: Magnolia Masquerading as Soap Opera," *Journal of Popular Film and Television* 33, no. 3 (2005).

[4]For example, see Dillman, "Twelve Characters," 147; Gwendolyn Audrey Foster, "Magnolia Film Analysis," *Senses of Cinema* (2015), http://sensesofcinema.com/2015/cteq/magnolia-a-savage-attack-on-masculinity-and-whiteness/; Christina Lane, *Magnolia* (Hoboken, NJ: John Wiley & Sons, 2011), 6.

[5]Kutter Callaway, *Scoring Transcendence: Contemporary Film Music as Religious Experience* (Waco, TX: Baylor University Press, 2013).

[6]Robert K. Johnston, *Useless Beauty: Ecclesiastes Through the Lens of Contemporary Film* (Grand Rapids, MI: Baker Academic, 2004), 73-92.

[7]Mario DeGiglio-Bellemare, "Magnolia and the Signs of the Times: A Theological Reflection," *Journal of Religion & Film* 4, no. 2 (2000), http://digitalcommons.unomaha.edu/jrf/vol4/iss2/4.

[8]Shane Hipps, "Magnolia: The Exodus for Kids," May 2003.

[9]Erin Runions, "Falling Frogs and Family Traumas: Mediating Apocalypse in Magnolia with Adrienne Gibb," in *How Hysterical* (New York: Palgrave Macmillan, 2003); David Congdon, "Reconsidering Apocalyptic Cinema: Pauline Apocalyptic and Paul Thomas Anderson," *Journal of Religion and Popular Culture* 24, no. 3 (2012).

[10]Jason M. Silverman, "We May Be Through with the Past," *Religion and the Arts* 20, no. 4 (2016).

Though scholars have pored over the scriptural minutiae of the mise en scène, Anderson has consistently denied any prior awareness of biblical allusions in his film. Instead, the director has claimed inspiration from paranormal chronicler Charles Fort, whose work includes reports of frogs falling from the sky, a phenomenon depicted in the film.[11] It was only when Anderson learned about the biblical connection after the fact that he began embedding scriptural allusions into the film as "a fun directorial, bored-on-the-set thing to do."[12] Well, that's the official line. But Silverman argues that Anderson perhaps wasn't as oblivious to the biblical echoes as he claims. How so? The film explicitly and repeatedly quotes a line from Bergen Evans's rationalist tome *The Natural History of Nonsense* (without acknowledging the source): "We may be through with the past, but the past is not through with us."[13] Evans references Charles Fort's work, dismissing his reports of frog rain. Silverman thus concludes, "This raises the suspicion that the inspiration [for the frog storm] originally came from Evans and was either forgotten/misremembered or Fort was given as a form of misdirection. Certainly one could hardly find more different sorts of authors."[14] This is significant only insofar as the quotation above is lifted from a chapter in which Evans skeptically addresses biblical curiosities, like whether or not Adam and Eve had bellybuttons. So it's likely then that Anderson was aware of the biblical connotations that a deluge of frogs would hold for many viewers.[15]

But while speculation about the Bible's role in Anderson's creative process is interesting, it is more pertinent to note Anderson's explicit comments about the biblical and religious facets of his artistic vision. Even if Anderson's claim of initial biblical ignorance is correct, the array of references to Exodus 8:2 discreetly peppered throughout the film is intentional. When, having explained the gimmicky nature of the Exodus allusions, an interviewer surmised a lack of a meaningful biblical connection, Anderson replied emphatically to the contrary. There *is* indeed a substantial link, he said, then refused

[11]For example, see Chuck Stephens, "Interview," in *Magnolia: The Shooting Script*, ed. Paul Thomas Anderson (New York: Dey Street Press, 2000).

[12]Chris Garcia, "All Paul Thomas Anderson Does," *The Austin American Statesman*, January 6, 2000, http://cigsandredvines.blogspot.co.nz/2000/01/interview-austin-american-statesman.html.

[13]Also, though not in the film, the published screenplay has a copy of Evans's book appear on Stanley's desk. Paul Thomas Anderson, *Magnolia: The Shooting Script*.

[14]Silverman, "We May Be Through with the Past," 467.

[15]Silverman, "We May Be Through with the Past," 466-68.

to elaborate.[16] Anderson was raised Catholic, and has said, possibly facetiously, that *Magnolia* is a form of personal confession.[17] In an interview with Anderson, journalist Edward Guthmann writes that *Magnolia* "grew from the fact that 'I [Anderson] have experienced a lot of death in my life the last couple of years' and says he 'latched on to a kind of spirituality' after that period."[18] According to Guthmann, "Anderson acknowledges a spiritual theme in *Magnolia,* and sees his film as something of a wake-up call—a cautionary tale about the ways in which we forget to be accountable to one another, and the importance of being morally responsible."[19] This seems to reflect his frequent reference to the notion of frogs as an index of a society's health,[20] frogs being what scientists term an *indicator species.* As an explanation for the frogs, Anderson says,

> Maybe there are certain moments in your life when things are so f——ed up and so confused that someone can say to you, "It's raining frogs," and that makes sense. That somehow makes sense as a warning; that somehow makes sense as a sign. I started to understand why people turn to religion in times of trouble, and maybe my form of finding religion was reading about rains of frogs and realizing that makes sense to me somehow. And then of course to discover it in the Bible and the reference that it makes there just sort of verifies it, like, "Hey, I guess I'm on the right track."[21]

In a similar vein, elsewhere Anderson says,

> It wasn't until after I got through with the writing that I began to discover what it might mean, which was this: You get to a point in your life, and sh—t is happening, and everything's out of your control, and suddenly, a rain of frogs just makes sense . . . I just found myself at a point where I was going through some sh—tty stuff and I was ready for some sort of weird religious experience, or as close as I could get to one.[22]

---

[16]Garcia, "All Paul Thomas Anderson Does."

[17]Lynn Hirschberg, "His Way," *The New York Times Magazine,* December 19, 1999, www.nytimes.com/1999/12/19/magazine/his-way.html.

[18]Edward Guthmann, "The Actor's Director," *San Francisco Chronicle,* January 2, 2000, www.sfgate.com/entertainment/article/The-Actor-s-Director-Magnolia-filmmaker-Paul-2814488.php.

[19]Guthmann, "Actor's Director."

[20]Stephens, "Interview."

[21]David Konow, "P.T.A. Meeting," *Creative Screenwriting,* January 2000, http://cigsandredvines.blogspot.co.nz/2000/01/interview-creative-screenwriting.html.

[22]Stephens, "Interview."

Anderson encourages divergent interpretations of the frogs: "There absolutely is no wrong way [to interpret the frog storm]. If you want to reference the Bible, that's good; if you want to link it to something else you can."[23] But clearly there's an association in his mind between the frog storm, religion, and spirituality.

Some viewers too have found *Magnolia* to be religiously meaningful. In 2003–2004, the film was included in the Museum of Modern Art's "The Hidden God" exhibition, a presentation of thirty films that have "simultaneously insinuated and disguised the mystery that believers call God,"[24] taking its place alongside staples of religious cinema. And the biblical allusions are not lost on audiences. Viewers remark on the "biblical style . . . [of the] last leg of the film,"[25] and "an apocalyptic, biblical ending."[26] One reviewer reasons that "these [characters'] problems are so big, it makes sense for something of biblical proportions to solve them,"[27] while another calls it a "secular interpretation of the Bible."[28] Others interpret the film not just biblically, but also theologically. According to various lay critics, the film suggests "a higher force,"[29] "the existence of a higher power,"[30] and that strange things "are caused by some higher power, God for most of us."[31] In the words of one reviewer, this is a "movie filled with broken people, unforgivable sins, and divine intervention,"[32] or to quote another, "Strange Occurrences and Divine Intervention."[33] It is, therefore, "a spiritual way to end such an epic piece of film making."[34]

---

[23]Konow, "P.T.A. Meeting."

[24]"The Hidden God: Film and Faith," Museum of Modern Art, 2003, accessed November 9, 2017, www.moma.org/calendar/film/787.

[25]Kwong C, "User Review of 'Magnolia' (Rotten Tomatoes)," 2012, www.rottentomatoes.com/m/magnolia/reviews/?page=21&type=user.

[26]Gregory G, "User Review of 'Magnolia' (Rotten Tomatoes)," 2011, www.rottentomatoes.com/m/magnolia/reviews/?page=40&type=user.

[27]John M, "User Review of 'Magnolia' (Rotten Tomatoes)," 2011, www.rottentomatoes.com/m/magnolia/reviews/?page=40&type=user.

[28]Shane S, "User Review of 'Magnolia' (Rotten Tomatoes)," 2010, www.rottentomatoes.com/m/magnolia/reviews/?page=51&type=user&sort=.

[29]Phisk, "A Film Which Impresses with Great Performances, a Great Storyline and Maybe the Best Beginning Ever," 2011, www.imdb.com/title/tt0175880/reviews?count=1452&start=30.

[30]Andrew M, "User Review of 'Magnolia' (Rotten Tomatoes)," 2011, www.rottentomatoes.com/m/magnolia/reviews/?page=48&type=user.

[31]TxMike, "Fascinating Film, Unique Story-Telling Approach, Great Ensemble Cast, Just Misses Its Mark, I Rate It 7 of 10," 2001, www.imdb.com/title/tt0175880/reviews?count=1452&start=1353.

[32]Kevin O, "User Review of 'Magnolia' (Rotten Tomatoes)," 2013, www.rottentomatoes.com/m/magnolia/reviews/?page=16&type=user.

[33]Aaron J, "User Review of 'Magnolia' (Rotten Tomatoes)," 2013, www.rottentomatoes.com/m/magnolia/reviews/?page=16&type=user.

[34]Bradley W, "User Review of 'Magnolia' (Rotten Tomatoes)," 2012, www.rottentomatoes.com/m/magnolia/reviews/?page=29&type=user.

Of course, just because a viewer writes a review referencing Scripture or even the divine doesn't necessarily mean that viewer has had a profound spiritual experience. Yet, for some, the film appears to elicit responses that are indeed religiously meaningful. One writes that it "makes you wonder if maybe, just maybe, the hand of God touches us sometimes."[35] For another, it is a "reminder that, regardless of how bad it might seem to be, there's still something out there beyond our comprehension that/who is watching us and basically letting us know it's okay . . . we're not that badly off."[36] Many reviewers remark on the emotional intensity of the film,[37] sometimes prompting responses that border on the religious:

> Just when you are drained of all emotion the astounding events of the climax pummel your soul with an intensity of human feeling the likes of which is ever so rarely experienced in life at large, let alone just the cinema. Grown men will weep and women will wail. . . . Somewhere inside this movie is a meaning for life for all people with a soul.[38]

The film holds significant personal meaning for blogger Matthew Jenner: "*Magnolia* was a spiritual experience for me. . . . The spontaneous musical number in the middle of this film, as well as the very famous scene toward the end that can only be described as biblical, there is something lurking beneath *Magnolia* that isn't clear."[39] Johnston mentions a student of his who claims to have had a divine encounter occasioned by *Magnolia*.[40] Matt Tinken makes this same claim:

> The people are saved by something outside themselves: thousands of frogs raining from the sky. Transcendence is unavoidable. . . . I had no other option

[35]Jorn-truyen, "Brilliant Epic with Emotional Depth," 2014, www.imdb.com/title/tt0175880/reviews?count=1452&start=420.

[36]Hungryhippo1970, "Great Flick!," 2001, www.imdb.com/title/tt0175880/reviews?count=1452&start=449.

[37]"An epic of awe-inspiring proportions. Flawless, emotional, truthful and heart-wrenching." StupidHumanSuit, "What Do We Forgive?," 2009, www.imdb.com/title/tt0175880/reviews?count=1452&start=56; "I will probably never be moved the same way or to the same degree by another movie," kbharris11, "Profound, Brilliant, Etc.," 2005, www.imdb.com/title/tt0175880/reviews?count=1452&start=61.

[38]Mike-parry1966, "Stunning, Powerful, Life Affirming, Deeply Moving . . . and Yes Black Humour Abounds. Don't Waste Another Day Without This Film in Your Life!!!!!!," 2010, www.imdb.com/title/tt0175880/reviews?count=1452&start=82.

[39]Matthew Jenner, "'Magnolia' (1999)," *Movies Unchained* (blog), November 9, 2017, https://moviesunchained.wordpress.com/2017/06/18/magnolia-1999/.

[40]Robert K. Johnston, *God's Wider Presence: Reconsidering General Revelation* (Grand Rapids, MI: Baker Academic, 2014), chap. 1.

> but to realize that God's hand is intimately involved in the dirty lives of cocaine addicts, misogynists, child molesters, losers, freaks, and child stars. I had no other option but to realize that God is intimately involved in this dirty life of mine also. . . . *Magnolia* provided for me a divine encounter.[41]

Others too have described their experience of watching the film as a spiritual experience.[42] That *Magnolia* is ranked highly on the *Arts & Faith* Top 100 suggests that it is a film that resonates at a spiritual level for some viewers.[43] Thus, Ron Reed writes, "There's no denying [*Magnolia* is] one of the most often cited favorites among Christian film buffs."[44]

General narrative and formal analysis. I suggest that the religious engagement with *Magnolia* has been largely shaped by three key characteristics: emotional intensity, biblical allusions, and the depiction of interconnectedness. We'll examine these first two characteristics before looking at the third more closely in the next section.

According to film scholar Christina Lane, a "distinguishing characteristic of *Magnolia* is its emotional excess."[45] Similarly, film scholar Joanne Clarke Dillman characterizes it as a "hysterical" text.[46] Herein lies a paradox of *Magnolia*: although an example of so-called smart cinema, hip and ironic examinations of dysfunction,[47] *Magnolia* resists the self-aware emotional detachment typical of similarly "smart" films, like those of Todd Solondz and Wes Anderson. And scholarship has sought to locate the film within postmodernism. Lane, for example, devotes substantial space to discussion of its reflexivity and intertextuality.[48] Film scholar Jason Sperb has likewise discussed *Magnolia* in terms of postmodernism, specifically with respect to a preoccupation with mediation—"*movies about movies*"[49]—and a reflection of

---

[41]Matt Tinken, "The Power of Film: Magnolia," *Reel Spirituality* (blog), Fuller Studio, March 28, 2012, https://fullerstudio.fuller.edu/the_power_of_film_magnolia/.

[42]For example, see TnMovieFan2, "User Comment on 'Magnolia' vs 'There Will Be Blood,'" 2016, www.flickchart.com/discussion/6D71646835/vs/7328EF1AD6.

[43]"Arts & Faith Top 100 Films."

[44]Ron Reed, "Moving Pictures," *Christianity Today*, June 22, 2004, www.christianitytoday.com/ct/2004/juneweb-only/top100films.html.

[45]Lane, *Magnolia*, 39.

[46]Dillman, "Twelve Characters," 146.

[47]Pat Brereton, "Smart Cult Classics: Case Studies of Donnie Darko, American Beauty and Magnolia," in *Smart Cinema, DVD: Add-Ons and New Audience Pleasures* (Springer, 2012), 64-65.

[48]Lane, *Magnolia*, 37-57.

[49]Jason Sperb, *Blossoms and Blood: Postmodern Media Culture and the Films of Paul Thomas Anderson* (Austin: University of Texas Press, 2013), 11; emphasis original.

the economic shift from material to immaterial commodities, which in turn is reflected in an aesthetic centered on surfaces.[50]

Unlike other films of its ilk, *Magnolia* eschews detached irony and instead encourages deep empathy with its characters.[51] The acting is a crucial factor. Ebert described the cast as "all swinging for the fences, heedless of image or self-protective restraint."[52] Tom Cruise's Frank arcs from vulgar, exaggerated machismo to body-shaking rage and grief. Julianne Moore's Linda vacillates between levelheaded calm and extreme agitation verging on incoherence. Thus, critics have described it as "an extraordinarily moving and serious film"[53] and "an emotional overload."[54] Ebert called it a "parable . . . expressed not in words but in emotions."[55]

Magnolia is a network narrative,[56] presenting us with several intersecting storylines rather than a single dominant storyline. Protagonists are multiple and often unrelated or only marginally so. It follows the large cast of characters over a twenty-four hour period, clustered around the eponymous boulevard that cuts through Los Angeles's San Fernando Valley, the hub of the television industry. The main characters are as follows:

- Earl Partridge (Jason Robards). An elderly, terminally ill media mogul on his deathbed, filled with regret for his many betrayals. When he deliriously calls for his estranged son, Frank, Earl's large-hearted nurse, Phil Parma (Philip Seymour Hoffman), tracks him down.
- Linda Partridge (Julianne Moore). Earl's trophy wife, formerly a "gold digger" who now genuinely loves her husband and is racked with guilt for her infidelities.
- Frank "T. J." Mackey (Tom Cruise). Earl's estranged son, a professional pickup artist, who loathes his father for his absence during his late mother's

[50]Sperb, *Blossoms and Blood*, 11-12.

[51]Lane, *Magnolia*, 6-7.

[52]Roger Ebert, "Magnolia," 2000, www.rogerebert.com/reviews/magnolia-2000.

[53]Tobyguise, "An Extraordinarily Moving and Serious Film," 2006, www.imdb.com/title/tt0175880/reviews?start=36.

[54]Theocharous_an, "An Absolute Masterpiece!," 2016, www.imdb.com/user/ur52871493/comments?order=alpha&start=10.

[55]Roger Ebert, "Great Movie: Magnolia," November 27, 2008, www.rogerebert.com/reviews/great-movie-magnolia-1999.

[56]David Bordwell, *The Way Hollywood Tells It: Story and Style in Modern Movies* (Berkeley: University of California Press, 2006), 72-103.

illness. After being interviewed at length by a reporter, Gwenovier (April Grace), Frank is summoned to his dying father's bedside.

- "Quiz Kid" Donnie Smith (William H. Macy). A hapless middle-aged man who achieved fame as a child for his achievements on the long-running quiz show "What Do Kids Know?" but is now lonely, misguided, and lovesick.
- Stanley Spector (Jeremy Blackman). A child prodigy on a winning streak on the current incarnation of "What Do Kids Know?," surrounded by exploitative adults, including his money-grubbing father, Rick (Michael Bowen).
- Jimmy Gator (Philip Baker Hall). The host of "What Do Kids Know?," an alcoholic estranged from his daughter, Claudia. The reason for the father-daughter rift becomes apparent when Jimmy's wife, Rose (Melinda Dillon), accuses him of sexually abusing Claudia as a child.
- Claudia Wilson Gator (Melora Walters). A cocaine addict angry at her abusive father, Jimmy. Her habit leads her to engage in illicit sex, but a glimmer of hope appears in her life when she takes a shine to straitlaced police officer, Jim.
- Jim Kurring (John C. Reilly). A compassionate, bumbling Christian police officer who strikes up a romantic relationship with Claudia during a callout. He dismisses clues to a crime delivered as a cryptic rap by the young Black child Dixon (Emmanuel L. Johnson).

These characters' lives are caught up in a common crisis when hit by a catastrophe that could be, and probably is, lifted right out of the Bible: a downpour of frogs. In the aftermath of this freak weather event, most of these characters achieve some sort of breakthrough—the capacity to forgive, an epiphany, or new resolve. The storylines are designed to elicit emotion. For example, the reconciliation of an estranged father to his son, best exemplified by Frank's fragile forgiveness of Earl, is an example of the separation-reunion theme that Tan and Frijda identify as a narrative structure particularly suited to eliciting a "sentimental" response.[57]

[57]Ed S. H. Tan and Nico H. Frijda, "Sentiment in Film Viewing," in *Passionate Views: Film, Cognition, and Emotion*, ed. Carl R. Plantinga and Greg M. Smith (Baltimore: Johns Hopkins University Press, 1999), 56-58.

Music makes an especially important contribution to the affective impact of the film. Much of it was penned by singer-songwriter Aimee Mann. Mann's music was an early inspiration for the film, with her lyrics incorporated into the screenplay as dialogue, and her music foregrounded in several ways.[58] Anderson even describes Mann as "another character" in the film,[59] while Lane calls Mann an "author" alongside Anderson.[60] Nowhere is Mann's creative presence felt more keenly than in the montage sequence in which her song "Wise Up" plays. Claudia sits alone in her apartment after an emotional episode, when the opening bars of "Wise Up" are heard—music that is seemingly nondiegetic until Claudia unexpectedly begins singing along. As if that were not surprising enough, the sequence cuts to Jim sitting alone, also singing along with the invisible Mann. One by one, each character is shown in isolation, joining in with the melancholy tune. Anderson likens this to people independently singing along to the radio,[61] but the actual effect is quite different. As viewers, we do not perceive it as purely diegetic, because there is no clear diegetic source and the music is of a high, consistent quality, even across cuts.[62] We thus find ourselves in a diegetic no man's land. Some are bothered by this stylistic idiosyncrasy, but for others it's an especially poignant moment, fueled in large part by Mann's music.

Several scholars have pointed out *Magnolia*'s televisuality. It is a film about the TV industry and, as such, its aesthetic borrows from TV. The TV-themed film *Network* (Sidney Lumet, 1976) was a touchstone in *Magnolia*'s development, and its influence can be clearly seen in the studio scenes.[63] Though television—production *and* consumption—features heavily in the mise en scène (e.g., studio scenes, TV sets in living rooms), it also informs the film's structure and a range of other formal characteristics. These coalesce in the notion of televisual "flow," in which the fragmented, disparate imagery of television is nevertheless experienced as continuous and unified.[64] Dillman

---

[58]Stephens, "Interview."

[59]Stephens, "Interview."

[60]Lane, *Magnolia*, 82.

[61]Mark Olsen, "Singing in the Rain," *Sight and Sound* 10, no. 3 (2000).

[62]Michael Slowik, "Isolation and Connection: Unbounded Sound in the Films of Paul Thomas Anderson," *New Review of Film and Television Studies* 13, no. 2 (2015): 157.

[63]In the "making of" documentary, Anderson screens *Network* for the *Magnolia* film crew. Mark Rance, "That Moment: Magnolia Diary" (USA 2000).

[64]Lane, *Magnolia*, 60-61.

observes that *Magnolia* is segmented, divvied up into sequences,[65] many of which are marked by clear-cut changes in editing, cinematography, musical foregrounding, and so forth (see table 6.1). Moreover, writes Dillman, "the infomercial, the interview, and the game show [mediate] the cuts between the diegetic real and the 'televisual real,'"[66] allowing us to move between the screen and the screen-within-a-screen seamlessly. Film scholar Gwendolyn Audrey Foster's description of *Magnolia* as a "sprawling and operatic music video" seems particularly apt.[67] As film scholar and critic Cynthia Fuchs puts it, "The film resembles three hours of channel surfing."[68]

Table 6.1. Breakdown of sequences

Act	Sequence	Sequence Title/Description	Timecode	Duration
1	A	prologue	00:00:19	00:05:29
	B	"One" credit sequence	00:05:48	00:06:15
	C	narrative setup	00:12:27	00:29:07
2	D	pre-taping at TV studio (sequence shots)	00:41:34	00:21:42
	E	whip-pan montage sequence	01:03:38	00:02:46
	F	narrative complications	01:06:24	00:57:06
	G	"Regret" monologue/montage sequence	02:03:30	00:09:02
3	H	"Wise Up" montage sequence	02:13:28	00:03:07
	I	character crises	02:16:35	00:22:25
	J	frog storm	02:39:00	00:06:19
	K	epilogue/denouement	02:45:19	00:08:14

It's not a film only of flow, but also of fluidity. Mobile framing is the film's dominant stylistic feature.[69] The camera regularly dollies from long- or midshot to closeup, repeatedly and relentlessly closing in on characters. This technique is quite pronounced, for example, in the "One" and whip-pan montage sequences. Though this is more cinematic than televisual, when combined with other televisual, MTV-esque stylistic elements, it contributes

[65]Dillman, "Twelve Characters," 146.

[66]Dillman, "Twelve Characters," 146.

[67]Foster, "Magnolia Film Analysis."

[68]Cynthia Fuchs, "TV Land," PopMatters, 2004, accessed November 29, 2017, https://web.archive.org/web/20091208070109/www.popmatters.com/film/reviews/m/magnolia2.shtml; cited in Lane, *Magnolia*, 71.

[69]Lane, *Magnolia*, 59.

to the sense of dynamism and kineticism. It also encourages character identification. "The cinematography creates a bond not only between the subject and the camera but also between characters and audience, characters and director, and in certain charged moments between characters and an implied all-knowing power."[70] I would add also that the constant drift inward toward characters' faces heightens our empathy, and the persistent movement deep into characters' personal space thus gives a sense of closeness, literally and figuratively, to the characters.[71] The camera's proximity and movement thus fosters a sense of intimacy with these people, thereby intensifying the viewer's emotional experience.

For certain scholars then, *Magnolia* is melodrama. Lane comments that the "heightened affect and definitive commitment to melodrama encourage character identification as well as a certain emotional engagement or immersion."[72] Likewise, Foster refers to its "ever-present sense of heightened melodrama."[73] Dillman has developed this notion further, positing that *Magnolia* stands in the tradition of soap opera. Overdetermined music, an abundance of closeups, and a reliance on dialogue all signify melodramatic excess.[74] Even the runtime of the film is excessive.[75] Dillman goes on to argue that by downplaying the goal-directedness typical of "masculine" narratives, "*Magnolia* positions the audience as female in its address and textual style."[76] Through this "feminization" of male characters and the conspicuous use of Mann's voice in the soundtrack, we are invited to adopt a female viewing perspective.[77] *Magnolia* has thus been hailed as a critique of patriarchy. In his work on smart cinema, Pat Brereton notes that "*Magnolia* has constantly been read . . . as symptomatic of a crisis in masculinity."[78] Indeed, though the misogyny of Frank is repugnant, the years

---

[70]Lane, *Magnolia*, 59-60.

[71]For discussion about the role of actors' faces in eliciting sympathy or empathy, see Carl R. Plantinga, "The Scene of Empathy and the Human Face on Film," in *Passionate Views: Film, Cognition, and Emotion*, ed. Carl R. Plantinga and Greg M. Smith (Baltimore: Johns Hopkins University Press, 1999).

[72]Lane, *Magnolia*, 7.

[73]Foster, "Magnolia Film Analysis."

[74]Dillman, "Twelve Characters," 145-46.

[75]"With a duration of three-plus hours, *Magnolia* seems to urge catharsis on the viewer by entrapping the viewer in a system of flow different to that found in a bounded film text." Dillman, "Twelve Characters,"147.

[76]Dillman, "Twelve Characters," 147.

[77]Dillman, "Twelve Characters," 144.

[78]Brereton, "Smart Cult Classics," 76.

of neglect at the hands of his own father, Earl, is worse. By the film's end, Frank seems more a victim than a perpetrator, though he is surely both. *Magnolia*'s patriarchs have wreaked irreparable damage on their children, haunting the personal histories of these characters. Thus, Foster writes that "all roads eventually lead back to pale men near death, men whose bodies are metastatic sites of a lingering, devastating form of cancer, their decaying bodies metaphors of white masculinity and patriarchy itself as a form of cancer."[79]

One striking feature of the scholarly literature is how often commentators reach for the language of "sin,"[80] seemingly taking their cue from the moment, easily missed, in which Donnie hunches over a toilet and partially quotes Exodus 20:5: "The sins of the father . . . lay upon the children." *Magnolia* derives affective power from the quagmire of sin that all characters find themselves in, sometimes as perpetrator but more often as victim. Film scholar George Toles makes this point with reference to the "Wise Up" sequence, which "charts a movement past solitary struggle to a vision of unified brokenness . . . [the] plausibility of this movement is what gives the 'Wise Up' interlude, for some viewers, its affecting power."[81] We empathize with most of these characters crippled by an insidious "cancer," thereby amplifying the emotional force of the film. Of course, there is nothing inherently religious about deeply felt emotion. Nevertheless, it is relevant to the religious engagement with *Magnolia*. How so? In his discussion of audience reception of Anderson's films, Callaway points out that "filmgoers often conceive of a film's spirituality and, indeed, its transcendence in affective and even sensual terms."[82] This is a crucial point. In the right context, emotionality itself may register for certain people as somehow spiritual. It seems likely, therefore, that the spiritual resonance of *Magnolia* stems, in part, from its emotional power.

The most direct invitation for theological engagement comes, however, from its biblical allusions. Many of these take the form of scriptural references

[79]Foster, "Magnolia Film Analysis." Media theorist Brian Michael Goss takes a slightly dissenting view, believing that *Magnolia* offers a partial critique of patriarchy and market ideology only to wind up ultimately affirming them. Brian Michael Goss, "'Things Like This Don't Just Happen': Ideology and Paul Thomas Anderson's Hard Eight, Boogie Nights, and Magnolia," *Journal of Communication Inquiry* 26, no. 2 (2002).

[80]For example, see Brereton, "Smart Cult Classics," 77; George Toles, *Paul Thomas Anderson* (Champaign: University of Illinois Press, 2016), 23.

[81]Toles, *Paul Thomas Anderson*, 15.

[82]Callaway, *Scoring Transcendence*, chap. 5.

that are simultaneously explicit and concealed. Signs and images that read "Exodus 8:2" or, more commonly, "82" for short are sprinkled liberally throughout the mise en scène's periphery.[83] The number shows up as the prisoner number for a hanged criminal, painted on the side of an airplane, and in the neat arrangement of coiled cables atop an apartment building. An intertitle with the weather forecast reads "82% chance of rain" and the booking ID in Marcie's (Cleo King) mugshot is "8208208208200." The *full* reference appears on a billboard and on a bus-stop sign as Jim sees Donnie scaling his workplace wall, and most conspicuously on a placard held aloft by a member of the studio audience, which, tellingly, is snatched away by a stagehand played by Anderson himself![84] There are over fifty such instances throughout the film,[85] and thus the scriptural passage acts as an interpretive key. Exodus 8:2 reads, "If you refuse to let them go, I will send a plague of frogs on your whole country." It thus foreshadows the eventual rain, inviting an interpretation of this event as *not* random (to quote the narrator, "This is not just 'something that happens' . . . this was not just a matter of chance. Oh, these strange things happen all the time"), and indeed as ordained by God, an instance of "divine intervention."

Of course, this isn't the only possible interpretation. Though the notion of the universe as random is challenged explicitly, any suggestion of divine involvement is only implicit. While watching in wide-eyed wonder as frogs fall from the sky, Stanley mutters this could just be "something that happens"—bizarre, but possibly explicable without invoking God. Yet, to quote Old Testament scholar Jason M. Silverman, "The citations of Exod. 8.2 . . . together with Catholic police officer Jim Kurring's role as a central moral 'heart,' does give the revelatory moment a potentially religious character."[86] Theologian David Congdon sees the deluge as "a test of the viewer's ability to see the film *parabolically* or *bifocally*. As a piece of apocalyptic cinema, *Magnolia* is a cinematic parable that paradoxically unites an 'immanent' natural phenomenon (movie qua film) and a 'transcendent' invasion of judgment and grace (movie qua parable)."[87]

[83]Anderson has confirmed that the "82"s are abbreviated references to Exodus 8:2, rather than the other way around. Sean Daly, "Director Has His Pick of Actors," *The Times Union*, 2000.

[84]Silverman, "We May Be Through with the Past," 470.

[85]Lane, *Magnolia*, 19.

[86]Silverman, "We May Be Through with the Past," 477.

[87]Congdon, "Reconsidering Apocalyptic Cinema," 413; emphasis original.

So while some characters—and viewers—might write it off as nothing more than a meteorological anomaly, others see it "bifocally," as natural *and* divine. Indeed, just such an interpretation is articulated by one of the film's characters. In an effort to help Officer Jim solve the murder case, Dixon, an aspiring rapper who calls himself "The Prophet," raps a verse that ends with "When the sunshine don't work / *The good Lord bring the rain in.*" Befuddled by the obscure content and rapid-fire delivery, Jim dismisses the boy's witness. Dixon has invited Jim to read the situation bifocally, but instead, Jim scorns Dixon's insight as he puts on dark glasses, literally and figuratively.

Magnolia thus handles Scripture with uncommon sophistication and nuance, as opposed to the standard Hollywood *modus operandi* of using biblical or even faux-biblical references as a superficial plot device.[88] Of course, Western culture is rife with biblical references, and such references alone do not make a Christian interpretation appropriate. That said, scriptural allusions are likely to prompt religious associations in the minds of at least some viewers. Hipps posits that the "true" meaning of the film is unlocked by the Exodus narrative, which, in this version, depicts children as enslaved to adults.[89] DeGiglio-Bellemare adopts a similarly liberationist approach, albeit written in a more academic register. For DeGiglio-Bellemare, *Magnolia*'s captives are enslaved to forces of structural sin, patriarchy, and freemarket capitalism as manifest in the television industry. "The G*d of Magnolia is the G*d of Exodus, a G*d who is at work in history, not above history, who cares for the slave, not the Pharaoh, who seeks change, not the status quo."[90]

Others have advanced apocalyptic interpretations. Runions describes *Magnolia* as apocalyptic not only because it depicts a cataclysmic event, but also because it is an "unveiling" of patriarchy.[91] An extreme closeup of a painting on Claudia's wall with the caption "but it did happen" encapsulates its unveiling quality as it affirms Claudia's version of events as true and by extension vindicates the other victimized children.[92] Congdon, too, takes an

[88]Nicola Denzey, "Biblical Allusions, Biblical Illusions: Hollywood Blockbuster and Scripture," *Journal of Religion & Film* 8, no. 1 (2004), http://digitalcommons.unomaha.edu/cgi/viewcontent.cgi?article=1712&context=jrf.

[89]Hipps, "Magnolia: The Exodus for Kids."

[90]DeGiglio-Bellemare, "Magnolia and the Signs of the Times," 9.

[91]Runions, "Falling Frogs and Family Traumas," 135. Silverman, however, has challenged Runions's interpretation of biblical apocalypticism. Silverman, "We May Be Through with the Past," 462.

[92]Runions, "Falling Frogs and Family Traumas," 152.

apocalyptic perspective, albeit significantly different to that offered by Runions. For Congdon, *Magnolia* is not an example of traditional apocalypticism, but of *Pauline* apocalypticism. While the former conjures up images of end-of-the-world catastrophes, the latter is about the divine invasion of Christ and the Holy Spirit into the present world—the arrival of new creation within the old. In this view, *Magnolia* is Pauline apocalyptic *par excellence*.[93]

Against such apocalyptic interpretations (especially Runions's), Silverman suggests a prophetic approach, which unites salvation and judgment in a single act, and calls for a response: "The rain of frogs within *Magnolia*, therefore, functions exactly like a prophetic sign in the biblical tradition: it reveals (connections and consequences of actions), judges (patriarchy, oppression, misogyny, pedophilia), and offers redemption (freedom from oppression, the past, towards love)."[94] One feature common to these divergent interpretive approaches is the two-sided nature of the amphibious downpour: simultaneously judgment *and* salvation.[95] Most fundamentally, these scriptural interpretations all see God's hand in the event and in the film as a whole.

The references to Exodus are usually so well-hidden and fleeting as to be accessible only to the repeat viewer or the especially eagle-eyed one. As Hipps writes, "The true meaning of the film lies in the margins."[96] Though marginal, these clues have been included in the frame deliberately and painstakingly. Plus, the film has other scriptural resonances that may be clear to even less attentive (or obsessive) viewers. The quotation of Bergen Evans mentioned above is frequently uttered by the narrator (Ricky Jay), nested within an oft-repeated line: "The book says, 'We may be through with the past, but the past is not through with us.'" What is the "book" in question? As discussed already, the book is a work by Bergen Evans, though this is never stated. Silverman convincingly argues, however, these ambiguous references to "the book" are intended to trick viewers into taking it as a reference to the Bible.[97] At least

[93]Congdon, "Reconsidering Apocalyptic Cinema," 406-8.

[94]Silverman, "We May Be Through with the Past," 477.

[95]For example, see Roy Anker, *Of Pilgrims and Fire: When God Shows Up at the Movies* (Grand Rapids, MI: Eerdmans, 2011), chap. 6, Kindle; Congdon, "Reconsidering Apocalyptic Cinema," 413; Hipps, "Magnolia: The Exodus for Kids"; Silverman, "We May Be Through with the Past," 476.

[96]Hipps, "Magnolia: The Exodus for Kids." Though I would not call this the "*true* meaning," his basic contention about the marginality of important interpretive clues is valid.

[97]Silverman, "We May Be Through with the Past," 466.

one IMDb user has flirted with this very mistake.[98] But even without awareness of the Exodus 8:2 motif, viewers may interpret the frog deluge as divine intervention. The freak weather event is an awesome disruption of ordinary life stemming from forces greater than any human, something insurance companies will categorize as an "act of God." Lane writes:

> *Magnolia* sets out to show that life's chain of events have a greater meaning—a grand design—and that, by extension, each individual's moral choices carry weight within a larger community. The film ultimately revolves around a question of faith—a refusal to believe only in chance. Its own style and structure *feel* as though nothing is left to chance, appearing to have an organic and pre-conceived architecture.[99]

For Lane, there is an "independently *moving* consciousness" in the film that becomes most apparent in the frog storm.[100] This, in conjunction with the theme of chance, gives rise to a sense of a higher power at work. Beneath the apparent chaos, there is purpose and meaning.

Not that a simple equivalence should be drawn between the transcendent other of *Magnolia* and the Christian God. Nevertheless, aspects of the film resonate deeply with a Christian conception of God. Thematically, there is significant congruence between *Magnolia* and Scripture, particularly with respect to forgiveness and reconciliation. Silverman points out the significance of specifically highlighting the second verse of Exodus 8, as opposed to the whole chapter, since it is "a verse explicitly linking the frogs as punishment for oppression."[101] In other words, it is not the frog plague itself but rather the *reason* for the plague (i.e., oppression) that make it spiritually meaningful. In this verse, God promises an infestation of frogs if the oppressor does not "let go" of God's people. Biblically, this is a warning to Pharaoh that he must release the Hebrews from their slavery in Egypt. In *Magnolia,* "let go" takes on a more metaphorical meaning. The oppressor—abusive, exploitative fathers—must let go of the oppressed, the children who continue to suffer at their hands even well into adulthood. As frogs fall, Earl breathes his last, and Jimmy's attempted suicide is turned into a "Rube Goldberg-style comic

[98]TxMike, "Fascinating Film."
[99]Lane, *Magnolia*, 15.
[100]Lane, *Magnolia*, 15; emphasis original.
[101]Silverman, "We May Be Through with the Past," 477.

death,"[102] a fatal electrical fire triggered by a falling frog. About Jimmy's death, Anderson says, "There is truly a sense of moral judgment at work with this character. I can't even let him kill himself at the end—he's got to burn. And that's what he deserves. I wanted it to be really clear that with this character, I'm saying 'No.' No to any kind of forgiveness for him."[103] In the case of Earl and especially Jimmy, the frogs are a judgment.

In contemporary idiom, however, to "let go" is synonymous with forgiveness and refusing to be in bondage to the past. So it is also the victims who are commanded to "let go," to forgive or simply move on. Frank's shift from spitting bitter profanities at his moribund father to desperately pleading "don't go away, you f—ing a—hole" implies a faltering, courageous forgiveness. Donnie's cleareyed assessment of his misguided attempts at finding love reveals a newfound wisdom, a recognition of the folly of his past strategies. Claudia's smile to the camera as Jim speaks healing words to her suggests she might emerge from the shadows of her past and forge meaningful relationships in the future. In his piece on *Magnolia* for the anthology released in conjunction with MoMA's "The Hidden God" exhibition, arts stalwart Richard Peña suggests, "All these things might have happened anyway, but in the context of the frog rain they take on the mantle of a kind of divine sanction."[104] Dillman rightly says these characters are "in search of metanoia, a profound sense of spiritual awakening."[105] This catastrophe calls these broken souls to metanoia, a gracious invitation to change for the better. Granted, as Toles argues, these are modest outcomes for such a cataclysmic event,[106] hence Johnston's dubbing it "the saddest happy ending."[107] But for *Magnolia*'s victims, the frogs signify genuine salvation—modest, yes, but hard-won and hopeful, divine action that breaks the shackles of the past.

Interconnectedness through editing. Another key ingredient in *Magnolia*'s spiritual power is the feeling of interconnectedness and shared humanity it fosters. Film scholar Michael Slowik writes that all Anderson's films are preoccupied with "the isolation one can feel from the rest of the

---

[102]Toles, *Paul Thomas Anderson*, 22.

[103]Stephens, "Interview."

[104]Richard Pena, "Magnolia," in *The Hidden God: Film and Faith*, ed. Mary Lea Bandy and Antonio Monda (New York: Museum of Modern Art, 2003), 237.

[105]Dillman, "Twelve Characters," 150.

[106]Toles, *Paul Thomas Anderson*, 22.

[107]Johnston, *Useless Beauty*, 85.

world, and the inherent difficulty—yet potential rewards—of forging relationships with others."[108] Toles likewise recognizes these same themes of community and isolation running through Anderson's oeuvre, but also sees a progression in how he handles them. Put simply, his pre-*Magnolia* films celebrate community, while his post-*Magnolia* films lament isolation. *Magnolia* is a transitional work, situated between these two periods in Anderson's body of work: "The millennial space carved out in *Magnolia* attests to Anderson's faith in a world where talk and group activity are plentiful and transformative. He pursues a vision of provisional community and reconciliation, though it is underwritten throughout by a relentless emphasis on estrangement and neediness."[109]

So while there is a drive toward human connection, there is also resistance to that impulse, isolation stubbornly refusing to be eliminated with a neat and tidy resolution. Human relationships in *Magnolia* are messy. Film scholar John Bruns likens *Magnolia* to musical polyphony, characterized by "simultaneity without unity."[110] Ultimately, however, *Magnolia* lands more on the side of community than of isolation. In fact, its messiness invests even greater meaning into the relational bonds that *are* formed against all odds. Here, intimacy and community are hard-won. The relational messiness notwithstanding, the sense of connection depicted and, I would argue, sometimes *elicited* is compelling. I agree with Slowik that "despite copious amounts of cancer, crying, pain, and loneliness, *Magnolia* offers Anderson's clearest vision of human connectedness."[111]

This connectedness, I suggest, is conveyed in part through editing.[112] The editing strategies vary depending on the sequence, many of which are formally demarcated. Table 6.1 gives an overview of the sequences that make up the film, some of which are delineated through particular editing techniques. This section will examine the editing by focusing especially on the second act. This act—which, at over ninety minutes long, represents half the film's runtime—is edited into a "weave," employing a range of techniques designed to draw multiple threads together to create a single, unified piece. Nevertheless, this formal

---

[108]Slowik, "Isolation and Connection," 150.

[109]Toles, *Paul Thomas Anderson*, 3.

[110]John Bruns, "The Polyphonic Film," *New Review of Film and Television Studies* 6, no. 2 (2008): 196.

[111]Slowik, "Isolation and Connection," 156.

[112]DeGiglio-Bellemare, "Magnolia and the Signs of the Times," 3.

theme is established much earlier, in the "One" sequence, which introduces each main character. The lyrics of the song ("One is the loneliest number that you'll ever do") establishes loneliness as the fundamental challenge facing these individuals,[113] yet the sequence's highly mobile camerawork and fluid editing, "threaded" around the motif of TV, visually unites these lonely characters. This credit sequence is a microcosm of a formal pattern that will be elaborated on later in the film.

The cornerstone of the film's editing is crosscutting. While crosscutting is a feature found in many films, it takes on a different character in network narratives. Network narratives necessitate that we flit from one storyline to the other, and even conventional, single-protagonist films do this when shifting between various subplots. Crosscutting, therefore, encourages consideration of the relationship between images, as evidenced by the so-called Kuleshov Effect, a foundational principle of editing. Early in the history of cinema, Soviet filmmaker Lev Kuleshov discovered that the same image of an actor wearing a neutral facial expression was interpreted differently depending on the images surrounding it. The Kuleshov Effect is a testament to the "gestalt impulse," the innate tendency to create meaning from juxtaposed images.[114] In a famous sequence from *The Godfather* (Francis Ford Coppola, 1972), Coppola cuts back and forth between a scene of Michael Corleone (Al Pacino) at the christening of his godchild while vowing to renounce Satan and a series of murders carried out under his orders, thereby creating an ironic incongruity. Kuleshov's student, the influential filmmaker and theorist Sergei Eisenstein, uses a similar technique with the opposite effect in his film *Strike* (Sergei Eisenstein, 1925). At the climax, Eisenstein intercuts a scene of strikers being gunned down with images of cows being slaughtered, thereby drawing a parallel between the two acts. In both instances, the editing adds new meaning, yet their meanings run counter to each other due to the content of the images. There is, therefore, an interplay between image and editing that shapes its meaning.

As network narratives crosscut from one storyline to another, they encourage the audience to consider the relationship between disparate characters. As such, they often deal with themes of connectedness. We see this

---

[113]Lane, *Magnolia*, 74.

[114]Ken Dancyger, *The Technique of Film and Video Editing: History, Theory, and Practice* (Waltham, MA: Focal Press, 2002), 189.

stated rather heavy-handedly by a character in the network narrative *Crash* (Paul Haggis, 2004): "In L.A., nobody touches you. We're always behind this metal and glass. I think we miss that touch so much that we crash into each other just so we can feel something." Its network form reinforces the theme of how strangers' lives intersect. There is an alternative way to create a multiprotagonist film, namely the anthology film, in which each of the film's storylines is presented uninterrupted in its entirety, positioned back-to-back with the others—essentially a linear series of shorts. Although most anthology films are united around a common element, the connections between the stories are typically less and looser. For example, the eight storylines of *Waru* (Chelsea Cohen et al., 2017) revolve around the tangi (a customary Māori funeral rite) of an abused child, but their linear arrangement suppresses any deep sense of interconnectedness. With the narrator's opening monologue about coincidence and fate, *Magnolia* uses the network form as a way of exploring the generic thematic material of connection, but does so in a more complex fashion than many other network narratives. It paradoxically creates a greater sense of dissimilarity *and* connectedness, a point to which we will return.

Editing is often about timing, and in *Magnolia* the timing and pace of the editing serves to draw disparate storylines together. More often than not, especially in the second act, Anderson and editor Dylan Tichenor (who previously worked on films by network narrative pioneer Robert Altman), do not allow a dramatic situation to resolve before cutting away. We see this, for instance, when Jim and Claudia meet while Jim is on a callout. Classical editing would normally allow the scene to continue uninterrupted, unless cutting away to indicate a *simultaneous* event. Here, however, it cuts away to other storylines before returning, picking up where we left off. Dillman writes, "From cut to cut and from segment to segment, time in the interlocking narratives seems to stand still."[115] Dillman observes that this way of handling time is an especially televisual technique,[116] though most films do this when depicting concurrent events. Here in *Magnolia* it too indicates simultaneity, but also interconnectedness. Narrative considerations are secondary; it is mostly a matter of keeping these sequences short, rhythmic, and therefore more tightly woven.

[115]Dillman, "Twelve Characters," 146.
[116]Dillman, "Twelve Characters," 146.

There is also ample use of quick cutting. I mean this in both a conventional and in a more idiosyncratic sense. First, there is the ordinary meaning: the splicing together of short shots, just seconds or even frames long, imbuing sequences with freneticism. Second, there is the shifting between *storylines*, not merely shots. At certain points, *Magnolia* grants a similar amount of screen time to each storyline. Immediately after Jim loses his gun, there is a passage of sixteen scenes across different storylines all six to forty-eight seconds in duration (a twenty-one-second average). Though the shot-lengths have not been slavishly matched, they're all brief. A short time later, Earl expresses his regret for letting "[his] love go." We hear this jeremiad in voiceover as it cuts from one character to another, the monologue giving the sequence formal unity. These images are all ten to twenty-nine seconds in duration (nineteen-second average).[117] Dedicating only a short amount of time to each storyline before cutting away is not only democratic, but also unifying.

Though important, the editing strategies discussed thus far are standard. Where *Magnolia*'s editing innovates is what I call its *weave*, an editing design that gives formal unity to most of the second act. Dillman refers to the "centripetal pull" of the quiz show "What Do Kids Know?," which I suggest can be attributed to the fact that the second act is edited to give special prominence to the television studio. The second act is introduced by an intertitle that gives the weather forecast, a device that also marks the beginning of the first act (after the prologue) and the third. Immediately following the intertitle is a tracking or dolly shot, following Stanley and his father, Rick, as they enter the studio.[118] The camera follows several characters, most notably Stanley and Jimmy, bouncing between various contestants and crew as they wend their respective ways through the studio maze in a series of complex dollies, reminiscent of Altman.[119] These sequence shots flag this as a set piece, and thus

[117]I have omitted a "hip-hop montage" nested within this sequence because it is a short, distinct sequence in which each shot is just a second or two long.

[118]I follow Bordwell and Thompson in using *dolly shot* and *tracking shot* interchangeably. David Bordwell and Kristin Thompson, *Film Art: An Introduction*, 10th ed. (New York: McGraw-Hill, 2012), 196.

[119]For example, the eight-minute tracking shot in *The Player* (Robert Altman, 1992). Altman's influence on Anderson is well known. Anderson served as standby director on Altman's *A Prairie Home Companion* for insurance purposes, understudy to his aging mentor. See David Carr, "Lake Wobegon Goes Hollywood (or Is It Vice Versa?), with a Pretty Good Cast," *New York Times*, July 23, 2005, www.nytimes.com/2005/07/23/movies/MoviesFeatures/lake-wobegon-goes-hollywood-or-is-it-vice-versa-with.html?_r=0.

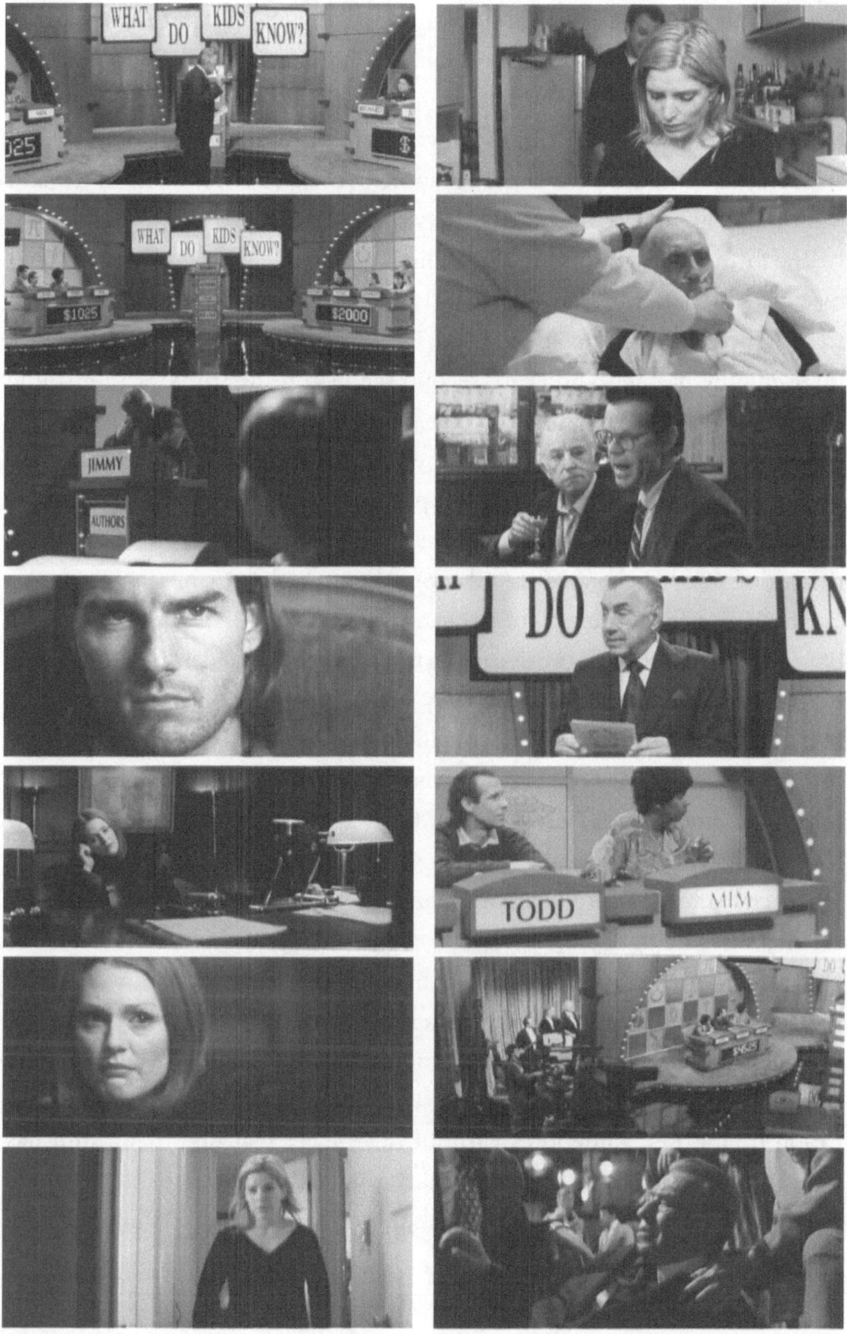

Figure 6.1. In this twenty-three-minute sequence from *Magnolia*, the TV studio acts as the thread "woven" through the other storylines, with almost every second scene taking place at the studio

establish the studio as of central importance. Expanding on the weave metaphor, we might say the studio is established as the unifying thread—"weft," if you prefer—that will be woven throughout the other locations and storylines. Before taping begins, the film cuts away from the studio to other storylines and returns to the studio twice. The taping of the quiz show finally starts and will run throughout almost the entirety of the second act.

The formal centrality of the TV studio is maintained and indeed intensified by cutting back to the studio frequently. In some passages, almost *every other scene* is back at the studio. In figure 6.1, every storyline is included in a twenty-three-minute passage, and every second scene is at the studio with just one exception. We're never away from the studio for long. The studio is the unifying thread of the second act. That the studio dominates cannot be chalked up simply to character or plot. It's important to note, however, that Stanley and Jimmy's storylines, which unfold at the TV studio, are no more important than those of other characters. Anderson edits according to theme, not plot.[120] The back-and-forth movement between various storylines sees them blend, blur, and bleed into each other, forcing the viewer to consider these storylines in relation to the quiz show at the story's center. The quiz show thus gives this part of the film formal unity, the thread that holds it all together.

The threads are drawn together even tighter through creative transitions. Match (or quasi-match) cuts are used to shift from one storyline to another, specifically by cutting on the quiz show, either in the studio itself or on TV sets in characters' various locations. For example, it cuts from a shot of the TV set in Dixon's living room to Earl's TV set, matching the on-screen images.[121] This type of graphic matching creates porous boundaries between storylines, locations, and characters, conveying a sense that the lives of these disparate characters are somehow connected, not least by this TV show. Television becomes a kind of portal that effortlessly transports the viewer from one location to another, sometimes without the viewer realizing that a shift has taken place. A similar effect is created through whip-pan transitions, where the cut comes on an extremely quick, blurry camera pan. Whip-pans are

[120]Lane, *Magnolia*, 2.

[121]Lane writes that the "source of fluidity is the use of numerous television screens and cameras; the omnipresence of the television medium develops an ongoing thread that runs throughout the film." Lane, *Magnolia*, 60.

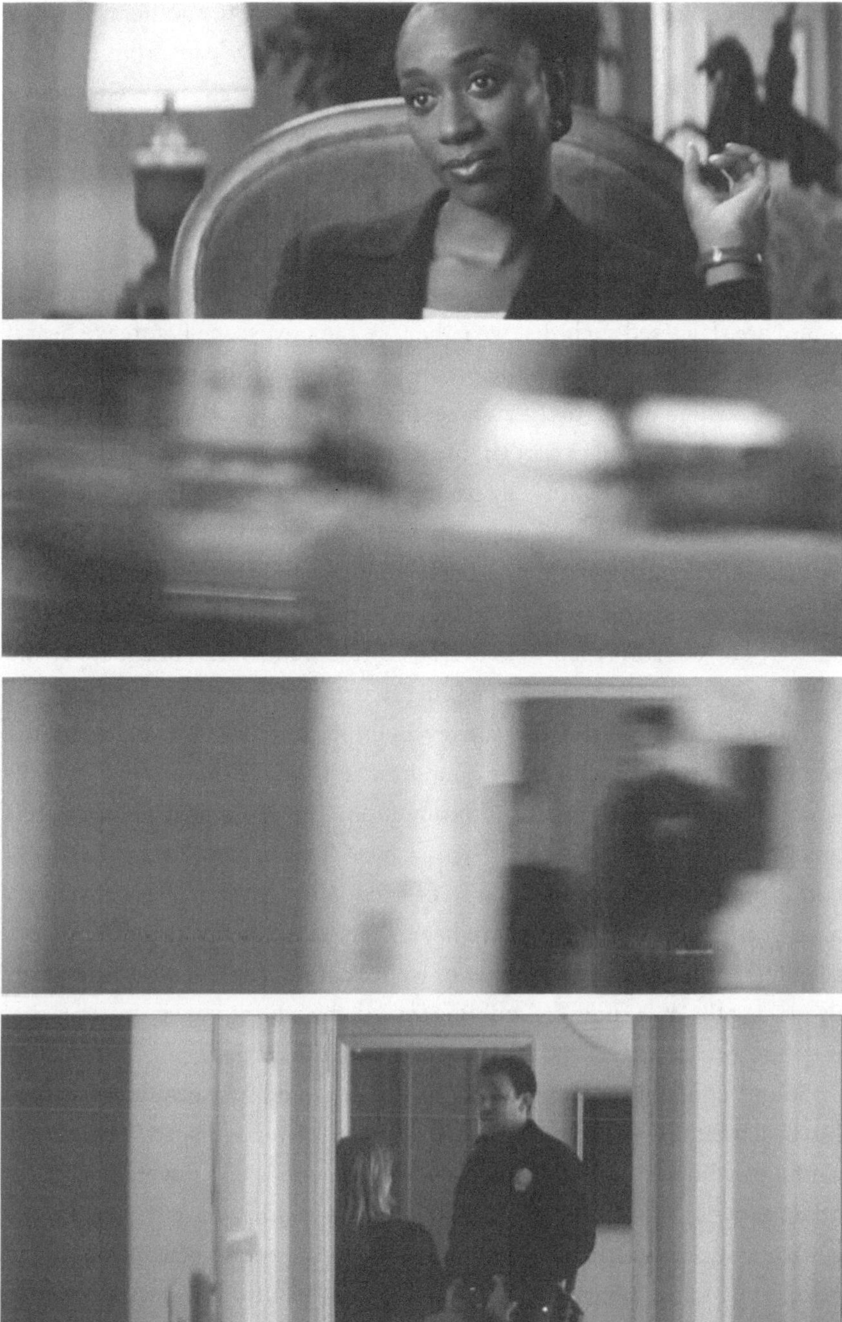

Figure 6.2. In *Magnolia*, cuts sometimes come on the whip-pan, seamlessly transporting us to another location such that storylines literally blur into one another

sometimes used to move the camera from one character to another within the same location, such as we see when the camera rapidly pans from Frank to Gwenovier. But then the camera similarly whip-pans right from Gwenovier not back to Frank, but to Jim and Claudia *in a different location* (fig. 6.2). Anderson has cut on the whip-pan, concealing the cut and thus seamlessly transporting us to another location. He repeats this technique on several occasions, so that one storyline quite literally blurs into another.

There are also a number of split edits, in which the cutting of image and sound are staggered such that we either see the next scene before we hear it (L-cut) or hear the next scene before we see it (J-cut). The most conspicuous example is when we cut to the audio of Frank's "Seduce and Destroy" seminar while the image of Phil in Earl's home remains on screen. For a full thirty-five seconds, we see Phil confusedly pacing around the living room while simultaneously hearing the wild applause and grandiose fanfare from Richard Strauss's *Also Sprach Zarathustra* that belongs properly to the following scene. These are two very different characters in very different settings, yet the split edit, a J-cut, suggests their lives overlap. These transitions contribute to the "porousness built into *Magnolia*'s editing structure."[122]

These formal strategies also convey an important idea. When, toward the end of the act, the credits of the quiz show roll, we see that "What Do Kids Know?" is a "Big Earl Partridge" production. The prolonged silence at this precise moment underscores its significance. It turns out that media mogul Earl is the central figure in this web of lives. What most of these characters have in common is that they have been affected—directly or indirectly, personally or professionally, for better or (more commonly) for worse—by Earl. By making the quiz show the unifying thread, the editing conveys an idea that is not otherwise articulated. The meaning is in the cutting.

Sound contributes significantly to the sense of connectedness as well. Hawksley details how sound weaves together the lives of disparate characters. Certain audio editing techniques ensure that one scene dovetails with another, allowing unrelated storylines to mesh. A sound match cut is used when cutting from the sound of rain in one scene to the sound of a shower in the next. Split cuts, mentioned above, likewise ensure that scenes overlap,

---

[122]Lane, *Magnolia*, 60.

creating linkages between the various characters and their storylines.[123] Slowik too has examined aural dimensions of Anderson's films with a particular emphasis on his use of "unbounded sound," in which the source of the sound cannot be unambiguously located within the frame. Unbounded sound therefore includes nondiegetic sound, but also offscreen diegetic sound and sound that exists somewhere between the two ends of the diegetic and nondiegetic spectrum.[124] We find a particularly foregrounded instance of unbounded sound in *Magnolia*'s "Wise Up" sequence, with which the second act culminates.

Callaway and Johnston have both offered theological analyses of this montage sequence.[125] In his theology of film music, Callaway considers *Magnolia* alongside two of Anderson's other films, *There Will Be Blood* (2007)[126] and *Punch-Drunk Love* (2002), and finds that the director uses "music to signify the presence of an immanent transcendence."[127] *Magnolia*'s deluge of frogs certainly points toward the transcendent other, but because this entity defies depiction, it is music that conveys it more effectively, especially through "Wise Up." Here the ostensibly nondiegetic music penetrates the "porous diegetic boundary" as the characters each take turns singing along with the song, "leaving us in diegetic limbo."[128] This blurring suggests a dissatisfaction "with the modern distinction between the noumenal and phenomenal worlds, the removal of the divine from our sensate experience, the separation of the sacred and the secular."[129] Though not writing from a theological perspective, Toles too has made a similar observation. In "Wise Up," the "many wrangling voices that Anderson himself has whipped up to fever pitch fall still for an interval, and in their place appears a voice from the *outside*, that of Aimee Mann. . . . Something large seems to be at work as Mann's ability to break through mental resistance spreads."[130] He goes on to describe the frog storm as "a more

[123]Theodora Hawksley, "But It Did Happen: Sound as Deep Narrative in P. T. Anderson's Magnolia (1999)," *Journal of Religion and Film* 13, no. 2 (2009).

[124]Slowik, "Isolation and Connection."

[125]Callaway, *Scoring Transcendence*; Johnston, *Useless Beauty*.

[126]Ranked #92, "Top 100 Films," *Arts & Faith*, 2011, accessed January 3, 2022, https://imagejournal.org/top-100-films/.

[127]Callaway, *Scoring Transcendence*, chap. 5.

[128]Callaway, *Scoring Transcendence*, chap. 3.

[129]Callaway, *Scoring Transcendence*, chap. 5.

[130]Toles, *Paul Thomas Anderson*, 16; emphasis original.

eruptive version of the female divinity or hidden force that intervenes in the 'Wise Up' sequence."[131] Music is the most conspicuous and innovative element of the "Wise Up" sequence, but the sequence equally depends on visual editing. In a manner of speaking, the cutting places unrelated characters close to each other, while the music is what connects them.

Bruns's examination of *Magnolia*'s multiplicity of characters is insightful. Borrowing a metaphor from music theory, Bruns argues for it as a rare example of a "polyphonic" film. Polyphony is a musical texture in which multiple melodies coexist, none of which have primacy over another. Harmonic music (homophony) involves multiplicity, but the harmonic lines are dependent upon and subordinate to the melody. The lines in polyphony, however, are independent. Applied to cinema, polyphony implies multiple "independent" protagonists of roughly equal importance.[132] Note, however, that network narratives are not necessarily polyphonic. *Crash* features multiple protagonists, yes, but a single authorial voice still emerges as characters develop and plots resolve all a little too neatly.[133] But *Magnolia* is messy. Even ostensibly minor characters appear with mysterious agendas of their own that seem somehow indifferent to or at cross-purposes with the narrative goals of the protagonists (e.g., Thurston Howell [Henry Gibson], who speaks in riddles).[134] At the risk of taking liberties with Bruns's argument, it's almost as if such characters were themselves heroes in another quite distinct film being shot in the same time and place. *Magnolia,* therefore, has "a quality of irreducible plurality."[135] Thus, writes Bruns, in *Magnolia* we find "simultaneity [that] provides little or no sense of unity."[136] For Bruns, even the apparent unity of "Wise Up" rings hollow, the superficial sentiment belied by the sequence's artifice, the possibility of such unity undermined by its very unreality.[137]

I find Bruns's notion of polyphony illuminating, for it offers a convincing account of the film's messiness. Ultimately, however, he pushes the interpretation too far. Few commentators or viewers take "Wise Up" to be ironically

---

[131]Toles, *Paul Thomas Anderson,* 21.
[132]Bruns, "Polyphonic Film," 189-90.
[133]Bruns, "Polyphonic Film," 205.
[134]Bruns, "Polyphonic Film," 202.
[135]Bruns, "Polyphonic Film," 203.
[136]Bruns, "Polyphonic Film," 206.
[137]Bruns, "Polyphonic Film," 208.

detached. "One's initial reaction is to scoff, as if Anderson has finally gone too far," writes critic Mark Olsen. "But the plaintive tone of the song maps the characters' connectedness in ways scene after scene of dialogue never could."[138] This may be a smart film, but it is one marked by uncommon sincerity.[139]

So while there is a complexity to *Magnolia*, there is also genuine unity in this sequence and indeed in the film as a whole. In the light of Bruns's articulation of polyphony, perhaps Johnston puts it too strongly when he writes that "*Magnolia*'s nine stories ultimately play out with one voice," yet his basic contention is correct.[140] The sense of community here is chastened, but genuine: polyphony and harmony. For Anderson, community is never easy, and here it is especially hard-won. The sense of collectivity is made more meaningful precisely because of the stubborn plurality. Perhaps this is why it resonates profoundly for some viewers, who may even be swept up in a feeling of connectedness themselves. As Lane puts it: "As the characters connect without necessarily even knowing it, we as spectators are encouraged to see ourselves as part of that community."[141]

Connectedness and Communion

Individual spirituality and communal religion. In his discussion of cinematic revelatory experience, Johnston refers to two types of transcendence: that "with a lowercase *t*" and that "with a capital *T*" respectively.[142] The former he describes as "delving more deeply into oneself and one's humanity,"[143] while the latter is "something independent of and outside ourselves and our cultures, even if it is known from within."[144] Thus, we might say that, for some, the film's deeply sympathetic portrayal of this *de facto* community may occasion transcendence, while the insinuation of divine presence may also occasion Transcendence—and the two experiences may even be mutually informative. I suggest then that the religious meaning of *Magnolia* is inextricably bound up in its portrayal of human community. Those parts of the film in which the

[138]Olsen, "Singing in the Rain," 27-28.

[139]Lane, *Magnolia*, 6-7.

[140]Johnston, *Useless Beauty*, 85.

[141]Lane, *Magnolia*, 26.

[142]Robert K. Johnston, *Reel Spirituality: Theology and Film in Dialogue*, 2nd ed. (Grand Rapids, MI: Baker Academic, 2006), 242-43.

[143]Johnston, *Reel Spirituality*, 243.

[144]Johnston, *Reel Spirituality*, 242.

divine seems particularly evident also have a collective orientation. The frog storm impacts all characters; "Wise Up" involves all characters; and providence seems to be threading all characters' lives together. If this is the divine, it is the divine at work in human community, not merely in individuals. Earlier, I described *Magnolia*'s editing design as a "weave." It surely comes as no surprise then that one of the film's marketing posters and DVD cover was composed of character images crisscrossing each other, so that the ensemble cast is literally woven together.

Toles notes that after *Magnolia,* however, Anderson shifted toward "estranged solitary,"[145] films that focus on individuals isolated from wider society. For example, when Anderson traded in the network narrative form for "100% straightforward old-fashioned storytelling,"[146] Anderson made a quasi-Western (his previous film, *Punch-Drunk Love,* also deviated from the network form favored in his earlier work),[147] a genre practically synonymous with individualism. But far from being a celebration of individualism, *There Will Be Blood* is rather an indictment. A self-proclaimed "family man," protagonist Daniel Plainview (Daniel Day-Lewis) cares for nobody but himself; his adoption of an orphan is motivated purely by the business opportunities it might bring. Plainview's unrelenting self-regard ultimately lands him in a prison of his own making. By contrast, *Magnolia*'s network form conveys connectedness—and thus invites connection. These films thus give expression to Anderson's apparent conviction of the necessity of community for human flourishing.

Like many Westerns, religion in the contemporary West is often construed in individualistic terms. In fact, "religion" hardly seems like the right word, since it has been usurped by "spirituality" in some settings, and the common self-descriptor "spiritual but not religious" may be understood as a rejection of a communal orientation in favor of an individual one. In the popular consciousness, spirituality is private and personal; religion is corporate and institutional. Were you to shop for books on New Age spirituality in a bookstore,

---

[145]Toles, *Paul Thomas Anderson,* 4.

[146]Kenneth Turan, "'There Will Be Blood,'" *LA Times,* December 26, 2007, www.latimes.com/entertainment/envelope/cotown/la-et-blood26dec26-story.html.

[147]The film has also been described as "western to its core." Michael Samuel, "Reclaiming Past, Resisting Progression: Existential Tensions in Rockstar's 'Red Dead Redemption,'" in *The New Western: Critical Essays on the Genre Since 9/11,* ed. Scott F. Stoddart (Jefferson, NC: McFarland, 2016); Turan, "There Will Be Blood."

you would likely be directed to the *self*-help section. Authority has been granted to the self, each individual free to selectively appropriate disparate elements from various traditions, designing a unique, tailormade, personal "faith." In this view, communion with the divine begins only where communion with others stops. Perhaps this is the reason this type of spirituality is often associated with images of nature—say, someone taking in the view from a mountaintop. Christians, too, may make this association. In contemporary evangelical worship settings, the lyrics to congregational music are often projected onto a screen against background images of nature—mountain vistas, clouds, soaring eagles.

These are innocuous examples of course, but they are symptomatic of the contemporary mindset: in matters of the soul, better to be alone "in nature" than be exposed to the sullying effects of human interaction. Human relationships are simply too messy to exist in the same exalted realm as private spirituality. The polyphonic arrangement of *Magnolia* counters that, the inevitable messiness notwithstanding, humans are fundamentally relational beings, and even presents that relationality as both "horizontally" aligned with fellow humans and "vertically" aligned with God.

Communion theology. The anthropology of *Magnolia* thus squares nicely with that of Christian tradition, which is committed to an account of our humanity that is essentially relational. Granted, private spiritual practices occupy an important place in Christian piety, and hermits that lived solitary lives in isolation from human community are counted among the church's most revered figures. But, taken as a whole, the Christian tradition conceives of human identity as irreducibly bound up in our relation to God, humanity, and the whole of the created order. The individualistic anthropology of contemporary Western culture is utterly alien to the Bible, which is relentlessly communal in orientation. According to Scripture, God is less interested in molding individuals on mountaintops with arms thrust triumphantly into the air than in forming a "chosen people," a "holy nation" (1 Pet 2:9), whose highest calling, after the injunction to love God, is to love *one another* (Mk 12:28-31).

Christians are not immune to the wider forces shaping society. As such, highly individualistic expressions of Christianity are common in our day and age. But the "communion theology" developed in the late twentieth century by Eastern Orthodox theologian and bishop John Zizioulas, among others, challenges the individualistic tendencies of the West, and has helped us see with new eyes the necessity of communion to our very being. Zizioulas's theology rests on his understanding of personhood, an appropriation of the Cappadocian Fathers' synthesis of biblical and classical thought on the matter.[148] The Greek for *person* (*prosōpon*) means literally that which is "before the eyes" and was typically used to refer to the masks worn by theater actors. In such a view, personhood is a mere mask without ontological content. In his summary of Zizioulas, theologian Veli-Matti Kärkkäinen writes that the "revolutionary insight of the Cappadocians was the identification of the hypostasis ('essence') with the 'person.'"[149] Therefore, in contrast to classical anthropology, "Communion is an ontological category."[150] Zizioulas himself puts it this way: "The person is no longer an adjunct to a being, a category which we add to a concrete entity once we have first verified its ontological hypostasis. *It is itself the hypostasis of the being.*"[151] Personhood is not tacked on to being, a mask worn by the individual; rather, it is *essential.*

This is as true of God as it is of humans. God's triune nature means that communion exists in the Godhead itself, making relationality essential to God's very being.

> Love is not an emanation or "property" of the substance of God . . . but is *constitutive* of His substance, i.e. it is that which makes God what He is, the one God. Thus love ceases to be a qualifying—i.e. secondary—property of being and becomes *the supreme ontological predicate.* Love as God's mode of existence "hypostatizes" God, *constitutes* His being.[152]

Evangelical theologian Stanley Grenz expresses a complementary idea:

> Were God a solitary acting subject, a person apart from Father, Son, and Spirit, God would require the world as the object of his love in order to be who he is, namely, the Loving One. But because God is triune, the divine reality already comprehends both love's subject and object.[153]

---

[148]John D. Zizioulas, *Being as Communion: Studies in Personhood and the Church* (Crestwood, NY: St. Vladimir's Seminary Press, 1985), 27-46.

[149]Veli-Matti Kärkkäinen, *The Doctrine of God: A Global Introduction* (Grand Rapids, MI: Baker Academic, 2004), Kindle, 136.

[150]Kärkkäinen, *Doctrine of God,* 135.

[151]Zizioulas, *Being as Communion,* 39; emphasis original.

[152]Zizioulas, *Being as Communion,* 46; emphasis original.

[153]Grenz, *Theology for the Community of God,* chap. 2.

The Johannine assertion that "God is love" (1 Jn 4:8) doesn't mean simply that love is God's dominant characteristic; it means that the Godhead *is* literally love (note, however, that this is quite different from saying that love is God).[154] According to Zizioulas, Greek ontology sees God as God first, Trinity second—an addendum to the divine. This is apparently the default ontology for many. Catholic theologian Karl Rahner has noted that "despite their orthodox confession of the Trinity, Christians are, in their practical life, almost mere monotheists."[155] Zizioulas's ontology of communion forces us to do more than pay lip service to trinitarianism, but truly consider its ramifications for the very being of God, being defined by communion.

This account of being holds significant explanatory power for theological anthropology. We are not merely human beings—autonomous, self-sufficient individuals—but human beings *in relation*. Thus, writes Kärkkäinen, "No individual apart from others can ever be a person, not even Christ."[156] In Zizioulas, we have a kind of philosophical expression of poet John Donne's famous dictum that "no man is an island"—only more radical.[157] Our relationships are not, to run with Donne's metaphor, merely a matter of adjacent territories forming one vast, unbroken continent; they are the very land itself. In a very real sense, we *are* our relationships. This leads quite naturally on to the matter of the church. Despite his creative use of theology proper, Zizioulas's seminal *Being as Communion* "is not a study about God, even less a systematic presentation of theology as a whole; it is a collection of essays about the church."[158] The entirety of his thought about being and God ultimately comes into focus on the issue of the church, of which he has a high view:

> The mystery of the Church, even in its institutional dimension, is deeply bound to the being of man, to the being of the world and to the very being of God. In virtue of this bond, so characteristic of patristic thought, ecclesiology assumes a marked importance, not only for all aspects of theology, but also for the existential needs of man in every age.[159]

---

[154]Grenz, *Theology for the Community of God*, chap. 2.

[155]Karl Rahner, *The Trinity* (London: Herder & Herder, 1970), 10.

[156]Veli-Matti Kärkkäinen, *Christology: A Global Introduction* (Grand Rapids, MI: Baker Academic, 2003), Kindle, 133.

[157]John Donne, *Devotions upon Emergent Occasions and Death's Duel* (New York: Vintage Books, 1999), 101.

[158]Kärkkäinen, *Doctrine of God*, 135.

[159]Zizioulas, *Being as Communion*, 15.

For Zizioulas, a human is presented with two modes of existence: "The hypostasis of biological existence" and "the hypostasis of ecclesial existence."[160] The fall is humanity's "refusal to make being dependent on communion," a withdrawal from God and thus a decline into disconnected individualism.[161] Biological existence is characterized by this individualism, both propelling us toward personhood and yet, in a tragic irony, simultaneously thwarting our attainment of personhood in the fullest sense. Because of Christ, who has realized authentic personhood, we may transcend biological existence to arrive at ecclesial existence. The ecclesial being realizes human potential, becoming the sort of human we are meant to be. It is ecclesial because, Zizioulas says, this actually happens in the church. Biology no longer determines a human's relationship with the world, allowing for love that transcends the typical tribal (biological) divisions. In other words, in the church there is true communion.[162]

The universal through the particular. If *Magnolia* can be fruitfully described as a weave, it may also be thought of as a photomosaic, a large picture comprised of a multitude of much smaller pictures. Images from the lives of a single character are arranged alongside those of other characters, allowing a larger "picture" of humanity to emerge. Photography renders its subject in the sort of detail that anchors it to a specific time and place, and cinema therefore excels at depicting the particular. But when edited together, images that are inescapably particular may confront the viewer with something approaching the universal.[163] Taken alone, photographic images tend toward particularity, but editing spatially and temporally discontinuous images together may tend toward universality: *this person in this place, plus that person in that place, equals all people in all places.* Like a photomosaic, the universal is constructed *out of* the particular.[164] The editing in *Magnolia* functions this way, affording us a glimpse of life that transcends the limited perspective of any one character. Viewers may likewise be drawn into the picture it presents, as if their own lives were a part of it.

---

[160]Zizioulas, *Being as Communion*, 50.

[161]Zizioulas, *Being as Communion*, 102.

[162]Zizioulas, *Being as Communion*, 50-56.

[163]I am using *universal* only in a relative sense.

[164]I suspect the "photomosaic effect" is partly what made the "The Blessing" videos that proliferated during the Covid-19 pandemic resonant for so many. For example, see More Than Music Mentor, "The Blessing Aotearoa" (New Zealand, 2020), www.youtube.com/watch?v=eZQPifs2kjo.

The analogy of a photomosaic is even more apt when applied to films like *Koyaanisqatsi* (Godfrey Reggio, 1982)[165] or *Samsara* (Ron Fricke, 2011). These nonnarrative documentary features are similar (*Samsara* director Ron Fricke was the cinematographer on *Koyaanisqatsi*), composed of diverse and disparate images of the world, natural and cultural, edited together to form a "big picture" of contemporary life. In some respects, these are fine examples of Eisenstein's "intellectual montage," generating ideas through the juxtaposition of unrelated images.[166] For many viewers, however, the experience of seeing these films is not primarily intellectual. Amateur reviewers of *Koyaanisqatsi*, for example, write that it "communicates to you from the realm beyond words. . . . It is a wordless, feeling thing,"[167] and that "the film works best on an emotional level so switch your brain off and just watch and listen."[168] Some reach for religious language to describe the viewing experience. For example, according to viewers, *Samsara* is "spirit lifting,"[169] "simply transcendent,"[170] "a kind of meditation,"[171] and "the most Intense, Mind Blowing, Movie [*sic*] I have ever seen."[172] Certainly the images themselves are arresting, with scarcely a dull shot to be found in either film (and, in the case of *Koyaanisqatsi*, certain visual effects were revolutionary at the time).[173] But it is the *arrangement* of these startling images into feature-length sensory onslaughts that gives them their distinct affective impact. Unrelated individual images are arranged to form a picture of humanity and our world that may make some viewers feel a part of that very picture. Thus, a viewer of *Samsara* remarks, "The level of connection to this planet and the people on it which *Samsara* can stimulate is truly something,"[174] while another concludes her review with "We are one."[175]

---

165 Ranked #71, "Top 100 Films," *Arts & Faith*, accessed January 3, 2022, https://imagejournal.org/top-100-films/.

166 David Bordwell, *The Cinema of Eisenstein* (New York: Routledge, 2005), 132-33.

167 Tostinati, "An Interiorized Film," 2001, www.imdb.com/title/tt0085809/reviews?ref_=tt_ql_3.

168 Epsilon3, "Breathtaking," 2005, www.imdb.com/title/tt0085809/reviews?ref_=tt_ql_3.

169 Braddugg, "Visual Imagery to Great Perfection and Detail," 2013, www.imdb.com/title/tt0770802/reviews?start=10.

170 Rosielarose, "The Greatest Visual Experience That My Eyeballs Have Ever Witnessed," 2011, www.imdb.com/review/rw2491086/.

171 Akasaka3, "Gorgeous," 2012, www.imdb.com/title/tt0770802/reviews?ref_=tt_ql_3.

172 Candim1970, "Mind Blowing!," 2012, www.imdb.com/title/tt0770802/reviews?start=10.

173 Greg Carson, *Essence of Life*, (USA, 2002).

174 WilyBasilisk, "A Reflection of the Poetry, Tragedy and Wonder to be Found throughout This World, Finding Coherence within the Disorder," 2014, www.imdb.com/user/ur53075887/.

175 Candim1970, "Mind Blowing!"

A similar sentiment is evoked by the crowdsourced documentary *Life in a Day* (Kevin Macdonald, 2011), which cuts together footage shot by amateur YouTube filmmakers from around the world on a single day. I attended its premiere during Sundance Film Festival 2011. During the postscreening Q and A, the filmmakers surprised and delighted the audience by bringing onto the stage many of the film's "stars," who had been flown to the United States from all corners of the globe. This offscreen spectacle reinforced the onscreen message: we are one.

Life in a Day is a compilation of images of ordinary life to create an extraordinary sketch of life itself. Indeed, the quotidian serves as rich material for these types of films or montage sequences. At the climax of *I Wish* (Hirokazu Koreeda, 2011), the main narrative action is interrupted by a montage sequence of routine details: a medical thermometer, an empty packet of chips, a folded school uniform, a baseball home plate etched into the dirt, a bicycle bell, an encouraging hand on the shoulder. These are the most mundane images, but, assembled in this way, they evoke something more significant: life itself. Such sequences are a gloss on the meditative style we explored in chapter one, but with one crucial difference: rather than relying on long-takes, quotidian montage sequences employ fast cutting. Despite this difference, they have a similar effect, illuminating the beauty—the sacred, even—beneath the humdrum surfaces of daily life. The viewer senses the connection between her life with the source of that very life, God, and the accompanying emotion is typically a feeling of greater connectedness.

It's possible, too, that in some cases a feeling of connectedness may morph into an "oceanic feeling," a vast, expansive sensation of oneness. Recall that vastness is an essential characteristic of awe, and, therefore, in such cases, it seems reasonable to suggest that a vast, "oceanic" feeling of connectedness may even mesh with awe. Perhaps it's not surprising then that Sigmund Freud's correspondent Romain Rolland, who was "never without the sensation,"[176] believed oceanic feeling to be the inspiration for religion itself. For his part, Freud hypothesized that oceanic feeling is the residual sense of undifferentiated unity with the mother and world experienced during infancy.[177] We

[176]Sigmund Freud, *Civilization and Its Discontents*, ed. Joan Riviere and James Strachey, rev. ed. (London: Hogarth, 1963), 1.

[177]Freud, *Civilization and Its Discontents*, 1-9.

could conceivably apply a parallel theological rationale to our desire for communion, one in which the desire is construed as a memory of Eden, a harking back to a primordial state of unspoiled communion with God. It may also be a pointer to the future. C. S. Lewis famously posited that "if I find in myself a desire which no experience in this world can satisfy, the most probable explanation is that I was made for another world."[178] A similar argument from desire could likewise be applied to our hunger for communion, suggesting that the very appetite attested to by *Magnolia* is evidence for its ultimate, eschatological reality. To again invoke Johnston's distinction, this is where transcendence and Transcendence meet. Our desires for communion with God and with our fellow humans are complementary. According to Tan and Frijda, the action tendency of oceanic feeling, and sentimental emotion more generally, is "to give up one's individual autonomy and lose oneself into the greater entity."[179] That impulse to surrender may be a picture of the *telos* of human life: to be not individuals but persons, human beings in relation, created beings in communion with the Uncreated.

Feelings of connectedness, of being "at one" with others, may serve as a reminder that we are made for communion. As I have maintained throughout, however, revelation always involves the work of the Holy Spirit. The formal qualities I have explored here, especially editing, invite particular affects from viewers, yet none "produce" revelation; revelation depends entirely on divine agency. Nevertheless, through narrative and stylistic strategies that elicit strong affective responses, imply divine action, and convey interconnectedness, *Magnolia* may act upon some viewers such that they respond with greater openness to revelation.

In his "Great Movie" review, Ebert touches on all three of what I consider to be *Magnolia*'s key factors in its religious quality. He calls it a "parable . . . expressed not in words but in emotions."[180] Of the frog storm he writes, "That this device has sometimes been joked about puzzles me. I find it a way to elevate the whole story into a larger realm of inexplicable but real behavior. We need something beyond the human to add another dimension."[181] Against

---

[178]C. S. Lewis, *Mere Christianity* (New York: HarperCollins, 2009), 136-37.

[179]Tan and Frijda, "Sentiment in Film Viewing," 64.

[180]Ebert, "Great Movie: Magnolia."

[181]Ebert, "Great Movie: Magnolia."

those who accuse "Wise Up" of being empty cinematic flash, Ebert sees it as a reflection of the fact that "Anderson sees these people joined at a level below any possible knowledge, down where fate and destiny lie . . . joined by their actions and their choices."[182] This triumvirate of attributes—radical emotionality, intimations of divine presence, and the theme of interconnectedness—means that, for some viewers, *Magnolia* registers as somehow religious. Viewers may experience a transcendence (lowercase *t*) that opens out into Transcendence (capital *T*), drawn toward both their fellow human beings and to God. The broken lives of *Magnolia* form the threads of a rich, intricate tapestry, into which the viewer may herself feel woven.

[182]Ebert, "Great Movie: Magnolia."

Conclusion

Seeing Is Believing

This may be the conclusion, but truth be told, any conclusions drawn here can only be provisional. When it comes to revelation, we simply cannot make many definitive claims. A project like this is fraught with indeterminacies. As I have repeatedly stated, experiences of revelation can't be proven. And at a more mundane level, viewer responses are usually ambiguous. Despite these unknowns, however, this book has sought, among other aims, to demonstrate that some viewers' experiences could plausibly be categorized as revelatory. As should be clear from the title of this book and this chapter, I think it's theologically legitimate to say that seeing is believing. But a title doesn't tell the whole story. As I mentioned in the introductory chapter, it would be more representative of my argument to say that seeing is feeling, and feeling is believing.

Seeing Is (Feeling Is) Believing

Seeing is feeling. Watching a film is rarely a purely intellectual exercise. Movies invite emotion. And while we cannot neatly disentangle the affective impact of narrative from that of style, since the two are mutually informative, it's clear that viewer emotion is elicited, in part, by formal structures—not least images. Images contain an affective potency that raw narrative information may often lack. With that in mind, we've explored how lighting is used in *Ordet* and its successor *Silent Light* in concert with other formal structures to create films about wonders that, in turn, elicit wonder. We've discussed how the mise en scène of *2001: A Space Odyssey*, specifically celestial bodies included in (or omitted from) the frame, works with other stylistic devices to prompt a sense of awe, sublimity, and even numinous feeling. We've examined how the editing in *Magnolia* intensifies the interwovenness of storylines typical of network narratives by adopting a "weave" pattern and employing creative transitions to create porous boundaries between disparate characters. These are, of course, merely specific instances of how film often functions more generally. What we take in with our eyes we often feel in our hearts. Seeing is feeling.

Feeling is believing. What we feel has implications for religious belief. We humans are creatures shaped by feeling even more fundamentally than we are shaped by thought.[1] Cognitive film theory has called attention to the "searchlight" function of emotion, the way it shifts our awareness to particular aspects of the environment pertinent to the situation.[2] Jacob's dream at Bethel is likewise a story about shifting awareness. God was present in that most unlikely of places, yet Jacob was oblivious to that presence. But during his sojourn there, Jacob has a revelatory dream and awakens exclaiming, "Surely the Lord is in this place, and I was not aware of it" (Gen 28:16). We can be in God's presence, and not know it. It took a dream to enable Jacob's waking self to become aware of the divine.

In an analogous way, emotion elicited by film images may awaken a viewer to God's presence by guiding her attention like a searchlight to aspects of reality through which God is disclosing Godself. Think of this as akin to tuning in to a TV signal. The images are, in a sense, already present via radio waves, yet they remain invisible until a receiver enables us to tune in to the correct frequency and perceive what is being broadcast. Likewise, the affect elicited by film images may help us "tune in" to what the Spirit is revealing. Film images and other formal characteristics invite certain emotions that may guide our attention to those aspects of reality through which God speaks. It bears repeating that form does not itself generate divine revelation—that remains the activity of God alone—but it may become the medium through which God reveals Godself by increasing receptivity to divine self-disclosure.

---

[1]James K. A. Smith, *Desiring the Kingdom: Worship, Worldview, and Cultural Formation*, Cultural Liturgies (Grand Rapids, MI: Baker Academic, 2009), Kindle; Smith, *Imagining the Kingdom*.

[2]Noël Carroll, "Film, Emotion, and Genre," in *Passionate Views: Film, Cognition, and Emotion*, ed. Carl R. Plantinga and Greg M. Smith (Baltimore: Johns Hopkins University Press, 1999), 28; Carl R. Plantinga, *Moving Viewers: American Film and the Spectator's Experience* (Berkeley: University of California Press, 2009), 79.

The Bethel paradigm is a form of general revelation, though not as we have traditionally conceived of it. Traditional theologies have limited general revelation to knowledge that is universally accessible, not the highly particular variety sometimes reported by filmgoers. Though willing to pay lip service to general revelation, evangelicals have been less enthusiastic in practice. Most have seen it as giving rise to little, if any, genuine knowledge of God, sufficient only to render humans inexcusable for sin. Such a pessimistic view will hold out little hope for the revelatory potential of film. Johnston offers a refreshingly optimistic account of general revelation. And when supplemented by Gunton's point that *all* knowledge is revealed by the Spirit,[3] we end up with a theology of general revelation capacious enough to accommodate both knowledge arrived at through human reason (the traditional view) *and* the form of knowledge that comes through particular experiences that are highly affective—like those sometimes experienced in a movie theater.[4] Feeling is believing.

Methodological value. But of what theological value is this approach to film? It strikes me as useful for at least three reasons. First, it helps us better appreciate the theological meaning of a film in a way that takes us beyond mere narrative and into the realm of style. In so doing, it does justice to the irreducibility of the film-viewing experience and honors the richness of the film-mediated revelatory event while avoiding "the heresy of paraphrase" that impoverishes some Christian engagement with film and leaves the spiritually attuned cineaste dissatisfied. Second, and relatedly, it gives due weight to the affective dimension of film-mediated revelation, which is often of central significance to the recipient but may easily be overlooked in theological discussion due to the difficulty of its articulation. Indeed, a reductionistic thematic or "narrative only" approach to film strikes some as "heresy" precisely because it is the crucial emotional component that often gets lost in translation. Third, it accounts for the religious significance of cinema as it is actually experienced by ordinary filmgoers, as opposed to the common scholarly strategy of constructing elaborate "readings" that, though clever, may have little to do with the real experience of religiously engaged viewers.

[3]Colin E. Gunton, *A Brief Theology of Revelation: The 1993 Warfield Lectures* (Edinburgh: T&T Clark, 1995).

[4]Robert K. Johnston, *God's Wider Presence: Reconsidering General Revelation* (Grand Rapids, MI: Baker Academic, 2014).

Though film-mediated revelation is difficult to study with precision or certitude, the topic nevertheless warrants our attention, for by giving careful thought to the matter, we gain insight into the locus of the Spirit's activity in culture. In an age when traditional religious institutions are increasingly seen as irrelevant, we must identify those cultural sites functioning religiously for contemporary people, even if those sites are nontraditional and ostensibly secular. If we discern that the Spirit of God is indeed at work in such places, places like cinema, then this will hold important implications for our understanding of contemporary Christian piety and mission.

We must be careful not to misapply these findings by seeing revelation as somehow just a matter of applying the right formal technique. Aside from being theologically problematic, such thinking could buttress spiritually manipulative practices that seek to conjure inauthentic religious experience. I suspect that the present culture has had its fill of religious fraud. We must insist, therefore, that God is the primary and essential agent of revelation and acknowledge the necessity of the mysterious work of the Spirit to impart genuine divine knowledge. The Bethel paradigm offers, nevertheless, a more comprehensive view of film-mediated revelation. It gives us a way to conceive of revelation that both preserves the essential primacy of God's agency in revelation *and* gives space for consideration of film form as being conducive to revelatory experience.

Next Questions

"Some questions are like matryoshka dolls," writes Turkish playwright Mehmet Murat Ildan. "Once opened, new ones come out!"[5] No surprise then that the questions explored in this book raise further questions, perhaps to be taken up by other scholars. As such, below are a few questions prompted by this project.

Do certain stylistic devices have an inherent tendency to invite religious engagement? I've zeroed in on a handful of films, analyzing how certain formal structures function to elicit particular affects that, in turn, invite religious engagement. It would be fascinating to know, however, if these same stylistic

[5]Mehmet Murat Ildan (@ildanquotations), Twitter, September 13, 2018, https://twitter.com/ildanquotations/status/1039864496209186817. Ildan confirmed to me via email that this was an authentic quotation of his. Mehmet Murat Ildan, August 15, 2020.

devices might have a similar effect in other films too. Do other films that use light similarly to *Silent Light* prompt the same sort of wonder? Are there other films that elicit awe through similar mise en scène strategies as *2001*? Not that simply employing a particular formal strategy would inevitably elicit a sense of the sacred. In fact, the received wisdom in film theory has typically rejected the notion that particular stylistic features express specific content.[6] Yet film scholar Lennard Højbjerg has argued that, while this is still essentially true, some stylistic devices have a *tendency* to express certain kinds of content, especially when rooted in our experiences of embodiment. Højbjerg's example is the circular camera movement used to express and elicit emotions associated with romantic love, grounded in the physical feeling of dizziness when falling in love.[7] Likewise, Fox has suggested that certain physical sensations may be elicited by formal strategies that mimic vitality affects—that is, the irreducible feelings of dynamic processes—such as the way a "floating" frame evokes the feeling of drifting on water.[8]

So while it would be naive to seek out techniques that *necessarily* elicit religious emotion, it seems plausible that some devices may be more likely to invite those sorts of feelings *if supported by concordant content*. For example, Bazin championed long-takes and mise en scène, aesthetic approaches traditionally favored by religious cinema, but I have a hunch that certain types of montage have their own religious resonance. So it might be fruitful to ascertain whether there's spiritual potential in montage. Research that explores a large number of films is required to determine whether or not particular formal strategies have a tendency to evoke religious experiences.

How do images function in commercial cinema? It would also be worthwhile to see similar research done with respect to more mainstream cinema. This book has focused on auteur films, which may be somewhat elitist in their appeal. Why this focus? Two reasons: (1) The films I chose reflect the preferences of a particular community of taste,[9] namely the *Arts & Faith* crowd,

[6]Lennard Højbjerg, "The Circular Camera Movement: Style, Narration, and Embodiment," *Projections* 8, no. 2 (2014): 71.

[7]Højbjerg, "Circular Camera Movement."

[8]Alistair Fox, *Speaking Pictures: Neuropsychoanalysis and Authorship in Film and Literature* (Bloomington: Indiana University Press, 2016), 88-89.

[9]Frank Burch Brown, *Good Taste, Bad Taste, and Christian Taste: Aesthetics in Religious Life* (Oxford: Oxford University Press on Demand, 2000).

and (2) the most visually striking and innovative films tend to be the least narrative-oriented and, therefore, also hold limited commercial appeal.

This second point possibly doesn't make intuitive sense, so let me explain. According to Richard Engnell, it's the context around everyday objects that leads us to view them instrumentally. But by putting a film frame (or, following Bazin, "masking") around the object, it's elevated out of its larger context, defamiliarized, and thereby enabled to take on a mysterious, even "spiritual" quality.[10] Similarly, onscreen objects tend to be viewed in a more utilitarian fashion when subservient to narrative.[11] Following Kracauer, Engnell distinguishes between "theatrical" stories, which give narrative primacy, and "cinematic" stories, which subordinate narrative to "scene," by which he means the imagery itself. When divorced from a strong narrative function, images ("scene") accentuate the significance and mystery of material reality, thus "[rescuing] physical reality from subordination to ordinary human purposes."[12]

This means there is an inherent trade off between intimating the sacred visually and doing so via narrative. Were *The Tree of Life* "more Hollywood"—that is, a so-called theatrical story—I suspect at least some of the visual richness that is so evocative of the spiritual would be undermined. As such, exploring the revelatory potential of image in mainstream cinema presents a unique challenge, though still an important one.[13] Some of the importance of theological engagement with film stems from cinema's popularity and accessibility. It's a populist medium, so there would be real value in exploring revelatory experiences occasioned by mainstream movies.

In what other ways does emotion relate to revelation? The Bethel paradigm is not the only possible way emotion is involved in revelatory experience. For example, there may well be instances in which an emotion like awe is only the *response* to divine encounter, rather than a kind of catalyst (indeed, this seems

[10]Richard Engnell, "The Spiritual Potential of Otherness in Film: The Interplay of Scene and Narrative," *Critical Studies in Mass Communication* 12, no. 3 (1995): 243.

[11]"The typical theatrical film, then, subordinates the thereness of the scene to the demands of effective storytelling, thus diminishing the potential of scene for renewing our contact with a now-strange physical reality. From the spiritual perspective, the theatrical story restricts the ability of the scene to open up a space for the Other." Engnell, "Spiritual Potential," 246.

[12]Engnell, "Spiritual Potential," 243.

[13]Engnell points out that there *is* spiritual potential in theatrical stories, namely in their ability to subvert norms, which he calls *parable* (as opposed to *myth*). Engnell, "Spiritual Potential," 246-48.

to be the standard biblical pattern; cf. Is 6:1-5). In fact, it seems likely that sometimes emotion itself may mediate a sense of the sacred, especially "exquisite" feeling that alone suggests to the viewer a higher order of existence. A film might elicit, say, wonder, an emotion that in turn becomes the object of wonder. These examples are merely illustrative. We've only scratched the surface of emotion and its significance to divine encounter. Affect and emotion are probably associated with revelation in multiple ways, and thus further research—potentially integrative approaches between theology and psychology—would be beneficial.

What might empirical research reveal? One of the challenges of a project like this is accurately interpreting user reviews. Rarely do ordinary filmgoers use theologically explicit and precise language in their written responses. It's rare, for example, for viewers to *explicitly* claim a film was "revelatory" in the theological sense. Of course, a sense of divine presence or communication does indeed seem to be implied, even if variously articulated, but there's no escaping the fact that there is often some ambiguity in viewer responses. Examining the religious reception of the films in this book has, therefore, entailed some responsible reading between the lines.

Similar projects might consider starting with empirical research to more accurately assess the plausibility that a viewer has experienced revelation (bearing in mind that revelation can never be definitively proven). Methodologically, this might look like a hybrid of Brant's approach and mine: empirical research to establish the plausibility of revelation having occurred, followed by the sort of analysis I've undertaken in these pages.

Returning to Bethel

Jacob's sojourn in Genesis 28 wasn't the last time he visited Bethel. In Genesis 35, God instructs him to return to this backwater where he had met God all those years prior. And, yes, it happens again: divine encounter. Once again, God appears to Jacob, blesses him, and renames him (Gen 28:9-15). This, I think, is one reason I keep going back to the movies. I'm returning to Bethel, hoping for revelation, hoping to be blessed, hoping even to be renamed. Occasionally, it happens.

As I explained at the outset, my first such experience came while watching *Magnolia*. But other films since have similarly become the medium for revelatory experience. Another such occasion was seeing *The Tree of Life* at a second-run theater in Pasadena, California, where I was living at the time. I went into the film having heard very little about it, except that it was by Terrence Malick. I quickly fell under its spell, utterly entranced, somehow feeling simultaneously calm and exhilarated. I left this 139-minute reverie with the sense that somehow God had met me there.

I also wondered if my experience had been unusual, since a chunk of the audience slunk out of the theater at some point during the lengthy—and stunning!—creation sequence, apparently too bored to stay any longer. But, it turns out, I wasn't the only one who had apparently encountered the holy through the film. Malick's masterpiece has inspired plenty of religious reflection, even entire books.[14] For my purposes, however, a quotation taken from an online user review will suffice to encapsulate my own response:

> Here is a film—like ALL Malick films—that uses images not to tell stories, but to evoke emotions. Malick is the visual poet of our era, a man who doesn't care about narrative or cause and effect, but lets his VISUALS speak for what he wants us to FEEL. . . . This is the most spiritual film I have EVER SEEN. There is a 20 minute passage of images and music that made me want to believe in God.[15]

It's all there in that statement: images, emotion, and revelation. I've sought in this book to explore these three dimensions of cinema and the relationships between them, an attempt to come to grips with how some films leave an indelible mark on our soul. Now that you've read this account, I encourage you to keep returning to Bethel. From time to time, you'll discover a film that leads you to utter, in a gloss on Jacob, "Surely the Lord is in this movie theater, and I was not aware of it!"

---

[14]For example, Peter J. Leithart, *Shining Glory: Theological Reflections on Terrence Malick's Tree of Life* (Eugene, OR: Wipf & Stock, 2013).

[15]G, "User review of 'The Tree of Life' (Rotten Tomatoes)."

Movies Cited

2001: A Space Odyssey (Stanley Kubrick, 1968)
American Beauty (Sam Mendes, 1999)
Bicycle Thieves (Vittorio De Sica, 1948)
Black Panther (Ryan Coogler, 2018)
Carl Th. Dreyer—My Metier (Torben Skjødt Jensen, 1995)
The Child (Jean-Pierre Dardenne and Luc Dardenne, 2005)
Close Encounters of the Third Kind (Steven Spielberg, 1977)
Crash (Paul Haggis, 2004)
Day of Wrath (Carl Theodor Dreyer, 1943)
Days of Heaven (Terrence Malick, 1978)
Faust (F. W. Murnau, 1926)
The Godfather (Francis Ford Coppola, 1972)
Hail, Caesar! (Ethan Coen, Joel Coen, 2016)
I Wish (Hirokazu Koreeda, 2011)
Inside Out (Pete Docter, 2015)
Interstellar (Christopher Nolan, 2014)
The Irishman (Martin Scorsese, 2019)
Japón (Carlos Reygadas, 2002)
The Keys of the Kingdom (John M. Stahl, 1944)
King Kong (Merian C. Cooper, Ernest B. Schoedsack, 1933)
Koyaanisqatsi (Godfrey Reggio, 1982)
The Last Temptation of Christ (Martin Scorsese, 1988)
Life in a Day (Kevin Macdonald, 2011)
Magnolia (Paul Thomas Anderson, 1999)
Memento (Christopher Nolan, 2000)
Moulin Rouge! (Baz Luhrmann, 2001)
Network (Sidney Lumet, 1976)
Of Gods and Men (Xavier Beauvois, 2010)
The Orator (Tusi Tamasese, 2011)
Ordet (Carl Theodor Dreyer, 1955)

Paris, je t'aime (Bruno Podalydès, Paul Mayeda Berges, Gurinder Chadha, Gus Van Sant, Joel Coen, Ethan Coen, Walter Salles, Daniela Thomas, Christopher Doyle, Isabel Coixet, Nobuhiro Suwa, Sylvain Chomet, Alfonso Cuarón, Olivier Assayas, Oliver Schmitz, Richard LaGravenese, Vincenzo Natali, Wes Craven, Tom Tykwer, Frédéric Auburtin, Gérard Depardieu, Alexander Payne, 2006)
The Passion of Joan of Arc (Carl Theodor Dreyer, 1928)
The Passion of the Christ (Mel Gibson, 2004)
The Piano (Jane Campion, 1993)
Pickpocket (Robert Bresson, 1959)
The Picture of Dorian Gray (Albert Lewin, 1945)
Places in the Heart (Robert Benton, 1984)
The Player (Robert Altman, 1992)
Punch-Drunk Love (Paul Thomas Anderson, 2002)
Raging Bull (Martin Scorsese, 1980)
Reason and Emotion (Bill Roberts, 1943)
Richard III (Laurence Olivier, 1955)
Samsara (Ron Fricke, 2011)
Silence (Martin Scorsese, 2016)
Silent Light (Carlos Reygadas, 2007)
The Son (Jean-Pierre Dardenne and Luc Dardenne, 2002)
Stranger Than Fiction (Marc Forster, 2006)
Strike (Sergei Eisenstein, 1925)
Tender Mercies (Bruce Beresford, 1983)
There Will Be Blood (Paul Thomas Anderson, 2007)
The Ten Commandments (Cecil B. DeMille, 1956)
The Tree of Life (Terrence Malick, 2011)
Triumph of the Will (Leni Riefenstahl, 1935)
Vampyr (Carl Theodor Dreyer, 1932)
Waru (Chelsea Cohen, Ainsley Gardiner, Casey Kaa, Renae Maihi, Awanui Simich-Pene, Briar Grace Smith, Paula Whetu Jones, Katie Wolfe, 2017)

Bibliography

"The 50 Greatest Films of All Time." Sight & Sound, BFI, 2012, accessed August 30, 2018, www.bfi.org.uk/news/50-greatest-films-all-time.

Abeel, Erica. "The Son (Le Fils)." Review of *The Son (Le Fils)* by Jean-Pierre and Luc Dardenne. Buying & Booking Guide, 2003.

Abrams, Nathan. "Stanley Kubrick: Midrashic Movie Maker." In *The Bible in Motion: A Handbook of the Bible and Its Reception in Film*. Berlin: De Gruyter, 2016.

"Account No. 000878." In *Archive of the Alister Hardy Religious Experience Research Centre*. Lampeter, UK: University of Wales Trinity Saint David, 1971. www.uwtsd.ac.uk/library/alister-hardy-religious-experience-research-centre/online-archive.

"Account No. 000959." In *Archive of the Alister Hardy Religious Experience Research Centre*. Lampeter, UK: University of Wales Trinity Saint David, 1970. www.uwtsd.ac.uk/library/alister-hardy-religious-experience-research-centre/online-archive.

"Account No. 002314." In *Archive of the Alister Hardy Religious Experience Research Centre*. Lampeter, UK: University of Wales Trinity Saint David, 1971. www.uwtsd.ac.uk/library/alister-hardy-religious-experience-research-centre/online-archive.

"Account No. 003734." In *Archive of the Alister Hardy Religious Experience Research Centre*. Lampeter, UK: University of Wales Trinity Saint David, 1977. www.uwtsd.ac.uk/library/alister-hardy-religious-experience-research-centre/online-archive.

"Account No. 003759." In *Archive of the Alister Hardy Religious Experience Research Centre*. Lampeter, UK: University of Wales Trinity Saint David, 1979. www.uwtsd.ac.uk/library/alister-hardy-religious-experience-research-centre/online-archive.

Adler, Renata. "The Screen: '2001' Is Up, Up and Away: Kubrick's Odyssey in Space Begins Run." *New York Times*, April 4, 1968. www.nytimes.com/movie/review?res=9a04e6da1530ee3bbc4c53dfb2668383679ede.

Agel, Jerome. *The Making of Kubrick's 2001*. New York: New American Library, 1970.

Almond, Philip C. *Rudolf Otto, An Introduction to His Philosophical Theology*. Chapel Hill: University of North Carolina Press, 1984.

Anderson, Joseph L., and Donald Richie. *The Japanese Film*. Edited by Donald Richie. New York: Grove Press, 1960.

Anderson, Paul Thomas. *Magnolia: The Shooting Script.* New York: Dey Street Books, 2000.

Anker, Roy. "Dazzle Gradually." *Books & Culture*, July/August 2009, 22.

———. *Of Pilgrims and Fire: When God Shows up at the Movies.* Grand Rapids, MI: Eerdmans, 2011. Kindle.

"Arts & Faith Top 100 Films." *Arts & Faith*, 2011. http://artsandfaith.com/top-100/.

"Arts & Faith Top 100 Films—2020." *Arts & Faith*, 2020. http://artsandfaith.com/index.php?/films/&do=year&id=8.

Ash, Carisa A. *A Critical Examination of the Doctrine of Revelation in Evangelical Theology.* Eugene, OR: Wipf & Stock, 2015. Kindle.

Astor, Maggie. "A Guide to the Charlottesville Aftermath." *New York Times*, August 13, 2017. https://www.nytimes.com/2017/08/13/us/charlottesville-virginia-overview.html?mcubz=1.

Athanasius. *On the Incarnation of the Word.* Amazon Digital Services, 2010. Kindle. https://www.amazon.com/St-Athanasius-Incarnation-Word-ebook/dp/B003ELPVJM.

Banerjee, Suparno. "2001: A Space Odyssey: A Transcendental Trans-Locution." *Journal of the Fantastic in the Arts* 19, no. 1 (2008): 39.

Barker, David. "'I've Never Understood a Traditional Screenplay:' Carlos Reygadas on Post Tenebras Lux." *Filmmaker Magazine*, May 1, 2013. http://filmmakermagazine.com/66943-ive-never-understood-a-traditional-screenplay-carlos-reygadas-on-post-tenebras-lux/#.Wd8jEIZx1E7.

Barlow, Helen. "Tusi Tamasese: A Voice from Samoa." *NZ Herald (New Zealand)*, September 8, 2011. www.nzherald.co.nz/entertainment/news/article.cfm?c_id=1501119&objectid=10750044.

Barna, George. *Revolution.* Carol Stream, IL: Tyndale House, 2005.

Barrett, Justin L. *Born Believers: The Science of Children's Religious Belief.* New York: Atria Books, 2014. Kindle.

Barth, Karl. *Church Dogmatics.* Edited by G. W. Bromiley and Thomas F. Torrance. Vol. I.1, Peabody, MA: Hendrickson, 2010.

———. *Church Dogmatics.* Edited by G. W. Bromiley and Thomas F. Torrance. Vol. IV.3. Peabody, MA: Hendrickson, 2010. Originally published: T&T Clark, 1961.

Barth, Karl, and Emil Brunner. *Natural Theology: Comprising "Nature and Grace" by Emil Brunner and the Reply "No!" By Karl Barth.* Translated by Peter Fraenkel. Eugene, OR: Wipf & Stock, 2002.

Amnon Barzel, *Light Art: Targetti Light Art Collection.* Milan: Skira, 2005.

Baxter, John. *Stanley Kubrick: A Biography.* London: HarperCollins, 1997.

Bazin, André. *What Is Cinema?* Edited by Hugh Gray, Jean Renoir, and François Truffaut. Berkeley: University of California Press, 2005.

Bebbington, David W. *Evangelicalism in Modern Britain: A History from the 1730s to the 1980s.* 1st ed. New York: Taylor and Francis, 2003. ebook.

Berkouwer, G. C. *General Revelation.* Grand Rapids, MI: Eerdmans, 1955.

Bernstein, Jeremy. "Beyond the Stars." In *Stanley Kubrick: Interviews,* ed. Gene D. Phillips, 17-20, 2001.

Bichard, Valerie. "O Le Tulafale/the Orator." Review of *The Orator* by Tusi Tamasese. *Journal of Pacific History* 48 (February 19, 2013): 101-2. https://dx.doi.org/10.1080/00223344.2013.769291.

Bird, Michael S. "Film as Hierophany." In *Religion in Film.* Knoxville: University of Tennessee Press, 1982.

Bordwell, David. *The Cinema of Eisenstein.* New York: Routledge, 2005.

———. *The Films of Carl-Theodor Dreyer.* Berkeley: University of California Press, 1981.

———. *The Way Hollywood Tells It: Story and Style in Modern Movies.* Berkeley: University of California Press, 2006.

Bordwell, David, and Kristin Thompson. *Film Art: An Introduction.* 10th ed. New York: McGraw-Hill, 2012.

Borowitz, Eugene B., and Frances Weinman Schwartz. *The Jewish Moral Virtues.* Philadelphia: Jewish Publication Society, 1999.

Brant, Jonathan. *Paul Tillich and the Possibility of Revelation Through Film.* Oxford: Oxford University Press, 2012. ebook.

Brayton, Tim. "The Bright and Happy Christians." *Alternate Ending,* 2012. www.alternateending.com/2012/04/the-bright-and-happy-christians.html.

Brazier, Paul. *C. S. Lewis—Revelation, Conversion, and Apologetics.* Eugene, OR: Pickwick, 2012.

Brereton, Pat. "Smart Cult Classics: Case Studies of Donnie Darko, American Beauty and Magnolia." In *Smart Cinema, D.V.D. Add-Ons and New Audience Pleasures,* 63-86. Springer, 2012.

Brown, Colin. *The New International Dictionary of New Testament Theology.* 2 vols. Grand Rapids, MI: Zondervan, 1978.

Brown, David. *Divine Generosity and Human Creativity: Theology Through Symbol, Painting and Architecture.* Abingdon: Routledge, 2017.

———. *Tradition and Imagination: Revelation and Change.* Oxford: Oxford University Press, 1999.

Brown, Frank Burch. *Good Taste, Bad Taste, & Christian Taste: Aesthetics in Religious Life.* Oxford: Oxford University Press on Demand, 2000.

———. *Religious Aesthetics: A Theological Study of Making and Meaning.* Princeton, NJ: Princeton University Press, 1989.

———. "The Lion, the Wicked, and the Wonder of It All: Psalm 104 and the Playful God." *Journal for Preachers* 29, no. 3 (2006): 15-20.

Brown, William P. *Sacred Sense: Discovering the Wonder of God's Word and World.* Grand Rapids, MI: Eerdmans, 2015.

———. "Wonder: Stewards of God's Mysteries." *Journal for Preachers* 36, no. 4 (2013): 11-15. http://search.ebscohost.com/login.aspx?direct=true&db=rfh&AN=ATLA0001939073&site=ehost-live&scope=site.

Brueggemann, Walter. *Genesis.* Atlanta: John Knox, 1982.

———. *In Man We Trust: The Neglected Side of Biblical Faith.* Richmond, VA: John Knox, 1973.

———. *Psalms.* Edited by W. H. Bellinger. New York: Cambridge University Press, 2014.

Bruns, John. "The Polyphonic Film." *New Review of Film and Television Studies* 6, no. 2 (2008): 189-212.

Buber, Martin. "Moses: The Revelation and the Covenant," Atlantic Highlands, NJ: Humanities Press, 1988.

Burgoyne, Robert. "Narrative Overture and Closure in '2001, a Space Odyssey.'" *Enclitic* V/2, no. Fall-Spring 81-82 (1981): 172-80.

Burnette-Bletsch, Rhonda. "2001: A Space Odyssey (1968)." In *Bible and Cinema: Fifty Key Films.* Edited by Adele Reinhartz. London: Routledge, 2013.

Calhoun, Dave. "Ordet." *Time Out*, 2016. https://www.timeout.com/london/film/ordet.

Callaway, Kutter. *Scoring Transcendence: Contemporary Film Music as Religious Experience.* Waco, TX: Baylor University Press, 2013. Kindle.

Callaway, Kutter, and Dean Batali. *Watching TV Religiously: Television and Theology in Dialogue.* Engaging Culture. Grand Rapids, MI: Baker Academic, 2016.

Calvin, John. *Institutes of the Christian Religion.* Translated by Henry Beveridge (1845). Digireads, 2014. Kindle. https://www.amazon.com/Institutes-Christian-Religion-John-Calvin-ebook/dp/B00KJ39IHO/.

Carr, David. "Lake Wobegon Goes Hollywood (or Is It Vice Versa?), with a Pretty Good Cast." *The New York Times*, July 23, 2005. www.nytimes.com/2005/07/23/movies/MoviesFeatures/lake-wobegon-goes-hollywood-or-is-it-vice-versa-with.html?_r=0.

Carroll, Noël. "Film, Emotion, and Genre." In *Passionate Views: Film, Cognition, and Emotion.* Edited by Carl R. Plantinga and Greg M. Smith. Baltimore: Johns Hopkins University Press, 1999.

———. *The Philosophy of Horror, or, Paradoxes of the Heart.* New York: Routledge, 1990.

Carson, Greg. *Essence of Life*. 25 minutes. USA, 2002.

Chang, Justin. "Nothing but the Truth." *Variety*, 2014, 60-63.

Clarke, Arthur C. *2001: A Space Odyssey*. London: Penguin, 1968.

Cliffe, Nicole. "Undone: How God Seriously Complicated My Happy Atheist Life." *Christianity Today*, June 2016. www.cbmcint.com/undone-how-god-seriously-complicated-my-happy-atheist-life/.

Collinson, Stephen. "Trump's Wish for an End to the Pandemic Contradicts Reality." CNN, June 16, 2020. https://edition.cnn.com/2020/06/16/politics/donald-trump-coronavirus-politics-oklahoma-election-2020/index.html.

Congdon, David. "Reconsidering Apocalyptic Cinema: Pauline Apocalyptic and Paul Thomas Anderson." *Journal of Religion and Popular Culture* 24, no. 3 (2012): 405-18.

Covolo, Robert, and Cory Willson. "When Is a Mall Just a Mall? The Complexity of Reading Cultural Practices." *The Other Journal*, February 2, 2012. http://theotherjournal.com/2012/02/02/when-is-a-mall-just-a-mall-the-complexity-of-reading-cultural-practices/.

Craig, Justin. "'Interstellar' Review: Matthew McConaughey Shines, but Anne Hathaway Is Miscast." Fox News. Updated August 31, 2014. www.foxnews.com/entertainment/2014/11/03/interstellar-review-matthew-mcconaughey-shines-but-anne-hathaway-is-miscast.html.

Daly, Sean. "Director Has His Pick of Actors." *The Times Union* (Albany), 2000.

Dancyger, Ken. *The Technique of Film and Video Editing: History, Theory, and Practice*. Waltham, CT: Focal Press, 2002.

Dardenne, Jean-Pierre, and Luc Dardenne. "Taking the Measure of Human Relationships: An Interview with Jean-Pierre Dardenne and Luc Dardenne." By Joan M. West and Dennis West. *Cineaste* 28, no. 3 (2003): 14-17.

Dargis, Manohla. "Into the Mennonite World to Explore One Man's Test of Faith." Review of *Silent Light* by Carlos Reygadas. *New York Times*, September 23, 2008.

Davis, Caroline Franks. *The Evidential Force of Religious Experience*. Oxford: Oxford University Press, 1989.

———. "Religious Experience." In *Philosophy of Religion: An Anthology*. Edited by Charles Taliaferro and Paul J. Griffiths. Hoboken, NJ: Blackwell, 2003.

De Luca, Tiago. *Realism of the Senses in World Cinema: The Experience of Physical Reality*. Tauris World Cinema Series. London: I. B. Tauris, 2014.

De Luca, Tiago, and Nuno Barradas Jorge. *Slow Cinema*. Edinburgh: Edinburgh University Press, 2016.

De Semlyen, Nick. "The Irishman Week: Empire's Martin Scorsese Interview." *Empire*, November 6, 2019. www.empireonline.com/movies/features/irishman-week-martin-scorsese-interview/.

DeGiglio-Bellemare, Mario. "Magnolia and the Signs of the Times: A Theological Reflection." *Journal of Religion & Film* 4, no. 2 (2000). http://digitalcommons.unomaha.edu/jrf/vol4/iss2/4.

Demarest, Bruce A. *General Revelation: Historical Views and Contemporary Issues.* Grand Rapids, MI: Zondervan, 1982.

Denzey, Nicola. "Biblical Allusions, Biblical Illusions: Hollywood Blockbuster and Scripture." *Journal of Religion & Film* 8, no. 1 (2004). http://digitalcommons.unomaha.edu/cgi/viewcontent.cgi?article=1721&context=jrf.

Desser, David. "Transcendental Style in Tender Mercies." *Religious Communication Today* 8 (1985): 21-27.

Detweiler, Craig. *Into the Dark: Seeing the Sacred in the Top Films of the 21st Century.* Cultural Exegesis. Grand Rapids, MI: Baker Academic, 2008.

Diehl, David W. "Evangelicalism and General Revelation: An Unfinished Agenda." *Journal of the Evangelical Theological Society* 30, no. 4 (1987): 441-55. http://search.ebscohost.com/login.aspx?direct=true&db=rfh&AN=ATLA0000981864&site=ehost-live&scope=site.

Dillman, Joanne Clarke. "Twelve Characters in Search of a Televisual Text: Magnolia Masquerading as Soap Opera." *Journal of Popular Film and Television* 33, no. 3 (2005): 142-50.

Doebler, Peter L. "Jest in Time: The Problems and Promises of the Holy Fool in *Francesco, Giullare Di Dio, Ordet,* and *Ikiru.*" *Journal of Religion & Film* 17, no. 1 (2013): 35.

Donne, John. *Devotions upon Emergent Occasions and Death's Duel.* New York: Vintage Books, 1999. First published 1624.

Doran, Robert. *Theory of the Sublime from Longinus to Kant.* Cambridge: Cambridge University Press, 2017.

Douthat, Roger. "Varieties of Religious Experience." *New York Times,* December 14, 2016. https://www.nytimes.com/2016/12/24/opinion/sunday/varieties-of-religious-experience.html.

Downing, Crystal. *Salvation from Cinema: The Medium Is the Message.* London: Routledge, 2015. ebook.

Dreyer, Carl Theodor. *Dreyer in Double Reflection.* Vol. 458. Perseus Books Group, 1973.

———. "Jesus of Nazareth—the Script." https://issuu.com/dreyer/docs/jesus_dreyer_dfi.

Dreyer, Carl Theodor, and Oliver Stallybrass. *Four Screenplays.* London: Thames & Hudson, 1970.

Dulles, Avery. *Models of Revelation.* Dublin: Gill and Macmillan, 1983.

———. *Poetic Theology: God and the Poetics of Everyday Life.* Grand Rapids, MI: Eerdmans, 2011. Kindle.

———. "Revelation and Discovery." In *Theology and Discovery: Essays in Honor of Karl Rahner, SJ.* Edited by William J. Kelly. Milwaukee: Marquette University Press, 1980.

Ebert, Roger. "Great Movie: 2001: A Space Odyssey Review." Review of *2001: A Space Odyssey* by Stanley Kubrick. March 27, 1997. www.rogerebert.com/reviews/great-movie-2001-a-space-odyssey-1968.

———. "Great Movie: Magnolia." Review of *Magnolia* by Paul Thomas Anderson. November 27, 2008. www.rogerebert.com/reviews/great-movie-magnolia-1999.

———. "Great Movie: Ordet." Review of *Ordet* by Carl Theodor Dreyer. March 8, 2008. www.rogerebert.com/reviews/great-movie-ordet-1955.

———. "Magnolia." Review of *Magnolia* by Paul Thomas Anderson. January 7, 2000. www.rogerebert.com/reviews/magnolia-2000.

Elwell, Walter A. *Evangelical Dictionary of Theology.* 2nd ed. Grand Rapids, MI: Baker Academic, 2001.

Engnell, Richard. "The Spiritual Potential of Otherness in Film: The Interplay of Scene and Narrative." *Critical Studies in Mass Communication* 12, no. 3 (1995): 241-62. https://doi.org/10.1080/15295039509366936.

Falsetto, Mario. *Stanley Kubrick: A Narrative and Stylistic Analysis.* Westport, CT: Greenwood, 2001.

Foltz, Jonathan. "Betraying Oneself: Silent Light and the World of Emotion." *Screen* 52, no. 2 (2011): 151-72.

Foster, Gwendolyn Audrey. "Magnolia Film Analysis." *Senses of Cinema*, February 2015. http://sensesofcinema.com/2015/cteq/magnolia-a-savage-attack-on-masculinity-and-whiteness/.

Foundas, Scott. "Silent Light (Stellet Lichte)." *Variety*, 2007, 23-24.

Fox, Alistair. *Speaking Pictures: Neuropsychoanalysis and Authorship in Film and Literature.* Bloomington: Indiana University Press, 2016.

France, R. T. *The Gospel of Matthew.* New International Commentary on the New Testament. Grand Rapids, MI: Eerdmans, 2007. Kindle.

Freud, Sigmund. *Civilization and Its Discontents.* Edited by Joan Rivière and James Strachey. Revised and newly edited by James Strachey. London: Hogarth, 1963. First published in 1930.

Fry, Carrol. "From Technology to Transcendence: Humanity's Evolutionary Journey in 2001: A Space Odyssey." *Extrapolation* 44, no. 3 (2003): 331-43. https://doi.org/10.3828/extr.2003.44.3.07.

Fuchs, Cynthia. "T.V. Land." PopMatters, 2004. https://web.archive.org/web/20091208070109/www.popmatters.com/film/reviews/m/magnolia2.shtml.

Fujimura, Makoto. *Culture Care: Reconnecting with Beauty for Our Common Life.* New York: The Fujimura Institute, 2017. Kindle.

Fuller, Jason D. "Dreaded Monoliths: Rudolf Otto's Das Heilige and 2001: A Space Odyssey." *Teaching Theology & Religion* 12, no. 1 (2009): 58-59.

Fuller, Robert C. *Spirituality in the Flesh: Bodily Sources of Religious Experience.* Oxford: Oxford University Press, 2008. ebook.

———. *Wonder: From Emotion to Spirituality.* Chapel Hill: University of North Carolina Press, 2006.

Garcia, Chris. "All Paul Thomas Anderson Does." *The Austin American Statesman,* January 6, 2000. http://cigsandredvines.blogspot.co.nz/2000/01/interview-austin-american-statesman.html.

Gelmis, Joseph. "The Film Director as Superstar: Stanley Kubrick." In *Stanley Kubrick: Interviews,* edited by Gene D. Phillips, 80-104. Jackson: University Press of Mississippi, 2001.

Gifford, Kathie Lee, and Kate Shellnutt. "Kathie Lee Gifford: How Billy Graham Led Me to Christ." *Christianity Today,* February 19, 2016. www.christianitytoday.com/ct/2016/march/kathie-lee-gifford-how-billy-graham-led-me-to-christ.html.

Goldingay, John. *Genesis for Everyone—Part 2.* Louisville, KY: Westminster John Knox, 2010.

González, Pedro Blas. "Stanley Kubrick's '2001': An Existential Odyssey." Senses of Cinema, September 2009. http://sensesofcinema.com/2009/feature-articles/stanley-kubricks-2001-an-existential-odyssey/.

Goodwin, Richard V. "An Old Film in a New Light: Lighting as the Key to Johannine Identity in 'Ordet.'" *Journal of Religion & Film* 22, no. 2 (2018). https://digitalcommons.unomaha.edu/jrf/vol22/iss2/2.

Gordinier, Jeff. "1999: The Year That Changed Movies." *Entertainment Weekly,* November 26, 1999. www.ew.com/ew/article/0,,271806,00.html.

Gorospe, Athena Evelyn O. "Myth." In *Global Dictionary of Theology: A Resource for the Worldwide Church,* edited by William A. Dyrness and Veli-Matti Kärkkäinen. Nottingham, UK: Inter-Varsity Press, 2008.

Goss, Brian Michael. "'Things Like This Don't Just Happen': Ideology and Paul Thomas Anderson's Hard Eight, Boogie Nights, and Magnolia." *Journal of Communication Inquiry* 26, no. 2 (2002): 171-92.

Gray, Richard. "The Other Side of Paradise: Tusi Tamasese on 'The Orator.'" *Metro Magazine: Media & Education Magazine,* 2012, 30-32.

Grenz, Stanley J. *Theology for the Community of God.* Grand Rapids, MI: Eerdmans, 2000. Kindle.

Greydanus, Steven D. "Reading the Eternities." *Image* (2011). https://imagejournal.org/2011/02/14/reading-the-eternities-the-2011-arts-faith-top-100-films/.

Gschwandtner, Christina M. "Might Nature Be Interpreted as a 'Saturated Phenomenon'?" In *Interpreting Nature: The Emerging Field of Environmental Hermeneutics*, 82-101. Bronx, NY: Fordham University Press, 2014.

Gunton, Colin E. *A Brief Theology of Revelation: The 1993 Warfield Lectures*. Edinburgh: T&T Clark, 1995.

Guthmann, Edward. "The Actor's Director." *San Francisco Chronicle*, January 2, 2000. www.sfgate.com/entertainment/article/The-Actor-s-Director-Magnolia-film maker-Paul-2814488.php.

Haitjema, Th. L. "Het 'Barthiaanse' Bezwaar Tegen Artikel Ii Der Nederlandse Geloofsbelijdenis." *Onder Eigen Vaandel*, 1938.

Hanson, Dirk. "Drowning in Light." *Nautilus*, February 28, 2014. http://nautil.us/issue /11/light/drowning-in-light.

Hardy, Ann. *Film, Spirituality and Hierophany: The Contemporary Search for Meaning*. Alister Hardy Religious Experience Research Centre, 2002. http://repository.uwtsd .ac.uk/441/.

Hawksley, Theodora. "But It Did Happen: Sound as Deep Narrative in P. T. Anderson's Magnolia (1999)." *Journal of Religion and Film* 13, no. 2 (2009).

Hebert, A. G. *The Bible from Within*. London: Oxford University Press, 1950.

Heschel, Abraham Joshua. *God in Search of Man: A Philosophy of Judaism*. New York: Octagon Books, 1972. First published 1955.

"The Hidden God: Film and Faith." Museum of Modern Art, 2003. www.moma.org /calendar/film/787.

Higgins, Gareth. *How Movies Helped Save My Soul: Finding Spiritual Fingerprints in Culturally Significant Films*. Lake Mary, FL: Relevant Books, 2003.

Hipps, Shane. "Magnolia: The Exodus for Kids." *Metaphilm*, May, 2003. https://web .archive.org/web/20030618153937/http://metaphilm.com/philm.php?id=96_0_2_0.

Hirschberg, Lynn. "His Way." *New York Times*, December 19, 1999. www.nytimes.com /1999/12/19/magazine/his-way.html.

Hoberman, J. "Divine Light." *The Village Voice* (New York), September 24–30, 2008.

Højbjerg, Lennard. "The Circular Camera Movement: Style, Narration, and Embodiment." *Projections* 8, no. 2 (2014): 71-88.

Honeycutt, Kirk. "Silent Light." *Hollywood Reporter* 399 (2007): 12.

Hopkins, Gerard Manley, and W. H. Gardner *Poems and Prose of Gerard Manley Hopkins*. Penguin Classics. New York: Penguin, 1985.

James, William. *Varieties of Religious Experience: A Study in Human Nature*. n.p.: n.p., 1902. Kindle.

Jasper, David. "On Systematizing the Unsystematic: A Response." In *Explorations in Theology and Film: Movies and Meaning*, edited by Clive Marsh and Gaye Ortiz, 235-44. Oxford: Blackwell, 1997.

Jenner, Matthew. "'Magnolia' (1999)." *Movies Unchained* (blog), November 9, 2017. https://moviesunchained.wordpress.com/2017/06/18/magnolia-1999/.

Jensen, Torben Skjødt. "Carl Th. Dreyer—My Metier." Steen Herdel & Co., Unni Straume Filmproduksjons, 1995. 96 minutes.

Jewett, Robert. *Saint Paul at the Movies: The Apostle's Dialogue with American Culture.* 1st ed. Louisville: Westminster John Knox, 1993.

Johnson, William. "Between Daylight and Darkness: Forever and Silent Light." *Film Quarterly* 61, no. 3 (2008): 18-23. https://doi.org/10.1525/fq.2008.61.3.18.

Johnston, Robert K. "Becoming Theologically Mature: The Task of Theological Education Today for American Evangelical Seminaries." *Ministerial Formation* Unit I: Unity and Renewal (April 1996): 41-49.

———. *God's Wider Presence: Reconsidering General Revelation.* Grand Rapids, MI: Baker Academic, 2014. Kindle.

———. *Reel Spirituality: Theology and Film in Dialogue.* 2nd ed. Grand Rapids, MI: Baker Academic, 2006.

———, ed. *Reframing Theology and Film: New Focus for an Emerging Discipline.* Grand Rapids, MI: Baker Academic, 2007.

———. *Useless Beauty: Ecclesiastes Through the Lens of Contemporary Film.* Grand Rapids, MI: Baker Academic, 2004.

Kärkkäinen, Veli-Matti. *Christology: A Global Introduction.* Grand Rapids, MI: Baker Academic, 2003. Kindle.

———. *The Doctrine of God: A Global Introduction.* Grand Rapids, MI: Baker Academic, 2004. Kindle.

Keats, Jonathan. "20 Ways to See the Light." *Nautilus*, March 6, 2014. https://nautil.us/issue/11/light/20-ways-to-see-the-light.

Keltner, D., and J. Haidt. "Approaching Awe, a Moral, Spiritual, and Aesthetic Emotion." *Cognition and Emotion* 17, no. 2 (2003): 297-314. https://doi.org/10.1080/02699930302297. Also accessible at www.scopus.com/inward/record.url?eid=2-s2.0-0037373507&partnerID=40&md5=76607adcbd21064facofa76f92b77eb0.

Konow, David. "P.T.A. Meeting." *Creative Screenwriting*, January, 2000. http://cigsandredvines.blogspot.co.nz/2000/01/interview-creative-screenwriting.html.

Kracauer, Siegfried. *Theory of Film: The Redemption of Physical Reality.* Princeton, NJ: Princeton University Press, 1997. First published, 1960.

Krämer, Peter. "'Dear Mr. Kubrick': Audience Responses to 2001: A Space Odyssey in the Late 1960s." *Participations* 6, no. 2 (2009).

Kuberski, Philip. *Kubrick's Total Cinema: Philosophical Themes and Formal Qualities.* London: A&C Black, 2012.

Kubrick, Stanley, and Gene D. Phillips. *Stanley Kubrick: Interviews.* Conversations with Filmmakers Series. Jackson: University Press of Mississippi, 2001.

Kuipers, Richard. "2001: A Space Odyssey (1968)." Review of *2001: A Space Odyssey* by Stanley Kubrick. 2001. www.urbancinefile.com.au/home/view.asp?a=4657&s=Reviews.

Labberton, Mark, ed. *Still Evangelical?: Insiders Reconsider Political, Social, and Theological Meaning.* Downers Grove, IL: InterVarsity Press, 2018.

Lakoff, George, and Mark Johnson. *Metaphors We Live By.* Chicago: University of Chicago Press, 1980.

Lane, Christina. *Magnolia.* Hoboken, NJ: John Wiley & Sons, 2011.

Leithart, Peter J. *Shining Glory: Theological Reflections on Terrence Malick's Tree of Life.* Eugene, OR: Wipf & Stock, 2013.

Lewis, C. S. "Essays Presented to Charles Williams." Edited by Charles Williams and Dorothy L. Sayers. London: Oxford University Press, 1947.

———. *God in the Dock: Essays on Theology and Ethics.* Grand Rapids, MI: Eerdmans, 1970.

———. *Mere Christianity.* New York: HarperCollins, 2009.

———. *Surprised by Joy.* London: Fount, 1998.

———. *The Weight of Glory.* Grand Rapids, MI: Eerdmans, 1949.

Lightfoot, Joseph Barber, John Reginald Harmer, and Michael William Holmes. *The Apostolic Fathers: Greek Texts and English Translations of Their Writings.* Grand Rapids, MI: Baker Academic, 1992.

Lindvall, Terry R., W. O. Williams, and Artie Terry. "Spectacular Transcendence: Abundant Means in the Cinematic Representation of African American Christianity." *Howard Journal of Communications* 7, no. 3 (1996): 205-20.

Locke, Richard. "Realism with a Heart: The Dardenne Brothers Bring an Idiosyncratic Sympathy to Their Portrayals of Belgian Lowlifes." *The American Scholar* 83, no. 2 (2014): 88-91.

Loughlin, Gerard. *Alien Sex: The Body and Desire in Cinema and Theology.* Hoboken, NJ: Blackwell, 2008.

Macquarrie, John. "Symbolism Case Study: Light as a Religious Symbol." In *The Bible in Its Literary Milieu,* edited by John Maier and Vincent Tollers, 396-410. Grand Rapids, MI: Eerdmans, 1979.

Marion, Jean-Luc. *In Excess: Studies of Saturated Phenomena.* New York: Fordham University Press, 2002.

Marsh, Clive. *Cinema and Sentiment: Film's Challenge to Theology*. Studies in Religion and Culture Series. Eugene, OR: Wipf & Stock, 2004.

Marsh, Clive, and Gaye Ortiz, eds. *Explorations in Theology and Film: Movies and Meaning*. Hoboken, NJ: Blackwell, 1998.

McCorristine, Shane. *Interdisciplinary Perspectives on Mortality and Its Timings: When Is Death?* London: Palgrave Macmillan, 2017.

McGilchrist, Iain. *The Master and His Emissary: The Divided Brain and the Making of the Western World*. New Haven, CT: Yale University Press, 2009.

McKim, D. K., and P. S. Chung. "Revelation and Scripture." In *Global Dictionary of Theology: A Resource for the Worldwide Church*, edited by William A. Dyrness and Veli-Matti Kärkkäinen. Downers Grove, IL: InterVarsity Press, 2008.

McKim, Kristi. *Cinema as Weather*. Abingdon: Routledge, 2015.

Michelson, Annette. "Bodies in Space: Film as Carnal Knowledge." *Artforum* 7, no. 6 (1969): 54-63.

Moltmann, Jürgen. *The Spirit of Life: A Universal Affirmation*. Minneapolis: Fortress, 1992.

Moreland, Kenneth R. "Crawling Towards Diversity: Reflections on the Arts & Faith Top 100 Spiritually Significant Films." *The Porch Magazine* (2020). https://www.theporchmagazine.com/recent/2020/6/3/crawling-towards-diversity-reflections-on-the-arts-amp-faith-top-100-spiritually-significant-films-kenneth-r-morefield.

Morton, V. J. "Tiff Capsules—Day 4." *Rightwing Film Geek*, 2007. https://vjmorton.wordpress.com/2007/09/12/tiff-capsules-day-4/.

Mouw, Richard J. *He Shines in All That's Fair: Culture and Common Grace*. Grand Rapids, MI: Eerdmans, 2001. Kindle.

Muilenburg, James. "Holiness." In *The Interpreter's Dictionary of the Bible*, edited by George Arthur Buttrick. New York: Abingdon, 1962.

Nannicelli, Ted, and Paul Taberham. *Cognitive Media Theory*. Afi Film Readers. New York: Routledge, 2014.

Nayar, Sheila J. "Reconfiguring the 'Genuinely' Religious Film: The Oral Contours of the Overabundant Epic." *Journal of the American Academy of Religion* 78, no. 1 (2010): 100-128. https://doi.org/10.1093/jaarel/lfp086.

Neergaard, Ebbe, Beate Neergaard, and Vibeke Steinthal. *Ebbe Neergaards Bog Om Dreyer*. Dansk Videnskabs Forlag, 1963.

New Zealand Film Commission Annual Report 2011–2012. New Zealand, 2011. www.nzfilm.co.nz/sites/default/files/NZFC_Annual_Report_2011-2012.pdf.

Nichols, Bill. "American Gigolo: Transcendental Style and Narrative Form." *Film Quarterly* 34 (1981): 8-13.

Nietzsche, Friedrich. *Thus Spoke Zarathustra: A Book for All and None*. Amazon Digital Services, 2012. Kindle. First published 1896.

Nolan, Steve. "Paul Tillich and the Possibility of Revelation Through Film: A Theoretical Account Grounded by Empirical Research into the Experiences of Filmgoers." *Journal of Contemporary Religion* 29, no. 1 (2014): 170-73. https://doi.org/10.1080/13537903.2014.864834.

Nordern, Eric. "Playboy Interview: Stanley Kubrick." In *Stanley Kubrick: Interviews*, edited by Gene D. Phillips, 47-74. Jackson: University Press of Mississippi, 2001.

O'Meara, Robert. "Stanley Kubrick, 2001: A Space Odyssey, 1968." *Screen* 10, no. 1 (January 1, 1969): 104-12.

Olsen, Mark. "Singing in the Rain." *Sight and Sound* 10, no. 3 (2000): 26-28.

Otto, Rudolf. *The Idea of the Holy: An Inquiry into the Non-Rational Factor in the Idea of the Divine and Its Relation to the Rational.* 2nd ed. Translated by John W. Harvey. London: Oxford University Press, 1950. First published 1917.

Pappademas, Alex. "Career Arc: Paul Verhoeven." *Grantland*, February 12, 2014. http://grantland.com/features/career-arc-paul-verhoeven/.

Pardes, Ilana. "Moses Goes Down to Hollywood: Miracles and Special Effects." *Semeia* (1996): 15-32.

Patterson, David W. "Music, Structure and Metaphor in Stanley Kubrick's '2001: A Space Odyssey.'" *American Music* 22, no. 3 (2004): 444-74.

Peña, Richard. "Magnolia." In *The Hidden God: Film and Faith*, edited by Mary Lea Bandy and Antonio Monda. New York: The Museum of Modern Art, 2003.

Penn, S. "The Time-Image in Carlos Reygadas' Stellet Licht: A Cinema of Immanence." *Bulletin Of Spanish Studies* 90, no. 7 (2013): 1159-81. https://doi.org/10.1080/14753820.2013.839147.

Pinnock, Clark H. *A Wideness in God's Mercy: The Finality of Jesus Christ in a World of Religions.* Grand Rapids, MI: Zondervan, 1992.

Plantinga, Carl R. *Moving Viewers: American Film and the Spectator's Experience.* Berkeley: University of California Press, 2009.

———. "The Scene of Empathy and the Human Face on Film." In *Passionate Views: Film, Cognition, and Emotion*, edited by Carl R. Plantinga and Greg M. Smith, 239-55. Baltimore: Johns Hopkins University Press, 1999.

Plantinga, Carl R., and Greg M. Smith. *Passionate Views: Film, Cognition, and Emotion.* Baltimore: Johns Hopkins University Press, 1999.

Plate, S. Brent. "Religion/Literature/Film: Toward a Religious Visuality of Film." *Literature and Theology* 12, no. 1 (1998): 16-38.

Poland, Lynn. "The Idea of the Holy and the History of the Sublime." *The Journal of Religion* 72, no. 2 (1992): 175-97. https://doi.org/10.1086/488862.

Pollard, Tom. *Sex and Violence: The Hollywood Censorship Wars.* Boulder, CO: Paradigm, 2009.

Powell, Anna. *Deleuze, Altered States and Film*. Edinburgh: Edinburgh University Press, 2007.

Puente, Maria. "Kevin Spacey Scandal: A Complete List of the 15 Accusers." *USA Today*, November 7, 2017. www.usatoday.com/story/life/2017/11/07/kevin-spacey-scandal-complete-list-13-accusers/835739001/.

Quicke, Andrew. "Phenomenology and Film: An Examination of a Religious Approach to Film Theory by Henri Agel and Amédée Ayfre." *Journal of Media and Religion* 4, no. 4 (2005): 235-50.

Rahner, Karl. *The Trinity*. London: Herder & Herder, 1970.

Rance, Mark. "That Moment: Magnolia Diary." 1 hour 13 minutes. USA, 2000.

Rapf, Maurice. "A Talk with Stanley Kubrick About 2001." In *Stanley Kubrick: Interviews*, edited by Gene D. Phillips, 75-79. Jackson: University Press of Mississippi, 2001.

Raphael, Melissa. *Rudolf Otto and the Concept of Holiness*. Oxford: Clarendon, 1997. ebook.

Rascaroli, Laura. "Like a Dream: A Critical History of the Oneiric Metaphor in Film Theory." *Kinema*, Fall 2002. https://openjournals.uwaterloo.ca/index.php/kinema/article/view/982/1053.

Reed, Ron. "Moving Pictures." *Christianity Today*, June 22, 2004. www.christianitytoday.com/ct/2004/juneweb-only/top100films.html.

Reygadas, Carlos. "Interview by Cinematographos." June 20, 2017. www.youtube.com/watch?v=lDUnG_d4ytY.

———. "Interview by Filminkmagazine." June 20, 2013. www.youtube.com/watch?v=pPfjDBFk44A.

———. "*Silent Light* or Absolute Miracle: An Interview with Carlos Reygadas at Cannes 2007." By Karin Luisa Badt. August 1, 2007. http://brightlightsfilm.com/silent-light-absolute-miracle-interview-carlos-reygadas-cannes-2007/.

Reygadas, Carlos, José Castillo, and Camino Detorrela. "Carlos Reygadas." *BOMB*, no. 111 (2010): 70-77.

Richmond, Scott C. *Cinema's Bodily Illusions: Flying, Floating, and Hallucinating*. Minneapolis: University of Minnesota Press, 2016.

Robinson, William R, and Mary McDermott. "'2001' and the Literary Sensibility." *The Georgia Review* 26, no. 1 (1972): 21-37.

Romney, Jonathan. "Carlos Reygadas: Silent Light." *Sight and Sound* 17, no. 7 (2007): 17.

Rosenbaum, Jonathan. "Mise En Scène as Miracle in Dreyer's *Ordet*." jonathanrosenbaum.net, 2008. https://jonathanrosenbaum.net/2022/03/mise-en-scene-as-miracle-in-dreyers-ordet/.

Rowe, Christopher. "The Romantic Model of '2001: A Space Odyssey.'" *Canadian Journal of Film Studies* (2013): 41-63. www.jstor.org/stable/24411807

Rudkin, Francesca. "Movie Review: Interstellar." *NZ Herald,* November 6, 2014. www.nzherald.co.nz/entertainment/news/article.cfm?c_id=1501119&objectid=11353493.

Rumsby, Martin. "The Ocean Is Our Prairie." *Millennium Film Journal,* no. 61 (2015): 86-95.

Runions, Erin. "Falling Frogs and Family Traumas: Mediating Apocalypse in Magnolia with Adrienne Gibb." In *How Hysterical.* New York: Palgrave Macmillan, 2003.

Ruthven, J. "Miracle." In *Global Dictionary of Theology: A Resource for the Worldwide Church,* edited by William A. Dyrness and Veli-Matti Kärkkäinen: Nottingham, UK: Inter-Varsity Press, 2008.

Ryken, Leland, and David L. Jeffrey. "Light." In *A Dictionary of Biblical Tradition in English Literature,* edited by David L. Jeffrey. Grand Rapids, MI: Eerdmans, 1992.

Samuel, Michael. "Reclaiming Past, Resisting Progression: Existential Tensions in Rockstar's 'Red Dead Redemption.'" In *The New Western: Critical Essays on the Genre Since 9/11,* edited by Scott F. Stoddart. Jefferson, NC: McFarland, 2016.

Schleiermacher, Friedrich. *On Religion: Speeches to Its Cultured Despisers.* Translated by John Oman. n.p.: Beloved Publishing, 2015. Kindle. First published and translated from German, 1799.

Schrader, Paul. *Transcendental Style in Film: Ozu, Bresson, Dreyer.* New York: Da Capo, 1988. First published 1972. http://catdir.loc.gov/catdir/enhancements/fy0830/88015974-d.html.

———. *Transcendental Style in Film: Ozu, Bresson, Dreyer.* Online resource vol. 1. Oakland: University of California Press, 2018. ebook.

Schrader, Paul, and Joseph Kickasola. "Paul Schrader on Revisiting Transcendental Style in Film (TIFF 2017)." In *TIFF Originals,* December 20, 2017. https://www.youtube.com/watch?v=m4F8I8OVmUU.

Scorsese, Martin. "Martin Scorsese: I Said Marvel Movies Aren't Cinema. Let Me Explain." *New York Times,* November 4, 2019. www.nytimes.com/2019/11/04/opinion/martin-scorsese-marvel.html.

Scorsese, Martin, and Michael Henry Wilson. *A Personal Journey with Martin Scorsese Through American Movies.* Hyperion Books, 1997.

Shiota, Michelle N. "Comment: The Science of Positive Emotion: You've Come a Long Way, Baby/There's Still a Long Way to Go." *Emotion Review* 9, no. 3 (2017): 235-37. https://doi.org/10.1177/1754073917692665.

Shiota, Michelle N., Dacher Keltner, and Amanda Mossman. "The Nature of Awe: Elicitors, Appraisals, and Effects on Self-Concept." *Cognition & Emotion* 21, no. 5 (2007): 944-63. https://doi.org/10.1080/02699930600923668.

Shoard, Catherine. "Francis Ford Coppola: Scorsese Was Being Kind—Marvel Movies Are Despicable." *New York Times,* October 21, 2019. https://www.the

guardian.com/film/2019/oct/21/francis-ford-coppola-scorsese-was-being-kind-marvel-movies-are-despicable.

Silverman, Jason M. "We May Be Through with the Past. . . ." *Religion and the Arts* 20, no. 4 (2016): 459-90.

Singer, Irving. *Cinematic Mythmaking: Philosophy in Film*. Cambridge, MA: MIT Press, 2010.

Sitney, P. Adams. *Modernist Montage: The Obscurity of Vision in Cinema and Literature*. New York: Columbia University Press, 1990.

Sklar, Robert. "The Terrible Lightness of Social Marginality: An Interview with Jean-Pierre and Luc Dardenne." *Cineaste* 31, no. 2 (2006): 19-21, 61.

Slowik, Michael. "Isolation and Connection: Unbounded Sound in the Films of Paul Thomas Anderson." *New Review of Film and Television Studies* 13, no. 2 (2015): 149-69.

Smith, Daniel. "Pixar's Mood Master: Can Pete Docter's New Movie Change the Way We Think About Our Emotions?" *The Atlantic*, 2015, 20-21.

Smith, Greg M. *Film Structure and the Emotion System*. Cambridge: Cambridge University Press, 2003. Kindle.

Smith, James K. A. *Desiring the Kingdom: Worship, Worldview, and Cultural Formation*. Cultural Liturgies. Grand Rapids, MI: Baker Academic, 2009. Kindle.

———. *Imagining the Kingdom: How Worship Works*. Cultural Liturgies. Grand Rapids, MI: Baker Academic, 2013. Kindle.

———. *Thinking in Tongues: Pentecostal Contributions to Christian Philosophy*. Grand Rapids, MI: Eerdmans, 2010, Kindle.

Sobchack, Vivian. *The Address of the Eye: A Phenomenology of Film Experience*. Princeton, NJ: Princeton University Press, 1992.

———. "Embodying Transcendence: On the Literal, the Material, and the Cinematic Sublime." *Material Religion* 4, no. 2 (2008): 194-203. https://doi.org/10.2752/175183408X328307.

———. "What My Fingers Knew: The Cinesthetic Subject, or Vision in the Flesh." In *Carnal Thoughts: Embodiment and Moving Image Culture*. Berkeley: University of California Press, 2004.

Spencer, Russ. "Where You Find It." *Salon*, 2000. www.salon.com/2000/03/25/ball_2/.

Sperb, Jason. *Blossoms and Blood: Postmodern Media Culture and the Films of Paul Thomas Anderson*. Austin: University of Texas Press, 2013.

Stephens, Chuck. "Interview." In *Magnolia: The Shooting Script*, edited by Paul Thomas Anderson, 197-208. New York: Dey Street, 2000.

Stone, Bryan P. *Faith and Film: Theological Themes at the Cinema*. Atlanta: Chalice Press, 2000.

Strang, V. "Wonderful Light: Affect and Transformation in Engagements with Light and Water." Conference paper. ASA Conference, Edinburgh, June 19-23, 2014.

Suber, Howard. "2001: A Space Odyssey." The Criterion Collection. Updated October 31, 2017. https://www.criterion.com/current/posts/819-2001-a-space-odyssey.

Sundararajan, Louise. "Religious Awe: Potential Contributions of Negative Theology to Psychology, 'Positive' or Otherwise." *Journal of Theoretical and Philosophical Psychology* 22, no. 2 (2002): 174-97. https://doi.org/10.1037/h0091221.

Tan, Ed S. *Emotion and the Structure of Narrative Film: Film as an Emotion Machine.* Routledge Companion Series. New York: Routledge, 1995.

Tan, Ed S. H., and Nico H. Frijda. "Sentiment in Film Viewing." In *Passionate Views: Film, Cognition, and Emotion,* edited by Carl R. Plantinga and Greg M. Smith. Baltimore: Johns Hopkins University Press, 1999.

Taylor, Barry. "The State of the Nation." Fuller Theological Seminary, Pasadena, April 5, 2010.

Taylor, Charles. *A Secular Age.* Cambridge, MA: Harvard University Press, 2009.

Teodoro, José. "On Earth as It Is in Heaven." *Film Comment* 45, no. 1 (2009): 48-51.

———. "Silent Light: An Interview with Carlos Reygadas." *Cineaste* 34, no. 2 (2009). https://www.cineaste.com/spring2009/carlos-reygadas-interview/.

Terrien, Samuel. "Fear." In *The Interpreter's Dictionary of the Bible,* edited by George Arthur Buttrick. New York: Abingdon, 1962.

Thomas, Owen C. "Spiritual but Not Religious: The Influence of the Current Romantic Movement." *Anglican Theological Review* 88, no. 3 (2006): 397-415.

Thomsen, C. Claire. "The Slow Pulse of the Era: Carl Th. Dreyer's Film Style." In *Slow Cinema,* edited by Tiago De Luca and Nuno Barradas Jorge. Edinburgh: Edinburgh University Press, 2016.

Tillich, Paul. *On Art and Architecture.* Edited by John Dillenberger and Jane Dillenberger. New York: Crossroad, 1987.

Tinken, Matt. "The Power of Film: Magnolia." *Reel Spirituality* (blog). *Fuller Studio,* March 28, 2012. https://fullerstudio.fuller.edu/the_power_of_film_magnolia/.

Toles, George. *Paul Thomas Anderson.* Champaign: University of Illinois Press, 2016.

Torrance, Thomas F. *Christian Theology and Scientific Culture.* Eugene, OR: Wipf & Stock, 1998.

Turan, Kenneth. "'There Will Be Blood.'" *LA Times,* December 26, 2007. www.latimes.com/entertainment/envelope/cotown/la-et-blood26dec26-story.html.

Valdesolo, P., and J. Graham. "Awe, Uncertainty, and Agency Detection." *Psychological Science* 25, no. 1 (2014): 170-78. https://doi.org/10.1177/0956797613501884; www.scopus.com/inward/record.url?eid=2-s2.0-84891953028&partnerID=40&md5=90c6732b69f2b2b2626f7b9d3165c96b.

Valdesolo, Piercarlo, Andrew Shtulman, and Andrew S. Baron. "Science Is Awe-Some: The Emotional Antecedents of Science Learning." *Emotion Review* 9, no. 3 (2017): 215-21. https://doi.org/10.1177/1754073916673212.

Van Hell, A. C. "Widening the Screen: Orthodox Protestant Film Viewers in the Netherlands and the Appropriation of Meaning in Relation to Their Religious Identity." Vrije Universiteit, 2016. http://dare.ubvu.vu.nl/handle/1871/54466.

Von Rad, Gerhard. *Genesis: A Commentary.* Philadelphia: Westminster, 1972.

Vander Stichele, Caroline. "Reframing Jesus: Dreyer's Lifelong Passion." In *The Bible in Motion: A Handbook of the Bible and Its Reception in Film,* edited by Rhonda Burnette-Bletsch. Handbooks of the Bible and Its Reception. Berlin: De Gruyter, 2016.

Vaughan-Johnson, Laura. "Cinemetrics Database." Review of *2001: A Space Odyssey* by Stanley Kubrick, 2019. http://cinemetrics.lv/movie.php?movie_ID=23779.

Veith, Gene Edward. "How Inner Mission Evangelizes." *Patheos: Cranach; The Blog of Veith,* March 15, 2016. www.patheos.com/blogs/geneveith/2016/03/how-inner-mission-evangelizes/.

Von Dosenrode, Sören, and Sören Zibrandt von Dosenrode-Lynge. *Christianity and Resistance in the 20th Century: From Kaj Munk and Dietrich Bonhoeffer to Desmond Tutu.* Vol. 8. Leiden: Brill, 2009.

Wahl, Jan. *Carl Theodor Dreyer and Ordet: My Summer with the Danish Filmmaker.* Screen Classics Series. Lexington: University Press of Kentucky, 2012.

Walker, Andrew. "Scripture, Revelation and Platonism in C. S. Lewis." *Scottish Journal of Theology* 55, no. 1 (2002): 19-35.

Wall, James M. "2001: A Space Odyssey and the Search for a Center." In *Image & Likeness: Religious Visions in American Film Classics,* edited by John R. May. New York: Paulist Press, 1992.

Waltke, Bruce K. *Genesis: A Commentary.* Edited by Cathi J. Fredricks. Grand Rapids, MI: Zondervan, 2001.

Walton, Kevin Anthony. *Thou Traveller Unknown: The Presence and Absence of God in the Jacob Narrative.* Carlisle, UK: Paternoster, 2003.

Warner, Rick. "Filming a Miracle: Ordet, Silent Light, and the Spirit of Contemplative Cinema." *Critical Quarterly* 57, no. 2 (2015): 46-71.

Wenham, Gordon J. *Genesis.* Waco, TX: Word Books, 1987.

Westermann, Claus. *Genesis 12–36: A Commentary.* London: SPCK, 1986.

Whidden, David L., III. *Christ the Light: The Theology of Light and Illumination in Thomas Aquinas.* Emerging Scholars. Minneapolis: Fortress, 2014.

Williams, Dale E. "2001: A Space Odyssey: A Warning Before Its Time." *Critical Studies in Media Communication* 1, no. 3 (1984): 311-22.

Wordsworth, William. *The Collected Poems of William Wordsworth*. Ware: Wordsworth Editions, 1994.

Yong, Amos. *Beyond the Impasse*. Grand Rapids, MI: Baker Academic. 2003.

Zizioulas, John D. *Being as Communion: Studies in Personhood and the Church*. Crestwood, NY: St. Vladimir's Seminary Press, 1985.

Zwissler, Laurel. "Black Panther as Spirit Trip." *Journal of Religion & Film* 22, no. 1 (2018): Article 41, 1-7. https://digitalcommons.unomaha.edu/cgi/viewcontent.cgi?article=1983&context=jrf.

Image Credits

Figure 1.1. *The Orator*, directed by Tusi Tamasese (Sydney, NSW: Transmission Films, 2011).

Figure 1.2. *The Son*, directed by Jean-Pierre Dardenne & Luc Dardenne (New York: New Yorker Video, 2004).

Figure 1.3. *Silent Light*, directed by Carlos Reygadas (New York: Palisades Tartan, 2010).

Figure 1.4. *Silent Light*, directed by Carlos Reygadas (New York: Palisades Tartan, 2010).

Figure 1.5. *Silent Light*, directed by Carlos Reygadas (New York: Palisades Tartan, 2010).

Figure 3.1. *The Tree of Life*, directed by Terrence Malick (Beverly Hills, CA: 20th Century Fox Home Entertainment, 2011).

Figure 3.2. *The Tree of Life*, directed by Terrence Malick (Beverly Hills, CA: 20th Century Fox Home Entertainment, 2011).

Figure 3.3. *The Tree of Life*, directed by Terrence Malick (Beverly Hills, CA: 20th Century Fox Home Entertainment, 2011).

Figure 3.4. Fourfold-source model (Wesleyan quadrilateral). Robert K. Johnston, *Reel Spirituality* (Grand Rapids, MI: Baker Academic, 2000, 2006). Used by permission.

Figure 3.5. Fivefold-source model. Robert K. Johnston, *Reel Spirituality* (Grand Rapids, MI: Baker Academic, 2000, 2006). Used by permission.

Figure 4.1. *Ordet*, directed by Carl Theodor Dreyer (Melbourne: Madman Entertainment, 2008).

Figure 4.2. *Ordet*, directed by Carl Theodor Dreyer (Melbourne: Madman Entertainment, 2008).

Figure 4.3. *Silent Light*, directed by Carlos Reygadas (New York: Palisades Tartan, 2010).

Figure 5.1. *2001: A Space Odyssey*, directed by Stanley Kubrick (Burbank, CA: Warner Home Video, 2001).

Figure 5.2. *2001: A Space Odyssey*, directed by Stanley Kubrick (Burbank, CA: Warner Home Video, 2001).

Figure 5.3. *2001: A Space Odyssey*, directed by Stanley Kubrick (UK/US: Warner Home Video, 2001).

Figure 5.4. *2001: A Space Odyssey*, directed by Stanley Kubrick (UK/US: Warner Home Video, 2001).

Figure 6.1. *Magnolia*, directed by Paul Thomas Anderson (Sydney, NSW: Roadshow Entertainment, 2000).

Figure 6.2. *Magnolia*, directed by Paul Thomas Anderson (Sydney, NSW: Roadshow Entertainment, 2000).

General Index

Scripture Index

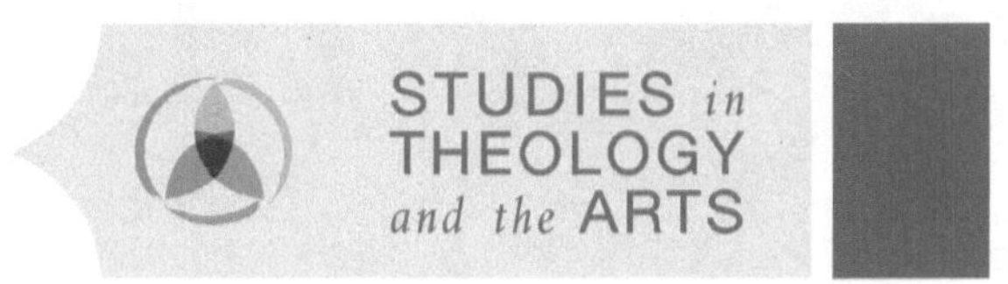

IVP Academic's Studies in Theology and the Arts (STA) seeks to enable Christians to reflect more deeply on the relationship between their faith and humanity's artistic and cultural expressions. By drawing on the insights of both academic theologians and artistic practitioners, this series encourages thoughtful engagement with and critical discernment of the full variety of artistic media—including visual art, music, literature, film, theater, and more—which both embody and inform Christian thinking.

Also Available in the
Studies in Theology and the Arts Series

Resisting the Marriage Plot
by Dalene Joy Fisher

God in the Modern Wing
Edited by Cameron J. Anderson and G. Walter Hansen

www.ingramcontent.com/pod-product-compliance
Lightning Source LLC
LaVergne TN
LVHW091032080826
845145LV00002B/467